The Bishop's School Cookbook

**Published in celebration of
the school's 85th anniversary**

September 1994

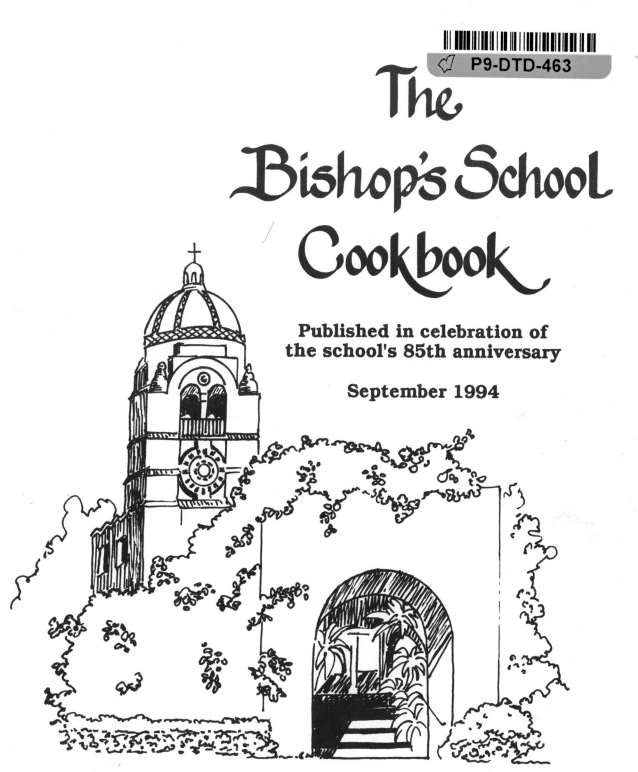

**Favorite recipes from our school family
in La Jolla, California, and beyond**

The Bishop's School Cookbook
Favorite recipes from our school family
in La Jolla, California, and beyond

First Edition

Copyright 1994 by

The Bishop's School
Parents' Association and Alumni Association

ISBN 0-9641931-0-8

Library of Congress Catalog Card Number 94-066673

Printed by
Vanard Lithographers, Inc.
San Diego, California

The Bishop's School Cookbook
7607 La Jolla Boulevard
La Jolla, CA 92037
(619) 459-4021

Additional copies of this book may be purchased at
The Bishop's School Alumni Office at the address above.
If you wish to have copies mailed to you,
please use the order forms in the back of the book.

The Bishop's School is a college preparatory, independent day school located in the center of La Jolla, California. Founded in 1909 by The Rt. Rev. Joseph H. Johnson, Bishop of the Episcopal Diocese of Los Angeles, the school's rich history includes gifts of land and money from Ellen Browning Scripps and her half-sister, Virginia Scripps, and buildings designed in the early 1900s by architect Irving Gill, noted for his California mission style. Originally a girls' boarding school, Bishop's became coed in 1971 when it merged with The San Miguel School for Boys. While maintaining its affiliation with the Episcopal church, the school enrolls students of all faiths.

The Bishop's of 1994 is exciting and alive with 600 students in grades seven through twelve, who strive for excellence and are challenged by a faculty unmatched for their dedication and talent. Strong academics, competitive athletics and dynamic arts allow Bishop's students to develop their own special talents and interests. Throughout its 85 years, Bishop's has been an educational leader in the community and the nation and has touched the lives of generations of young people and their families.

To honor this exceptional school on the occasion of its 85th anniversary, The Parents' Association and the Alumni Association launched the cookbook project in the fall of 1993. Requests for "favorite recipes" were mailed to our extended school family and we were thrilled to receive more than 600 responses from current and past students, parents, grandparents, faculty, staff, trustees and friends from as far away as Greece and New Zealand, and from all corners of the U.S. Results from our 120 recipe testers prove beyond a shadow of a doubt that The Bishop's School produces not only great minds, but very talented cooks, as well.

This unique collection of recipes offers a wide variety of types of foods and styles of cooking and reflects the rich cultural, ethnic and geographical diversity of our school family. Some of the recipes are old-fashioned and historical and very, very special, while others, equally special, exemplify the latest trends in contemporary cuisine. You will find many quick and easy recipes for new cooks and for busy cooks of all ages who are wondering, "What *can* I make for dinner tonight?" You will also be pleased to find a complete sampling of sophisticated dishes for your most elegant brunches, luncheons and dinner parties. Many of the recipes are original, some are adaptations, most are available in print for the first time ever in this cookbook. We know for a fact that they are all favorites, tried and true.

The Cookbook Committee hopes that you will enjoy preparing and sharing these recipes with your family and friends, and that they will become your favorites too. Happy cooking!

Betty Vale
Cookbook Chairman

This cookbook is a joint project of
The Bishop's School
Parents' Association and Alumni Association

Cookbook Committee Members

John Amberg
Marilyn Bilger
Lucy Borsenberger '69
Lois Case
Patricia Clark
Dana Dahlbo
Nancy Deems
Karin Donaldson
Heidi Dorris

Joni Ann Ganley
Nancy Gordon
Kimberly Miller
Pat Miller
Eileen Pue
Susy Smith '64
Judith Strada '63X
Betty Vale
Suzanne Baral Weiner

Cover painting of The Bishop's School campus
and interior pen and ink drawings
by Lisa Hill
La Jolla artist and former Bishop's parent.

Very special thanks

to the many members of our school family
who generously shared their favorite recipes with us and
helped us test and taste each and every one,

to our computer team,
John Amberg, Dana Dahlbo, Nancy Deems,
for their dedication and diligence,

to the staff and faculty for all of their help with this project

and to Headmaster Michael Teitelman
for his support and enthusiastic encouragement.

The committee also wishes to thank
our friend, Gloria Andujar,
for freely giving of her time and expertise.

All proceeds from the sale of this cookbook are contributed to
The Bishop's School Faculty Endowment Fund.

The following members of The Bishop's School family
provided invaluable assistance with
mailings, recipe testing and proof reading

Mary Adamske
Alicia Amberg
Jessie Amberg '96
Terri Antman
Kathy Applen
Sharon Arbelaez
Liz Armstrong
Paddi Arthur
Christine Bagley
Brenda Baker
Lori Bantz
Charlotte Bentley '79
Joan Black
Catherine Blair
Lasley Hanlon Bober '73
Sandra Bogart '70
Mary Boggs
Robin Brey '69
Ilana Brown
Marilyn Bruker
Mimi Lee Bulkley '64X
May Bull
Bruce Burgener '61
Elsie Burke
Lisa Salcido Burke '84
Robert Case
Lynn Cassidy
Margaret Cooke '62
Galen Cooper
Linda Costello
Molly Crabtree
Liz Crowell
Susan Delhamer
Andrew Dennis '97
Evan Dennis '97
Jendy Dennis '94
Jamie Clinton Detweiler '61
Ellie Dillemuth
Sheryl Durkin
Mary Eikel
Dottie Engel
Marci Gessay
Anne Gilchrist
Nisha Goyal

Carol Guess
Helga Halsey
Sarah Henriksen
Janice Hinds
Heather Drake Holden '68
Linda Hull
Dee Jerge
Jane Jones
Alysun Kayser-Ortiz '79
Gordon (Zeke) Knight
Betsy Menard Kurtz '69
Ruth Lira
Irene Ma
Keggie Gillmor Mallett '63
Cheryl Mallory
Susan McClellan
Sandy McCreight
Christopher Means '96
Jeanie Fawcett Merrill '42
Dotti Millbern
Carole Mills
Nancy Minton
Dick Mitchell
Pat Warner Mitchell '45
Linda Morefield
Elaine Muchmore
Tracy Nelson
Mary Newberry
Nancy Nolan
Christina Brooks
  Nowacki '83
Susan Oliver
Ann Marie Osterwalder
Marilyn Ott
Candy Cassidy Pagano '73
Pam Fadem Palisoul '68
Ann Payne
Lori Perkins
Arlene Powers
Lauren Izner
  Ramenofsky '72X
Anne Ricchiuti
Annette Ritchie
Linda Robinson

Jeanette Ruchlewicz
Tim Rutherford '71
Mary Ruyle
Gail Saivar
Alice Saunders
Tom Sayer '77
Nancy Scull
Mary Sease
Gail Shaw
Betsy Gill Sherman '65
Diane Shockley
Annellen Simpkins
Bonnie Sipe
Elsie Lee Collier Smith '34
Jeanne Smith
Susanna Smith
Marjie Entz Smoot '65
Kathleen Snyder
Margarget Sottosanti
Susie Spanos
Kristina Starkey '68X
Kathleen Parnell Steele '80
Sara Sweet
Suthisiri Tilakamonkul
Ellin Todd '68
Cary Tremblay
Kerri Sandstrom
  Trowbridge '88
Vivien U
Elizabeth Vale '92
Susannah Vale '95
Jocelyn Vortmann
Nancy Walter
Carol Ware
Marilee Burchfiel
  Warfield '69X
Christine Wenger '92
Joni Wexler
Sharri Woods
Carol Yates
Chris Young
Irene Metaxas Zafiriou '57
Maggie Zures

Recipe Couriers

Laurie Amberg '98, Alison Dahlbo '97, Jeremy Deems '94

"People ask me: Why do you write about food, and eating and drinking? Why don't you write about the struggle for power and security, and about love, the way others do?

The easiest answer is to say that, like most other humans, I am hungry. But there is more than that. It seems to me that our three basic needs, for food and security and love, are so mixed and mingled and entwined that we cannot straightly think of one without the others. So it happens that when I write of hunger, I am really writing about love and the hunger for it, and warmth and the love of it and the hunger of it...and then the warmth and richness and fine reality of hunger satisfied...and it is all one.

We must eat. If, in the face of that dread fact, we can find other nourishment, and tolerance and compassion for it, we'll be no less full of human dignity."

Mary Frances Kennedy Fisher '27X

Excerpted from the Foreward to The Gastronomical Me *by M.F.K. Fisher, originally published in 1943. We thank Miss Ruth Jenkins, Headmistress Emeritus, for sharing with us her copy of the book,* The Art of Eating, *a compilation of the works of M.F.K. Fisher, in which this piece appears. Permission for use of this material granted by Macmillan Publishing Company.* The Art of Eating, *copyright 1990 by M.F.K. Fisher.*

* * * * *

"The best food I have ever been served in an institution, outside my own family, was at The Bishop's School for Girls! Wonderful fresh milk, delicious home-grown vegetables, the best hot chocolate in the world at our elevenses...and of course, a special flavor to the vintage Hershey Bars..."

Mary Frances Kennedy Fisher '27X

Excerpted from a note written by M.F.K. Fisher in 1982 to Betty Knox, President of the Board of Trustees, 1982-88. Mrs. Knox kindly made this material available to us for publication in our cookbook.

Table of Contents

Bread & Breakfast

Apricot Cream Cheese Nut Bread

Yields 9" x 5" x 3" loaf

INGREDIENTS:

2 eggs
1/2 cup orange juice
1/2 cup water
1 nut bread boxed mix
3/4 cup chopped diced
   dried apricots
1/2 cup chopped walnuts

2 3-ounce packages
   cream cheese
1/3 cup sugar
1 tablespoon flour
1 teaspoon grated
   orange peel

PROCEDURE:

Preheat oven to 350°. Combine 1 of the eggs, orange juice and water with the nut bread mix. Stir in diced apricots and nuts. Set aside. Combine cream cheese, sugar, flour, the remaining egg and orange peel. Blend well in electric mixer or food processor. Pour 1/2 of bread batter into a 9" x 5" x 3" loaf pan which has been greased and floured heavily. Spoon cream cheese mixture over top. Spoon remaining bread mixture on top. Bake for 1 hour. Cool for 10 to 15 minutes in pan and then remove from pan to a rack to cool completely. When cool, wrap tightly and store in refrigerator. Slice after refrigerating for at least 2 hours.

Best after being refrigerated overnight. Great with a cup of coffee or tea.

Marilee Burchfiel Warfield '69X
Parent, Tyler Warfield-Wilkinson '95

Kona Banana Bread

Yields 2 8" x 4" x 2" loaves

INGREDIENTS:

2 cups sugar
1 cup shortening or
   margarine
6 ripe bananas, mashed

4 eggs, well-beaten
2 1/2 cups flour
1 teaspoon salt
2 teaspoons baking soda

PROCEDURE:

Preheat oven to 350°. Cream the sugar and shortening (or margarine) until light and fluffy. Add the 6 mashed bananas and the well-beaten eggs. Mix flour, salt and baking soda together. Blend the flour mixture gradually into the banana mixture. Important: DO NOT OVERMIX. Divide batter between 2 well-greased 8" x 4" x 2" loaf pans. Bake 45 to 50 minutes or until tester comes out clean. Cool in pans on racks for 15 minutes. Turn out onto racks to cool completely before slicing.

Gildee Abercrombie Vaughn '64

Banana Nut Bread

Yields 9" x 5" loaf

INGREDIENTS:

1 cup sugar
1/2 cup (1 stick) butter
2 very, very ripe
   bananas
2 eggs
3 tablespoons milk
2 teaspoons vanilla
   extract

2 cups flour
1/2 teaspoon baking
   powder
1/2 teaspoon baking soda
1/4 teaspoon salt
3 to 5 ounces chopped black
   walnuts

PROCEDURE:

Preheat oven to 350°. Cream together sugar and butter. Add bananas, eggs, milk, vanilla and mix well. Then add flour, baking powder, baking soda and salt. Mix well. Add chopped black walnuts and mix until blended. Pour into a greased and floured 9" x 5" bread pan. Bake for 50 to 60 minutes. Cool in pan for 10 minutes. Remove from pan and cool on rack.

Can be frozen. Great way to use bananas too ripe to eat. Good served with creamed cheese.

Phyllis Johnson
Grandparent, Chad M. Johnson '94

Date Nut Bread

Yields 9" x 5" x 3" loaf

INGREDIENTS:

- 1 cup boiling water
- 1 cup chopped dates
- 1 teaspoon baking soda
- 3 tablespoons shortening
- 1 cup sugar
- 1 egg or egg white
- 1/2 cup nuts
- 2 cups flour (white or whole wheat)

PROCEDURE:

Preheat oven to 300°. In a medium size bowl pour boiling water over dates and baking soda and let stand until cool. With an electric mixer, cream shortening and sugar. Add egg, nuts and date mixture and blend at slow speed. Add flour and mix until well-blended. Pour mixture into greased and floured 9" x 5" x 3" bread pan. Bake for about 1 hour.

To increase sweetness, add bananas and more dates instead of adding more sugar. Add cinnamon and nutmeg for extra spice!

Ann Bethea '73

3

Cranberry Cream Cheese Loaf

Serves 12

INGREDIENTS:

- 1/2 cup (1 stick) butter, room temperature
- 8 ounces cream cheese, room temperature
- 1 cup sugar
- 1/4 cup brown sugar
- 2 eggs
- 1 teaspoon vanilla
- 2 cups flour
- 1 teaspoon baking powder
- 1/2 teaspoon baking soda
- 1/4 teaspoon salt
- 1/4 teaspoon cinnamon
- 1/4 cup cold milk
- 1/4 cup (packed) dried cranberries (or 1 cup fresh)
- 1/2 cup chopped pecans (optional)

PROCEDURE:

Preheat oven to 350°. Grease and flour a 9" x 5" loaf pan. In a large bowl mix the butter and room temperature cream cheese; beat well. Add sugars and mix. Add eggs 1 at a time; beat well. Add vanilla. Add flour, baking powder, baking soda, salt and cinnamon and mix well. Stir in cold milk, cranberries and nuts. Pour the thick mixture into loaf pan. Bake 55 to 60 minutes or until tester inserted into center comes out clean. Cool 20 minutes.

Chocolate chips (or drained canned cherries) can be used instead of cranberries. Freezes very well.

Annette Ritchie
Parent, Natalie Ritchie '99

Cranberry Bread

Yields 9" x 5" loaf

INGREDIENTS:

Grated peel of 1 orange
1 1/2 cups (12-ounce bag) fresh cranberries
1 egg
2/3 cup sugar
1/2 cup orange juice

2 tablespoons oil
2 1/4 cups flour
1 teaspoon baking powder
1/2 teaspoon baking soda
1/4 teaspoon salt

PROCEDURE:

Preheat oven to 325°. Grate orange peel and set aside. Wash cranberries. Slice large ones in half and discard soft ones. Set aside. Grease and flour a 9" x 5" bread pan and set aside. Beat well the egg and sugar. Add orange juice and oil and mix well. Mix dry ingredients together. Add 1/2 of the dry ingredients to egg mixture, beat well. Then add the remainder and mix well. (There should be no lumps after each addition of dry ingredients.) Stir in cranberries and orange peel. Fill bread pan with batter. Bake in middle or slightly upper level of preheated oven for 1 hour. Loaf is done when sharp knife is inserted and comes out without any batter sticking to it. Cool in pan on rack for 30 minutes. Turn out on rack to cool. May need to run a knife around the edges of pan to loosen. Let cool completely before slicing.

Can be frozen up to 9 months. To freeze, wrap in wax paper, then in foil. (Cranberries tend to discolor the foil.) This is good served with soft cream cheese.

Gwen Foss
Parent, Sandy Foss '92X and Lynne Foss '95

Lemon Poppy Seed Bread

Yields 4 6" x 3" loaves

INGREDIENTS:

2 2/3 cups all-purpose flour
1 1/2 teaspoons double
   acting baking powder
1/2 teaspoon salt
1/4 cup poppy seeds
1 cup (2 sticks) butter
  (or margarine),
  softened
1 1/4 cups sugar

2 tablespoons lemon zest
  (freshly grated)
1 1/2 teaspoons vanilla
3 large eggs
1/3 cup milk

Syrup:
1/2 cup lemon juice
1/2 cup sugar

PROCEDURE:

Preheat oven to 350°. Sift together flour, baking powder and salt. Stir in poppy seeds. In another bowl cream butter and sugar together with an electric beater. Beat in zest and vanilla. Beat in eggs 1 at a time, then add milk and beat until well-blended. Add the flour mixture and mix until combined. Divide the batter into 4 buttered and floured 6" x 3" loaf pans. Bake in middle of oven for 40 to 45 minutes or until tester comes out clean.

Poke tops of bread all over with skewer and brush with approximately 1/2 of the syrup. After 5 minutes of cooling in pan, invert breads onto rack and poke all over and brush with remaining syrup. Let cool, then wrap with plastic wrap and foil. Will keep in refrigerator for 1 week or frozen for 1 month.

Syrup: While bread is baking, make syrup by boiling lemon juice and sugar until sugar is dissolved.

The best! Doubles easily.

Susan Oliver
Parent, Josh Oliver '96 and Hunter Oliver '98

Persimmon Bread

Yields 9" x 5" x 3" loaf

INGREDIENTS:

2 cups all-purpose flour
1 teaspoon baking
   powder
1 teaspoon baking soda
1/2 teaspoon salt
1/2 teaspoon ground
   cinnamon
1/2 teaspoon ground
   nutmeg
1/2 cup persimmon pulp

2/3 cup brown sugar,
   packed lightly
3 egg whites
3 tablespoons light olive
   or vegetable oil
1/3 cup chopped prunes
1 cup chopped walnuts

PROCEDURE:

Preheat oven to 325°. Lightly grease a 9" x 5" x 3" loaf pan and cut a piece of wax paper to fit in bottom. In a large bowl stir together flour, baking powder, soda, salt, cinnamon and nutmeg. In a smaller bowl, stir together persimmon pulp, brown sugar, egg whites and oil until blended. Add persimmon mixture to dry ingredients and stir until just combined. Stir in prunes and walnuts. Pour into prepared pan. Bake approximately 1 hour, until a toothpick inserted in center comes out clean. Let loaf cool in pan 5 minutes before removing from pan and cooling completely on a rack.

This recipe is delicious and very low in fat (no cholesterol). Since the bread is very moist, refrigerate after a day or so wrapped in foil.

John Miller
Parent, Kristin Miller '87 and Patrick Miller '93

Pumpkin Tea Bread

Yields 2 9" x 5" loaves

INGREDIENTS:

Vegetable oil or
shortening to grease
pan
3 1/3 cups sifted flour
2 teaspoons baking soda
2 teaspoons baking
powder
1 1/2 teaspoons salt
1 teaspoon cinnamon

1 teaspoon pumpkin pie
spice
1 1-pound can pumpkin
2/3 cup water
2/3 cup shortening
2 2/3 cups sugar
2 eggs
1 cup golden raisins

PROCEDURE:

Preheat oven to 350°. Grease 2 9" x 5" x 3" loaf pans with vegetable oil or
shortening. Sift together in a large bowl the first 6 dry ingredients. Combine the
pumpkin with the water and set aside in a small bowl. In a medium bowl,
combine the solid shortening with the sugar and eggs. Beat at high speed with a
hand-held electric mixer for 2 minutes. Using a large spoon, mix the pumpkin
mixture with the shortening mixture and blend well. Add this mixture to flour
mixture. Beat on low speed until all ingredients are combined. Add golden
raisins by stirring gently with a large spoon. Divide batter between the 2 loaf
pans. Bake 1 hour or until a toothpick inserted in the center comes out clean.

Freezes well. Good for breakfast also. A Thanksgiving and Christmas tradition.

Carol Guess
Parent, Graham Guess '90, Garrett Guess '92,
Gillian Guess '95X, Gaylen Guess '98

Ginny's Pumpkin Bread

Yields 2 9" x 5" loaves

INGREDIENTS:

Vegetable oil spray for
pans
3 cups sugar
1 cup oil
4 large eggs
2 cups puréed cooked
pumpkin (fresh or
canned)

1/2 cup water
3 1/2 cups flour
1 1/2 teaspoons salt
1 teaspoon cinnamon
1 teaspoon nutmeg
1 teaspoon ground
cloves
2 teaspoons baking soda

PROCEDURE:

Preheat oven to 350°. Spray 2 9" x 5" loaf pans with vegetable spray. In a
mixing bowl combine all ingredients and mix well by hand. Pour into loaf pans,
dividing equally. Bake 1 hour or until a toothpick inserted in center comes out
clean. Cool in pans on racks for 30 minutes. Turn out on racks. May serve
warm or leave on racks until completely cool before storing.

*Perfect plain or toasted. For cranberry bread, delete pumpkin and substitute 1 16-
ounce can of whole cranberry sauce, add 1 cup of chopped nuts and substitute 1/2
cup orange juice for the 1/2 cup water.*

Wendy Blair
Parent, Tom Blair '95

Pumpkin Bread

Yields 1 bundt pan

INGREDIENTS:

4 large eggs
2 cups sugar
1 cup oil
3 cups sifted flour
2 teaspoons baking soda

1 teaspoon salt
2 teaspoons baking powder
3 1/2 teaspoons cinnamon
1 1-pound can pumpkin

PROCEDURE:

Preheat oven to 350°. In a large bowl, beat eggs at a high speed. Add sugar and beat until thick and a light lemon color. Pour in oil and blend. In another bowl mix together flour, baking soda, salt, baking powder and cinnamon. Add these dry ingredients to the egg mixture and blend well on medium speed. Add pumpkin and mix well. Bake for 45 minutes to 1 hour in a greased and floured bundt pan.

Great for fall luncheons or a Thanksgiving dessert.

Lasley Hanlon Bober '73

Zucchini Bread

Yields 2 9" x 5" x 3" loaves

INGREDIENTS:

1 2/3 cups sugar
1/2 cup brown sugar
1 cup salad oil
3 eggs, slightly beaten
2 teaspoons vanilla
2 cups peeled and grated zucchini

1/2 cup chopped walnuts
3 cups flour, sifted
1 teaspoon baking soda
1 teaspoon salt
1 teaspoon cinnamon
1/4 teaspoon black pepper

PROCEDURE:

Preheat oven to 350°. In a large bowl, mix the sugars and oil together and blend well. Add the eggs and beat until well-blended. Add vanilla, zucchini and walnuts and mix well. In a small bowl mix together the remaining (dry) ingredients. Add dry ingredients to wet, mixing until well-blended. Pour batter into 2 lightly-greased 9" x 5" x 3" bread pans. Bake for about 1 hour. Test for doneness.

Terri Antman
Parent, Bryan Antman '97

Wheat Germ Zucchini Bread

Yields 2 9" x 5" loaves

INGREDIENTS:

3 eggs
1 cup vegetable oil
1 cup granulated sugar
1 cup firmly packed
    brown sugar
3 teaspoons maple
    flavoring
3 cups coarsely shredded
    zucchini
2 1/2 cups regular all-
    purpose flour,
    unsifted

1/2 cup toasted wheat
    germ
2 teaspoons baking soda
1 teaspoon salt
1/2 teaspoon baking
    powder
1 cup finely chopped
    walnuts
1/3 cup sesame seeds

PROCEDURE:

Preheat oven to 350°. With a rotary beater, beat the eggs to blend. Add the oil, sugars and maple flavoring and continue beating until mixture is thick and foamy. Using a spoon, stir in the shredded zucchini. In another bowl, combine flour, wheat germ, baking soda, salt, baking powder and walnuts. Stir gently into zucchini mixture just until well-blended. Divide batter between 2 greased and flour-dusted 9" x 5" loaf pans. Sprinkle with sesame seeds. Bake for 1 hour or until wooden toothpick inserted in center comes out clean. Cool in pan 10 minutes; turn out on wire racks to cool completely.

Yummy and moist thanks to zucchini. You may also cook in 3 8" x 3" pans, in which case cooking time will be less than 1 hour. Check at 50 minutes.

Toni Eisenhauer
Parent, Lars Eisenhauer '94

Yeasted Apple Breakfast Bread

Yields 2 9" x 5" loaves

INGREDIENTS:

1 cup water
1 teaspoon sugar
1/2 tablespoon yeast
1 1/2 cups unbleached flour

1 cup apple juice
1 cup warm water
1 green apple, peeled and grated
3 tablespoons sugar
2 teaspoons salt

1 teaspoon cinnamon
1/2 tablespoon yeast
1 cup rye flour
4 cups unbleached white flour

1/2 cup chopped pecans
1 cup chopped dates
1 cup raisins, soaked in hot water for 5 minutes, then drained

PROCEDURE:

Mix water, sugar, yeast and 1 1/2 cups flour together. Beat 300 times with a wooden spoon and let stand at room temperature covered for at least 4 hours or overnight. (Alternatively you may omit the sugar and leave in refrigerator for up to 1 week. Let warm to room temperature before proceeding because the cold will significantly retard the yeast.)

Add juice, water, apple, sugar, salt, cinnamon and additional yeast. Mix the 2 flours together, then beat the flour into the apple mixture 1/2 cup at a time until a stiff batter forms and dough pulls away from sides of bowl. (The exact amount of flour is dependent upon the humidity of the day.) Turn out onto a lightly floured board and knead for 15 minutes (fold dough over, press, turn a quarter turn and repeat). If you examine the dough at this point, you will be able to see tiny bubbles just below the surface. Knead in pecans, dates, raisins. Turn dough into oiled ceramic bowl and let rise until doubled, approximately 1 1/2 hours. Punch down and let rise again 45 minutes or so.

Preheat oven to 400°. Punch dough down, shape into 2 loaves and place on lightly greased cookie sheet, perforated pans, or 2 9" x 5" bread pans. Let rise 20 to 25 minutes, until doubled. Bake for 35 to 40 minutes if you use cookie sheets, or 55 minutes in bread pans. When done, turn out onto cooling rack.

This is good toasted. It can be cut after cooling for 30 to 40 minutes and is wonderful with a dab of butter. (Note that I do not use oil in the dough.)

Elaine Muchmore
Parent, Mary-Beth Muchmore '96

Sally Lunn Bread

Serves 6

INGREDIENTS:

1 package yeast
3/4 cup milk, lukewarm
1/4 cup warm water
1/2 cup (1 stick) butter

1/3 cup sugar
3 eggs, beaten
4 cups flour
1 teaspoon salt

PROCEDURE:

Preheat oven to 350°. Mix yeast, milk and water together. Let yeast sit until it activates. Melt butter, then add sugar, eggs and flour mixed with salt. Combine yeast and butter mixtures. Let dough rise until it doubles, then punch down. Put dough in greased angel food cake pan and let rise again. Bake for 1/2 hour, until golden brown. When done, turn out onto cooling rack.

Marion Steefel
Summer neighbor, Jessie Amberg '96 and Laurie Amberg '98

Blueberry Coffee Cake

Serves 8 to 10

INGREDIENTS:

1/4 cup (1/2 stick) butter
3/4 cup sugar
1 egg
1/2 cup milk
2 cups sifted flour
2 teaspoons baking powder
1/2 teaspoon salt

1 1/2 cups blueberries (fresh or frozen)

Topping:
1/2 cup flour
1/2 cup sugar
3 teaspoons cinnamon (or more to taste)
1/4 cup (1/2 stick) butter

PROCEDURE:

Preheat oven to 375°. Cream together the butter and sugar. Add the egg and beat 1 to 2 minutes. Then add milk and beat 1 more minute. Add flour, baking powder and salt and mix well. Then add blueberries and stir in with a spoon. Put batter into 9" greased and floured round glass pie plate. Make topping by mixing together with fingertips the flour, sugar, cinnamon and butter until crumbly. Cover top of cake with this mixture. Bake for 45 to 50 minutes.

This is great warm out of the oven but still wonderful if it cools to room temperature. It can be reheated for 5 minutes if you want to bake it ahead and serve it warm.

Nancy Scull
Parent, Anna Scull '94

14

Danish Coffee Cake

Serves 12

INGREDIENTS:

1 cup (2 sticks) butter, room temperature
2 cups granulated sugar
2 eggs
1 cup (1/2 pint) sour cream
1 teaspoon almond extract
2 cups flour
1 teaspoon baking powder
1/4 teaspoon salt

Topping:
4 tablespoons brown sugar
1 cup chopped pecans
1/2 teaspoon ground cinnamon

Powdered sugar to sprinkle on top

PROCEDURE:

Preheat oven to 350°. In the bowl of an electric mixer cream butter and sugar. Add eggs and beat again. Fold in sour cream and almond extract. In another bowl mix together the flour, baking powder and salt. Add these dry ingredients to butter mixture and mix well. In a small bowl, mix together the topping ingredients. Spoon half of batter into greased bundt pan. Sprinkle with half of topping mixture. Spoon in rest of batter, then finish with remaining topping mixture. Press in topping slightly. Bake for 45 to 60 minutes. (Check after 45 minutes. Done when tester inserted in center comes out clean.) Cool and turn out onto a plate. Sprinkle with sifted powdered sugar.

Mary Ruyle
Parent, Chad Ruyle '96

Pineapple Coconut Coffee Cake

Serves 9 to 12

INGREDIENTS:

1/4 cup brown sugar, packed
1/2 teaspoon cinnamon
3 tablespoons brown sugar
2 1/4 cups Bisquick
3 tablespoons granulated sugar
3 tablespoons butter, melted

1 egg, lightly beaten
2/3 cup milk
3/4 cup shredded coconut

Pineapple Glacé:
3/4 cup crushed pineapple with syrup
1/3 cup brown sugar, packed
3 tablespoons butter

PROCEDURE:

Preheat oven to 400°. Prepare glacé according to directions below. Mix the 1/4 cup brown sugar and cinnamon and set aside. Sprinkle greased round, 9" pan with the 3 tablespoons brown sugar. Combine Bisquick, granulated sugar, butter, egg, milk and beat vigorously for 1/2 minute. (Batter will be very thick.) Spread half the batter in the pan. Sprinkle brown sugar mixture over batter. Spoon remaining batter over the sugar mixture, spreading very carefully. Spoon the pineapple glacé evenly over the batter and sprinkle with coconut. Bake 25 minutes or until coconut is browned. (Cover loosely with aluminum foil if coconut begins to burn.) Serve warm.

Glacé: Heat all ingredients to a boil, stirring constantly. Boil and stir for 3 minutes. Cool before pouring over cake.

Quick and easy. (Spreading the batter is easier the second time.) Looks elegant on crystal cake plate.

Maggie Zures
Parent, Julie Zures '95 and Jeffrey Zures '98

Prune and Apricot Coffee Cake

Serves 12

INGREDIENTS:

3/4 cup dried, pitted
   prunes
3/4 cup dried, pitted
   apricots
2/3 cup light brown sugar,
   firmly packed
1 tablespoon flour
1 tablespoon cinnamon
2 cups unsifted flour
2 teaspoons baking
   powder

1/2 teaspoon salt
3/4 cup shortening
3/4 cup granulated sugar
2 eggs
1 teaspoon vanilla
3/4 cup milk
6 tablespoons (3/4 stick)
   butter, melted
1/3 cup chopped walnuts

PROCEDURE:

Let prunes and apricots stand in hot water, to cover, 5 minutes. Drain fruit and chop finely. Set aside.

Preheat oven to 350°. Lightly grease and flour a 9" tube pan. In a small bowl, combine the brown sugar, 1 tablespoon flour and cinnamon. Set aside. Sift the 2 cups flour with the baking powder and salt. Set aside. In large bowl, with electric mixer at high speed, beat shortening, granulated sugar, eggs and vanilla until light and fluffy, about 5 minutes. At low speed, beat in flour mixture (in thirds), alternately with milk (in halves) beginning and ending with flour mixture; beat just until combined. With rubber scraper, gently fold in fruit.

Turn 1/3 of batter into pan, spreading evenly. Sprinkle with 1/3 of brown sugar mixture, then with 2 tablespoons of melted butter. Repeat layering twice. Sprinkle top with walnuts. Bake 55 minutes or until tester inserted near center comes out clean. Let cool in pan on wire rack about 25 minutes. Remove from pan and serve warm. (Room temperature is fine too.) Dust with sifted powdered sugar.

Mary Ruyle
Parent, Chad Ruyle '96

Yum Yum Coffee Cake

Yields 9" x 12" cake

INGREDIENTS:

1/2 cup (1 stick) margarine
1 cup sugar
1 cup (1/2 pint) sour cream
2 eggs, beaten
1 teaspoon vanilla
2 cups flour
1 teaspoon baking soda

1 teaspoon baking powder
1 teaspoon salt

Topping:
1/4 cup brown sugar
1/4 cup granulated sugar
1 teaspoon cinnamon
1 cup chopped nuts

PROCEDURE:

Preheat oven to 325°. Blend margarine and sugar. Add sour cream, beaten eggs and vanilla and mix until well-blended. In another bowl, mix together the flour, baking soda, baking powder and salt. Add this dry mixture to the margarine mixture and blend well. Mix together topping ingredients. Put half of cake mixture in greased 9" x 12" pan. Sprinkle on half of topping. Then add remaining batter and remaining topping. Bake for 35 to 40 minutes.

Barbara Tardy
Staff, Business Office

Diamond J Cinnamon Muffins

Serves 10 to 12

INGREDIENTS:

1/3 cup soft margarine
1/2 cup sugar
1 1/2 cups flour
1 1/2 teaspoons baking
    powder
1/2 teaspoon salt
1/2 teaspoon nutmeg

1/2 cup milk

Topping:
1/2 cup (1 stick)
    margarine, melted
1/2 cup sugar
2 teaspoons cinnamon

PROCEDURE:

Preheat oven to 350°. In an electric mixer, cream together the margarine and sugar. Sift the dry ingredients together into another bowl. Add the dry ingredients to the creamed mixture alternately with the milk, blending after each addition. Lightly grease muffin cups (or spray with non-stick cooking spray) and fill with batter 2/3 full. Bake 20 to 25 minutes until brown. Test with toothpick which should come out clean when done.

While muffins are cooking, prepare topping ingredients: Melt margarine; mix the sugar and cinnamon together in a small bowl. While muffins are still warm, dip tops and bottoms in melted margarine. Then roll the whole muffin in the cinnamon sugar mixture. All of this can be done ahead; just reheat muffins before serving.

These muffins always make a hit with our guests in Montana. They are quick and easy and have no eggs. Especially good with turkey, chicken or ham.

Jinny Beardsley Combs '48

Grant Corner Inn Orange Muffins

Yields 1 dozen

INGREDIENTS:

Muffin Batter:
1 cup (2 sticks) unsalted
  butter
1 cup sugar
2 eggs
1 teaspoon soda
1 cup buttermilk
2 cups all-purpose flour

Grated peel of 2
  oranges
1/2 cup raisins

Glaze:
1 cup brown sugar
Juice of 2 oranges

PROCEDURE:

Preheat oven to 400°. In medium mixing bowl cream butter with sugar until light and fluffy. Beat in eggs. Set aside. In small bowl, mix soda and buttermilk. Add buttermilk alternately with flour to creamed ingredients. Stir in grated peel and raisins. Fill paper-lined muffin cups 2/3 full. Bake for 15 to 20 minutes, or until golden brown. Mix glaze ingredients, pour over muffins and immediately remove from the tins. Serve warm.

Louise Stewart '65

Grant Corner Inn Carrot Muffins

Yields 36 muffins

INGREDIENTS:

4 cups all-purpose flour
1 cup packed light
  brown sugar
1 1/2 cups sugar
4 teaspoons baking soda
4 teaspoons cinnamon
1 teaspoon mace
1 teaspoon salt

1 pound carrots, peeled
  and grated
1 cup golden raisins
1 15-ounce can crushed
  pineapple
6 eggs, beaten
1 cup vegetable oil
4 teaspoons vanilla

PROCEDURE:

Preheat oven to 350°. Into large mixing bowl sift flour, sugars, baking soda, cinnamon, mace and salt. Add carrots and raisins, tossing to coat and separate; set aside. In medium mixing bowl combine pineapple, eggs, oil and vanilla. Pour into dry ingredients, stirring well to blend. Pour batter into muffin cups which have been well-greased or lined with papers, filling 3/4 full. Bake for 30 minutes, or until tops spring back when touched. Let muffins cool for at least 10 minutes before removing from pans.

The favorite muffin at our inn, according to our guests. These freeze beautifully; taste almost like tiny carrot cakes. Frost them with cream cheese icing and you have carrot cupcakes!

Louise Stewart '65

Muffins Your Dad Grew Up On

Yields 18 muffins

INGREDIENTS:

2 cups 100% whole
   wheat flour
1/3 cup brown sugar
1/4 cup vegetable oil

1 teaspoon baking soda
1/2 teaspoon salt
1 1/2 cups buttermilk
1 egg

PROCEDURE:

Preheat oven to 375°. Mix first 5 ingredients thoroughly. Add buttermilk and the egg and mix until well-blended. Bake in lightly-greased muffin pans for 20 minutes.

I mix dry ingredients and keep in refrigerator until needed. These muffins are great served hot out of the oven with butter, margarine or cream cheese and jam.

Joyce Armstrong Wayman '49

Popovers

Serves 6

INGREDIENTS:

1 1/4 cups low fat milk
1 1/4 cups unbleached flour

1/2 teaspoon salt
3 jumbo (or 4 large) eggs

PROCEDURE:

Preheat oven to 425°. Generously grease popover cups. Pour milk into mixing bowl. Add flour and salt. With rotary beater or wire whisk, beat until well-blended. Do not overbeat. Add eggs, 1 at a time, beating in each until blended. Pour batter into popover cups, filling 3/4 full. Bake for 20 minutes. Reduce oven temperature to 325° and continue baking 15 to 20 minutes. Serve immediately.

Good with roast beef. If you do not have popover cups, you may cook this batter in an iron skillet or muffin tins.

Jocelyn Vortmann
Parent, Anna Vortmann '90, Cady Vortmann '93,
Jocelyn Vortmann '97

Williamsburg Spoon Bread

Serves 6

INGREDIENTS:

1 cup cornmeal
1 1/2 teaspoons baking soda
1/2 teaspoon baking
   powder
Dash cinnamon
Dash nutmeg

2 cups low fat
   buttermilk*
1 cup milk
3 tablespoons butter or
   margarine, melted
1/2 teaspoon salt
3 large eggs

*To make without buttermilk: Substitute 2 cups whole or low fat milk for buttermilk, eliminate baking soda and use 3 teaspoons baking powder.

PROCEDURE:

Preheat oven to 350°. Butter a 2-quart casserole dish. Mix cornmeal, baking soda, baking powder, cinnamon and nutmeg together in a large mixing bowl. In a 2-quart saucepan heat buttermilk, milk, butter and salt over medium heat until just below a simmer. (Scald. Do not allow to boil or milk will separate.) Add hot milk mixture gradually to the cornmeal mixture while stirring. Beat eggs with wire whisk and stir into cornmeal and milk mixture. Pour into casserole dish and bake for 25 minutes. (Should have a custard consistency.)

Serve in small bowls with butter and honey or jam for breakfast or dinner. The best tasting spoon bread is made with whole grain, stone ground cornmeal like the kind you can buy in Williamsburg, Virginia!

Nancy and Ward Deems
Parents, Jeff Deems '91 and Jeremy Deems '94

New England Corn Bread

Serves 6 to 8

INGREDIENTS:

2 eggs
2 tablespoons butter
2 tablespoons honey
2 cups buttermilk
1/2 cup flour (preferably whole grain)

1 teaspoon baking soda
2 cups cornmeal (preferably stone ground)

PROCEDURE:

Preheat oven to 425°. Beat eggs in a large mixing bowl. Melt butter in 10" cast iron frying pan. Add honey and buttermilk to eggs and stir well. Mix together the flour and soda and add to egg mixture. Mix in cornmeal. Pour in hot melted butter and stir well. Pour batter into hot frying pan (in which butter was melted). Place pan in oven and bake 20 minutes. Serve from pan.

The whole grain flour and cornmeal are readily available in bulk or packaged and give a wonderful flavor!

Charlotte Brazell
Parent, Charles Brazell '69

Custard Corn Bread

Serves 4 to 6

INGREDIENTS:

3/4 cup yellow corn meal
1/2 cup flour
1 teaspoon baking powder
1 teaspoon salt

3 tablespoons (packed) brown sugar
1 egg, lightly beaten
2 tablespoons butter, melted
1 1/2 cups milk

PROCEDURE:

Preheat oven to 400°. Mix together the corn meal, flour, baking powder, salt and brown sugar. Then add egg, butter and 1 cup of the milk and mix until well-blended. Pour batter into a greased 9" x 6" pan. Then pour the remaining 1/2 cup milk over batter. Bake for 20 minutes or until golden brown. (There will be a soft "custard" layer in the middle.) Serve immediately.

Marion Steefel
Summer neighbor, Jessie Amberg '96 and Laurie Amberg '98

Christmas Breakfast

Serves 10 to 12

INGREDIENTS:

6 slices bread
8 eggs, beaten
1 pound bulk sausage, crumbled, cooked and drained

2 cups milk
1 cup grated sharp cheddar cheese
Salt to taste
1 teaspoon dry mustard

PROCEDURE:

Cut bread into pieces, approximately 1/2" square. Mix all ingredients together. Put in greased 9" x 13" casserole. Chill for at least 12 hours. Preheat oven to 350°. Bake for 35 minutes.

This has always been a big hit at my brunches.

Tempe Pell
Aunt, Elizabeth Vale '92 and Susannah Vale '95

Baumers' Banana Pancakes

Yields 8 6" pancakes

INGREDIENTS:

1 cup Aunt Jemima
　 Original pancake mix
1/2 cup instant oatmeal
1/4 cup oat bran
1/4 cup wheat germ
1 cup milk (or more)
2 jumbo eggs

2 small, ripe bananas,
　 mashed
1 tablespoon canola oil
1/2 teaspoon vanilla
　 Optional: A few shakes
　 of "Molly McButter"

PROCEDURE:

Combine ingredients, stir with large wooden fork. Add more milk if too thick.
Lightly grease griddle or skillet and place over high heat. When griddle is very
hot, turn heat down slightly and pour batter onto griddle to form 3" pancakes.
Turn when pancakes bubble and bottoms are golden brown. Cook until other
side is brown. Serve with honey.

Carol Baumer
Parent, Michael '86 and Stephen '91

Cottage Cheese Pancakes

Serves 4

INGREDIENTS:

6 large eggs, separated
2 cups cottage cheese
　 (low or nonfat)
3/4 cup flour
1/4 teaspoon salt
1/2 teaspoon cinnamon

1/4 teaspoon nutmeg
　 (optional)
2 tablespoons sugar
1/4 teaspoon cream of
　 tartar (optional)
　 Safflower oil for
　 cooking

PROCEDURE:

Beat egg yolks in a bowl. Add cottage cheese, flour, salt, cinnamon, (optional) nutmeg and sugar. Mix well. Beat egg whites and (optional) cream of tartar in separate bowl with electric mixer until almost stiff. Fold into cottage cheese mixture. Heat lightly oiled griddle. Spoon batter onto griddle to form 3" pancakes and cook over medium heat, turning once.

These are deliciously light and fluffy! Serve with Lyle's Golden Syrup and fruit for a real treat. (Can use egg substitute for yolks, but real egg whites are essential for lightness.)

Nancy Diehl Deems
Parent, Jeff Deems '91 and Jeremy Deems '94

Sour Cream Pancakes

Yields 16 to 20 pancakes

INGREDIENTS:

1/2 teaspoon salt	1 egg
1 teaspoon baking soda	1 cup (1/2 pint) sour
1 tablespoon sugar	cream
1 cup flour	1 cup milk

PROCEDURE:

In a small bowl combine and sift together all the dry ingredients (salt, baking soda, sugar and flour) and set aside. In a large bowl blend egg and sour cream with a fork just until all lumps have disappeared. Stir in milk. Then slowly add flour mixture to egg, sour cream and milk mixture. Stir until well-combined and there are no lumps. DO NOT BEAT. Pour silver dollar size pancakes onto preheated griddle. As bubbles form, turn over and cook until golden. Serve at once.

Quick and easy! These pancakes are delightful with maple syrup or with just a dusting of powdered sugar.

Liz Armstrong
Parent, Mac Armstrong '93 and Annie Armstrong '96

Oatmeal Blueberry Pancakes

Serves 6 to 8

INGREDIENTS:

2 cups old-fashioned
   oats
1/2 cup whole-wheat flour
1/2 teaspoon baking soda
1/2 teaspoon baking
   powder
1 tablespoon sugar

2 cups buttermilk
1/4 cup oil
2 eggs (or 1 egg plus 2
   egg whites)
1 cup blueberries
   (optional)
Your favorite syrup

PROCEDURE:

In a large mixing bowl combine the oats, whole wheat flour, baking soda, baking powder and sugar and stir to blend. Add the buttermilk, oil and eggs and stir until well-mixed. Add blueberries if desired and stir gently to mix in. Cook on hot, lightly-oiled griddle. Serve with your favorite syrup.

Our family's favorite for breakfast.

Sara Sweet
Staff, Director of Food Service

Puffy Pear Pancake

Serves 2

INGREDIENTS:

2 1/2 tablespoons granulated
   sugar
1/2 teaspoon cinnamon
2 ripe Bosc pears, peeled,
   cored and thinly
   sliced
2 tablespoons lemon
   juice

1/2 cup all-purpose flour,
   sifted
2 large eggs
1/3 cup milk
1 tablespoon butter
1 tablespoon vegetable
   oil

PROCEDURE:

Preheat oven to 450°. In a small bowl combine sugar and cinnamon; set aside. In another small bowl combine pears with 1 tablespoon lemon juice and 1 tablespoon cinnamon/sugar mixture. In a third bowl put flour and 1 tablespoon cinnamon/sugar. In yet another bowl mix together the milk and eggs with whisk until well-combined. Whisk the milk and eggs into the flour until well-mixed. (Batter can be slightly lumpy; do not over beat.)

Heat 1 tablespoon butter and 1 tablespoon oil in a 10" heavy iron or ovenproof frying pan on top of range. When butter is melted, pour batter into pan, rotating to cover pan bottom. Arrange pear mixture evenly over top of batter. Cook for about 2 minutes until batter is just set and transfer pan to hot oven. Bake for about 8 minutes until pancake starts to puff up and barely brown. Put rest of cinnamon-sugar mixture on top and bake about 8 minutes more until fluffy and golden brown. Remove to plate and serve immediately. Can sprinkle rest of lemon juice over top to lessen sweetness or dust with powdered sugar.

This is a great weekend breakfast or brunch dish. It is also good as a simple dessert. These can also be made with other fruit or just plain.

Patrick Miller '93

Dutch Baby

Serves 4

INGREDIENTS:

4 large eggs
1/2 cup milk
1/2 teaspoon sugar
1/2 cup flour, sifted

3 tablespoons butter
Powdered sugar
Syrup

PROCEDURE:

Preheat oven to 425°. In a blender mix eggs, milk, sugar and flour until smooth. Melt butter in 10" or 11" iron skillet over low heat. Add batter. Bake in oven for 20 minutes. Reduce heat to 300° and bake 10 minutes more. Serve with powdered sugar and syrup.

Kids love this when they have sleepovers. Goes well with fresh fruit and yogurt.

Sarah Henriksen
Parent, Nicholas Henriksen '98

The Big Pancake

Serves 4

INGREDIENTS:

2 eggs
1/2 cup milk
1/2 cup flour
1/4 cup (1/2 stick) butter
   (or margarine),
   melted

Topping:
1 lemon, cut in wedges
Powdered sugar
1 cup fruit

PROCEDURE:

Preheat oven to 450°. Mix together the eggs, milk and flour. In a 10" iron skillet melt butter (or margarine). Put batter in hot pan and then in the oven for 12 minutes. Serve with lemon wedges, powdered sugar and fruit. The lemon is a must. The fruit topping can vary from fresh peaches, frozen blueberries to orange marmalade.

Have your guests seated when the pancake comes out of the oven. It makes quite a show but falls quickly.

Ursula Banning
Grandparent, Casey Bonaguidi '94

Rich Belgian Style Waffles

Yields 6 to 8 waffles

INGREDIENTS:

1 egg yolk
1 cup (1/2 pint) sour
   cream
1/2 cup milk
3 tablespoons butter,
   melted
1 cup flour

2 teaspoons sugar
1 teaspoon baking
   powder
1/2 teaspoon salt
1/4 teaspoon baking soda
1 egg white, stiffly
   beaten

PROCEDURE:

Preheat waffle maker. Put all ingredients except egg white in the bowl of an electric mixer. Beat on low until moistened. Increase speed to medium, mix until smooth. Whisk egg white separately until it forms stiff peaks. Fold egg white gently by hand into batter. Pour 1/2 cup of the batter over center of grids. Close waffle maker. Bake until golden, about 2 1/2 minutes. Repeat.

Serve hot with warmed maple syrup (the real stuff!) or Strawberries Romanoff. May be frozen and then re-crisped in oven. I use this recipe for "everyday" waffles. It is very popular.

Debra (Kip) Durney '71

Three-Berry French Toast

Serves 4

INGREDIENTS:

2 teaspoons sugar	1 cup nonfat milk
1 cup strawberries	1 teaspoon vanilla
1/2 cup raspberries	8 slices cinnamon-raisin
2 teaspoons cornstarch	bread
2 teaspoons water	Vegetable oil spray (or
1/2 cup blueberries	2 tablespoons butter
2 eggs	or margarine)

PROCEDURE:

Put sugar and red berries in medium size saucepan; let stand 10 minutes. Heat on medium heat for 3 to 5 minutes. Mix cornstarch with water, then add to berries. Stir and cook on high until thick and clear; then add blueberries. Turn off heat. Beat eggs with wire whisk in medium bowl. Add milk and vanilla to eggs, stir. Heat large fry pan or electric skillet to medium. Spray with vegetable spray (or melt butter or margarine). Dip bread in egg mixture. Cook bread in fry pan or skillet approximately 2 minutes each side or until brown. Serve 2 slices per person with sauce on top.

Great Sunday or holiday brunch. Low fat/low cal treat (without butter/margarine). Can substitute favorite berries in season. Can be easily multiplied for larger groups.

Jenny Bantz '95

Breakfast In A Glass

Serves 2

INGREDIENTS:

- 1 cup orange juice
- 1 cup nonfat plain yogurt
- 2 cups frozen or fresh fruit (strawberries, raspberries or peaches)

- 1 banana, frozen and cut into about 6 pieces
- 1 teaspoon vanilla
- 2 tablespoons sugar (or more to taste)

PROCEDURE:

Place all ingredients in blender and blend until completely mixed. Pour into 2 10-ounce glasses.

Good way to use very ripe bananas. Peel and freeze ripe bananas in plastic bags to have whenever you want to make a quick breakfast in a glass.

Jeff Deems '91 and Jeremy Deems '94

"Tutti Frutti" Breakfast Frappé or Dessert Sorbet

Yields 4 3/4 cup servings

INGREDIENTS:

2 cups pineapple juice (unsweetened)
1 peeled frozen banana

1 cup fresh strawberries, washed and stemmed (or frozen strawberries)

PROCEDURE:

Place all ingredients in a blender and blend. Pour into glass and serve immediately as delicious breakfast frappé or pour into dessert glasses and chill or freeze as dessert sorbet. (Can also be poured into popsicle molds and frozen as flavorful and nutritious popsicles.)

A great breakfast or dessert for busy kids or parents. All natural, contains no sugar. Light and healthy. Great use for leftover bananas; simply peel bananas, place in ziploc bag and freeze. They are ready to go to make this quick nutritious treat.

Ellen Moffat Fry '69
Trustee and
Parent, Beth Fry '94 and Rob Fry '95

Appetizers

Hummus
(Chickpea Dip)

Yields 1 1/2 cups

INGREDIENTS:

**1 16-ounce can
    chickpeas (garbanzo
    beans), drained
1/2 cup olive oil
3 tablespoons fresh
    lemon juice**

**2 garlic cloves
   Middle Eastern
      pocketbread (pita) to
   accompany**

PROCEDURE:

Place all the above ingredients (except pita) in a blender. Process at low speed until the mixture is a rough purée. Taste and add more garlic or lemon juice as desired. Serve as dip with Middle Eastern pocketbread (pita).

Little bowls filled with different mixtures to taste are so appealing. Our curiosity is raised. We can hardly wait to sample each offering. What a fine way to begin a pleasant gathering. In the Middle East the practice of serving dishes of softly colored, fragrant purées has been refined to an art. These purées, often garnished with shiny black olives and red paprika, are eaten with small pieces of pita. Sometimes called Middle Eastern pocketbread, pita is widely available on supermarket bread shelves. Hummus and the 3 following recipes are examples of popular varieties which are easy to prepare and fun to serve.

Marianne Engle
Parent, Lindsey Engle '94 and Jordan Engle '98

Baba Ghanoush
(Eggplant Tahini Dip)

Yields 1 1/2 cups

INGREDIENTS:

1 large or 2 medium
   eggplants
1 to 2 cloves garlic
2 tablespoons tahini
   (ground toasted
   sesame seeds)
3 tablespoons lemon
   juice

1/4 teaspoon ground
   cumin
1/2 teaspoon salt
   Middle Eastern
   pocketbread (pita) to
   accompany

PROCEDURE:

Pierce the eggplant with a fork in 2 places. Broil the whole eggplants, turning them occasionally, until the skins turn black and the flesh is juicy (or, you may bake the eggplants at 500°). Cooking takes about 20 minutes if broiled, longer if baked. Cool slightly. Slice eggplants in half, scoop out the flesh from the shell and let it drain in a colander. Gently press out the juice with the back of a spoon. Combine the eggplant, the garlic squeezed through a press and the remaining ingredients (except pita). Mix thoroughly with a fork. Taste and adjust seasonings. Serve as dip with Middle Eastern pocketbread (pita).

Marianne Engle
Parent, Lindsey Engle '94 and Jordan Engle '98

Tahini Cream Dip

Yields 1 1/2 cups

INGREDIENTS:

1/2 cup tahini (ground toasted sesame seeds)
2 garlic cloves
1/4 cup fresh lemon juice (or more to taste)
1/2 teaspoon ground cumin

3/4 cup water
Salt to taste
1/2 cup minced parsley (optional)
Middle Eastern pocketbread (pita) to accompany

PROCEDURE:

Place all the above ingredients (except pita) in a blender. Process to a smooth purée. Adjust seasoning. Add parsley, if desired. Serve as dip with Middle Eastern pocketbread (pita).

Marianne Engle
Parent, Lindsey Engle '94 and Jordan Engle '98

Yogurt with Mint

Yields 1 1/2 cups

INGREDIENTS:

1 cup (1/2 pint) plain yogurt
1/2 cup fresh mint, or parsley and dried mint, minced

1 clove garlic, pressed
1/4 teaspoon salt
Middle Eastern pocketbread (pita) to accompany

PROCEDURE:

Combine above ingredients (except pita) in a bowl. Adjust seasoning. The yogurt, garlic and salt combined without the mint is also delicious. Serve as dip with Middle Eastern pocketbread (pita).

Marianne Engle
Parent, Lindsey Engle '94 and Jordan Engle '98

Ortega Dip

Yields 1 to 2 cups

INGREDIENTS:

3 medium tomatoes
1 4-ounce can diced
   green chiles
2 2.25-ounce cans diced
   black olives

3 diced green onions
1 tablespoon oil
2 tablespoons vinegar
   Salt, pepper, garlic salt
   (to taste)

PROCEDURE:

Dice tomatoes (with or without skin). Add all other ingredients and stir.

Allow salsa to sit for 30 to 60 minutes for flavors to blend. May also add 1/2 cup fresh cilantro for extra flavor. Serve with any Mexican-type meal.

Susanna Smith
Parent, Troy Smith '97 and Adam Smith '98

Mexican Dip

Yields approximately 2 cups

INGREDIENTS:

3 avocados, diced
2 tomatoes, diced
1 7-ounce can diced
   green chiles (do not
   drain)

1 4.25-ounce can
   chopped black olives,
   drained
2 to 3 green onions, chopped
   Dash wine vinegar
   Garlic salt to taste

PROCEDURE:

Mix the first 5 ingredients together. Then add the wine vinegar and garlic salt to taste.

Low cal! Serve with tortilla chips. Easy! Make at last minute because the avocado darkens.

Susan Delhamer
Parent, Brent Delhamer '98

Guacamole
(Avocado Paste)

Yields 1 1/2 cups

INGREDIENTS:

2 ripe avocados
2 tablespoons lime juice
2 tablespoons finely
   minced green onions

Salt to taste
Pinch oregano

PROCEDURE:

Remove skins and pits from avocados. Mash with silver fork. Add lime juice and blend to a smooth paste. Add onion, salt and oregano, stirring lightly. Cover, chill and serve on lettuce leaves, accompanied by tortillas.

May be served in a small bowl as a dip with tortilla chips or vegetables. Better if made ahead. Can set pits in guacamole to help retard darkening. For another version of guacamole, you may substitute cumin for oregano, add a little hot sauce and chopped tomatoes if desired.

Pauline Cornford
Grandparent, Lauren Slater '97

Grande Tostada Dip

Serves 4 to 6

INGREDIENTS:

1 avocado
Juice of 1 lemon
1 16-ounce can refried beans
1 cup (1/2 pint) sour cream
1 4-ounce can diced green chiles
1 4-ounce can sliced black olives

2 green onions, chopped, including tops
2 fresh tomatoes, chopped
Salsa, to taste
1 cup grated cheddar cheese
1 cup grated Monterey jack cheese
Large tortilla chips

PROCEDURE:

Mash avocado and mix with the lemon juice. Layer ingredients thinly on a large shallow platter or dish in the following order: Beans, avocado, sour cream, chiles, olives, green onions, tomatoes, salsa and cheeses. Once prepared, let sit in the refrigerator for 15 minutes. Surround with tortilla chips just before serving.

Extremely easy and always a winner as a meal or appetizer.

Melissa Hansch '90

Super Nachos

Serves 4 to 6

INGREDIENTS:

8 ounces lean ground beef
1/2 package taco seasoning mix
1/2 cup water
1 15-ounce can vegetarian refried beans
1/2 cup shredded Monterey jack cheese
1/2 cup shredded cheddar cheese

1 tablespoon chopped green chiles
1 cup shredded iceberg lettuce
2 tomatoes, chopped
1 8-ounce package tortilla chips
1 avocado, sliced
1/2 cup (1/4 pint) sour cream or plain yogurt

PROCEDURE:

In a large skillet cook meat until browned. Drain fat. Add taco seasoning and water. Bring to boil. Reduce heat and simmer 15 to 20 minutes or until meat is cooked and flavors blended. Set aside. Spread beans to cover bottom of 12" to 14" pizza pan. Sprinkle with cheeses. Top with meat mixture. Sprinkle with chiles. Broil 5 to 7 minutes until cheese is bubbly and brown. Around edge of pan arrange ring of lettuce then tomatoes, then tortilla chips, then avocado slices. Top with sour cream in center. Serve extra tortilla chips in basket.

Kids love this for dinner although it's great as an hors d'oeuvre.

Sarah Henriksen
Parent, Nicholas Henriksen '98

Cheese and Green Chile Pie

Serves 12 to 15 as appetizer
or 6 to 8 as main course

INGREDIENTS:

1 **pound Monterey jack cheese, grated**
1 **pound longhorn cheese, grated**
6 **eggs, lightly beaten**
1 **5-ounce can evaporated milk**

2 **4-ounce cans chopped green chiles**

Optional:
1 **pound cooked ham, sausage or other desired meat**

PROCEDURE:

Preheat oven to 350°. Combine the cheeses, eggs and milk. Line a 9" x 13" glass dish with the chiles and optional meat. Cover with the cheese mixture. Bake for 40 minutes. When used as an hors d'oeuvre, omit the meat, if desired; cool and cut into bite size squares. When used as a main course, include meat, if desired, and cut into larger pieces to serve.

When used for brunch serve with fresh fruit compote and pastry (or variety of pastries). When used as a luncheon dish serve with tossed green salad and croissants. This may be frozen and reheated. This is perfect for Christmas morning; prepare everything in advance and then enjoy after the gifts have been opened.

Anne G. Branch
Parent, Allen Branch '84

Chile Con Queso

Serves a crowd

INGREDIENTS:

1 tablespoon margarine (or butter)
1 large onion, chopped
1 4-ounce can diced jalapeño peppers
1 28-ounce can whole peeled tomatoes, drained (squeeze out excess liquid), diced
1 pound Monterey Jack cheese, cubed
1 pound mild cheddar (or Colby) cheese, cubed
1 rounded tablespoon flour
2 tablespoons half and half
Tortilla chips

PROCEDURE:

In a large skillet melt margarine (or butter). Add onion and cook until translucent. Then add peppers. (If you prefer dish less spicy, do not use the whole can of peppers.) Sauté 1 or 2 minutes and add diced, drained tomatoes. Simmer on low heat while cubing cheeses. Place cheese cubes in a plastic bag and add flour. Close bag tightly and shake cheese to coat. Add to skillet. Keep heat on low. Add half and half. Stir carefully every few minutes until cheese is melted all the way through. Keep on low heat until ready to serve. Serve with a bowl of tortilla chips.

The key to this dish is keeping cheese over low heat. Too high heat causes oil in cheese to separate. Great dip. You can also use crudités for dipping. When reheated, it will be a little oily but still tastes great.

Carolyn Slack Standley '73

Chili Dip

Serves 8

INGREDIENTS:

1 16-ounce can Dennison's chili (no beans)
8 ounces cream cheese
Blue corn chips or regular tortilla chips to accompany

PROCEDURE:

Mix the chili and cream cheese in a saucepan. Place over low heat and stir until cheese is melted and mixture is well-blended. Serve with blue corn chips or regular tortilla chips.

Easy picnic or barbecue treat. May use nonfat cream cheese. Dip will not look as good, but will taste great.

Dee Jerge
Parent, Kari Jerge '98

Gazpacho

Serves 5 as appetizer

INGREDIENTS:

1 1/2 **cups tomato juice**
1 **beef bouillon cube**
1 **tomato, chopped**
1/4 **cup chopped unpeeled cucumber**
2 **tablespoons chopped green pepper**
2 **tablespoons chopped onion**
2 **tablespoons red wine vinegar**
1 **tablespoon salad oil**
1/2 **teaspoon salt**

1/2 **teaspoon Worcester-shire sauce**
3 **drops Tabasco (more or less to taste)**

Accompaniments:
Herbed croutons and about 1/3 cup each of chopped tomato, unpeeled cucumber, green pepper and onion

PROCEDURE:

Heat tomato juice to boiling. Add bouillon cube. Stir until dissolved. Stir in remaining ingredients except accompaniments. Blend slightly in food processor. Chill several hours. Serve topped with accompaniments (or allow guests to choose their own).

Delicious on a hot summer day and a real crowd pleaser at parties. Easy to prepare a day ahead!

Brenda Hayward
Parent, Richard Caleel '88

Cheddar Cheese Cookies

Yields 3 to 4 dozen

INGREDIENTS:

2 cups grated sharp cheddar cheese
1/2 cup (1 stick) unsalted butter
1 cup flour
1 teaspoon garlic salt

3/4 cup finely chopped pecans
OR
2 tablespoons chopped chives

PROCEDURE:

Cream the cheese and butter together. (A food processor works well and is quick.) Gradually add flour, salt and 1 of the last 2 ingredients. Blend well together. Form into a log roll about 12" long and 2" wide. Wrap roll in wax paper. Refrigerate until ready to bake.

Preheat oven to 375°. When dough is chilled, cut off slices 1/4" thick and place on ungreased cookie sheet. Bake for approximately 10 to 12 minutes. Do not overbake or the cookies will be too crunchy.

The roll can be made ahead and refrigerated or frozen.

Mary Griffin
Parent, Amy Griffin '94 and Robert Griffin '96

Sesame Cheese Wafers

Yields 4 dozen

INGREDIENTS:

1/2 pound Tillamook sharp cheddar cheese, grated
2 tablespoons butter, softened
3/4 cup flour

1 teaspoon Worcestershire sauce
1/2 teaspoon salt
Dash liquid hot pepper seasoning
1/4 cup sesame seeds

PROCEDURE:

Combine grated cheese with butter, flour, Worcestershire sauce, salt and liquid red pepper seasoning. Mix thoroughly. Form the cheese dough into 1" diameter logs. Roll in sesame seeds, gently pressing the seeds into the dough. Wrap in foil and refrigerate until cold.

When ready to cook, preheat oven to 450°. Slice dough rolls about 1/8" thick. Place on cookie sheets. Bake wafers for 8 to 10 minutes. Watch closely so they do not burn.

If you like, more sesame seeds can be pressed onto the surface of the wafers just before baking. Variations: For a south-of-the-border wafer, use Monterey jack cheese and add 1 tablespoon finely minced jalapeño peppers with seeds and veins removed. For Italian flavored wafers, use 4 ounces freshly grated Parmesan cheese, 4 ounces grated Provolone cheese and 1 tablespoon fresh basil or oregano finely minced (or 2 teaspoons dried herbs).

Carolyn Yorston
Headmaster's Advisory Council and
Parent, Wendy Yorston Stevens '75

Cheese Cookies

Yields 12 to 14 dozen

INGREDIENTS:

1 cup (2 sticks) butter, softened
3/4 pound grated sharp or New York cheddar cheese
2 cups bread flour

1 1/2 teaspoons salt
1/4 teaspoon cayenne pepper

PROCEDURE:

Soften and cream butter in large bowl with a wooden spoon. Grate cheese on fine grater. Add cheese to soft butter and blend thoroughly with pastry blender. Sift flour, salt and cayenne pepper into small bowl. Add flour to cheese/butter mixture in 3 parts, blending between each addition. Blend final mixture until it forms a solid ball and no longer sticks to the bowl. Cut mixture into 4 even parts. Roll each part into a cylinder on wax paper until it is almost as long as the width of wax paper. Refrigerate overnight or until firm (4 to 6 hours).

Preheat oven to 400°. Cut cookies about 3/8" thick. Place on large ungreased cookie sheet about 1/2" apart. Bake 9 to 10 minutes until edges are golden brown. Remove immediately. Serve warm.

Best if warmed in 150° to 170° oven before serving. Cheese cookies can be kept in plastic container in freezer indefinitely (at least 6 months). Great for cocktails anytime or served with soup or salad. When I store them I use the wax paper they were rolled in between the layers.

Beverly Huse Ryburn '38

Parmesan Tortillas

Yields 12 tortillas

INGREDIENTS:

12 flour tortillas
Olive oil

Shredded Parmesan cheese

PROCEDURE:

Preheat oven to 350°. Brush or spray tortillas with olive oil. Sprinkle liberally with Parmesan. Bake until golden.

These are so light, they make an excellent accompaniment to cocktails before dinner. They are also good cold. Kids love them!

Gail Saivar
Parent, Jesse Saivar '95

English Muffin Tidbits

Serves 12

INGREDIENTS:

1 **cup shredded cheddar cheese**
1 **small onion, finely chopped**
1 **2.25-ounce can pitted olives, finely chopped**
1 **4-ounce can chopped mushrooms, sautéed**

1/2 **cup mayonnaise**
Salt and pepper to taste

6 **English muffins, split**

PROCEDURE:

Mix all the topping ingredients in a bowl. Spread each muffin half with mixture. Cut each muffin half into 6 sections. Place on cookie sheet and freeze. When frozen, remove from sheet and place in plastic bags for final freezing.

When ready to serve, preheat oven to 350°. Take out quantity desired and bake on cookie sheet for 15 minutes.

Quick and easy. Good for drop-in guests.

Anna Louise Whitehouse White '33

47

Quick Greek Cheese Pie

Serves 6

INGREDIENTS:

1 cup (2 sticks) butter
4 eggs
1 cup flour
3 teaspoons baking
  powder
1 cup milk
1 cup (1/2 pint) yogurt

7 1/2 ounces Edam cheese,
  grated
7 1/2 ounces feta cheese
  (white goat cheese),
  grated
Pepper to taste

PROCEDURE:

Preheat oven to 350°. Beat the butter until smooth. Add eggs, 1 at a time, beating after each addition until well-blended. Add flour and baking powder and beat until well-mixed. Blend in milk, yogurt and cheeses. Add pepper to taste. Pour mixture into a 12" round ceramic tart pan and bake for approximately 30 minutes or until the blade of a knife comes out dry.

You can serve immediately, but can also keep in the refrigerator and warm in microwave. Quick and easy and freezes beautifully.

Irene Metaxas Zafiriou '57

Blue Cheese Spread

Serves 6 to 8

INGREDIENTS:

8 ounces cream cheese
4 ounces blue cheese
1/2 cup sliced almonds

1 cup sliced red or green
seedless grapes

PROCEDURE:

Preheat oven to 350°. Beat room-temperature cream cheese together with blue cheese. Place in 9" pie plate (or similar size ovenproof serving dish) and spread evenly. Sprinkle almonds over top. Bake for 10 minutes. Remove from oven and press sliced grapes into top. Serve hot with crackers

This is also good with steak as a side sauce.

Marcy Baugh
Parent, Michael Baugh '95

Curried Cream Cheese Spread

Serves 8

INGREDIENTS:

8 ounces cream cheese
1/2 cup Major Grey's
(mango) chutney
1/2 cup slivered almonds,
chopped

1 teaspoon curry powder
1/2 teaspoon dry mustard

Crackers to
accompany

PROCEDURE:

Combine all ingredients (reserving a few chopped almonds for topping) and stir to blend well. Place in serving bowl and refrigerate. Sprinkle almonds on top and serve with crackers

Easy and delicious!

Kimberly Miller
Parent, Camden Miller '94X, Trent Miller '96, Derek Miller '98

Brie with Sun-dried Tomatoes

Serves 16

INGREDIENTS:

1 2-pound Brie wheel
5 tablespoons parsley, minced
5 tablespoons Parmesan cheese, grated
10 sun-dried tomatoes in oil, chopped
2 1/2 tablespoons oil from tomatoes

6 cloves garlic, minced
2 tablespoons minced fresh basil
3 tablespoons toasted pine nuts, chopped
Basil leaves for garnish

PROCEDURE:

Chill Brie well before handling. Remove rind from top of cheese and place cheese on serving plate or platter. Mix other ingredients (except basil) together. Spread on top of Brie. Garnish with basil leaves. Serve at once or refrigerate. For best flavor allow Brie to stand 30 to 60 minutes after removing from refrigerator.

Colorful. Great with water crackers or melba toast.

Sarah Henriksen
Parent, Nicholas Henriksen '98

Artichoke Spread

Serves 6 to 8

INGREDIENTS:

1 14-ounce can artichokes, drained and roughly chopped
1 cup onions, minced
1 cup mayonnaise
1/2 cup Swiss cheese (Emmenthal), grated

1/2 cup Parmesan, grated
Garlic powder and pepper to taste

Crackers to accompany

PROCEDURE:

Preheat oven to 350°. Mix all ingredients except for 1/4 cup of Swiss cheese together in a bowl and put into an ovenproof casserole or serving dish. Sprinkle top with the remaining 1/4 cup Swiss cheese. Cook in oven until golden, approximately 20 to 30 minutes. Serve as spread with crackers, preferably "Carr's" wafers.

You may cook this 1 day ahead, minus 10 minutes of total cooking time and, when ready to serve, reheat at 350° for 10 minutes. It's a very delicious appetizer to serve at any type of gathering. Always a success!

Kathleen Wahab
Parent, Carl Wahab '88, Stephanie Wahab '86, Stephen Wahab '88

Artichoke Dip in Bread Bowl

Serves 10

INGREDIENTS:

1 8.5-ounce can
   artichoke hearts
1/2 cup mayonnaise
1 garlic clove, diced

1 cup grated Parmesan
   cheese
1 round bread loaf
1 baguette (optional)

PROCEDURE:

Preheat oven to 350°. Blend together artichoke hearts (drained), mayonnaise and diced garlic. Use blender or food processor and blend on medium-high speed until mixture is creamy. Pour into a bowl. Add Parmesan cheese and mix with spoon. Pour mixture into a glass or metal bread loaf pan. Place pan into oven and bake for 20 minutes. Test dip by looking for bubbling and browning around pan edges. Remove pan and set aside for a moment. Cut the top section off round bread loaf and pull out the inside bread to make a bowl out of bread loaf. Pour dip mixture into bread loaf. Cut up the remaining bread pieces to place around bread loaf for dipping. (May cut up a baguette as well for additional pieces.) Serve warm.

A wonderful appetizer. Very quick and easy to make. Goes well with Italian, Spanish or American dishes.

Sharon S. de Moyano
Wife, Rafael Moyano, Faculty, Foreign Language Department

Hot Bread Dip

Serves 8 to 12

INGREDIENTS:

1/4 cup butter
3 or 4 green onions, chopped
1 clove garlic, minced
2 cups (1 pint) sour
   cream
8 ounces cream cheese
8 ounces cheddar
   cheese, grated
1 large (8" to 10") round
   loaf sourdough or any
   crusty bread

Optional (use any, all
   or none):
1/4 cup bacon bits
1 7-ounce can chopped
   clams
1 8-ounce jar marinated
   artichoke hearts,
   chopped

PROCEDURE:

Preheat oven to 300°. In medium frying pan, melt 1/4 cup butter and sauté chopped green onions and minced clove of garlic until soft. Set aside. In large mixing bowl, combine sour cream, cream cheese, cheddar cheese. Add 1 or more optional ingredients if desired. Add sautéed onions and garlic to the mixture and stir with wooden spoon until thoroughly mixed. Cut the top off of a round loaf of sourdough/crusty bread (making an opening about 5" to 6" in diameter). Save top for the lid. Scoop out loaf of bread and break or cut the inside bread into bite size pieces for dipping. Pour cheese mixture into hollowed out bread. Replace lid. Wrap entire loaf in aluminum foil, place on baking sheet and bake 1 1/2 hours. In the last 1/2 hour to 45 minutes, place bread pieces, also wrapped in foil, on the same sheet to bake. For crisper bread pieces, open foil.

For extra bread dipping pieces, cut up hard rolls and bake along with bread pieces.

Janet Houts
Parent, Kathryn Houts '97 and Fred Houts '95

Artichoke Dip

Serves 4 to 6

INGREDIENTS:

1 4-ounce can or jar
artichoke hearts
1 8-ounce package
cream cheese
1 cup mayonnaise

2/3 cup Parmesan cheese

Seasoned bagel chips
or spicy crackers to
accompany

PROCEDURE:

Preheat oven to 350°. Drain and chop artichoke hearts. Soften cream cheese to room temperature. Mix all ingredients together until mixture is creamy, but not overly blended. (Do not purée artichokes!) Spoon into ceramic baking dish. (A fluted quiche dish works very well.) Bake for 25 to 30 minutes or until golden brown on top. Serve with seasoned bagel chips or any spicy cracker.

This is a warm and satisfying appetizer that is easy to make if you are short of time and energy!

Elsie Burke
Parent, Tara Burke '97

Suzie's Dip

Serves 15

INGREDIENTS:

1 cup mayonnaise
1 cup chopped artichoke
hearts
1 cup grated Parmesan
cheese

Crackers to
accompany

PROCEDURE:

Preheat oven to 350°. Mix dip ingredients together and put in ovenproof serving dish, uncovered. Bake for 45 minutes or until top is browned. Serve warm with crackers.

Margo Armbruster Halsted '56

Cheesy Artichoke Dip

Serves 10 to 20

INGREDIENTS:

2 14-ounce cans
   artichoke hearts in
   water
8 ounces cheddar
   cheese, grated
1 1/2 cups freshly grated
   Parmesan cheese

2 cups mayonnaise
1 teaspoon dill
   Dash garlic powder (or
   more to taste)

Crackers (stoned
   wheat or water)

PROCEDURE:

Preheat oven to 350°. Drain artichoke hearts and chop into small to medium pieces. Mix artichokes together with the other dip ingredients in a large bowl. Spoon into a baking dish and bake for 20 to 30 minutes. Mixture should be bubbling. Serve as a dip with water crackers or other crackers of your choice.

Can be assembled 1 to 2 days ahead and cooked just prior to serving. If dish has been in the refrigerator, allow 5 minutes longer for cooking.

Katherine Yarborough
Parent, Mitchell Price '92 and Taylor Price '99

Gourmet Stuffed Broiled Mushrooms

Serves 12

INGREDIENTS:

2 pounds large
   mushrooms
3/4 cup (1 1/2 sticks)
   butter or margarine
1/4 cup Worcester-shire
   sauce
1 teaspoon Tabasco
   sauce
   Dash garlic powder,
   Cajun spice, lemon
   pepper
1 tablespoon sherry

1 teaspoon olive oil
1 bunch parsley, finely
   chopped
1/2 cup chopped fresh
   basil
1 1/2 cup prepared bread
   crumbs
1/2 cup grated sharp
   cheddar cheese
1 cup freshly grated
   Parmesan cheese

PROCEDURE:

Wash mushrooms under cold running water and lay on paper towels to dry. Carefully break off mushroom stems and reserve. Melt butter in large saucepan. Add Worcestershire and Tabasco sauce, spices, sherry and stir until fully blended. Place mushroom caps into the saucepan and baste with sauce. When all mushrooms are coated, remove and place in broiling pan coated lightly with olive oil. Reserve sauce. Mince mushroom stems and add to reserved sauce in saucepan along with the parsley, basil, bread crumbs, cheddar cheese and 1/2 cup of the Parmesan cheese. Blend thoroughly and stuff caps with mixture. Sprinkle with remaining 1/2 cup Parmesan cheese. Broil for 8 to 10 minutes, watching carefully.

I have never made this recipe without having to say, "I'm sorry there isn't any left".

Delisa McArdle
Sister, David Harper '90 and Labrina Harper '87

Potato Pancakes

Yields 12 pancakes

INGREDIENTS:

2 cups grated potatoes	3 tablespoons grated onion
3 large eggs, well-beaten	Vegetable oil for frying
1 1/2 tablespoons all-purpose flour	Applesauce and/or sour cream to accompany
1 1/4 teaspoons salt	

PROCEDURE:

After grating potatoes, wring in a paper towel to remove as much water as possible. Combine potatoes and eggs. Sift together the flour and salt and add to potato mixture. Add the grated onion and stir to blend. Heat the oil (about 1/8" deep) in heavy skillet. Put spoonfuls of potato batter in hot oil to make pancakes. Brown and turn to other side and cook until crisp. Serve hot with applesauce and/or sour cream.

Make small for appetizers.

Jocelyn Vortmann
Parent, Anna Vortmann '90, Cady Vortmann '93,
Jocelyn Vortmann '97

Bruscetta Tomato Toast

Serves as many as you like

INGREDIENTS:

Crusty bread, sliced
Olive oil
Garlic cloves, peeled
and cut in half
Fresh tomatoes, sliced

Fresh basil leaves,
coarsely chopped
Vinegar (balsamic, red
wine or rice)

PROCEDURE:

Toast the bread. Then brush lightly with olive oil and rub with garlic. Add a slice or two of tomato and some coarsely chopped basil leaves and sprinkle a little vinegar to taste on top.

Use the very best ingredients possible; the quality of the bread and olive oil and the freshness of the tomatoes and basil make all the difference. Simple, but simply scrumptious. Good with soup or salad for a light supper.

Diana Binkley
Parent, Pepper Binkley '97

Salmon or Tuna Dip

Serves 6

INGREDIENTS:

1 6-ounce can tuna or
   salmon, drained
1/2 8-ounce package
   cream cheese
2 tablespoons chili sauce

1 teaspoon parsley flakes
   (or chopped fresh
   parsley)

Crackers to
   accompany

PROCEDURE:

Mix 1 can salmon (or tuna) with cream cheese and chili sauce until creamy.
Make into a round mold on round platter and sprinkle parsley flakes over to
garnish. Put into refrigerator for about 1 hour (or all day if desired). Serve with
crackers around the mold.

*You cannot ruin this recipe. You can use 8-ounces of cream cheese instead of
4-ounces and vary the amount of chili sauce to taste. Men especially seem to like the
salmon dip.*

Susan Fleet Welsch '63
Honorary Lifetime Trustee

Smoked Salmon Appetizer

Serves 6 to 8

INGREDIENTS:

8 ounces smoked salmon
   or canned salmon,
   deboned and flaked
3 tablespoon lemon juice
1/4 cup chopped red onion

2 tablespoons capers
1/8 cup mayonnaise

Water crackers, to
   accompany

PROCEDURE:

Mix all together (except crackers) and serve with water crackers

Terry Lakenan Rismon '73X

Tuna Dill Mold

Serves 6

INGREDIENTS:

1 envelope (1 tablespoon)
   unflavored gelatine
2 tablespoons lemon
   juice
1 chicken bouillon cube,
   dissolved in 1/2 cup
   warm water
1/4 cup mayonnaise
1/4 cup plain nonfat
   yogurt
1/4 cup milk
2 tablespoons finely
   chopped parsley

1 tablespoon minced
   green onion
1 teaspoon dry mustard
1 teaspoon finely
   chopped dill weed
1/4 teaspoon pepper
1 7-ounce can tuna,
   well-drained and
   mashed with a fork
1/2 cup seeded, grated
   cucumber

PROCEDURE:

In a bowl stir together gelatine and lemon juice. Let stand 5 minutes to soften.
Stir in chicken broth to dissolve completely. In a large bowl, mix together all
remaining ingredients. Then add gelatine mixture to this mixture. Pour into a 2-
cup mold and chill until set.

Better if made a day ahead. I serve it with Triscuits or Rye Crisp.

Kathy Applen
Parent, Ethan Applen '92 and Ellie Applen '99

Cajun Shrimp

Serves 6

INGREDIENTS:

1 pound extra-large
   shrimp in shells
1 tablespoon fresh lime
   juice
1/2 tablespoon paprika
1/2 teaspoon garlic powder
1/2 teaspoon onion powder
1/4 teaspoon thyme
1/4 teaspoon oregano

1/4 teaspoon salt
1/8 teaspoon black pepper
1/8 teaspoon white pepper
1/8 teaspoon cayenne
   pepper
Olive oil spray
Lime wedges for
   garnish

PROCEDURE:

Peel and clean shrimp, leaving tails on. Toss shrimp with lime juice in large
bowl. Mix all dry ingredients and sprinkle over shrimp. Toss to coat well.
Arrange shrimp on skewers. Spray with olive oil and grill on barbecue over high
flame with cover closed, approximately 4 minutes a side for very large shrimp. Or,
sauté in large skillet lightly coated with olive oil until shrimp are pink. Chill,
covered, at least 1 hour. Garnish with lime wedges.

*These are best grilled. Make sure you take 1 before serving, as they disappear
instantly. Recipe may be doubled or tripled for a large party. Serve as first course
or hors d'oeuvre.*

Gail Saivar
Parent, Jesse Saivar '95

Grilled Shrimp and Prosciutto

Serves 6

INGREDIENTS:

1 cup dry white wine
1 cup olive oil
1/4 cup fresh lemon juice
2 tablespoons Dijon
   mustard
1/2 cup chopped fresh
   basil
   Freshly cracked black
   peppercorns, to taste

24 jumbo shrimp, peeled
   and deveined,
   tails left on
24 whole large basil leaves
24 thin slices prosciutto
   (Italian ham), fat
   trimmed

PROCEDURE:

Combine first 6 ingredients. Pour over shrimp in a shallow bowl. Marinate in the refrigerator at least 3 hours, turning the shrimp occasionally. Prepare hot coals with a generous amount of mesquite for grilling the shrimp. Remove the shrimp from the marinade, reserve the marinade. Wrap the middle of each shrimp first with a basil leaf and then with a slice of prosciutto. Thread 4 shrimp lengthwise starting at the head on each of 6 metal skewers. Grill the shrimp, basting with the reserve marinade, for several minutes on each side. Serve immediately.

This looks as beautiful as it tastes. Always a hit. Send leftovers to Arline!

Arline Greene
Parent, Cheryl Greene '98

Herbed Shrimp

Serves 10

INGREDIENTS:

1 cup dry white wine
1 teaspoon mustard
    seeds
3 bay leaves
    Juice of 1 lemon
4 tablespoons chopped
    fresh basil
2 tablespoons chopped
    fresh rosemary
1 tablespoon chopped
    fresh tarragon
2 cloves garlic, minced
1 tablespoon dill or other
    herbed mustard

1 cup olive oil
1 small green bell
    pepper, diced
1 small red bell pepper,
    diced
1 small yellow bell
    pepper, diced
    Salt and pepper to
    taste
2 pounds jumbo shrimp,
    peeled, cleaned and
    cooked

PROCEDURE:

Combine all ingredients (except shrimp) in a bowl large enough to hold shrimp and mix well. Add cooked shrimp and toss to coat well. Cover bowl and refrigerate <u>overnight</u>. Serve with toothpicks and crusty bread.

Susan McClellan
Parent, Ryan McClellan '96

Spicy Shrimp

Serves 8

INGREDIENTS:

2 1/2 pounds large shrimp,
    shelled and deveined
1/4 cup finely chopped
    parsley
1/4 cup finely chopped
    shallots
1/4 cup tarragon vinegar
1/4 cup white wine
    vinegar

1/4 cup olive oil
4 tablespoons Dijon
    mustard
2 teaspoons crushed red
    pepper
2 teaspoons salt
    Pepper to taste

PROCEDURE:

Boil shrimp in a large pot of salted water for approximately 10 minutes. When done, drain and cool. Mix together all the other ingredients and pour over cooled shrimp. Mix well so every shrimp is covered. Cover and refrigerate for 2 hours.

Sheryl Durkin
Parent, Kimberly Durkin '96 and Kristin Durkin '98

Fresh Crab Mold

Serves 12

INGREDIENTS:

1 10-ounce can cream of
    mushroom soup
1 package unflavored
    gelatine
3 tablespoons cold water
8 ounces cream cheese,
    room temperature

1 cup mayonnaise
1 tablespoon Worcester-
    shire sauce
1 cup finely chopped
    celery
1/2 pound fresh crab meat

PROCEDURE:

Heat soup in a saucepan (undiluted). Dissolve gelatine in the water and add to the warmed soup. Remove from heat and gently stir in the remainder of the ingredients. Pour mixture into a 4-cup mold and refrigerate overnight. Gently unmold onto serving platter and serve with crackers or crudités.

To impress your friends, use a fish-shaped mold and put an olive half in the indentation for the fish eye before pouring in the mixture. When carefully unmolded, it really becomes an "eye-catching" hors d'oeuvre.

Marilyn Bilger
Parent, Lauren Bilger '93 and Whitney Bilger '96

Crab Cocktail Spread

Serves 6 to 8

INGREDIENTS:

1 8-ounce package
  cream cheese
1 7-ounce can good crab
  meat, drained
1 12-ounce jar seafood
  cocktail sauce

Parsley flakes (or
  chopped fresh parsley)

Crackers to
  accompany

PROCEDURE:

Place cream cheese on round serving dish. Pour approximately 1/2 bottle cocktail sauce over and around cheese. Sprinkle crab meat (drained) over sauce. Sprinkle parsley over the top. Serve with crackers.

This is very fast to prepare and the platter always comes back to the kitchen empty.

Sibby Hull Toland '44

Chili Crab Dip

Serves 6

INGREDIENTS:

1/2 medium onion, finely
    chopped
8 ounces cream cheese
2 tablespoons
    mayonnaise
2 tablespoons Worcester-
    shire
1 tablespoon lemon juice
    Dash garlic salt
    Dash Tabasco

1 12-ounce jar
    Homemade Brand
    Chili Sauce
1 7-ounce can crab meat

    Crackers to
    accompany

PROCEDURE:

Using a mixer, blend well all ingredients but chili sauce, crab and crackers in a medium bowl at medium speed. Spread mixture in bottom of a flat serving dish. Top with approximately 1/2 jar of the chili sauce. Top with crab. Chill for 1 hour before serving. Serve with crackers.

Joan Heylman
Faculty, Physical Education Department

Elegant Smoked Turkey in Radicchio

Serves 8 to 10

INGREDIENTS:

6 slices smoked turkey
1/2 cup mayonnaise
1 tablespoon Dijon
    mustard
1 4-ounce jar sliced
    pimentos

3 bunches radicchio
    leaves
2 bunches chives,
    soaked in water

PROCEDURE:

Chop smoked turkey in food processor or by hand. Add next 3 ingredients and mix with turkey. Place approximately 1 tablespoon of the turkey mixture in each radicchio leaf. Roll up lengthwise. Tie roll with bow made of soaked chive.

People are crazy for this. It is so pretty. To make easier, put turkey mixture in bowl and surround with radicchio or endive leaves.

Ann Gilchrist
Parent, Jennifer Gilchrist '94

Chinese Foil Wrapped Chicken

Serves 20 to 25

INGREDIENTS:

2 **pounds boned and skinned chicken breasts, cut into 1" x 1" pieces**
1 **egg white**
1/4 **cup hoisin sauce**
1/4 **cup plum sauce**
1/2 **cup Chinese parsley or cilantro, chopped**
6 **ginger slices (fresh)**

1 **tablespoon sesame oil**
6 **peeled and mashed garlic cloves**
2 **tablespoons soy sauce**
1/4 **teaspoon white pepper**
2 **tablespoons black bean sauce**
2 **tablespoons vermouth**
24 **4" foil squares (approximately)**

PROCEDURE:

Mix all ingredients, (except foil and chicken), together to form a marinade. Marinate chicken for at least 4 hours or overnight in this mixture. Preheat oven to 350°. Remove raw garlic and ginger from marinade. Place 1 piece of chicken in the center of each foil square. Fold over to form a triangle. Double fold the edges and flatten to remove air. Bake foil packets in a single layer on a cookie sheet for approximately 20 minutes. Serve in foil packets. Each person unwraps his own and eats with fingers.

A terrific make ahead appetizer that children love to help with. Packets may be frozen for up to 2 months, if uncooked and stored in plastic or ziploc bag. The marinade contains egg white as a tenderizer. All the Chinese products are readily available in the Asian grocery section or specialty store.

Nora Hom Newbern
Parent, Camille Newbern '99

Chopped Chicken Liver

Serves 8 to 10

INGREDIENTS:

1 pound fresh chicken
   livers
1 tablespoon white
   vinegar
3 medium onions,
   chopped
2 cloves garlic, minced
2 tablespoons vegetable
   oil
3 hardboiled eggs

1 to 2 tablespoons
   mayonnaise
Salt and pepper to
   taste

Crackers or small
   rounds of rye or
   pumpernickel bread
   to accompany

PROCEDURE:

Wash livers in cold water and place in a saucepan with enough cold water to
cover. Add the vinegar to the water. Bring to a boil and lower heat. Simmer for
approximately 15 minutes. Drain and set aside. Sauté the onions and garlic in
the oil until lightly browned. Place cooked livers, sautéed onions and garlic and
hardboiled eggs in a food processor. Blend until smooth. Add the mayonnaise,
salt and pepper and mix well. Place in a bowl and refrigerate. When cold, serve
as an hors d'oeuvre on crackers or small rounds of rye or pumpernickel bread.

*This is a great party favorite. You will probably find that you will have to double
this recipe for parties, since it is the first hors d'oeuvre to be finished off.*

Sylvia Schwartz
Grandparent, Adam Schwartz '97

Liver Pâté

Serves 6 to 8

INGREDIENTS:

Pâté:
1 pound chicken livers
1 14-ounce can chicken broth
1/2 cup (1 stick) margarine
1/2 cup (1 stick) butter
1 large shallot
1/2 teaspoon salt
4 turns of pepper grinder
1/4 generous teaspoon freshly grated nutmeg
1/8 generous teaspoon ground cloves

1/2 teaspoon powdered mustard
4 tablespoon sweet Marsala wine

Gel Topping:
1/2 envelope unflavored gelatine
1 cup canned chicken broth
1 scallion

Toast and cornichons to accompany

PROCEDURE:

Wash livers in cold water, removing yellow fatty parts. Simmer broth in medium saucepan. Add drained livers and lightly simmer about 10 minutes, covered, until done and slightly pink when cut. Drain livers. (Remaining broth may be offered to cats.) Melt margarine and butter. Place livers, margarine and butter in blender and add all pâté remaining ingredients. Blend 30 seconds at medium speed. Stop and push down contents once and blend again, about 30 seconds. Mixture should be completely smooth. Chill in small terrine covered airtight with plastic. When chilled, top with gel, if desired.

Gel: Dissolve gelatine in broth according to package directions. Cool. Spoon gel over chilled pâté to cover about 1/8" depth. Chill until firm. Cut 2 to 3 green scallion leaves 4" to 5" long and slice lengthwise to form narrow lily of the valley leaves. Place flat on gelatine, with green strips close together at the base of the plant and fanning out at top. Cut white part of scallion crosswise in 1/8" thick slices and place along leaves to form buds. Press lightly into gel. Carefully coat with a second 1/8" gel. Chill to firm and serve only slightly below room temperature, with toast and cornichons.

Anne Rolph Barton '44

French Country Pâté

Yields 5 to 6
8-ounce French glass jelly jars

INGREDIENTS:

1 medium onion, minced
2 shallots, minced
1 pippin apple, peeled
  and minced
2 tablespoons oil
2 tablespoons butter
8 ounces hot pork
  sausages
8 ounces chicken livers
1 cup apple brandy
2 8-ounce packages
  cream cheese
1 1/2 teaspoons dry tarragon

1/4 teaspoon white pepper
1/8 teaspoon thyme
1/8 teaspoon allspice
1 tablespoon garlic salt
1 cup walnuts, toasted

Gelatine topping:
1 envelope unflavored
  gelatine
1 10-ounce can beef
  consommé
2 tablespoons sherry or
  Madeira

PROCEDURE:

Sauté onion, shallots and apple in 1 tablespoon oil and 1 tablespoon butter. Then put in food processor. Sauté sausage and chicken livers in 1 tablespoon oil and 1 tablespoon butter and put in food processor. Heat brandy and flame. Pour into food processor. Process for 30 seconds (using On/Off button.) Add broken bits of cream cheese and then process (On button) until blended. Add all seasonings. Add walnuts (On/Off button quickly) All ingredients should be well-blended by this point.

Gelatine topping: Mix gelatine ingredients in small saucepan and heat until gelatine dissolves. Let cool.

Pour pâté into jars. Let cool. Carefully pour cooled gelatine mixture on top of pâté so surface of pâté does not break. Refrigerate until gelatine sets.

Serve in jelly jar with French bread and a great champagne. Wrap up and give as gifts. Recipients will rave!

Heather Drake Holden '68

Tomato Soup

Serves 6 to 8

INGREDIENTS:

2 tablespoons butter
2 tablespoons olive oil
1 large onion, thinly
   sliced (2 cups)
4 sprigs fresh thyme (or
   1/2 teaspoon dried)
4 to 6 fresh basil leaves,
   chopped (or 1/2
   teaspoon dried)
4 cups chopped fresh
   ripe (or canned)
   tomatoes

3 tablespoons tomato
   paste
1/4 cup flour
4 cups chicken broth
1 teaspoon sugar
1 cup (1/2 pint) half and
   half for richer soup
   (optional)
Salt and freshly
   ground black pepper
   to taste

PROCEDURE:

Heat butter and oil in large heavy pot. Add onion, thyme and basil and cook slowly until onion is wilted and soft (approximately 10 minutes), stirring occasionally to prevent burning. Add tomatoes and tomato paste. Stir well and simmer for about 10 minutes. Put the flour in a small mixing bowl and add about 1/4 cup of the chicken broth, stirring or whisking until well-blended. (Add more broth if necessary.) Stir this into the tomato/onion mixture in pot. Add the remaining broth and simmer about 30 minutes, stirring frequently all over the bottom of pot so soup does not stick or burn. Put soup through food mill to remove seeds and tomato skins. Return soup to heat and add sugar. Add salt and pepper to taste. (Optional: Add half and half if desired at this point.) Correct seasonings.

Serve plain with crusty French bread or with garlic croutons sprinkled over top. This soup can be made very light or richer with the addition of the half and half. It has a delicious robust flavor and is best made when fresh home grown tomatoes are in season.

Pat Miller
Parent, Kristin Miller '87 and Patrick Miller '93

French Onion Soup

Serves 6 to 8

INGREDIENTS:

- 4 tablespoons (1/2 stick) butter
- 6 onions, shredded or sliced
- 4 cups chicken stock
- 2 cups beef stock
- 1/2 cup dry white wine or dry white vermouth
- 1 cup shredded mild Swiss cheese (preferably Gruyere)
- 8 slices dry French bread
- Grated Parmesan cheese (optional)

PROCEDURE

Melt butter in a large heavy saucepan and sauté the onions over low heat, stirring frequently, 20 to 30 minutes. This slow sauté allows the onions to slowly release their sugar while giving up their pungent taste. Increase the heat, stir and sauté the onions until they are a deep, rich golden brown. Add the stocks and the wine and simmer, partially covered for 15 minutes or so to blend the flavors. Ladle the hot soup into individual heatproof bowls, top with a slice of dry bread, cover generously with shredded cheese. Sprinkle on a little Parmesan cheese if desired. Pop under a hot broiler. Serve as soon as the cheeses bubble and brown a little.

Judith Lamphier Strada '63X
Parent, Nick Strada '92 and Catherine Strada '95

Leek and Wine Soup

Serves 6 to 8

INGREDIENTS:

6 tablespoons (3/4 stick) butter
2 pounds leeks, cleaned and sliced
2 baking potatoes, peeled and cubed
2   14-ounce cans chicken broth

1 cup white vermouth or dry white wine
Salt to taste
1 cup (1/2 pint) heavy cream
Freshly ground pepper
2 to 4 tablespoons vermouth

PROCEDURE:

Melt the butter in a heavy soup pot. Add the leeks and cook gently for 5 minutes. Add the cubed potatoes, broth, vermouth (or wine) and salt. Cook until the potatoes are tender, about 20 minutes. Turn off the heat. Purée the soup in a blender. This will have to be done in 2 lots. Return soup to pot. On low heat, stir in the cream. Season with freshly ground pepper and more salt, if needed. Add 2 to 4 tablespoons vermouth just prior to serving, if desired. Serve warm or cold.

Marianne Engle
Parent, Lindsey Engle '94 and Jordan Engle '98

Split Pea Soup

Serves 6

INGREDIENTS:

2 cups dried split peas
Ham bone
1/2 pound cubed ham
1/2 cup chopped onions
1 clove garlic (smashed)

1 bay leaf
Dash sugar
Salt and pepper to
taste

PROCEDURE:

Wash the peas, cover with fresh water for 15 minutes. Strain the water into a large pot. Add the peas and enough water to make 10 cups. Add the ham bone and cubed ham and bring to a boil. Reduce heat to lowest setting and cook covered for approximately 3 hours. Stir the mixture occasionally making sure that peas do not settle to the bottom. Add the onions, garlic, bay leaf, sugar, salt and pepper and cook at least 30 minutes more. Remove the ham bone, stir the mixture and refrigerate. When cold, skim the congealed fat from the soup. Reheat to serve.

Although many recipes call for the addition of a beurre manié (equal parts of flour and butter) to bind the soup, I feel that this is just too much added fat. For a thicker consistency, try using more split peas in the recipe or cook it down further after the fat has been skimmed. The ham I traditionally serve at Christmas is boned by the butcher prior to preparation. I freeze the ham bone for the pea soup I will prepare in the coming weeks.

Neely Swanson
Parent, Reid Swanson '94X

Fresh Pea Soup

Serves 4 for first course
or 2 for luncheon

INGREDIENTS:

2 cups fresh shelled peas
  (or frozen)
2 cups chicken broth,
  homemade or canned
  Salt and pepper to
  taste

Freshly grated nutmeg
1 cup (1/2 pint) half and
  half (or milk)

PROCEDURE:

Cook the fresh (or frozen) peas in rapidly boiling water for 3 to 4 minutes. Drain.
Reserve a few whole peas for garnish and place the rest in food processor fitted
with steel knife. Purée. Pour purée into a medium saucepan and stir in the
chicken broth. Season with salt, pepper and a few gratings of fresh nutmeg.
Cook while stirring over low heat until well-blended. Add the half and half (or
milk) and continue to stir over low heat until piping hot. (Do not boil.) Serve in
white bowls. Top with a few whole peas.

*Wonderful light soup for first course or for lunch with crisp French bread and
assorted cheeses. May use nonfat milk; soup will be thinner but just as tasty.*

Betty Vale
Parent, Elizabeth Vale '92 and Susannah Vale '95

Corn Chowder

Serves 4 to 6

INGREDIENTS:

1 large onion, chopped
1 large potato, diced
2 cups water
1 14-ounce can chicken broth
1 carrot, thinly sliced
1 stalk celery, thinly sliced
1/4 teaspoon sage
1/2 teaspoon pepper

1/2 teaspoon garlic salt
2 cups low fat or whole milk, warmed
3 cups frozen small kernel corn
1 tablespoon butter or margarine
4 tablespoons flour
1/3 cup cold water

PROCEDURE:

Place the chopped onion and potato with 2 cups water in a 4-quart saucepan and cook over medium heat for about 15 minutes. Add the chicken broth, carrot, celery, sage, pepper and garlic salt and cook for an additional 15 minutes. Add warmed milk and increase heat to bring soup to a low boil. Heat the frozen corn with butter or margarine in the microwave for about 5 minutes on high to defrost, stirring once. Set aside. Mix the flour with the cold water and add slowly to the soup, stirring constantly to thicken the soup. Reduce heat to low and stir in the warmed corn. Taste and add more garlic salt and pepper if necessary.

For a heartier soup add 1 to 2 cups cooked, diced chicken. Makes a tasty meal with English muffins.

Sherryl Parks
Parent, Josh Parks '91 and Cameron Parks '94

Cream of Broccoli Soup

Serves 12 (1/2 cup servings)

INGREDIENTS:

2 10-ounce packages
frozen chopped
broccoli
1/4 cup chopped onion
2 cups regular strength
chicken or beef broth
2 tablespoons butter

1 tablespoon flour
Salt to taste
1/8 teaspoon mace
(or nutmeg)
Dash pepper
2 cups (1 pint) half and
half or milk

PROCEDURE:

In a medium size pan, combine broccoli, onion and chicken broth. Simmer until tender, approximately 10 minutes. Whirl broccoli mixture in blender or food processor until very smooth. Melt butter in pan. Add flour, salt, mace and pepper, stirring until smooth. Slowly stir this mixture into the half and half. Return half and half mixture and broccoli purée to pan; stir to blend and cook over medium heat, stirring often, until soup bubbles. Serve hot.

Can be made ahead of time. Cool and keep in refrigerator until time for reheating. I like to serve in decorative coffee cups before going into dinner.

Cheryl Mallory
Parent, Edward Mallory '98

Zucchini Soup

Serves 8

INGREDIENTS:

2 large onions, chopped
2 tablespoons unsalted
  butter
2 pounds zucchini,
  thinly sliced
4 cups chicken stock (or
  canned chicken
  broth)
1 1/2 tablespoons white
  wine vinegar

1 garlic clove, minced
1/2 teaspoon salt
  Pepper to taste
2 potatoes, peeled and
  sliced
  Sour cream or plain
  yogurt for garnish

PROCEDURE:

In a large, heavy pot cook onion in butter over moderate heat for 5 minutes or until soft. Add zucchini, chicken stock, vinegar, garlic, salt and pepper. Bring liquid to a boil stirring occasionally. Add potatoes. Simmer the soup covered for 30 minutes. Let soup cool. Purée the soup in batches in blender or food processor. Chill, covered, for at least 2 hours. Serve in chilled bowls. Garnish with dollop of sour cream or plain yogurt.

A great chilled soup conveniently made a day ahead. If preferred, may heat and serve hot.

Patricia Clark
Parent, Ryan Clark '92 and Ashley Clark '95

Fresh Mushroom Soup

INGREDIENTS:

2 tablespoons chopped
   shallots
2 tablespoons unsalted
   butter
1/2 pound mushrooms,
   thinly sliced
1 1/2 cups chicken broth

2 tablespoons flour
1/2 cup half and half
2 tablespoons white
   wine
Salt and pepper to
   taste

PROCEDURE:

Sauté shallots in butter until soft. Add mushrooms. Cook until just tender.
Add chicken broth, flour and then slowly add half and half. Add splash of wine
at the end and salt and pepper to taste.

*Quick, easy, very rich. A treat. Serve with good French bread, a large green salad
and a plate of fresh fruit.*

Shannon Turner
Parent, Katie Turner '95 and Annie Turner '97X

Pumpkin Soup

Serves 4

INGREDIENTS:

1/4 cup (1/2 stick) butter
1 large onion, diced
2 1/2 cups chicken stock
1 pound fresh pumpkin, peeled and cut into 1" cubes

2 1/2 cups hot milk
Dash allspice
Salt and pepper to taste
Chopped parsley for garnish

PROCEDURE:

Melt half the butter, reserving 4 pats for garnish and sauté diced onion until tender. Add chicken stock and bring to boil. Add pumpkin cubes. Simmer until tender. Purée in blender. Add hot milk and spices to taste. Serve with a pat of butter on top. Garnish with parsley.

Goes well with a nice butter lettuce salad, garnished with sliced almonds and Mandarin oranges, tossed with honey poppy seed dressing and served with crusty bread!

Susy Smith '64
Staff, Director of Alumni

Root Soup

Serves 4 to 6

INGREDIENTS:

2 Idaho potatoes
4 large carrots
1 rutabaga
2 parsnips
3 medium leeks, white
   and light green part
   only

8 cups (2 quarts)
   chicken or vegetable
   stock
1 bunch parsley, finely
   chopped
1 tablespoon sherry
   (more or less to taste)
   Salt and pepper to
   taste

PROCEDURE:

Wash and coarsely chop roots. Place them in the 2 quarts chicken or vegetable stock in a large pot and bring to boil. Lower heat to medium and continue to cook until vegetables are tender. Using a slotted spoon, lift out all vegetables and place in a bowl, leaving remaining stock in pot. Place vegetables (a few at a time) in a blender jar (so jar is 1/2 or 3/4 full). Add about 1/2 cup of the reserved stock. Blend until puréed. Pour mixture back into stock in pot. Repeat blending steps until all vegetables have been puréed and returned to pot. Add parsley, sherry, salt and pepper to taste.

Any roots may be added or deleted and in any ratio. For carrot only soup, add 1 teaspoon vanilla and a dash of nutmeg. Quick and easy. Serve with thick pieces of your favorite hearty bread and green salad made with pears, chèvre (goat cheese) and toasted walnuts.

Erin Fray Kerr '80

Black Bean Soup

Serves 6 to 8

INGREDIENTS:

1 pound black beans
3 tablespoons cumin
4 teaspoons oregano
8 teaspoons chili powder
2 tablespoons tomato
   paste
1/2 medium onion, diced

1 tablespoon salt
1/4 teaspoon pepper
5 teaspoons processed
   garlic
1/2 cup chopped cilantro
   Sour cream or plain
   yogurt for garnish

PROCEDURE:

Cover beans and soak in water overnight. Drain and rinse. Place beans in large heavy pot and add all ingredients except cilantro and sour cream. Add enough water to cover beans by 2" and simmer covered for 2 hours or until tender. You can also purée some of the beans for a thicker soup. For better flavor, allow ingredients to mingle overnight. Reheat and serve topped with cilantro and sour cream or yogurt.

Gray Kristofferson
Parent, Cannon Kristofferson '90X and Karen Kristofferson '93

Sherried Wild Rice Soup

Serves 8 to 12

INGREDIENTS:

2/3 cup raw wild rice
2 cups water
1/2 teaspoon salt
1 medium leek
6 green onions
12 medium to large
   mushrooms
1 stalk celery, chopped
1 large clove garlic,
   sliced and chopped
1/2 cup (1 stick) butter
1 tablespoon fresh
   squeezed lemon juice

1/2 cup flour
8 cups (2 quarts)
   chicken broth
1 teaspoon Beau Monde
   seasoning
   Dash cayenne pepper
1 cup (1/2 pint) light
   cream
3 tablespoons dry sherry
   (Marsala is good)
   Salt and pepper to
   taste

PROCEDURE:

Rice: Thoroughly wash rice and place in a heavy saucepan with water and salt. Bring to a boil and simmer, covered, until tender but not too soft (about 45 minutes). Fluff with a fork and simmer another 5 minutes, uncovered. Wash and drain well.

While rice is cooking: Wash and trim the leek and green onions, leaving some of the green parts of both. Chop. Wash and slice the mushrooms. (I like to cut mushroom stems flush at the bottom of the cap.) Then chop, saving about 2/3 of the mushroom slices for adding later to the soup. Sauté the chopped ingredients in butter, along with lemon juice, in a large saucepan (big enough to become the soup pot) until just tender (about 3 minutes). Stirring with a wooden spoon, sprinkle in flour and cook 1 minute. Slowly add chicken broth, blending well. Simmer for about 15 minutes and then remove as many of the solids as possible (I use a ladle with holes). Place the solids and a small amount of broth in a blender and blend about 30 seconds. Return the mix to the broth. Add rice, then mushroom slices, Beau Monde and cayenne pepper. Whisk until thickened, then add the cream and sherry and stir to blend. Remove from heat before soup comes back to a boil. Season with salt and pepper to taste.

Doris and Roger Lindland
Parents, Stuart Lindland '89

Wild Mushroom and Brie Soup

Serves 6 to 8

INGREDIENTS:

1 pound fresh wild mushrooms (any combination of Portobello, shiitake, oyster, etc.), sliced

1/2 pound white regular mushrooms, sliced

1/2 cup finely chopped shallots

1/4 cup (1/2 stick) butter

1/2 cup Marsala wine

4 cups chicken broth

4 to 6 ounces Brie cheese (soft, very ripe)

2 cups (1 pint) heavy cream

Salt and freshly ground pepper to taste

Garnish:

2 tablespoons butter

1 large carrot, julienned

1 large celery stalk, julienned

1 large Portobello (or other wild) mushroom, julienned

1/4 cup chopped chives

PROCEDURE:

Wash the mushrooms under running cold water and lay out on paper towels to dry. Combine the mushrooms, shallots, butter, Marsala wine and 2 cups of the chicken broth and cook slowly reducing the entire mixture by half, (about 20 minutes on a low simmer). Purée the mushroom mixture along with the Brie (rind and all). Return the mixture to the pan and add the remaining 2 cups of chicken broth and heavy cream. Simmer on very low heat about 5 more minutes. Add salt and pepper to taste. While the soup is simmering sauté the garnish vegetables (except chives) in the butter until heated through. Ladle soup into bowls. Distribute the sautéed garnish evenly among the bowls and sprinkle with the chives. Enjoy! Soup should be thick and rich. If too thick for your taste, add chicken broth to thin.

Serve with a winter vegetable salad and crusty Italian bread. This soup is very rich, but you must use heavy cream or soup will separate and curdle. I recommend Portobello mushrooms for their excellent earthy flavor.

Pamela Fuller LaMantia '73

White Bean Soup with Swiss Chard

Serves 6 to 8

INGREDIENTS:

1 cup dried great
  northern beans
2 large onions, chopped
3 garlic cloves, minced
3 tablespoons olive oil
2 carrots, peeled and
  chopped
1/2 pound Swiss chard (or
  spinach)

5 cups chicken stock
2 cups water
1 bay leaf
1 teaspoon salt
1/2 teaspoon black pepper
3 tablespoons parsley,
  chopped
  Grated Parmesan
  cheese

PROCEDURE:

Cover and soak beans overnight. Drain. In a large pot sauté onions and garlic in oil, stirring, about 5 minutes or until soft. Add carrots and sauté for 3 minutes. Add chard and cook until wilted. Add the beans, along with chicken stock, 2 cups water and bay leaf. Partially cover and simmer until beans are tender (1 hour). Purée half of soup in food processor. Return to pot with remaining soup. Add salt, pepper and parsley. Serve hot sprinkled with Parmesan cheese.

Great served with Italian flatbread (focaccia)!

Patricia Clark
Parent, Ryan Clark '92 and Ashley Clark '95

Mine Tour Minestrone

Serves 8

INGREDIENTS:

1 large onion, chopped
2 stalks celery, chopped
2 carrots, chopped
1 tablespoon olive oil
1 teaspoon chopped
  garlic
8 cups (2 quarts)
  chicken broth
1/2 pound cooked Italian
  sausage, chopped
3 potatoes, diced
1 14-ounce can
  tomatoes, drained
  and chopped

2 zucchini, diced
3 tablespoons basil
  leaves, minced
1 cup cooked white
  beans
2 cups shredded fresh
  spinach
Salt and pepper to
  taste
Grated Parmesan or
  Romano cheese for
  garnish

PROCEDURE:

In a large soup pot cook the onion, celery and carrots in the olive oil for 5 minutes over medium heat. Stir in garlic and continue cooking for 2 minutes. Add the chicken broth, sausage, potatoes, tomatoes, zucchini and basil. Simmer until the vegetables are tender. Add the beans, spinach and salt and pepper to taste and simmer 10 minutes more. Sprinkle with grated Parmesan or Romano cheese for garnish.

Served at the Tourmaline Mine Tour picnics which were auctioned off at The Bishop's School Auction in 1992 and 1993.

Molly Hannan
Parent, Mimi Hannan '92

Minestrone Soup alla Lizz

Serves 8 to 10

INGREDIENTS:

1 cup white beans
1/2 cup chopped onion
2 leeks, rinsed thoroughly and chopped
2 carrots, chopped
2 potatoes, peeled and chopped
2 garlic cloves, minced (optional)
3 tablespoons extra virgin olive oil
4 cups hot water
4 cups chicken stock

1 teaspoon dried sweet basil
2 tomatoes, chopped
Salt and pepper to taste
1 cup chopped cabbage
1 cup washed spinach leaves
1 cup chopped zucchini
1 cup spaghetti noodles broken into 2" to 3" pieces
Freshly ground Parmesan cheese for table (optional)

PROCEDURE:

Soak beans in water to cover over night. Rinse well, put in saucepan, cover with water and boil for 30 minutes. Drain and set aside. In a large pot sauté onion, leeks, carrots potatoes and garlic in olive oil on low heat. Sauté until veggies are tender but not cooked through. Add reserved beans along with hot water, chicken stock, basil, tomatoes, salt and pepper. Raise heat to medium high and bring to almost boiling. Reduce heat to simmer, cover and cook for 1 hour. Add cabbage, spinach, zucchini and spaghetti. Continue to simmer for 10 to 15 minutes or until pasta and vegetables are cooked. Correct seasoning. Serve with freshly grated Parmesan cheese if desired.

A wonderful cold weather soup! Served cold in the summertime, it makes a nice light meal, that is tasty and very healthful. Should be served with either plain baguette or garlic bread.

Elizabeth (Lizz) Cavanaugh Grimes '78X

Homemade Minestrone Soup

Serves 6 to 8

INGREDIENTS:

2 1/2 tablespoons olive oil
3 carrots, peeled and cut in 1" slices
2 large celery stalks, cut in 1" pieces
1 large onion, chopped
1 15-ounce can diced tomatoes in juice
1 15-ounce can clear chicken broth
1 8-ounce can tomato sauce
3 1/2 cups water
Salt and pepper, parsley flakes, oregano, sweet basil (your choice), to taste

1 15-ounce can red kidney beans
1 15-ounce can white kidney beans (cannellini beans)
1 10-ounce package frozen spinach or 1/2 of 10-ounce bag fresh, prewashed spinach
1/2 small green cabbage, shredded
1 cup elbow macaroni, cooked separately according to package directions
Freshly grated Parmesan cheese

PROCEDURE:

Heat the olive oil in a 6-quart soup pot. Add the carrots, celery and onion and cook in the oil until the onions are transparent and the celery and carrots are somewhat softened. Add the tomatoes, chicken broth, tomato sauce and water. Bring the ingredients to a boil and immediately lower heat so that soup is lightly bubbling. Add seasonings of your choice. Cover and cook for 20 minutes. Add the red and white kidney beans, spinach, cabbage and cooked macaroni. Cook about 10 to 15 minutes more so everything is heated through and cabbage and spinach are soft. Correct seasoning. Serve with freshly grated Parmesan cheese on top.

This soup is great served immediately and is just as good several days after it is made. I always serve it with warm, crusty French bread. This recipe is easy to prepare. It is low in fat, nutritious and filling.

Gail Finegold
Parent, Todd Finegold '94

Hearty Lentil Barley Soup

Serves 6 to 8

INGREDIENTS:

1/2 pound Italian sausage
1 medium onion, chopped
3 cloves garlic, minced
1/3 cup pearl barley
8 cups chicken broth (or 4 cups broth and 4 cups water)

1 whole skinless chicken breast (approximately 1 pound)
1 cup lentils
1 15-ounce can garbanzo beans
1 12-ounce jar mild salsa
1 pound fresh spinach, cleaned and chopped (optional)

PROCEDURE:

Remove sausage casings and crumble meat in a 5 to 6-quart pot over medium-high heat. Stir often until browned. Remove meat from pan with a slotted spoon and set aside. Add onion, garlic and barley to the pan drippings. Cook, stirring often, until onion is limp and barley is toasted. Add chicken broth and bring to a boil. Add chicken and lentils. Bring back to a boil, cover and simmer until chicken is white in the thickest part, about 30 minutes. Remove chicken and when cool enough to handle, shred meat and return to pot. Drain the garbanzo beans and add to soup. Also add sausage meat and salsa. Heat to simmering. Stir spinach into soup and then ladle into bowls.

A satisfying, yet quick soup. Be creative. You can eliminate the spinach if desired and add sliced carrots, minced parsley, a bit of dill, whatever your family prefers.

Joni Ann Ganley
Parent, Brendan Ganley '99

Ian's Hearty Steak Soup

Serves 6

INGREDIENTS:

6 tablespoons butter
1/3 cup all-purpose flour
5 cups beef stock
2 beef bouillon cubes
   (optional)
1/2 cup canned tomatoes
1/2 cup diced celery
1/2 cup diced carrots
1/2 cup chopped onion
1 pound ground round
   steak

1 10-ounce package
   frozen mixed
   vegetables
1 1/2 teaspoons freshly
   ground black pepper
1 1/2 teaspoons Maggi
   Salt to taste
   Chopped parsley for
   garnish

PROCEDURE:

Place butter in soup pot and melt without burning. Add the flour and stir constantly to form a smooth paste. Cook over medium heat for 3 minutes, stirring occasionally. Slowly add the beef stock and stir until smooth. Add the (optional) bouillon cubes. Bring to a boil and add tomatoes and fresh vegetables. Regain the boil, reduce heat, cover and simmer for 30 minutes. While stock is simmering, sauté the ground beef in a little butter in a large skillet, until lightly browned (approximately 10 minutes). Drain and set aside. When stock has finished simmering, add meat. Simmer for 15 minutes. Add frozen vegetables. Simmer another 5 to 10 minutes. Add pepper, Maggi and salt to taste. Serve in warmed soup bowls. Garnish with parsley.

This is a truly delicious family dinner recipe and should be served with warm French bread. It is a recipe that freezes very well. Particularly good on a cold winter night.

Jane and Ian Jones
Parents, Victoria Jones '97 and Andra Jones '99

Sopa de Albondigas

Serves 8 to 10

INGREDIENTS:

Broth:
1 medium onion,
    chopped
3 cloves garlic, minced
2 tablespoons olive oil
1 15-ounce can tomato
    sauce
8 cups beef stock
4 cups chopped fresh
    tomatoes
1 to 2 teaspoons curry
    powder
1 to 2 teaspoons cumin
1 teaspoon crushed
    oregano
1 to 2 teaspoons salt

Meatballs:
1 pound ground pork
1 pound extra lean
    ground beef or turkey

1/2 cup uncooked rice
2 tablespoons chopped
    mint leaves
1 teaspoon pepper
1/2 teaspoon salt
2 eggs, beaten
2 tablespoons chopped
    fresh parsley

Condiments:
Chopped avocado
Chopped fresh cilantro
**Chopped fresh
    tomatoes**
Jalapeño slices
**Sour cream (or nonfat
    yogurt)**
**Grated Monterey jack
    cheese**

PROCEDURE:

To make the broth, sauté onions and garlic in the olive oil. Add tomato sauce, beef stock, fresh tomatoes, curry powder, cumin, oregano and salt. (These spices may be adjusted to suit your family.) Heat to boiling. Meanwhile, mix together ingredients for meatballs (albondigas). Shape into little balls and drop into boiling mixture. Cover and cook 45 minutes. Serve with assortment of condiments.

This is a wonderful dinner, served with herbed French bread, for a rainy day, football dinner, or when everyone in the house will be eating at different times. It holds well on the stove, can last a week in refrigerator and freezes well also.

Pamela Fadem Palisoul '68
Parent, Philip Palisoul '96

Tortilla Soup

Serves 6

INGREDIENTS:

2 large chicken breasts
1 dozen corn tortillas
1/2 cup vegetable oil
1/2 bunch cilantro, chopped
2 cloves garlic, peeled and chopped
2 yellow onions, diced
4 tomatoes, diced
2 teaspoons cumin, or more to taste

1/2 fresh jalapeño (or to taste)
8 cups (2 quarts) chicken stock

Garnish:
Cilantro
Diced avocado
Grated cheese
Tortillas

PROCEDURE:

Preheat oven to 350°. Wrap chicken in foil and bake approximately 1 hour. Cut tortillas into 1/2" strips. Heat 1/4 cup of the oil in a frying pan and fry tortilla strips until crisp. (Add more oil as needed). Drain and set aside. In a large pot heat 2 or 3 tablespoons oil and add cilantro, garlic, onions and tomatoes. Cook over medium heat, stirring until onions are limp (5 minutes). Add cumin, jalapeño and chicken stock (in order). Simmer for 15 minutes (or longer) until soup thickens slightly. Turn off heat. Add half the tortilla strips. Shred the cooked chicken and add to soup. Stir to mix. Serve soup in individual bowls and garnish with cilantro, diced avocado, grated cheese and the remaining tortilla strips.

Great for large groups and can be doubled easily!

Mary Jane Babcock Sexton '77

Creamy Chicken and Vegetable Rice Soup

Serves 4 to 6

INGREDIENTS:

1/2 cup uncooked white rice
1 1/2 cups water
4 cups canned chicken broth
1/4 cup chopped green pepper
1/2 cup diced celery
1/4 cup diced onion
1/4 cup shredded carrot
1/4 cup chopped mushrooms

1/2 teaspoon minced garlic
2 tablespoons margarine, melted
1/2 cup all-purpose flour
1 1/2 cups shredded cooked chicken (white meat)
1/4 teaspoon salt
1/4 teaspoon white pepper
1 cup evaporated nonfat milk

PROCEDURE:

Combine rice and water in large saucepan. Cover and bring to a boil. Reduce heat and simmer 15 minutes or less. Add chicken broth to rice in saucepan. Cover and simmer 30 minutes. Remove from heat and set aside. Sauté green pepper, celery, onion, carrot, mushrooms and garlic in margarine in large skillet until tender. Stir in flour and cook over medium heat 1 to 2 minutes. Add chicken, salt, pepper and rice to mixture in skillet, a little at a time at first, stirring constantly, so flour will not lump. Stir in evaporated nonfat milk. Cook over medium heat, stirring frequently until thoroughly heated. DO NOT BOIL.

One of the best soups ever. Even though it is low fat, it is quite hearty, needing only a good bread and a crisp salad to complete the meal. Wonderful for an afternoon in front of the fire watching your favorite football game. No muss, no fuss, no bother.

Penny Palmer Lumpkin '57

91

Tom Yum Kai
(Spicy, Sour, Hot Chicken Soup)

Serves 4

INGREDIENTS:

8 cups chicken stock
**1 lemon grass, cut into
    4" strips and smashed**
**1 pound boneless
    chicken, cut into
    pieces**
1 1/2 cups sliced mushrooms
**4 tablespoons fresh lime
    juice**
4 Kaffir lime leaves

**3 Kai (Laos Root)
    Galanga (similar to
    ginger root)**
6 tablespoons fish sauce
**1 tablespoon shrimp
    curry paste**

Garnish:
**Green onions and
    cilantro, roughly
    chopped**

PROCEDURE:

Boil stock in large saucepan. Add lemon grass and continue to boil for 5 minutes. Add chicken pieces and the rest of the soup ingredients. Continue to cook until boiling resumes. Pour into soup tureen or 4 individual soup bowls. Garnish with onion and cilantro. Serve immediately.

Lemon grass is used medicinally in Thailand, similar to America's chicken soup. Especially good for colds. This soup is served at all meals to help aid digestion. Ingredients may be found in Asian markets.

*Suthisiri Tilakamonkul
Parent, Pongsiri Prachyarata-Nawooti '98*

Chawan-Mushi
(Steaming Egg Custard Soup)

Serves 4

INGREDIENTS:

3 eggs
4 cups chicken broth
2 teaspoons salt

2 boneless, skinless
    chicken breasts,
    cooked and diced
4 shrimp, peeled and
    cooked

PROCEDURE:

Bring steamer* to a boil. In a bowl, beat eggs and add cooled chicken broth and salt. Divide chicken and shrimp among 4 small heat-resistant soup bowls. Pour the egg mixture into soup bowls. Place bowls in boiling steamer. Steam for 15 minutes. Serve hot.

* Circular bamboo steamer with removable lid. These come in various sizes. For this recipe, you will need at least a 14" diameter steamer to accommodate the 4 bowls. Place the steamer with lid inside a wok with enough water to reach just below steamer base. Bring the water to a boil before placing food inside steamer.

Mariko Nonaka
Parent, Daisuke Nonaka '98

Shrimp and Artichoke Soup

Serves 8

INGREDIENTS:

1 10-ounce can cream of
mushroom soup,
undiluted
1 10-ounce can cream of
celery soup, undiluted
2 1/2 soup cans milk
1 14-ounce can
artichoke hearts,
drained and coarsely
chopped

1 cup finely shredded
carrots
1/2 teaspoon curry powder
Freshly ground pepper
to taste
Dash ground allspice
1/4 teaspoon onion powder
1 pound fresh shrimp,
peeled and boiled

PROCEDURE:

About 20 minutes before serving combine all ingredients (except for shrimp) in a large pot. Simmer uncovered for 10 minutes. Add shrimp. Cover and return to simmer. Uncover and continue simmering for 5 minutes.

Very quick and easy. Delicious!

James H. Branard Jr.
Grandparent, Elizabeth Vale '92 and Susannah Vale '95

Rita's Crabmeat Soup

Serves 6 to 8

INGREDIENTS:

1 10-ounce can "lite" condensed tomato soup

1 10-ounce can condensed split pea soup

1 10-ounce can "lite" condensed cream of mushroom soup

1 15-ounce can "lite" evaporated milk

1 clove garlic, crushed

2 6 1/2-ounce cans crabmeat (good quality)

Salt and pepper to taste

Nonfat milk (optional)

1/4 cup dry sherry (or to taste)

Sprig of mint or parsley

PROCEDURE:

Heat the 3 cans of soup (undiluted) with the evaporated milk and the crushed garlic in a large, heavy pot. Bring just to a boil then turn to low and simmer for 10 minutes. Add crabmeat and salt and pepper to taste. Simmer for 3 to 5 minutes, stirring until crab is heated. (Be careful not to overheat.) Thin with nonfat milk if desired. Add sherry just prior to serving. Pour into bowls. Garnish with mint or parsley. Can easily be expanded by adding more soup and/or crabmeat.

Very easy, but looks and tastes festive. Great for dinner parties or soup and salad suppers. Low fat, if "lite" selections used. (My mother's version went right to the hips!)

Lori Bantz
Trustee and
Parent, Jenny Bantz '95

Seafood Wonton Soup

Serves 4 to 6

INGREDIENTS:

Filling:
1/2 pound salmon fillet
1/2 pound scallops, fresh
3 large green onions,
    finely chopped
1 tablespoon grated
    fresh ginger (or more)
2 teaspoons chili oil
1 teaspoon soy sauce
1/2 teaspoon salt
1/2 teaspoon pepper

2 packages wonton skins
    (in refrigerator
    section of grocery
    store)

Soup:
8 cups (2 quarts)
    chicken broth
4 baby bok choys
1 cup pea pods
1 cup bean sprouts
    Soy sauce to taste

PROCEDURE:

Finely chop salmon and scallops into a paste or very small bits. Add the next 6 filling ingredients and mix thoroughly.

(To make wontons, you will need a small dish filled with water to have handy and 2 plates or trays.) Place 1 square skin on 1 plate (or tray) and spoon small amount of filling (about a teaspoon) onto center of skin. Then dip index finger into water and spread along 2 adjacent edges of skin to moisten. Fold skin over in half, so that square becomes a triangular pocket (like a turnover). Then wet 2 outside corners and pinch them together. Place wonton on second tray until ready to use. Continue production until all filling is used. In a medium stock pot heat broth to boiling. Drop in wontons, bok choy, pea pods and bean sprouts. Cook until wontons float to top and greens are tender (3 to 4 minutes). Serve with soy sauce to taste.

Wontons can be made a day ahead and refrigerated until ready to use. Other wonderful combinations for filling: 1/2 pork and 1/2 shrimp or 1/2 chicken and 1/2 pork. Feel free to add more vegetables, or vary to include spinach, mushrooms, Chinese broccoli, etc. I serve in large Chinese soup bowls with Chinese soup spoons.

Erin Fray Kerr '80

Seafood Cucumber Soup

Serves 6

INGREDIENTS:

2 cucumbers, peeled and
finely chopped
1 to 2 green onions, finely
chopped
1 teaspoon Maggi
1 drop Tabasco sauce (or
more to taste)
2 teaspoons dried dill
weed
1/2 cup finely chopped
parsley

4 cups (1 quart)
buttermilk
2 cups (1 pint) plain
yogurt
1 pound lump crabmeat
or tiny shrimp (or 1/2
pound of each),
cooked

PROCEDURE:

Stir all ingredients together in a large bowl. Refrigerate covered for several hours
until thoroughly chilled.

Rosamond Larmour Loomis
Headmistress, 1953-62

Cold Cucumber Soup

Serves 4 to 6 cups

INGREDIENTS:

2 10-ounce cans cream
   of potato soup
1 10-ounce can cream of
   chicken soup
1 to 2 cucumbers, unpeeled
   and coarsely chopped

2 cups (1 pint) sour
   cream
4 to 6 thin slices cucumber
   for topping

PROCEDURE:

Put all ingredients in a blender and blend until cucumber is pureed. Serve cold.

Very "gourmet" but super easy and quick. Serve in a small crystal bowl with 1 slice of cucumber floating on top. "Good, good, good."

Susanna Smith
Parent, Troy Smith '97 and Adam Smith '98

Cold Beet Borscht

Serves 2 to 4

INGREDIENTS:

1 15-ounce can sliced or
   shoestring beets
1 14-ounce can chicken
   broth
2 tablespoons dried
   onion flakes
1 clove garlic, sliced in
   half

1/2 cup fresh lemon juice
3 tablespoons sugar
   Salt and pepper to
   taste
1 cup (1/2 pint) sour
   cream

PROCEDURE:

Place all ingredients (except for sour cream) in a saucepan and bring to a boil.
Lower heat and let simmer for approximately 10 minutes. The secret to this
recipe is in the flavoring of the sugar and lemon. Taste and add either more
lemon juice or sugar, or both for desired taste. Add salt and pepper to taste.
Pour contents into glass container and place in refrigerator for at least 4 hours
until cold. When cold, pour half of cold borscht into a blender and blend for 15
seconds. Pour into a soup tureen or other large container. Pour the other half
of borscht into blender. Add the sour cream and blend. Pour this batch into the
first batch and mix well.

*Diced cucumber can be added to the borscht or a hot (peeled) boiled potato. After the
sour cream has been added to the borscht, it becomes a beautiful shade of hot pink.
Adding the hot white boiled potato to the cold soup, makes this dish a real culinary
treat!*

Sylvia Schwartz
Grandmother, Adam Schwartz '97

Gazpacho

Serves 4 to 6

INGREDIENTS:

5 tomatoes, peeled,
   seeded and chopped
2 cucumbers, peeled,
   seeded and chopped
1 red onion, chopped
1 green pepper, chopped
2 cloves garlic, crushed

2 teaspoons coarse salt
1/2 teaspoon sweet
   Spanish paprika
1/2 cup water
1/3 cup olive oil
1/3 cup red wine vinegar

PROCEDURE:

Purée the first 7 ingredients in 4 batches in a blender. Strain purée into a bowl. Return the purée to a blender. Mix together the water, olive oil and red wine vinegar. Add the olive oil/vinegar mixture by pouring a slow stream into blender while motor is running. Chill before serving.

Cecile Reed Renaudin '64
Parent, Reed Renaudin '93 and Claire Renaudin '98

Curried Cranberry Soup

Serves 10 1-cup servings

INGREDIENTS:

6 cups chicken stock
3 cups fresh cranberries
1 medium onion, finely chopped
4 tablespoons honey
3 cups (1 1/2 pints) half and half
3 teaspoons corn starch

3 teaspoons curry powder
Salt to taste
1/4 teaspoon cayenne
4 teaspoons fresh lemon juice
Orange slices for garnish

PROCEDURE:

In large heavy soup pot, stir together chicken stock, cranberries, onion and honey. Heat to boiling. Reduce heat and simmer 15 minutes or until cranberries begin to pop open. In small bowl whisk together until smooth, half and half, corn starch, curry powder, salt and cayenne. Stir cream mixture into cranberry mixture. Simmer 10 minutes. Do not let soup boil! Remove pan from heat and allow to cool slightly. Purée half of soup in food processor or blender. Stir puréed soup into remaining soup. Stir in lemon juice. Serve immediately or refrigerate covered for 3 to 4 hours to serve cold. Garnish with orange slices. Can be made the day before and reheated in double boiler.

This is a new twist for the all-American cranberry. Perfect starter for a holiday meal and nice change from canned sauce. Can make a cold turkey sandwich a complete meal.

Cindy Ker Elrod '64X

Cold Apricot Soup

Serves 8 to 10

INGREDIENTS:

1 16-ounce can apricot
   halves, undrained
1/4 cup lime juice
2 cups orange juice
1 cup apricot preserves

2 cups (1 pint) plain
   yogurt
Toasted almonds for
   topping

PROCEDURE:

Combine all ingredients (except for toasted almonds) in a blender and process on medium speed until smooth. Serve cold topped with toasted almonds.

Excellent first course for a summer dinner. Keeps for several days if refrigerated in an air-tight container.

Margaret Cooke '62

Salad

Vinaigrette au Moutarde

Yields 1 1/3 cups

INGREDIENTS:

1/3 cup good white wine
    vinegar
3 tablespoons Dijon
    mustard

1/2 teaspoon salt
    Freshly ground pepper
1 cup good olive oil

PROCEDURE:

Place first 4 ingredients in a bowl and whisk thoroughly to combine ingredients.
Gradually whisk in olive oil. Store in a glass bottle in refrigerator.

Anne Otterson
Parent, Eric Otterson '87 and Helen Otterson '89

Vinaigrette Salad Dressing

Yields 1/2 cup

INGREDIENTS:

1/2 cup (scant) "extra lite"
    olive oil
2 tablespoons red wine
    vinegar (or balsamic
    vinegar)
1/4 teaspoon dry mustard

1 teaspoon salt
    Freshly ground pepper
    to taste
1 large (or 2 small) cloves
    garlic, minced

PROCEDURE:

Just before serving, combine all ingredients and mix well.

Best served over a salad of romaine lettuce (or mixed exotic lettuces including arugula) with Roma tomatoes and/or small yellow tomatoes.

Variation: Make dressing 20 minutes before serving, add approximately 1/4 cup crumbled Feta or blue cheese and refrigerate to let flavors meld. Mix again just before pouring over salad greens.

Dawn Fletcher Matthiesen '64X

Walnut Oil Salad Dressing

Yields 1 1/3 cups

INGREDIENTS:

1/2 cup walnut oil
1/2 cup olive oil
1/3 cup red wine vinegar
2 teaspoons sugar

2 teaspoons salt
1/4 teaspoon freshly
    ground pepper

PROCEDURE:

Combine all ingredients in a container with a tight fitting lid. Shake well.
Refrigerate. Shake again before pouring over salad.

Will keep up to a week if refrigerated.

Peg Andrews Barnard '38

Italian Salad Dressing

Yields 2 cups

INGREDIENTS:

1 1/3 cups olive oil
3/4 cup red wine vinegar
1/4 cup grated Parmesan
    cheese
1 tablespoon honey
1 teaspoon salt

1 teaspoon celery seed
1/2 teaspoon white pepper
1/2 teaspoon dry mustard
1/4 teaspoon paprika
1 clove garlic, crushed

PROCEDURE:

Combine all ingredients in a screw-top jar. Cover and shake to mix well. Chill.
Shake again just before serving. Store unused dressing in refrigerator up to 1
month.

*Great green salad dressing. I also use this dressing to marinate sliced eggplant and
zucchini before I barbecue them.*

Karen Chiappetta
Parent, Trey McKelvey '98

Left Bank Dressing

Yields 1 cup

INGREDIENTS:

2 tablespoons Dijon
    mustard
2 tablespoons
    mayonnaise (light or
    nonfat is OK)

2 tablespoons red wine
    vinegar
1 cup canola oil
    Salt and pepper to
    taste

PROCEDURE:

Mix mustard into mayonnaise. Then add vinegar, oil, salt and pepper. Place into container with tightly fitting lid. Shake to blend ingredients. Store in refrigerator. Before each use, shake or stir to mix ingredients as they will separate.

Use on salad greens, cole slaw, pasta. A little goes a long way. Can also be used as a dip for fresh vegetables.

Mary Newberry
Staff, Development Office and
Parent, Nancy Newberry '97X

Oil and Vinegar Salad Dressing

Yields 2 1/2 cups

INGREDIENTS:

2 cups olive oil
1/2 cup tarragon red wine
    vinegar
1 teaspoon salt
2 teaspoons pepper

2 teaspoons Worcester-
    shire sauce
2 teaspoons prepared
    mustard
1 1/2 cloves garlic, minced

PROCEDURE:

Place all ingredients in a bottle and shake well before using.

Alice Saunders
Parent, Paul Saunders '96 and Carl Saunders '98

Caesar Salad Dressing

Yields 1 cup

INGREDIENTS:

1 clove garlic
4 anchovies
1/3 cup olive oil
1 tablespoon Worcester-
    shire sauce

1/4 cup lemon juice
1 egg, slightly cooked
    (boiled for 3 minutes)
2 teaspoons Dijon
    mustard

PROCEDURE:

Finely chop garlic and anchovies. Combine all ingredients in blender. Blend until smooth.

Best served over romaine lettuce and croutons with a generous sprinkle of freshly grated Parmesan or Romano cheese. Keeps well in the refrigerator.

Kathryn Adelstein '88

Salad with Fennel Seeds

Serves 8

INGREDIENTS:

4 types of salad greens (for 8), washed, dried and torn into bite size pieces

Vinaigrette:
1/4 cup white wine vinegar
2 tablespoons Dijon mustard

1 tablespoon fennel seeds, partially crushed
1 clove garlic, finely chopped
Salt and freshly ground black pepper

3/4 cup olive oil
1 tablespoon cream

PROCEDURE:

Prepare salad greens for 8 and place in salad bowl. Mix vinegar, Dijon mustard, fennel seeds, garlic, salt and pepper together well. Whisk in olive oil slowly, then, drop by drop, the cream. Pour over greens and toss well. Serve immediately.

Anne Otterson
Parent, Eric Otterson '87 and Helen Otterson '89

Lass' Tossed Salad

Serves 4

INGREDIENTS:

Dressing:
- 4 teaspoons sugar
- 1/2 teaspoon salt
- 1/2 cup salad oil
- 6 teaspoons white wine vinegar

Salad:
- 6 to 8 slices bacon
- 1 head lettuce, prepared for salad
- 1/2 cup Chinese noodles
- 4 green onions, sliced
- 3 ounces sliced almonds, toasted
- 4 teaspoons sesame seeds, toasted

PROCEDURE:

Stir or shake all ingredients for the dressing. Refrigerate. Fry the bacon, drain, cool and crumble. Place lettuce, bacon, Chinese noodles and onions in a large salad bowl. Add toasted sliced almonds and sesame seeds to salad bowl. Just before serving, stir or shake dressing ingredients to blend well and pour dressing over salad. Toss and serve.

Good with steak, chicken or lasagne.

Lasley Hanlon Bober '73

Avocado and Mushroom Salad

Serves 4 to 6

INGREDIENTS:

Dressing:
1/3 cup olive oil
2 to 3 tablespoons sherry
2 tablespoons chopped
  parsley
2 cloves garlic, crushed
1 teaspoon salt
Dash pepper
Juice of 1 lemon

Salad:
2 avocados, thinly sliced
1/2 pound mushrooms,
  thinly sliced
Romaine lettuce,
  washed and roughly
  cut or torn
Parsley sprigs to
  garnish

PROCEDURE:

Dressing: Combine dressing ingredients and mix well.

Salad: Layer sliced avocados and mushrooms on bed of romaine lettuce.
Carefully pour dressing over and marinate 1 hour. Garnish with parsley sprigs.

You may also marinate avocados and mushrooms in dressing and arrange over romaine at time of serving.

Cary Tremblay
Parent, Maurile Tremblay '88 and Sean Tremblay '98

Sally's Salad

Serves 8 to 10

INGREDIENTS:

Dressing:
1/3 cup sugar
1 teaspoon salt
1 teaspoon dry mustard
1/3 cup apple cider
   vinegar
1 small onion, finely
   chopped
1 cup salad oil
1 tablespoon celery
   seeds

Salad:
2 heads romaine lettuce,
   prepared for salad
2 10-ounce cans
   Mandarin oranges,
   drained
1 purple onion, sliced
   very thin
1 cup chopped pecans
4 ounces blue cheese,
   crumbled

PROCEDURE:

Mix dressing ingredients together and let sit <u>overnight</u>. Place salad ingredients in a bowl. Pour dressing over and toss gently to blend.

This recipe is from my friend, Sally Tyson Schipa '61.

Alicia Amberg
Parent, Jessie Amberg '96 and Laurie Amberg '98

BB Tennis Team Cobb Salad

Serves 12

INGREDIENTS:

Dressing:
1 cup white wine
   vinegar
1 cup "extra lite" olive
   oil
3 large cloves garlic,
   minced
2 teaspoons dry mustard
4 teaspoons sugar
1 teaspoon salt
1 teaspoon freshly
   ground pepper
8 ounces blue cheese,
   crumbled

Salad:
4 whole chicken breasts,
   skinned
6 small heads butter
   lettuce, prepared for
   salad
1 pound bacon, cooked,
   drained and crumbled
8 Roma tomatoes, sliced
4 avocados, sliced and
   tossed with lemon
   juice
8 ounces blue cheese,
   crumbled
1/2 medium red onion,
   thinly sliced
   (optional)
4 hard boiled eggs,
   chopped

PROCEDURE:

Dressing: The night before serving, combine the dressing ingredients and mix
well. Cover and refrigerate overnight.

Salad: Simmer chicken breasts in lightly salted water until done (approximately
15 minutes). Cut into bite size pieces. Place lettuce leaves in a large, shallow
salad bowl. Sprinkle the chicken, bacon, tomatoes, avocados, blue cheese,
onions (optional) and hard boiled eggs over the lettuce. Just before serving, mix
the dressing again, pour over salad and toss well.

A sure winner!

Dawn Fletcher Matthiesen '64X

Salad Niçoise

Serves 8 to 10

INGREDIENTS:

Salad:
Lettuce leaves,
   prepared for salad
3 cups sliced boiled new
   potatoes, chilled
1 1/2 pounds fresh green
   beans, cooked and
   chilled
3 7-ounce cans chunk
   white tuna, drained
6 hard-cooked eggs,
   chilled and quartered
2 8-ounce cans
   artichoke hearts,
   drained
2 green peppers, seeded
   and cut into strips
2 red peppers, seeded
   and chopped

4 ripe tomatoes, seeded
   and cut into sixths
1 cup Italian-cured
   olives
1 3/4-ounce can flat
   anchovies, drained
   (optional)
Capers (optional)

Dressing:
2/3 cup olive oil
1/3 cup red wine vinegar
Salt and pepper to
   taste
1 tablespoon sugar
2 tablespoons Dijon
   mustard
1 teaspoon oregano
2 cloves garlic, split

PROCEDURE:

Salad: Line a large platter with crisp lettuce greens. Arrange potatoes, beans, tuna, eggs, artichokes, peppers and tomatoes over the greens. Scatter olives, anchovies and capers over all and chill.

Dressing: Combine all ingredients in jar with tight-fitting lid. Shake well to blend. Refrigerate for at least 1 hour before serving.

At serving time pour half of dressing over the salad. Pass the remaining dressing.

Cecile Reed Renaudin '64
Parent, Reed Renaudin '93 and Claire Renaudin '98

Spinach Salad

Serves 6 to 8

INGREDIENTS:

1 large bunch fresh
   spinach, washed and
   patted dry
1 8-ounce can sliced
   water chestnuts
4 strips bacon, cooked
   and crumbled
4 hard boiled eggs, sliced
1 pound fresh or canned
   bean sprouts
6 to 8 large fresh
   mushrooms, sliced

Dressing:
1/2 medium onion (more
   or less to taste)
1 cup oil (canola, olive or
   vegetable)
1/4 cup vinegar
1/4 cup sugar (or more to
   taste)
1/3 cup ketchup
1/2 teaspoon salt
2 tablespoons Worcester-
   shire sauce

Sunflower seeds
(optional)

PROCEDURE:

Dressing: Grate or finely chop onion in blender or food processor. Add other dressing ingredients and blend until well mixed. Let this "marry" in refrigerator for at least 1 hour.

Toss first 6 ingredients together.

Pour dressing over salad ingredients and sprinkle with sunflower seeds (optional).

Betsy Gill Sherman '65

Spinach Salad
with Sesame Seed Dressing

Serves 10

INGREDIENTS:

1 pound fresh spinach
1/3 cup sliced almonds
2 cups firm
   strawberries, sliced

Dressing:
1 tablespoon sesame
   seeds
1/4 cup cider vinegar

3 tablespoons vegetable
   or walnut oil
3 tablespoons water
1 tablespoon sugar
1 teaspoon poppy seeds
1/4 teaspoon paprika
1/4 teaspoon Worcester-
   shire sauce
1 green onion, minced

PROCEDURE:

Preheat oven to 350°. Trim, wash and dry spinach. Tear into bite size pieces.
Place in salad bowl and set aside. Sprinkle almonds on baking sheet and roast
in oven for 5 minutes or until golden brown. Set aside.

Sesame Seed Dressing: Place sesame seeds in ungreased skillet and stir over
medium-high heat until lightly browned. In bowl or jar, combine sesame seeds,
vinegar, oil, water, sugar, poppy seeds, paprika, Worcestershire sauce and green
onion. Mix well.

Just before serving, pour dressing over spinach and toss well to coat. Add
strawberries and almonds. Toss lightly.

Beth Oakes
Parent, Ashleigh Oakes '96

Tropical Spinach Salad

Serves 6

INGREDIENTS:

1 bunch fresh spinach
2 red apples
2 oranges
1/2 jicama
10 medium mushrooms, sliced

1 8-ounce bottle Roquefort or blue cheese dressing
6 boneless chicken breasts, skinned

PROCEDURE:

Wash and dry spinach and trim all stems. Let crisp in a plastic bag. Peel and cut up apples and oranges into bite size pieces and place in salad bowl. Peel and julienne jicama and add to bowl. Add mushrooms and spinach. Toss all the above with the dressing to taste. Chill salad while grilling the chicken breasts about 5 minutes per side. Then cut the breasts in diagonal slices. Lay the chicken on top of the salad and serve.

This is a wonderful light entrée. The cold salad and warm chicken are a nice contrast.

Judy Nelson Ebright '63

Spinach and Salmon Salad

Serves 4

INGREDIENTS:

1 bunch fresh spinach
1 hard-boiled egg
4 slices bacon
1 tablespoon olive oil
1 1-pound salmon filet

2 tablespoons rice
  vinegar
1 teaspoon soy sauce
1 tablespoon sesame
  seeds

PROCEDURE:

Arrange cleaned and dried spinach leaves on 4 plates. Chop hard-boiled egg and sprinkle over spinach. Fry bacon in large frying pan over medium heat until crisp. Remove bacon and drain on paper towels and pour out almost all the bacon fat (leave just a trace in the pan for flavor). Crumble the bacon and sprinkle over the 4 salads.

Add the olive oil to the pan and cook the salmon filet over medium high heat. (For medium rare, cook 8 minutes on 1 side and 5 on the other for a 3/4" thick filet.) When cooked, remove the salmon to a cutting board and cut into strips or large chunks. Divide the salmon pieces on the spinach leaves on the 4 plates. Then add the vinegar and soy sauce to the frying pan with the oil and heat just until the vinegar starts to boil. Pour this mixture over the four salads. The spinach will wilt slightly. Top with the sesame seeds. Serve immediately.

Great for lunch.

Heidi Lorenz Truax '73

Bacon Caesar Salad

Serves 8 to 10

INGREDIENTS:

Dressing:
3 large cloves garlic, peeled
6 anchovy fillets
2 tablespoons fresh lemon juice
1 teaspoon Worcestershire sauce
1/2 teaspoon salt
1/2 teaspoon cracked pepper
1/2 teaspoon Dijon mustard

1 egg
1/2 cup olive oil

Salad:
2 heads romaine lettuce
4 ounces Parmesan cheese, grated coarsely
1 cup croutons
3/4 pound bacon, cooked, drained and chopped

PROCEDURE:

Put garlic, anchovies, lemon juice, Worcestershire sauce, salt, pepper and mustard in blender and blend. Add egg and blend. Add olive oil, a little at a time, blending after each addition to thicken. Refrigerate dressing and blend again before serving. Tear romaine into bite size pieces and chill. Place romaine, Parmesan cheese, croutons and crumbled bacon in wooden salad bowl. Slowly pour dressing over all while tossing lightly.

You can make the dressing several days ahead, store in blender jar in refrigerator and blend again before using.

Betty Compo
Grandparent, Catherine Bagley '95 and Sarah Bagley '99

Caesar Salad I

Serves 6 to 10

INGREDIENTS:

4 **cloves garlic**
1 **tablespoon capers**
1/3 **cup olive oil**

1/2 **cup olive oil**
2 **tablespoons lemon juice (or more to taste)**
2 **tablespoons Worcester-shire sauce**

2 **teaspoons coarsely ground pepper**
1 **teaspoon dry mustard**

2 **heads romaine lettuce**
1 **cup freshly grated Parmesan cheese Croutons, to taste**

PROCEDURE:

Mince the garlic. Make a paste of the first 3 ingredients in a small bowl using a wooden spoon. Blend this paste with the next 5 ingredients in food processor. Add more olive oil to taste. Tear romaine and toss with dressing and Parmesan cheese. Add croutons, if desired.

Some say it's even better than Sammy's.

Janna L. Hernholm
Trustee and
Parent, Melissa Hernholm '92, Sarah Hernholm '94X, Matthew Hernholm '97

Caesar Salad II

Serves 4

INGREDIENTS:

1 3/4-ounce tin
   anchovies with
   capers
1 clove garlic, minced
1 1/2 teaspoons Dijon
   mustard
1/3 cup olive oil
2 tablespoons tarragon
   vinegar
Juice of 1 lemon

1 head romaine lettuce,
   washed, dried and
   torn into large bite
   size pieces
Croutons
3/4 cup grated Parmesan
   cheese

PROCEDURE:

In a large salad bowl, mash anchovies with minced garlic. Add mustard, oil, vinegar and lemon juice and mix. Add romaine lettuce, croutons and Parmesan cheese and toss.

I make my own croutons by cutting up good crusty French bread into bite size pieces and toasting on a cookie sheet for 15 to 20 minutes at 350˚ (or until brown). I don't add any seasonings as the croutons pick up the dressing taste and are great. People love this! A real company salad, but the only 1 my family will eat!

Galen Cooper
Parent, Tyler Cooper '96X and Megan Cooper '98

Chinese Chicken Salad
with Romaine

Serves 6 to 8

INGREDIENTS:

2 heads romaine lettuce, prepared for salad

3 green onions (tops only), chopped

1 10-ounce package frozen tiny peas

1 3-ounce package Ramen noodle soup mix (chicken flavor)

1 3-ounce package sliced almonds

1/2 cup safflower oil

4 tablespoons rice vinegar

4 tablespoons sesame oil

4 tablespoons sugar (or 3 packages Equal sweetener)

1 cooked chicken, skin removed and cut into bite size pieces

PROCEDURE:

Place cut up lettuce and chopped tops of green onions in large bowl. Defrost peas and add to lettuce and onions. Crush the Ramen noodles with your hands and sauté with the sliced almonds in a frying pan (with no oil) until they begin to brown. Watch closely. Remove from pan when mostly browned and set aside. Mix the safflower oil, chicken flavor package from the soup mix, rice vinegar, sesame oil and sugar (or sweetener). Put aside for dressing. Add the bite size chicken pieces to lettuce mixture. Just before serving, add the browned noodles and almonds and top with dressing.

You can add mandarin oranges for decoration. This recipe is quick and easy and everybody loves it.

Deborah Kohn
Parent, Sydney Kohn '94

Chinese Chicken Salad
with Cabbage

Serves 4 to 6

INGREDIENTS:

3 chicken breast halves,
  cooked, cooled, cubed
1 small head green
  cabbage, shredded
4 green onions, sliced
  with tops
1 3-ounce package Top
  Ramen oriental
  noodle soup mix
2 tablespoons toasted
  sesame seeds
1/2 cup toasted, slivered
  almonds

Dressing:
1/2 cup salad oil
1 tablespoon sugar
2 tablespoons cider
  vinegar
1 teaspoon chicken
  bouillon granules
1 teaspoon soy sauce

PROCEDURE:

Toss together: Chicken, cabbage and green onions. Chill several hours.
Combine dressing ingredients and mix well. Chill until ready to serve. When
ready to serve, crumble oriental noodles in soup package. (Discard seasoning
packet.) Toss dressing with salad. Add sesame seeds, almonds and dry noodles
at the very last minute and serve. If added too soon, they become soggy.

*Good served with warm muffins (spice, blueberry, bran, etc.). A good picnic dish;
just pack dressing and crunchy items separately and mix right before serving.*

*Catherine Blair
Parent, Trevor Blair '95 and Peter Blair '97*

Crunchy Chinese Salad

Serves 10 to 12

INGREDIENTS:

Salad:
2 packages Top Ramen
   Chicken Sesame
   Noodles
2 tablespoons butter
1/2 cup sesame or
   sunflower seeds
1/2 cup slivered almonds
1 1/2 heads Chinese cabbage
4 to 5 green onions

Dressing:
1/2 cup corn oil
1/4 cup red wine vinegar
1/2 cup sugar
1 teaspoon soy sauce

PROCEDURE:

Salad: Crumble the noodles in a bowl. Save the sesame oil packet and discard the seasoning packet. Heat the butter in a 12" frying pan over medium-low heat and brown the noodles in the butter. Add the seeds and almonds and brown. Add the sesame oil packet from the noodles. Watch carefully because it burns easily. Cool. Cut off end of Chinese cabbage. Slice lengthwise into quarters. Chop Chinese cabbage into 1/4" to 1/2" strips. Slice green onion tops crosswise, approximately 1/4" to 1/2" wide. Discard white root end.

Dressing: Measure oil, vinegar, sugar and soy sauce into a wide mouth bottle with secure top. Shake well to blend.

Toss noodle mixture with cabbage mixture just before serving. Noodles will become soggy if mixed ahead. Shake dressing, pour over salad and enjoy.

The dressing can be made ahead and chilled. This dish is delicious. I always get requests for the recipe when I serve it at parties.

Betsy Menard Kurtz '69

Fumi Chicken Salad

Serves 6

INGREDIENTS:

Dressing:
1 1/2 teaspoons black pepper
1 teaspoon salt
1/4 cup sugar
6 tablespoons rice vinegar
1 1/4 cups olive oil

Salad:
3 tablespoons fresh sesame seed oil
1/3 cup sliced almonds

1/3 cup sesame seeds
3 pounds chicken breasts, boned, skinned, cooked, cooled, cubed
12 green onions, finely sliced (white part only)
2 small heads cabbage (remove all of white core), finely chopped
1 8-ounce package Oriental style noodles

PROCEDURE:

Make dressing by combining ingredients and stirring until well-blended and sugar is dissolved. Heat sesame seed oil in small skillet. Brown almonds and sesame seeds. Cool. Combine all salad ingredients in a GLASS container. Pour dressing over and toss well. Cover and refrigerate. Must be made the day before.

Serve with fresh fruit salad and 7-grain rolls for a perfect family or company dinner.

Nancy Walter
Parent, Colette Walter '94X, Jacquelyn Walter '96X, Brenton Walter '99

Taco Salad

Serves 10 to 12

INGREDIENTS:

2 pounds lean ground beef
Oil for browning meat
2 packages Lawry's Taco Seasoning
1 1/2 cups water
1 head lettuce, prepared for salad
1 package tortilla chips, crushed
2 or 3 tomatoes, diced
1 15-ounce can kidney beans, drained

1 cup grated cheddar cheese
2 7-ounce cans pitted black olives
2 cups (1 pint) sour cream
4 avocados
Juice of 1 lemon
Chili powder, to taste
Garlic salt, to taste

PROCEDURE:

Brown the ground beef well in a little oil. Drain fat and add Lawry's Taco Seasoning and the water. Simmer for 20 minutes. In a large salad bowl, layer sequentially the lettuce, tortilla chips, tomatoes, kidney beans, ground beef mixture, cheddar cheese, pitted olives and sour cream. Mash the avocados and season with the lemon juice, chili powder and garlic salt. (Lemon juice keeps the avocados from turning brown.) Spread avocado mixture on top of salad.

This salad is wonderful for a luncheon main dish. It has always had raves.

Cheryl Mallory
Parent, Edward Mallory '98

Mexican Salad

Serves 8 to 10

INGREDIENTS:

1 large head iceberg
lettuce, shredded
4 tomatoes, chopped
1 large onion, chopped
2 avocados, chopped
1 pound ground beef (or
turkey), browned
1 16-ounce can kidney
beans, drained

1 package taco
seasoning
8 ounces longhorn
cheese, grated

1 12-ounce bottle
Thousand Island
dressing
1 large bag tortilla chips

PROCEDURE:

In a large salad bowl, layer the first 8 salad ingredients in the order listed. Just before serving, toss with the Thousand Island dressing. Crumble the tortilla chips and sprinkle over the top.

This is a great salad and I always receive compliments and recipe requests for it. Be sure to use iceberg lettuce!

Marilyn Ott
Parent, Carter Ott '94

Tossed Taco Salad

Serves 6

INGREDIENTS:

1 pound lean ground
   beef
1 package taco
   seasoning
1 head lettuce or mixed
   lettuces
2 tomatoes, chopped
1 cucumber, chopped

1/4 red onion, chopped
8 ounces cheddar
   cheese, chopped into
   small pieces
1 8-ounce bottle French
   dressing
1 bag tortilla chips

PROCEDURE:

Sauté ground beef in skillet with taco seasoning according to directions on package. Set aside. Tear lettuce into bite size pieces and place in a salad bowl. Add vegetables and cheese and toss gently. Add cooled ground beef and French dressing and mix well. Break up half of the tortilla chips slightly, toss chips with salad and serve at once. Serve remaining chips on the table.

Serve with warm bread and a glass of red wine for a delicious meal.

Susan Lauer
Parent, Jennifer Lauer '94

126

Jade Noodle Salad

Serves 6

INGREDIENTS:

- 1 red bell pepper, julienned
- 1 yellow bell pepper, julienned
- 1 bunch cilantro, leaves only, chopped
- 1/2 pound Chinese pea pods
- 1 cup peanuts
- 1 bunch scallions, with tops, finely sliced
- 1 14-ounce can chicken broth
- 4 chicken breast halves, skinned and boned
- 1 pound linguine
- 1 12-ounce jar Williams-Sonoma Jade Szechwan Peanut Sauce

PROCEDURE:

Condiments: Put peppers, cilantro, pea pods, peanuts and scallions in individual serving bowls.

Bring chicken stock to a boil in a large saucepan. Add chicken breasts, reduce heat to a simmer. Poach chicken breasts partially covered until done (about 20 minutes). While still hot, slice chicken into serving size pieces and return to broth to keep warm. In the meantime, cook linguine according to package directions. Strain it and put into serving bowl. Strain chicken and add to linguine. Pour half of bottle of Jade Sauce over, toss and taste. Add more if desired. (It is spicy!) Serve and allow each person to add own condiments.

Alternative method: After adding Jade Sauce to linguine and chicken, add condiments, toss and serve. This method works better for a buffet. Can be served hot or at room temperature. Can be made a day ahead and brought back to room temperature before serving. If made a day ahead, add peanuts at the last minute.

This is so good. I am always asked for the recipe when I serve it.

Susie Spanos
Parent, John Spanos '99

Rice Salad
with Capers and Pine Nuts

Serves 10

INGREDIENTS:

Dressing:
2 tablespoons fresh
   lemon juice
2 tablespoons sherry
   vinegar
1 tablespoon Dijon
   mustard
1 tablespoon minced
   shallot
3/4 teaspoon salt
4 dashes hot pepper
   sauce (Tabasco)
1/2 cup olive oil

Rice:
4 cups water
1 cup long-grain rice
1 cup wild rice
1 1/2 teaspoons salt
2 bay leaves
2 tablespoons chopped
   fresh oregano (or 2
   teaspoons dried,
   crumbled)
1/2 cup pine nuts, toasted
1/3 cup drained capers
3 tablespoons chopped
   fresh chives
1/4 cup sliced sun-dried
   tomatoes
   Freshly ground pepper
   to taste

PROCEDURE:

Dressing: Whisk first 6 ingredients in bowl. Gradually whisk in oil. (Can be made 1 day ahead. Cover and chill.)

Rice: (Cook long-grain rice and wild rice in 2 separate saucepans. Prepare wild rice by rinsing prior to cooking as instructed on package.) Bring 2 cups of water to boil in each saucepan. Add rice, 3/4 teaspoon salt and 1 bay leaf to each pan and stir well. Cover, reduce heat to low and cook until water is absorbed, (about 20 minutes for long-grain rice and 40 minutes for wild rice). Remove bay leaves. Transfer rice to large bowl. Add dressing and oregano and toss well. Cover and refrigerate until cool, about 2 hours. (Can be prepared 1 day ahead.) Mix pine nuts, capers, chives and sun-dried tomatoes into rice. Season with pepper and serve.

Enjoyed by all at Auction '93 "Dining at Sweet's" luncheon in the Ellen Browning Scripps Drawing Room.

Sara Sweet
Staff, Director of Food Service

Curried Rice Salad

Serves 4 to 6

INGREDIENTS:

1 box chicken Rice-a-
  Roni
1/3 cup mayonnaise
1 8-ounce jar marinated
  artichoke hearts,
  drained and chopped
1/8 teaspoon curry powder

8 chopped black olives
  (optional)
1/2 green pepper, chopped
2 green onions, chopped

Garnish:
Whole black olives
  (optional)

PROCEDURE:

Cook rice as directed on box, let cool. Make dressing of mayonnaise, artichoke hearts and curry powder. Combine both mixtures. Stir in olives, green pepper and onions. Chill several hours (better if made a day ahead).

May increase curry powder to taste. Looks beautiful molded in a jello mold with black olives in the middle.

Linda Shick Juwvipart '72

Versatile Low Fat Chicken Salad

Serves 6

INGREDIENTS:

6 chicken breast halves, all skin and fat removed
1 1/2 cups nonfat milk
2 teaspoons chopped chives (or 2 tablespoons chopped fresh green onions)
1 tablespoon lemon juice
1 8-ounce can sliced water chestnuts
2 tablespoons nonfat mayonnaise (or nonfat or low fat sour cream)

Optional:
Pepper, garlic, curry powder to taste
1/4 cup sherry (mixed into mayonnaise or sour cream)
4 celery stalks, chopped
1 hard boiled egg, diced or mashed and sprinkled over salad
3 tablespoons orange juice concentrate (mixed into mayonnaise or sour cream)
1/2 cup chopped walnuts

PROCEDURE:

Preheat oven to 350°. Place chicken breasts and milk in a casserole dish. Cover casserole and bake in oven for 20 to 30 minutes or until chicken is cooked through. Remove chicken from dish and let cool. Discard milk. Dice the cooled chicken into bite size cubes and place in a mixing bowl. Mix in chives (or onions), lemon juice, water chestnuts and mayonnaise (or sour cream). Use any of the optional ingredients (according to individual taste and time available) and add to the salad mixture or use as topping. Serve cold.

The chicken can be prepared a day or two in advance and refrigerated in an airtight container to hold moisture, or prepared several weeks ahead of time and frozen. Great as a lunch served over rice or oriental noodles. As a lighter meal, serve in a tomato or bell pepper.

Joanne Callan
Trustee and Parent, Megan Callan '91

Turkey Supper Salad

Serves 3 to 4

INGREDIENTS:

1/4 cup olive or vegetable oil

4 green onions, chopped in large pieces (green tops, too)

1 clove garlic, minced

1 1/2 cup julienned, cooked turkey (or chicken)

1 cup julienned red bell pepper

1/4 cup white wine vinegar or lemon juice

1 teaspoon dried basil, crushed

1/4 teaspoon dry mustard

Salt and pepper to taste

1 head romaine lettuce, washed and torn for salad (4 cups)

1 avocado, sliced or cubed (optional)

1/2 cup shredded Monterey jack or mozzarella cheese

1/2 cup chopped, shelled natural pistachios

4 green onions, finely chopped

PROCEDURE:

Heat the oil in a large skillet. Sauté onions and garlic in oil until brown, then discard them, reserving the oil. Turn off heat. Add turkey and red pepper to oil and stir to coat with oil. Then add vinegar, basil, mustard, salt and pepper and stir to blend the ingredients. Pour this mixture over romaine in a large salad bowl and toss well. Top with avocado (optional), cheese, pistachios and remaining green onions. Serve immediately.

Everyone I have served this to has loved it! A good full meal salad.

Arlene Powers
Parent, David Powers '97

Variation on a Caprese

Serves 6

INGREDIENTS:

4 Roma tomatoes
4 ounces fresh goat cheese (Montrachet is best)
1 small bunch fresh oregano leaves

Salt to taste
1/4 cup extra virgin olive oil
Freshly ground pepper to taste

PROCEDURE:

Slice tomatoes approximately 1/4" thick. Slice cheese 1/4" thick or less. Wash and pick oregano leaves from stems. Arrange 3 slices of tomato on each salad plate. Sprinkle them lightly with salt if desired. Drizzle a small pool of olive oil over each plate. Top tomatoes with cheese slices. Grind pepper over each plate. Garnish with oregano leaves.

Leslie Collins Cook '81

Avocado and Tomato Salad Elegante

Serves 4

INGREDIENTS:

2 large avocados, sliced
2 medium ripe
     tomatoes, sliced
1/2 yellow bell pepper, cut
     into 1/4" to 1/2"
     squares
1/4 green bell pepper, cut
     into 1/4" to 1/2 "
     squares

1 2-ounce can sliced
     black olives
   Any good olive oil-
     based vinaigrette
   Feta cheese, crumpled
   Fresh basil, chopped
     (reserve sprig for
     each serving)

PROCEDURE:

Fan tomatoes and avocados on dinner sized plate forming a butterfly pattern, tomatoes on 1 side, avocados on the other. Sprinkle peppers and olives attractively over entire plate. Drizzle vinaigrette sparingly over all. Sprinkle feta cheese and basil over all. Garnish with basil sprig between tomatoes and avocados. Chill until ready to serve.

The "presentation" is what makes this salad a jaw-dropper. Must be served as a course, not as side dish!

Janed Guymon Casady '59

Corn and Black Bean Salad

Serves 4 to 6

INGREDIENTS:

1 cup canned white
   corn, drained
1 cup canned black
   beans, rinsed and
   drained
1 cup diced ripe
   tomatoes
3 tablespoons finely
   diced purple onion

1 cup coarsely chopped
   fresh cilantro leaves
2 tablespoons jalapeño
   sauce (more or less to
   taste)
2 tablespoons lime juice
2 tablespoons olive oil
Salt and pepper to
   taste

PROCEDURE:

Combine all ingredients and refrigerate for at least 1/2 hour before serving.

This salad is even better after aging a day or so.

Barbara Sanderson Kruming '64

Corn and Pea Salad

Serves 6

INGREDIENTS:

1 17-ounce can peas
   (Leseur Green Giant
   Small Early Peas),
   drained
1 12-ounce can corn
   (Green Giant White
   Shoe Peg Corn),
   drained
1 cup chopped celery
1 bunch green onions,
   chopped

1 2-ounce jar sliced
   pimentos
1 8-ounce can sliced
   water chestnuts

Dressing:
3/4 cup vinegar
3/4 cup sugar
1/2 cup vegetable oil
1 tablespoon water
1 teaspoon salt
1/2 teaspoon pepper

PROCEDURE:

Combine vegetables in a salad bowl. Combine dressing ingredients in a saucepan and bring to a boil. Remove from heat and cool. Pour dressing over salad and chill in refrigerator. Drain before serving.

Keeps several days in refrigerator.

Linda Strauss
Parent, Barbie Strauss '89

Marilyn's Healthy Bean Salad

Serves 6 to 8

INGREDIENTS:

3 cups dry pinto beans
6 cups water
1 6" strip Kombu
  seaweed
1 teaspoon salt
2 large yellow onions,
  chopped
1 tablespoon olive oil
3 to 4 tablespoons chopped
  cilantro leaves

Dressing:
6 tablespoons lemon
  juice
4 tablespoons shoyu
  (soy sauce)
2 teaspoons Dijon
  mustard
1 tablespoon Tahini
2 tablespoons water

PROCEDURE:

Wash and soak beans 4 to 6 hours (or overnight). (Quick method: Bring beans to boil then let sit 1 hour.) Pour off soaking water. Simmer beans in a large covered pot for 2 to 3 hours or pressure cook beans with seaweed in 6 cups of water for 35 minutes. When pressure is down, remove lid, add salt, stir, then simmer uncovered an additional 10 minutes. Drain off water. Lightly sauté onions in oil. Place beans, onions and cilantro in a bowl. Make dressing and add to salad mixture. Toss well and allow to marinate 2 hours or overnight in refrigerator.

Dressing: Combine ingredients in small bowl or blender and mix well. Add to bean salad.

Serve at room temperature or cold. Good with tortilla chips or rolled in soft corn tortillas with shredded cabbage or lettuce. Makes a great tostada. Ingredients available in natural food stores.

*Pauline Hays
Staff, Business Office*

Winter Vegetable Salad

Serves 4

INGREDIENTS:

10 ounces fresh or frozen
   Italian green beans,
   cut into bite size
   pieces
10 ounces fresh or frozen
   cauliflower, broken
   into flowers
2 carrots, peeled and
   thinly sliced in
   circles
1/2 cup pimento-stuffed
   green olives, sliced

1 small red onion, sliced
   into thin rings

Dressing:
1 large clove of garlic,
   peeled
1/2 teaspoon salt
1/4 cup balsamic vinegar
3 tablespoons extra
   virgin olive oil
   Freshly ground pepper
   to taste

PROCEDURE:

Steam the Italian green beans, cauliflower and carrots until just tender, about 5 to 10 minutes. While the vegetables are cooking, make the dressing (see directions below).

Dressing: Mash the garlic with the salt in the bottom of a wooden salad bowl; whisk in the vinegar, oil and pepper.

Add the vegetables to the salad bowl. Gently mix. Add the olives and onions and mix again. Add pepper to taste. You may serve at once or allow the dressing to be absorbed a bit and serve the salad at room temperature.

Serve with Wild Mushroom and Brie Soup (see recipe, page 82) and crusty Italian bread.

Pamela Fuller LaMantia '73

Broccoli Salad

INGREDIENTS:

- 1 bunch broccoli
- 1/2 pound bacon
- 1/4 small red onion
- 1/2 cup raw sunflower seeds
- 1 cup raw peanuts
- 1 cup raisins

Dressing:
- 3/4 cup light mayonnaise
- 2 tablespoons red wine vinegar
- 1/4 cup sugar

PROCEDURE:

Preheat oven to 350°. Rinse broccoli and cut into even pieces. Chop quite finely in food processor. Cook bacon until crisp. Drain, let cool, then crumble into small pieces with hands. Cut onion into chunks and dice finely in food processor. Roast sunflower seeds on baking sheet in oven until light tan in color, about 10 minutes. Redistribute them once or twice during roasting. (Do not leave too long or they will get bitter. When you start to smell them, they are nearly done.) Cool. Repeat roasting procedure with peanuts. Chop both in food processor. In a small bowl mix mayonnaise, vinegar and sugar with a small whisk until sugar is dissolved. Combine all ingredients in a large bowl and allow flavors to blend in refrigerator for several hours before serving.

Take this to a potluck and you'll get two questions: What's in it? May I have the recipe?

Margaret Sottosanti
Parent, Wayne Sottosanti '87, Mark Sottosanti '89,
Paul Sottosanti '98

Potato Salad from Alsace

Serves 4

INGREDIENTS:

4 to 6 large red potatoes, cut
    into 1/2" cubes
    (6 cups)
    Water to cook potatoes
    Dash salt
4 strips lean bacon,
    chopped
1 small onion, finely
    chopped
1 stalk celery, finely
    chopped
1/4 cup white wine
    vinegar

1/4 cup water
1 small dill pickle, finely
    chopped
1 teaspoon sugar
1/4 teaspoon dry mustard
1/4 teaspoon paprika
1/8 teaspoon salt
2 tablespoons chopped
    parsley (optional)
1 tablespoon chopped
    chives

PROCEDURE:

In a large saucepan combine potatoes with enough lightly salted cold water to cover. Cover and bring to a boil over high heat, then reduce heat to moderately low. Cook partially covered over medium heat until tender when pierced with fork. Drain and pat dry with paper towels. While potatoes are cooking, cook bacon in a large skillet for over medium heat until crisp. Drain on paper towels. Pour off all but 2 tablespoons of bacon fat and return skillet to moderate heat. Add onions and celery to skillet and sauté for 5 minutes (until onions are translucent). Add the vinegar, water and pickle and bring mixture to a boil over high heat. Reduce heat to low and stir in sugar, mustard, paprika and salt. Add potatoes and bacon to skillet. Toss gently to coat with dressing. Transfer to serving dish. Garnish with parsley and chives. Serve warm.

My great-grandfather came from Alsace-Lorraine as a boy. This recipe dates back to his family.

Dana Dahlbo
Parent, Alison Dahlbo '97

Sweet Potato Salad

Serves 8

INGREDIENTS:

1 40-ounce can sweet
potatoes or yams
1 or 2 tablespoons Durkee's
Famous Sauce
1/2 cup chopped green
onions

1 cup chopped celery
3 hard boiled eggs,
chopped
Pepper to taste

PROCEDURE:

Drain the sweet potatoes or yams and put into large mixing bowl. Mash until smooth. Moisten with Durkee's Famous Sauce. Add the green onions, celery and hard boiled eggs. Add pepper to taste. Mix well and turn into a serving bowl. Refrigerate and serve chilled.

Quick and easy. Everyone loves it. Surprisingly delicious. It is a perfect addition to holiday meals. Great with turkey, chicken, ham. Family favorite. My most requested recipe. Great for picnics.

Joan M. McKenna
Parent, Mary McKenna '82, Maria McKenna '86, Chris McKenna '88,
Sean McKenna '90X, Matthew McKenna '98

Warm Chile Salad

Serves 4 to 6

INGREDIENTS:

12 poblano chiles (2 to 3 per person)
Olive oil (enough to cover bottom of a baking dish)
Gruyere cheese (sliced thin, about 4 slices per chile)

1 1/2 cups blush wine vinaigrette ("Briannas" or a raspberry vinegar salad dressing)
Herb pepper blend spice

PROCEDURE:

Cooking is a dream on a barbecue grill and in the microwave. Preheat grill to high. Cut off the stems of the chiles and clean out seeds. Place in the baking dish with olive oil. Coat the outside of the chile with olive oil. Place chiles directly on hot grill. Continually brush chiles with olive oil and turn to grill on all sides. The skin will turn black and bubble. Grill for about 5 minutes. Place chiles in a paper bag, close tightly, let sit for about 15 minutes. This will help separate the skin from the chile. Scrape skin off of chiles. This is messy work, but will worth it. Also, wash hands carefully after handling chiles, to remove spice from fingers.

Stuff chiles with gruyere cheese. Place chiles in microwave safe pan. Microwave on high to melt cheese, about 1 to 1 1/2 minutes. Allowing about 1/4 cup of salad dressing per serving, shake (4 good shakes) herb pepper blend into dressing, mix and microwave for about a minute, until warm. Pour over chiles and serve.

I prefer "The Spice Hunter" herb pepper blend spice. I like to serve this with rice and grilled Ahi or swordfish as the entrée. My favorite fish marinade is olive oil, garlic, salsa and cheap tequila. This is a hit with everyone and isn't as spicy as it sounds. Note: Chiles vary in their spiciness during the year. January and February seem to be the spiciest months.

Janet Starkey Marsten '78

Molded Gazpacho

Serves 6 to 10

INGREDIENTS:

2 envelopes unflavored
  gelatine
1 20-ounce can tomato
  juice
1/3 cup red wine vinegar
1 teaspoon salt
Few drops Tabasco
  (optional)
1 cup peeled, diced
  tomatoes

1 cup pared, diced
  cucumber
1/2 cup diced green
  peppers
1/4 cup finely chopped red
  onion
1 tablespoon chopped
  chives

PROCEDURE:

In medium saucepan, sprinkle gelatine over 3/4 cup of tomato juice. Place over low heat until gelatine is dissolved. Stir in remaining tomato juice, vinegar, salt and Tabasco. Set saucepan in a bowl of ice until liquid has the consistency of beaten egg whites. Fold in vegetables until well-combined. Pour into 1 1/2-quart mold rinsed in cold water. Refrigerate 6 hours.

This is beautiful red salad mold. Serve with cold shrimp as a summer luncheon or with steamed broccoli and lamb for a showy red and green Christmas dinner buffet.

Susanna Smith
Parent, Troy Smith '97 and Adam Smith '98

Tomato Aspic

Serves 4 to 6

INGREDIENTS:

3 cups tomato juice
1/2 teaspoon salt
1 teaspoon sugar
1 teaspoon lemon juice
Onion juice to taste
Dash Tabasco
2 envelopes unflavored
  gelatine
1/2 cup water

1 avocado, chopped
1/2 cup chopped celery
1/2 cup pimento-stuffed
  olives, cut in half

Garnish:
Avocado slices
Artichoke hearts

PROCEDURE:

Boil tomato juice with the next 5 ingredients. Turn off heat and let sit 10 to 15 minutes. Soften gelatine in the water and add to tomato juice mixture. Stir until gelatine has melted. Cool until mixture begins to thicken. Prepare vegetables and olives and add to aspic when it begins to thicken and stir to mix with gelatine. Pour into ring mold and refrigerate until firm. Turn out on a serving platter. Garnish with avocado slices and artichoke hearts.

Cecile Reed Renaudin '64
Parent, Reed Renaudin '93 and Claire Renaudin '98

Avocado Salad Mold

Serves 8 to 10

INGREDIENTS:

1 3-ounce package
  lemon jello
1 cup boiling water
1/2 cup mayonnaise
3 tablespoons lemon
  juice

1 teaspoon salt
1 cup mashed avocado
1 cup (1/2 pint) heavy
  cream, whipped
Grapes and watercress
  for garnish

PROCEDURE:

In a large bowl, mix jello and boiling water. Stir until jello is completely dissolved. Place in refrigerator to chill. When partially set, whip slightly with egg beater. Add mayonnaise, lemon juice and salt. Blend well. Fold in avocado and whipped cream. Turn into individual molds or a ring mold. Chill until firm. Garnish with grapes and watercress.

Heather Gallagher
Parent, Kielty Gallagher '94

Corned Beef Salad

Serves 6 to 8

INGREDIENTS:

3/4 cup boiling water
1 3-ounce package lemon jello
1 1/2 cups coarsely chopped canned corned beef
1/2 cup chopped celery
1 5-ounce bottle pimento-stuffed olives, cut in half (optional)

1 cup mayonnaise
2 tablespoons chopped green pepper
3 hard boiled eggs, chopped
1 teaspoon grated onion

PROCEDURE:

In a large bowl pour boiling water over jello to dissolve. Cool until it begins to set. Mix in the remaining ingredients. Transfer to a mold if desired. Refrigerate until firm.

Makes a nice luncheon dish.

Dorothy Bain Ede '27

143

Special Albacore Salad

Serves 12

INGREDIENTS:

2   10-ounce cans tomato
     soup
4   3-ounce packages
     lemon jello
2   3-ounce packages
     cream cheese
1/2 cup Miracle Whip salad
     dressing
3/4 cup chopped celery
1/2 cup chopped green
     pepper
1/2 cup water
1/4 cup chopped green
     onions

1   12-ounce can albacore
     tuna (in water),
     drained
3/4 cup sliced green olives
     (with pimento)

Topping:
1   cup (1/2 pint) sour
     cream
1   cup mayonnaise
2   hard cooked eggs (12
     slices)

PROCEDURE:

Heat soup and dissolve jello in it. Soften cream cheese and add soup/jello
mixture to it. Beat in blender until very smooth. Blend in Miracle Whip salad
dressing. Stir in remaining ingredients. Pour into a 9" x 13" pan. Chill until
firm. Mix together sour cream and mayonnaise and spread on top of chilled jello
mixture. Slice into 12 squares. Slice hard cooked eggs and place 1 on each
square.

*This salad makes a lovely presentation either on 1 large serving platter or
individually on the plate. Goes well with plain crackers. You will swear that you
are eating salmon. This is 1 of my best salads and I hope you, too, will like it!*

Sandy McCreight
Parent, Julie McCreight '92 and Matthew McCreight '94

Lite n' Lively Sassy Suzy's Salad

Serves 6

INGREDIENTS:

18 strawberries, sliced
   horizontally
2 cucumbers, peeled,
   seeded and cubed
2 bananas, sliced
   horizontally 1/4"
   thick
2 avocados, cubed or
   sliced
2 heads butter lettuce,
   washed and torn into
   pieces
3 kiwi fruit, peeled and
   sliced horizontally
1/2 cup cashews (optional,
   but tasty)

Dressing:
1/4 cup raspberry wine
   vinegar
1/4 cup rice wine vinegar
1/2 cup safflower oil
   Poppy seeds
   Honey to taste
   Dijon mustard to taste
   Salt to taste
   Fresh ground pepper
   to taste

PROCEDURE:

Place cut up fruits and vegetables in a large salad bowl, omitting the lettuce and kiwi fruit.

Dressing: Place all ingredients in a small bowl and whisk briskly until well-blended.

To serve, place lettuce on salad plates. Pour dressing over fruits and vegetables and toss gently. Arrange fruits and vegetables attractively on lettuce. Garnish with sliced kiwi fruit. Sprinkle with cashews. Grind more fresh pepper over top as desired.

May use raspberries, blueberries, boysenberries. May substitute any store-bought poppyseed or honey-Dijon salad dressing. Wonderful with room temperature Brie cheese and cracked wheat rolls. Great for parties.

Suzanne Miller Halstead '80

Watercress Salad with Pears and Pecans

Serves 6

INGREDIENTS:

4 cups (lightly packed) watercress sprigs, rinsed and crisped
4 cups butter lettuce, rinsed, crisped and torn into bite size pieces
2 small firm ripe pears, cored and cut into thin slices (brush with lemon to prevent browning)
2 tablespoons sugar

1 tablespoon water
1/2 cup pecan halves
1/2 cup blue cheese, crumbled

Dressing:
2 tablespoons lemon juice
1/2 cup olive oil
1 large shallot, minced
1/2 teaspoon pepper
1/2 teaspoon sugar

PROCEDURE:

In a large bowl combine watercress, lettuce and pears. Set aside. Pour the sugar into a 7" to 8" frying pan over medium-high heat. Shake until sugar melts and turns amber color. Add water. Cook, stirring until sugar melts. Add pecan halves. Stir until all of sugar mix clings to nuts. Spread nuts on a piece of foil. Cool.

Dressing: In a small bowl mix lemon juice with oil, shallot, pepper and sugar.

Add pecans and dressing to watercress mix. Toss gently. Spoon mixture onto 6 salad plates. Sprinkle with blue cheese.

Sarah Henriksen
Parent, Nicholas Henriksen '98

Pineapple and White Cheddar Salad

Serves 6 to 8

INGREDIENTS:

1 tablespoon sesame
  seeds
1 head romaine or
  combination of
  lettuces
6 ounces sharp <u>white</u>
  cheddar cheese

1 20-ounce can chunk
  pineapple
4 tablespoons juice from
  pineapple
3 tablespoons
  mayonnaise

PROCEDURE:

Lightly toast sesame seeds in a skillet over medium heat. Set aside. Rinse and dry lettuce and tear into bite size pieces. Place in salad bowl. Coarsely shred white cheddar and toss with lettuce. Reserve 4 tablespoons of the juice from the pineapple and drain remaining juice. Cut pineapple chunks in half and add to the salad. Combine the reserved pineapple juice with mayonnaise and mix until smooth. Pour over the salad and toss well. Sprinkle toasted sesame seeds over the salad and serve at once.

Sharp white cheddar and good mayonnaise are necessary for the delightful combination of flavors in this salad. This was a favorite recipe of Jeff and Jeremy's great-grandmother, Clara Sinclair.

Peggy Diehl Candler
Aunt, Jeff Deems '91 and Jeremy Deems '94

147

Exotic Fruit Salad

Serves 4

INGREDIENTS:

3 cups strawberries, sliced

2 ripe kiwi fruit, peeled and sliced (1 cup)

1 cup fresh raspberries

2 medium size ripe star fruit, sliced crosswise (1 cup)

1 small ripe papaya, peeled, seeded and thinly sliced

Mint sprigs to garnish

Dressing:

8 ounces low fat plain yogurt

3 ounces cream cheese, softened

1 tablespoon honey

1/4 teaspoon ground cinnamon

2 tablespoons lemon juice

1/2 teaspoon grated lemon peel

PROCEDURE:

Combine fruit in a large bowl.

Dressing: In blender or food processor fitted with a metal blade, blend dressing ingredients for 1 minute or until smooth. Transfer dressing to 4 small bowls or cups. Spoon fruit onto serving plates. Garnish with mint springs. Serve chilled or at room temperature with dressing on the side.

Very attractive salad to serve when fresh fruit is available.

Dana Dahlbo
Parent, Alison Dahlbo '97

Grandma Evans' Holiday Salad

Serves 6

INGREDIENTS:

2 cups boiling water
1 6-ounce package lime
jello
1 20-ounce can crushed
pineapple, drained
(reserve syrup)
1 8-ounce package
cream cheese,
softened

3/4 cup whipping cream
1/2 cup finely chopped
celery
2 tablespoons
mayonnaise or salad
dressing
Salad greens

PROCEDURE:

Pour boiling water on gelatine in 1 1/2-quart bowl. Stir until gelatine is dissolved. Add enough water to reserved pineapple syrup to measure 1 cup. Stir into gelatine. Pour 3/4 cup gelatine into 7-cup mold or 9" x 9" x 2" pan. Refrigerate until firm. Gradually beat remaining gelatine into cream cheese until smooth. Refrigerate until slightly thickened, 1 to 1 1/2 hours. Beat until smooth. Beat whipping cream in chilled bowl until stiff. Fold pineapple, whipped cream, celery and mayonnaise into cream cheese mixture. Pour over gelatine in mold. Refrigerate until firm, at least 2 hours. Unmold on salad greens.

Ellen Evans
Grandparent, Todd Yates '98 and Scott Yates '99

"Healthy" Lemon Jello Mold

Serves 8 to 16

INGREDIENTS:

4 ounces water
1 20-ounce can
   pineapple cubes
   (packed in syrup)
1 6-ounce box lemon
   jello

16 ounces plain or lemon
   yogurt
2 large bananas, sliced
1/2 basket large
   strawberries, halved
   (optional)

PROCEDURE:

In a small saucepan, mix the water with the syrup from can of pineapple. Bring to a boil. Place jello in a large mixing bowl. Pour hot water/syrup mixture over jello and stir until jello is dissolved. Stir in the yogurt with wire whisk. Stir in the pineapple and sliced bananas. Large halved strawberries may also be added to make mold healthier as well as more colorful. Refrigerate.

Quick and easy. Can be made 1 day prior to serving. Can be surrounded by fresh fruit. (Tupperware mold works best.)

Bobbi Susselman
Parent, Jordan Susselman '96, Brandon Susselman '99,
Dalton Susselman '99

California Summer Salad

Serves 5

INGREDIENTS:

2 cups sliced fresh
   apricots
1 1/2 cups sliced fresh
   strawberries
1 1/2 cups pared, sliced kiwi
   fruit

1/4 cup apricot nectar
1/4 cup flaked coconut,
   lightly toasted
1 tablespoon finely
   chopped mint leaves

PROCEDURE:

Combine all ingredients in a medium bowl. Refrigerate 20 minutes or until slightly chilled. To serve, arrange fruit on individual plates or in bowls.

Quick and easy.

Dana Dahlbo
Parent, Alison Dahlbo '97

Spencer's Mango Salad

Serves 6 to 8

INGREDIENTS:

3 cups boiling water
3 3-ounce boxes lemon
   jello
1 27-ounce can mangos
   (available in Latin
   markets)

1 cup juice from mangos
1 8-ounce package
   cream cheese
Sour cream and brown
   sugar for garnish

PROCEDURE:

Pour boiling water over jello and stir until jello dissolves. In a blender or food processor fitted with a metal blade, blend mangos, juice and cream cheese until smooth. Stir creamed mixture and jello together until well-blended. Chill until firm. Serve with some sour cream sweetened with brown sugar.

Delicious!

Susan Oliver
Parent, Josh Oliver '96 and Hunter Oliver '98

Strawberry Salad

Serves 10 to 12

INGREDIENTS:

2 3-ounce packages
   strawberry jello
2 cups boiling water
3 ripe bananas, mashed
2 cups frozen thawed
   strawberries (with
   juice)

1 cup crushed pineapple,
   undrained
1 cup chopped pecans
1 cup (1/2 pint) sour
   cream

PROCEDURE:

Place jello in a mixing bowl. Pour boiling water over and stir until jello is completely dissolved. Add all remaining ingredients except for sour cream and stir to blend well. Pour 1/2 of the mixture into a mold and refrigerate both halves for 1 1/2 hours. Spread the sour cream on jellied mixture in the mold and pour remaining half of jello mixture over this. Place in refrigerator for at least 3 hours.

Great with Thanksgiving turkey.

Alicia Amberg
Parent, Jessie Amberg '96 and Laurie Amberg '98

Persimmon Salad

Serves 8 to 10

INGREDIENTS:

1 6-ounce box orange
  jello
1 cup very hot water
1 16-ounce can
  grapefruit sections
  (drain and save juice)
1 1/2 cups persimmon pulp
  (very ripe fresh
  persimmons puréed
  in food processor)

Pinch salt
Butter lettuce for 8 to
  10 salads
Mayonnaise or sour
  cream for garnish
  (optional)

PROCEDURE:

Dissolve jello in 1 cup very hot water. Stir until jello is completely dissolved, then place in refrigerator to cool but not congeal. Mix grapefruit juice with enough water to make 1 1/4 cups. Add to cooled jello along with persimmon pulp and grapefruit sections. Add salt and stir to mix well. Chill until set. Serve on butter lettuce with a dollop of mayonnaise or sour cream on top (optional).

Beautiful for Thanksgiving and Christmas. Ripe persimmons may be puréed and frozen until needed.

Jocelyn Vortmann
Parent, Anna Vortmann '90, Cady Vortmann '93, Jocelyn Vortmann '97

Twenty-four Hour Salad

Serves 10 to 12

INGREDIENTS:

2 16-ounce cans white cherries halved and pitted
1 20-ounce can diced pineapple
1 8-ounce can diced pineapple
2 cups orange sections (3 oranges)
2 cups miniature marshmallows
1/4 pound chopped almonds

2 eggs
2 tablespoons sugar
1/4 cup light cream
Juice of 1 lemon
1 cup (1/2 pint) heavy cream, whipped

Garnish:
Red maraschino cherries
Seedless grapes

PROCEDURE:

In a medium bowl combine well-drained fruits; add marshmallows and nuts. Beat eggs until light; gradually add sugar, light cream and lemon juice and mix well. Cook the egg mixture in a double boiler until smooth and thick, stirring constantly. Cool, then fold in whipped cream. Pour over fruit mixture and mix lightly. Chill 24 hours. DO NOT FREEZE. Garnish with red maraschino cherries and tart-sweet seedless grapes (if available).

Better if made a day ahead. It lasts very well in the refrigerator until consumed.

Ruth H. Edmiston
Grandparent, Jordyan Edmiston '98

Holiday Cranberry Salad

Serves 6 to 8

INGREDIENTS:

2 3-ounce packages
  raspberry jello
2 cups boiling water
1 6-ounce can crushed
  pineapple, drained
1 16-ounce can whole
  cranberry sauce
3/4 cup Tawny Port wine

1 cup mayonnaise
1 cup chopped pecans

Dressing:
1 cup (1/2 pint) sour
  cream
1 3-ounce package
  cream cheese

PROCEDURE:

Pour jello into a large mixing bowl. Pour boiling water over and stir until dissolved. Add the remaining salad ingredients and pour into a large mold. Chill until set.

Dressing: Blend dressing ingredients together and spoon into a serving bowl. Chill until ready to serve.

To serve, turn out salad on a serving platter. Serve dressing on the side.

This is an elegant salad, worthy of a special occasion.

Joan Black
Faculty, Chairman History Department

Eggnog Cranberry Salad

Serves 6

INGREDIENTS:

1 12-ounce package
   fresh cranberries
1 cup sugar
2 cups water
1 3-ounce package
   raspberry jello
1/2 cup chopped celery

1 11-ounce can
   Mandarin oranges,
   drained
1/4 cup slivered almonds
1 3-ounce package
   instant jello vanilla
   pudding
2 cups milk for pudding
   Nutmeg for garnish

PROCEDURE:

Boil the cranberries, sugar and 1 cup of the water gently for about 10 minutes, stirring occasionally, then remove from heat. In another pan boil 1 cup water; remove from heat. Add raspberry jello to water and stir until dissolved. Add jello mixture to cranberries and stir to blend. Stir in celery, oranges and almonds. Pour into a serving bowl. Chill until firm. Make pudding by following package directions. Pour pudding over cranberry gelatine. Chill. When pudding is firm, top with nutmeg.

Gerri Lewis
Parent, Matthew Lewis '95

Frozen Cranberry Salad

Serves 6 to 8

INGREDIENTS:

3 ounces cream cheese
1/4 cup mayonnaise
1/4 cup confectioners' sugar
1 16-ounce can whole cranberry sauce

3 tablespoons lemon juice
1 cup (1/2 pint) heavy cream, whipped
1 cup chopped nuts

PROCEDURE:

In a mixing bowl combine cream cheese, mayonnaise and sugar. In another bowl crush cranberry sauce and lemon juice with fork and add to cream cheese mixture. Fold in whipped cream and nuts. Turn into an 8" x 8" pan and freeze until firm.

This was a recipe from my grandmother, invented before concerns about cholesterol. It's great for a Thanksgiving or Christmas dinner. To reduce fat, substitute low fat or nonfat versions of ingredients.

Carol Hudgins Jackson '61

Pasta, Pizza & Risotto

Pasta Primavera

Serves 4 to 6

INGREDIENTS:

1 red sweet pepper
1 yellow sweet pepper
1 orange sweet pepper
2 small green zucchini, sliced
2 small yellow zucchini, sliced
1 cup broccoli, cut into small flowerets
2 cloves garlic, chopped
4 tablespoons olive oil

8 fresh basil leaves, chopped (or 1 teaspoon dried)
Salt and freshly ground pepper to taste
1 pound spaghetti or linguine pasta
1 cup freshly grated Parmesan cheese
Additional Parmesan cheese for table

PROCEDURE:

Put a large pot of lightly salted water (for cooking pasta) over high heat and bring to a boil while preparing sauce. Wash peppers; remove seeds and fibers. Slice into lengthwise strips approximately 1/2" wide. Prepare the other vegetables and the garlic. Heat oil and cook garlic over medium heat for 1 minute. Add peppers, zucchini, broccoli and basil. Cover and cook over medium heat for 10 minutes. Remove cover and cook for 5 minutes. Vegetables should be done but not mushy. Add salt and pepper to taste. Turn off heat and cover to keep warm. Cook pasta in the boiling water according to package directions, being careful not to overcook. Drain and pour into a serving bowl. Pour vegetables over. Sprinkle with Parmesan cheese. Toss to mix and serve immediately.

Fast and yummy.

Elizabeth Vale '92

Uncooked Fresh Tomato Pasta

Serves 3 to 4

INGREDIENTS:

2 cups fresh tomatoes (tasty home grown or farm grown), chopped, uncooked

1/4 cup extra virgin olive oil

2 to 3 cloves garlic, put through garlic press

2 to 4 tablespoons chopped fresh basil

Salt and pepper to taste

1/2 pound angel hair pasta (capellini)

Freshly grated Parmesan cheese for table

PROCEDURE:

In a medium bowl, combine chopped tomatoes, olive oil, garlic and basil. Season with salt and pepper. Set aside. In a large pot, boil pasta according to package directions. Cook until barely done (al dente). Pour pasta into a large bowl. Pour tomato sauce over top and combine (toss well). Serve with freshly grated Parmesan cheese.

This is a very fast, light and delicious summer meal. The sauce is uncooked and depends on ripe, flavorful home grown or farm grown tomatoes. Best made in the summer when fresh tomatoes are plentiful.

Kristin Miller '87

Spaghetti with Tuscan Tomato Sauce

Serves 4 to 6

INGREDIENTS:

2 tablespoons olive oil
1 medium onion, chopped
2 cloves garlic, chopped
2 14-ounce cans whole tomatoes
1/2 teaspoon sugar

Salt and freshly ground black pepper to taste
1 pound spaghetti (or pasta of your choice)
1 cup freshly grated Parmesan cheese

PROCEDURE:

Heat the oil and sauté the onion and garlic stirring frequently over medium heat until softened but not browned. Add the tomatoes with their juice, sugar, salt and freshly ground pepper to taste. Cook over medium heat, uncovered, for about 20 minutes, stirring occasionally. When sauce is reduced and thickened, pass the sauce through the medium disc of a food mill or use food processor to purée. (Leave slightly coarse.) Check seasoning. Return to pan and keep warm. Cook the pasta, following directions on the package. Avoid over-cooking. Drain the pasta and pour into a serving bowl. Add half the Parmesan cheese, mixing thoroughly. Add the sauce. Mix well and add the rest of the cheese and serve immediately.

Delicioso! Canned tomatoes come closest to approximating the Tuscans' fresh "sauce" tomatoes which are very soft, juicy and sweet and, as far as I know, unavailable in the U.S.

Betty Vale
Parent, Elizabeth Vale '92 and Susannah Vale '95

Pasta with Pesto al Fresco

Serves 4 to 6

INGREDIENTS:

12 Roma tomatoes
    (medium firm with
    deep red color)
2 ounces fresh basil
4 ounces pine nuts
1 pound capellini (angel
    hair) pasta (or pasta
    of your choice)
    Olive oil, extra virgin

Garlic salt, to taste
Pepper (or red pepper
    flakes), to taste
Freshly grated
    Parmesan cheese to
    taste

PROCEDURE:

Chop tomatoes into bite size chunks. Chop basil leaves into small pieces. Toast pine nuts in oven. (Watch carefully; they burn easily.) Cook pasta according to package directions, until barely done (al dente). Drain pasta and return to pot. Drizzle with olive oil until lightly coated. Sprinkle with garlic salt and pepper to taste. Transfer immediately to 4 dinner plates. Distribute the Parmesan cheese, tomatoes, basil and pine nuts evenly on top of the 4 plates of pasta.

Serve with Caesar salad, French bread and Chardonnay wine with fresh fruit or sorbet for dessert. All ingredients in this recipe can be increased or decreased as tastes prefer. Experiment with different fresh herbs and vegetables; this recipe is a versatile beginning for many combinations.

Suzanne Powell '81

Pesto Genovese

Serves 4 to 6

INGREDIENTS:

1 bunch fresh basil
5 cloves garlic
1 potato (russet preferably)
1/2 cup extra virgin olive oil
3 ounces fresh grated Parmesan cheese

1 1-pound box spaghetti pasta (durum grain)
1 teaspoon salt
Splash of olive oil
Extra grated Parmesan cheese for table

PROCEDURE:

Use a very sharp chopping knife on a cutting board to cut up the basil leaves, discarding the stems. Continue chopping until the basil is very fine, almost a liquid. On the same cutting board, chop up the peeled cloves of garlic and mix in with the basil. Peel the potato and chop it very fine, mixing it with the basil and garlic. Scrape the mixture into a small bowl. Mix in the olive oil and the grated Parmesan cheese. Your sauce is ready.

Cook the spaghetti pasta in a large pot of boiling water to which you have added 1 teaspoon of salt and a splash of olive oil. After 7 minutes test the pasta. Do not overcook. Make sure it is al dente. Pour into a strainer or colander. Place in a serving dish and pour the pasta sauce on top. Serve immediately with additional Parmesan to taste.

The key is fresh ingredients, fine chopping and good quality dry pasta.

Sonya Solinsky '89

Quick Veggie and Tofu Pasta

Serves 4

INGREDIENTS:

1 medium onion, sliced
8 ounces mushrooms,
  sliced
2 medium broccoli
  stalks, chopped
1 large carrot, peeled
  and grated

16 ounces firm tofu,
  cubed
1 16-ounce jar spaghetti
  sauce (your favorite)
1 pound pasta, cooked
  Grated Parmesan
  cheese to top

PROCEDURE:

In a large frying pan cook onion and mushrooms in 2 tablespoons water on medium heat. When onion is limp, add broccoli, carrot, tofu and spaghetti sauce. Cook for 10 minutes over medium heat. Serve sauce over your favorite pasta. Garnish with Parmesan cheese.

You may use any combination of your favorite vegetables and pasta.

Ellen Banning Anderson '75

Spaghetti Pugliesi

Serves 4 to 6

INGREDIENTS:

- 3 garlic cloves, peeled and chopped
- 3 tablespoons olive oil
- 1 1.75-ounce can anchovies, drained (reserve the oil)
- 1 28-ounce can Italian tomatoes, drained and puréed in blender
- 1 7-ounce can chopped clams
- 10 pimento stuffed green olives, sliced
- 10 black pitted olives, sliced
- 1 tablespoon capers
- 1 teaspoon dried basil (or 1 tablespoon chopped fresh)
- 1/2 teaspoon dried oregano (or 1 teaspoon fresh leaves)
- Cayenne pepper to taste
- 1 pound spaghetti, spaghettini or linguine
- 1 tablespoon butter
- 1 garlic clove, peeled and left whole

PROCEDURE:

Sauté garlic in the olive oil in a wide saucepan. When it begins to soften, add the anchovies and stir until they are broken apart. Add the tomatoes and the juices from the clams. Simmer for 10 minutes. Stir in the olives, capers, basil, oregano and cayenne. Simmer for 15 to 20 minutes until the sauce has thickened. Stir in the clams. Turn off the heat. Cook the pasta according to package directions until it is al dente, just tender. Drain without rinsing and toss in the butter. Reheat the sauce and taste for seasoning. Add a bit of the anchovy oil if you wish. Alternatively, squeeze in a clove of garlic for a more pronounced flavor. Pour over the buttered pasta, toss with 2 forks and serve immediately.

This Spaghetti Pugliesi is as good a red clam sauced pasta as there is. It is even delicious without the clams. By controlling the amount of anchovies and cayenne, you can make it as salty or spicy as you wish. I first had a version of this sauce in Bolzano, Italy, and I have been making it ever since.

Marianne Engle
Parent, Lindsay Engle '94 and Jordan Engle '98

Pierogi
(Filled Pasta)

Yields 60

INGREDIENTS:

Pasta:
4 cups unbleached flour
4 large eggs
2 tablespoons olive oil
1/2 teaspoon salt
Water as needed

Filling:
12 ounces farmers
    cheese, crumbled
8 ounces feta cheese,
    crumbled
3 tablespoons olive oil
2 eggs

1/2 teaspoon dried
    oregano
1/2 teaspoon dried
    dillweed
2 cloves garlic, crushed
    Freshly ground black
    pepper to taste

Butter to taste for
    topping
Freshly grated
    Parmesan cheese for
    table

PROCEDURE:

In a food processor, blend the flour, eggs, oil, salt and 2 tablespoons water until mixture begins to form a ball, adding more water drop by drop if dough is too dry. Cover and let dough stand at room temperature 1 hour. Mash cheeses (may use food processor). Stir in olive oil, eggs and seasonings, combining thoroughly.

To assemble: Roll out dough to approximately 1/8" thick (may use pasta machine). Cut out circles 4" in diameter. Fill with 1 tablespoon cheese mixture. Fold in half. Moisten edges with water or egg white and press to seal.

To cook: Bring water to boil in a large pot. Drop pierogi in one by one and cook until done (approximately 5 minutes). Drain and place in serving bowl. Top with butter and Parmesan cheese to taste.

Freezes well. Serve with romaine salad. Time consuming but worth it.

Clela Borysiewicz
Grandparent, Rebecca Horner '97

Penne Pasta with Sweet Pepper Sauce

Serves 4 to 6

INGREDIENTS:

2 pounds sweet red
  peppers (or a mixture
  of red, yellow and
  orange)
4 tablespoons olive oil
4 cloves garlic, chopped
  Salt and freshly
  ground black pepper
  to taste

1 pound penne pasta

  Italian parsley,
  chopped, for garnish
  Freshly grated
  Parmesan cheese, for
  garnish

PROCEDURE:

Place a large pot of lightly salted water over high heat and bring to a boil while
preparing sauce (so it will be ready to cook pasta). Wash peppers, remove seeds
and fibers and cut into strips about the same size as the pasta. In a large skillet
heat the oil, add the chopped garlic and sauté over medium heat for about 1
minute. Add the peppers. Cover and cook over medium-low heat for 10 minutes.
Remove cover and turn heat to high. Cook for another 5 minutes, stirring
occasionally. Add salt and pepper to taste. Remove from heat and cover to keep
warm. Cook the pasta al dente according to package directions, being careful not
to overcook. Drain, pour into a serving bowl and stir in the pepper mixture.
Serve at once. May sprinkle top of each serving with chopped parsley and/or
Parmesan cheese.

Betty Vale
Parent, Elizabeth Vale '92 and Susannah Vale '95

Spaghetti Sauce Bolognese

Serves 8 to 10

INGREDIENTS:

2 1/2 pounds onions, chopped
1/4 cup olive oil
3 1/2 pounds lean ground beef
3 tablespoons Italian seasoning
1 head garlic, separated into cloves (peel cloves and leave whole)

1 6-ounce can tomato paste
Salt and pepper to taste
4 beef bouillon cubes
1/2 cup water
2 pounds spaghetti pasta, cooked

PROCEDURE:

In a large heavy pot cook chopped onions slowly in 1/2 the olive oil until they lose their water and are slightly brown (but not burned). Add meat, cook on medium heat until it is no longer pink. Add Italian seasoning, garlic, tomato paste, salt and pepper. Mix well. Dissolve beef bouillon cubes in 1/2 cup warm water and pour into meat mixture. Simmer uncovered for 10 minutes. Remove from heat and stir in other half of olive oil. Serve on cooked spaghetti.

Can be made in advance and reheated.

Jean Rivier
Parent, Lauraine Rivier '93 and Cedric Rivier '96X

Sausage Sauce and Shells

Serves 6 to 8

INGREDIENTS:

- 1 **pound hot Italian sausage (fresh)**
- 1 **28-ounce can crushed tomatoes**
- 1 **bay leaf**

- 1 **pound small pasta shells**
- **Grated Parmesan cheese to taste**

PROCEDURE:

Remove sausage from casing and break into saucepan. Add tomatoes and bay leaf. Simmer covered for 30 to 45 minutes. Cook pasta in lightly salted boiling water. Drain pasta in a colander when done and pour into a serving bowl. Serve sauce over pasta. Top with Parmesan cheese.

Sauce freezes well.

Melissa (Missie) Herrick Burman '71

Sun-dried Tomato and Pepperoni Tortellini Sauce

Serves 10 to 12

INGREDIENTS:

1/4 pound sliced pepperoni
1 cup sun-dried tomatoes
1 tablespoon Dijon mustard
2 cloves garlic
2 teaspoons lemon juice

1 tablespoon red pepper flakes
3 tablespoons onion
2/3 cup olive oil
3 to 4 pounds large tortellini
Fresh chopped basil leaves for garnish

PROCEDURE:

Put first 7 ingredients in food processor and process for 30 seconds. While machine is running, add the olive oil in a slow stream. Cook tortellini according to package directions. Drain. Place in bowl and add sauce. Toss and garnish with fresh basil.

This is especially good served at room temperature. Makes a great picnic dish or side dish for grilled meats or chicken. So easy and different. Great with salad and bread!

Sarah Burton
Parent, Jorie Burton '99

Marda's "To Die For" Pasta

Serves 4 to 6

INGREDIENTS:

1 2-ounce tin anchovies,
  undrained
8 garlic cloves, mashed
1/2 cup olive oil
1 4-ounce jar capers,
  drained
1 4-ounce can chopped
  black olives

2 15-ounce cans
  tomatoes
Dash red pepper flakes
1 pound spaghetti pasta
  (do not use a thin
  noodle like angel hair)
1 cup freshly grated
  Parmesan cheese

PROCEDURE:

Mash anchovies and garlic together. Heat olive oil in a pan large enough to hold sauce ingredients. Add anchovy/garlic mixture to olive oil and sauté for 1 or 2 minutes. Add capers, olives, tomatoes with their juice (shred tomatoes with fingers) and red pepper flakes. Simmer 30 to 45 minutes. Cook spaghetti according to package directions. Drain and pour into serving bowl. Pour sauce over pasta. Sprinkle with the Parmesan cheese and toss to mix. Serve immediately.

Good cold the next day!

Galen Cooper
Parent, Tyler Cooper '96X and Megan Cooper '98

Seafood Tetrazzini

Serves 8 to 10

INGREDIENTS:

1 pound thin spaghetti
3/4 cup chopped onion
3/4 cup chopped green
    pepper
1/2 cup butter
1 cup flour
2 teaspoons salt
1/4 teaspoon pepper
4 cups (1 quart) half and
    half
1 6-ounce can
    mushrooms
1 1/2 cups shredded sharp
    cheddar cheese
1 teaspoon lemon juice

1 teaspoon dry mustard
1/2 teaspoon Worcester-
    shire sauce

1 pound lobster meat,
    cut into chunks and
1 pound cooked
    crabmeat and
1/2 pound shrimp
    OR
1 pound imitation
    crabmeat and
1 pound shrimp
1/3 cup grated Parmesan
    cheese

PROCEDURE:

Cook and drain spaghetti and place into 3-quart oven-proof serving dish. Sauté onion and green pepper in butter in a large skillet over low heat until soft. Slowly stir in flour, salt and pepper. Gradually add half and half and stir until thickened. Add mushrooms, cheddar cheese, lemon juice, dry mustard and Worcestershire sauce. Simmer until cheese melts. Stir in seafood. Pour seafood mixture over spaghetti. Sprinkle Parmesan over top. Place under broiler until cheese browns.

Serve with crusty bread and green salad. Great dish for formal or informal entertaining.

Mary Boggs
Parent, Katie Boggs '96

Pro Pasta Lake Oswego

Serves 4 to 6

INGREDIENTS:

1 pound chicken
    breasts, skinned,
    boned and cubed
Olive oil for sautéing
2 cups chopped fresh
    broccoli
1 zucchini, thinly sliced
1 cup thinly sliced
    carrots
Juice of 1 lemon
3 cloves garlic, crushed

3/4 pound fresh mush-
    rooms, thinly sliced
1/2 red pepper, thinly
    sliced
1/2 green pepper, thinly
    sliced
1 pound crab meat
1 pound favorite pasta
3/4 cup grated Parmesan
    cheese

PROCEDURE:

Sauté chicken in 1 or 2 tablespoons olive oil until crispy and brown. Meanwhile, in another pot cook broccoli, zucchini and carrots in lightly salted water until just tender. Drain vegetables and put in large bowl. Sprinkle lemon juice over vegetables. Sauté garlic in olive oil remaining from chicken breasts for about 1 minute. Add the mushrooms and red and green peppers and sauté for an additional 3 minutes. Add this mixture to vegetables in bowl. In same pan, add (if necessary) an additional bit of olive oil and sauté crab for 1 or 2 minutes and add to vegetables. Cook pasta of your choice in lightly salted water according to package directions. Drain pasta and place in your favorite pasta bowl or dish. Sprinkle Parmesan cheese over and toss until coated. Pour chicken, vegetables and crab over pasta, season with salt and pepper and watch the "pros" dive in.

This recipe is relatively quick and easy. Even my "Team Northwest" tennis students enjoy it and so will the pros in your family. Very healthy! Substitute freely as seasonal vegetables dictate. May also use scallops additionally or in place of crab or chicken. Add Italian herbs of your choice. Be creative!

Anni Bennett Miller '65

Linguine with Clam Sauce

Serves 8

INGREDIENTS:

- 8 cloves garlic, minced
- 2 tablespoons olive oil
- 3 7-ounce cans chopped clams (drain and reserve liquid)
- 5 tablespoons chopped parsley
- 1 teaspoon salt
- 1 1-pound box linguine
  Grated Parmesan cheese for table (optional)

PROCEDURE:

Sauté garlic in olive oil until somewhat soft, approximately 1 to 2 minutes. Remove from heat and add reserved clam juice, parsley and salt. Return to heat, bring to a boil, then simmer for 5 minutes. Add clams and simmer for another 10 minutes. Begin to cook pasta 5 minutes after starting the clam sauce. Drain and place on warmed platter. Pour sauce over and toss. Serve immediately.

Also good cold for lunch. Serve with Caesar salad and crusty bread.

Nancy Gordon
Parent, Lindsay Gordon '95 and Alison Gordon '98

Clams in Alfredo Sauce

Serves 6 to 8

INGREDIENTS:

- 1/3 Spanish red onion, chopped
- 2 cloves garlic, minced
- 6 tablespoons (3/4 stick) butter
- 1/4 cup oil
- 4 cups (1 quart) half and half
- 2 tablespoons chopped fresh basil
- 2 tablespoons chopped parsley
- 2 hard-boiled eggs, grated
- 1/2 cup grated Romano cheese
- 1 1/4 cups ricotta cheese
- 2 7-ounce cans whole baby clams
  Salt and pepper to taste
  Romano cheese for table

PROCEDURE:

Sauté onion and garlic in butter and oil until they soften (do not let them brown). Remove from heat and slowly add, while stirring, half and half, basil and parsley. Return to heat at low temperature. Add eggs, Romano cheese and ricotta cheese and heat until warm. Add 1 can clams undrained and 1 can clams drained. Season with salt and pepper to taste. Heat until warm.

Serve over fresh pasta and top with additional grated Romano cheese.

JoAnn Vasil
Parent, Stephen Vasil '93 and Stacy Vasil '95X

Spaghetti with Clam Sauce

Serves 4 to 6

INGREDIENTS:

- 6 tablespoons olive oil
- 3 cloves garlic, smashed, peeled and chopped
- 1/2 cup dry white vermouth or dry white wine
- 2 7-ounce cans chopped clams
- 1 pound spaghetti or linguine pasta
- 1 tablespoon butter, softened
- 3 tablespoons chopped parsley
- 1 clove garlic, peeled and left whole
- Salt and pepper, to taste

PROCEDURE:

Heat olive oil in a wide frying pan. Sauté chopped garlic briefly until it just begins to color. Immediately pour in wine and liquid from canned clams. Reduce liquid by half over a fast flame. Turn off heat. Cook pasta according to package directions until it is al dente (just tender). Drain and put into a serving bowl. Toss pasta with softened butter. Reheat sauce and add clams. Stir in parsley. Squeeze remaining garlic clove into sauce through a garlic press. Immediately pour hot sauce over pasta. Toss with 2 forks and season to taste with salt and pepper. Serve.

Sometimes I am hungry but too tired to cook. Sometimes friends arrive, dinner time is near and there is not much in the refrigerator. The solution is the same: Raid the pantry. With a package of pasta and a can of clams, dinner is at hand.

Marianne Engle
Parent, Lindsey Engle '94 and Jordan Engle '98

Vegetable Lasagne I

Serves 6

INGREDIENTS:

4 cups homemade
  Tomato Mushroom
  Sauce (see following
  recipe)
1 1-pound eggplant
4 tablespoons olive oil
  Salt
12 ounces lasagne noodles
3 1/2 cups grated mozzarella
  cheese
1 cup grated Parmesan
  cheese
1 package frozen
  spinach (thawed and
  squeezed dry)
3 plum tomatoes, sliced

Cream Sauce with
  Herbs:
1/4 cup butter
1/4 cup flour
2 cups milk
  Salt and white pepper
  to taste
  Nutmeg to taste
1 cup (1/2 pint)
  whipping cream
1/2 teaspoon dried thyme
2 tablespoons chopped
  fresh basil

PROCEDURE:

Make homemade Tomato Mushroom Sauce (see following recipe) and set aside.
Halve eggplant lengthwise, slice crosswise 3/8" thick. Heat 2 tablespoon olive oil
in large non-stick frying pan over medium-high heat. Add eggplant and sauté for
2 to 3 minutes per side. Transfer to paper towels to drain and add 2 more
tablespoons olive oil to pan and sauté remaining eggplant.

Prepare Cream Sauce with Herbs: Melt butter in a medium saucepan over low
heat. Whisk in flour and cook, whisking 2 minutes until foaming but not
brown. Remove from heat; whisk in milk. Cook over medium-high heat,
whisking constantly, until mixture thickens and comes to a boil. Add a pinch of
salt, white pepper and nutmeg. Simmer sauce over low heat, whisking often, for
10 minutes. Whisk in cream and bring to a simmer. Stir in thyme and basil. Set
aside.

Bring a large pot of water to boil. Add salt and lasagne noodles; cook according
to package directions.

Preheat over to 375°. Butter a 9" x 13" x 2" pan. Spoon 2/3 cup cream sauce on
bottom of pan, spreading evenly. Top with 1 layer lasagne noodles. Top with all
of the eggplant. Spoon 1 1/2 cups tomato sauce over eggplant. Sprinkle with
1 1/4 cups mozzarella, then with 1/3 cup Parmesan. Top with another layer of

noodles. Add 2/3 cup cream sauce and spread carefully with spatula. Top will all of spinach and spoon remaining tomato sauce over spinach. Sprinkle with 1 1/4 cups mozzarella, then 1/3 cup Parmesan. Top with another layer of noodles. Add remaining cream sauce and carefully spread smooth. Sprinkle with remaining mozzarella. Arrange tomato slices over center. Sprinkle with remaining Parmesan over all. Bake in preheated oven 30 to 40 minutes or until bubbling and lightly browned. Let stand 15 minutes before cutting .

Lasagne can be kept, covered, 1 day in refrigerator. Bring to room temperature before cooking.

Carole Markstein
Parent, Kyle Markstein '99

Tomato Mushroom Sauce

Yields about 3 quarts

INGREDIENTS:

- 1 **cup dried Italian mushrooms**
- 3 **tablespoons olive oil**
- 1 **cup packed chopped parsley**
- 3 **stalks celery, chopped**
- 2 **onions, chopped**
- 3 **cloves garlic, minced**
- 1/2 **teaspoon dried rosemary**
- 3 **carrots, grated**
- 3 **16-ounce cans tomato sauce**

- 2 **1-pound cans chopped tomatoes, plus liquid**
- 1 1/2 **teaspoons Italian spices**
- 1/2 **teaspoon dried sage leaves**
- 4 **fresh basil leaves, chopped**
- 1/4 **teaspoon dried red chili pepper**
- 1 1/2 **teaspoons salt**

PROCEDURE:

Place mushrooms in a small bowl and barely cover with hot water; set aside. In a large saucepan heat oil and add parsley, celery, onion, garlic, rosemary and carrots. Cook, stirring, until vegetables are soft. Stir in tomato sauce, tomatoes and liquid and the remaining herbs and spices. Pour all but the dregs of the mushroom soaking liquid into the saucepan. Chop mushrooms and add to sauce. Cover and simmer slowly for 3 hours, stirring occasionally. Add salt to taste. Serve hot or let cool.

Carole Markstein
Parent, Kyle Markstein '99

Vegetable Lasagne II

Serves 6 to 8

INGREDIENTS:

10 whole wheat or regular
    lasagne noodles
3 tablespoons olive oil
2 pounds spinach
1/2 pound mushrooms,
    sliced
2 large carrots, grated
1 onion, chopped
4 cloves garlic, minced
1 1/2 cups (15-ounce can)
    tomato sauce
1 1/2 cups (12-ounce can)
    tomato paste
2 teaspoons dried
    oregano

2 1/2 teaspoons dried basil
    or 4 teaspoons
    chopped fresh basil
2 eggs
3 cups ricotta cheese
4 cups (16 ounces)
    grated Monterey jack
    cheese
OR a mixture of
    2 cups (8 ounces)
    grated Mozzarella
    cheese and 2 cups
    (8 ounces) grated
    Monterey jack cheese
1 cup (4 ounces) freshly
    grated Parmesan
    cheese

PROCEDURE:

Fill a large pot with lightly salted water. Bring water to a full boil. Add lasagne noodles and cook until tender. Drain. Mix 2 teaspoons oil with noodles and set aside. Rinse spinach well. In a medium size saucepan cook spinach over low heat, covered, without water except for the drops that cling to the leaves after rinsing. Reduce heat when steam forms and cook 3 to 5 minutes. Drain and chop.

Preheat oven to 375˚. Oil a 9" x 13" ovenproof casserole. In a large saucepan, heat the remaining oil, cook mushrooms, carrots, onion and garlic until tender but not brown. Stir in tomato sauce, tomato paste, oregano and basil.

In a small bowl, beat eggs into ricotta cheese until smooth. In the casserole layer 1/2 the noodles, then 1/2 of the ricotta cheese mixture, spinach, Monterey jack cheese and tomato/vegetable sauce. Repeat layers. Bake for 30 to 40 minutes. Sprinkle with 1/2 of the Parmesan cheese. Let stand about 10 minutes before slicing. Serve with the remaining Parmesan cheese.

Great with a green salad and garlic bread. May be made a day ahead.

Eileen Pue
Parent, Sean Pue '93 and Lisa Pue '96

Vegetarian Lasagne

Serves 10 to 12

INGREDIENTS:

12 lasagne noodles
3 zucchini, grated
3 carrots, grated
1 medium onion, chopped
4 large garlic cloves, chopped
8 ounces mozzarella cheese, grated
3 cups ricotta cheese

1 2-ounce can sliced black olives
1/2 pound fresh mushrooms, thinly sliced
1 26-ounce jar marinara sauce, homemade or store bought
1/2 cup grated Parmesan cheese

PROCEDURE:

Preheat oven to 350°. Cook lasagne noodles in large pot of lightly salted boiling water until al dente. Lightly butter a 9" x 13" glass baking pan. Drain noodles. Place 1 layer of noodles in the pan. Cover with approximately 1/3 of the zucchini, carrots and onions and sprinkle with some of the garlic. (Reserve remaining garlic for top layer). Add grated mozzarella cheese and ricotta cheese, a layer of sliced olives, a layer of sliced mushrooms (uncooked) and 1/4 cup marinara sauce over first layer. Add second layer of noodles and continue layering vegetables and cheeses until pan is full (3 to 4 layers in all). Cover top layer of noodles with remainder of marinara sauce and sprinkle with remainder of garlic and a thin layer of Parmesan cheese. Bake 45 minutes and serve.

I always make 2 or 3 at a time and freeze the other 2 for later! Freezes well and is easy to reheat after defrosting in refrigerator overnight. Serve with salad and garlic bread.

To make "unvegetarian", sauté ground turkey with onions and garlic and layer turkey mixture with zucchini, carrots, cheeses, mushrooms, olives and marinara sauce.

Belinda Balaski '65

Baked Lasagne

Serves 12

INGREDIENTS:

1/2 onion, diced
1/4 cup olive oil
1 pound lean ground meat
3/4 pound sweet Italian sausage
1 6-ounce can tomato paste
1 46-ounce can tomato juice
1 28-ounce can Italian crushed tomatoes

Seasonings: Salt, pepper, chopped parsley, sweet basil, garlic powder to taste
1 tablespoon sugar
2 eggs
2 pounds ricotta cheese
1 pound grated Romano cheese
1 1-pound box lasagne noodles
1 pound mozzarella cheese, sliced

PROCEDURE:

Meat sauce: In a large heavy pot brown onion in olive oil. Add the ground meat and sausage. Brown lightly. Add the tomato paste, 1 tomato paste can full of water, tomato juice, tomatoes, seasonings and sugar. Simmer this mixture over low heat for 2 1/2 hours. Remove excess fat from the top during the simmering.

Add the eggs to the ricotta cheese and mix well. Add salt, pepper, chopped parsley and about 2 tablespoons of the grated Romano cheese. Mix well.

Cook the lasagne noodles for approximately 10 minutes in lightly salted boiling water. (Do not overcook. Noodles should be somewhat firm when squeezed between 2 fingers.) Drain and rinse in clean water.

Preheat oven to 350°. Pour enough meat sauce into a 9" x 13" pan to cover the bottom of the pan. Lay 1 layer of the cooked lasagne noodles in the pan covering the bottom. Spread some of the ricotta mixture over the noodles and top with a sprinkling of grated Romano cheese and mozzarella slices. Repeat the above steps using all of the noodles. (Criss-crossing the noodles as you build the layers is recommended.) Cover pan with foil and cook in oven until the cheese is bubbling (about 30 minutes). Let stand for about 10 minutes before cutting into portions.

Angelina Guidone
Grandparent, Eric Hansen '98

Sausage Lasagne

Serves 8 to 10

INGREDIENTS:

Sauce:
1/4 cup olive oil
1 medium onion, finely chopped
2 cloves garlic, minced
1 pound mild Italian sausage
2 28-ounce cans Italian style tomatoes
1/4 cup dried parsley
1 teaspoon salt
1/4 teaspoon ground black pepper
1/2 teaspoon dried oregano

Filling:
1/2 pound fresh mushrooms, sliced

2 tablespoons margarine
2 cups (1 pint) ricotta cheese
1 10-ounce package chopped frozen spinach
1 teaspoon salt
2 eggs, beaten
1/2 cup grated Parmesan cheese

Other:
8 strips lasagne noodles
6 ounces mozzarella cheese, sliced
6 ounces Monterey jack cheese, sliced
6 ounces provolone cheese, sliced

PROCEDURE:

Sauce: Heat oil in skillet; sauté onion and garlic 3 minutes. Remove casing and brown sausage in another skillet, stirring often; drain well. Chop tomatoes, undrained, and simmer in a large saucepan. Add remaining sauce ingredients and simmer uncovered all day.

Filling: Sauté mushrooms in margarine until tender and mix with ricotta. Cook spinach as directed and drain well. Blend spinach, salt, eggs and Parmesan cheese into ricotta mixture.

Preheat oven to 350°. Other: Parboil lasagne noodles and drain well. Cover bottom of a 9" x 13" baking dish with a thin layer of sauce. Top with a layer of lasagne noodles. Spread ricotta filling over lasagne, top with the 3 cheeses. Continue making layers, ending with mozzarella, Monterey jack and provolone cheeses on top. Bake uncovered for 45 minutes or until bubbling and golden. Let stand 15 to 20 minutes for easier slicing.

Use hot Italian sausage if you like food spicy. This sauce is also great with spaghetti. The sauce may be made a day ahead.

Christine Bagley
Parent, Catherine Bagley '95 and Sarah Bagley '99

Kelly Rifat's Southern Hospitality Pizza

Serves 4

INGREDIENTS:

Dough:
1 packet yeast
3 1/4 cups whole wheat flour
1 pinch salt
1 teaspoon minced fresh garlic
1 teaspoon crushed sweet basil
1 teaspoon dill weed
1 tablespoon olive oil
1 tablespoon honey
1 cup cool water
1/4 cup hot water

Handful of corn meal
Olive oil to brush crust
Pizza sauce to cover dough (homemade or store-bought)

Suggested Toppings:
3 to 4 cups grated mozzarella cheese
Tomatoes, sliced red onions, pesto sauce, sliced jalapeños, crumbled feta cheese

PROCEDURE:

To make dough with bread machine: Add all ingredients for dough (first 10 ingredients) in order in bread machine. For best results, place yeast in side of bread pan. Run bread machine through manual cycle. You may let dough stand for 1 hour following close of manual cycle to allow for extra rising.

To make dough by hand: Proof yeast in the 1/4 cup "hot" water (warmer than body temperature but not too hot) by sprinkling the yeast on the surface of the water. If the yeast is going to work, it releases that characteristic yeasty smell. Combine about 2 1/2 cups of the flour with the salt, garlic, herbs, olive oil, honey and remaining water. Mix well. If dough is still sticky, add more flour until you can handle the dough well enough to begin kneading. Sprinkle kneading surface (a chopping board works well) with some of the remaining flour and begin kneading, adding more flour to the board if the dough sticks. Knead 8 to 10 minutes, until the dough is a little shiny and resilient. Form into ball and place in a greased bowl in a warm spot. (A 105° to 110° oven works well.) Cover with a moist cloth. Let rise until doubled in size (about 1 hour). Punch down and let rise again until doubled in size.

Preheat oven to 425°. Powder a cookie sheet with corn meal. Empty dough onto center of cookie sheet and press from center of dough outward, forming a round crust of whatever thickness and shape you desire. Pinch edges to form raised crust to contain your toppings. Brush crust lightly with olive oil. Spoon on pizza sauce to cover dough. Cover with thin layer of mozzarella cheese. Top with sliced tomatoes, red onion, jalapeños or whatever you fancy. Brush vegetables with some pesto, if you wish. Cover completely with thick layer of mozzarella (and feta if you want). Bake 15 to 20 minutes.

This recipe is a feast after a long day at the office. Serve with ice cold beer and take outside to eat under a blossoming magnolia on a cool Southern fall evening.

Kelly and Matthew Rifat '87

Quick Pizza Dough

Yields 1 11" pizza crust

INGREDIENTS:

1 1/2 cups all-purpose flour
   1/4 teaspoon sugar
1 1/4 teaspoon quick-rising
        yeast
   1/2 cup hot water
   1/2 teaspoon salt

1 tablespoon olive oil
1 tablespoon yellow corn
   meal plus additional
   for sprinkling the pan
Your favorite pizza
   toppings

PROCEDURE:

Preheat oven to 500°. In a food processor, using the plastic blade, combine 1/2 cup of the flour with the sugar and the yeast. With the motor running, add 1/2 cup hot water and turn the motor off. Add the remaining 1 cup flour, the salt, oil and 1 tablespoon of the cornmeal and blend the mixture until it forms a ball. Oil an 11" black steel pizza pan and sprinkle lightly with cornmeal. Pat the dough out on pan, making the crust slightly thicker around the edge. Brush the crust with a good-quality olive oil and top with your favorite embellishments, including some fresh herbs (like basil or oregano), if your have them. Finish by drizzling a little olive oil over the toppings. Bake for 15 to 20 minutes, or until crust is golden brown.

With this basic and quick crust recipe, it's fun to try out new pizza toppings (or to use up leftovers) and even to mimic pizzas served at all those wonderfully creative Italian restaurants.

Lois Case
Parent, Robert Case '99

Pizza with Tomatoes and Cheese

Serves 2 to 4

INGREDIENTS:

Dough:
3/4 cup plus 1 tablespoon warm (110°) water
3/4 teaspoon dry yeast
1/4 teaspoon sugar
1/4 teaspoon salt
1 1/2 cups all purpose flour
Extra 1/4 to 1/2 cup flour as needed for kneading
2 teaspoons olive oil for bowl

Sauce:
1 8-ounce can tomato sauce
2 garlic cloves, minced or crushed
5 to 6 medium to large basil leaves, chopped

Mozzarella cheese, thinly sliced to cover surface of pizza
1 to 2 tomatoes, thinly sliced to cover surface of pizza

PROCEDURE:

Dough: Dissolve yeast and sugar in warm (110°) water. Let sit about 10 minutes or until foamy. Put salt and 1 1/2 cups flour into medium bowl and add yeast and water mixture. Rinse cup with extra 1 tablespoon water and add to flour. Stir with wooden spoon until dough is smooth and barely sticky. If necessary, add a small amount of extra flour to achieve correct consistency. Turn dough out onto floured board and knead, adding about 1/4 cup more flour. Dough should be soft but not sticking to hands when done (about 5 minutes). Put dough back into clean oiled bowl (roll dough around to coat with oil). Cover bowl with plastic wrap and a towel and let rise until at least doubled in volume, 1 to 1 1/2 hours.

Preheat oven to 475°. Turn dough onto greased 12" round pizza pan, patting out evenly.

Sauce: Mix sauce ingredients (tomato sauce, garlic and basil) together and spread over dough. Cover sauce with mozzarella slices. Cover mozzarella slices with tomato slices. Bake for 16 to 18 minutes until brown. Rotate pizza in last few minutes to insure even browning. Serve immediately!

Once you master the dough making, which isn't hard, it is easy to whip up several of these to serve to friends for dinner.

Kristin Miller '87

John's California Pizza

Yields 1 12" pizza

INGREDIENTS:

Dough for 1 12" pizza (see recipe, page 184)
1 to 2 slices prosciutto (1 to 2 ounces, thickly sliced, cut into 3/4" pieces)
6 to 8 marinated artichoke hearts, each cut in half or thirds
1 to 2 ounces fontina cheese, cut into 1/4" pieces
1 to 2 ounces goat cheese, cut into 1/4" to 1/2" pieces
6 to 8 sun-dried tomatoes in oil, each cut into 2 to 3 pieces

1 tablespoon fresh rosemary (1 teaspoon dried)
1/2 teaspoon dried leaf marjoram
Freshly ground pepper to taste
1/2 teaspoon crushed red pepper flakes (optional)
1 small onion, thinly sliced
2 to 3 fresh plum tomatoes, thinly sliced
Salt to taste

PROCEDURE:

Preheat oven to 475°. Place dough on greased 12" round pan and pat evenly over pan. Put the ingredients on the pizza in the following order, allowing for even distribution over 8 slices. First put on prosciutto, 2 to 3 pieces per slice. Next put on 2 artichoke pieces per slice. Distribute fontina and goat cheeses evenly over pizza. Put 2 sun-dried tomatoes per piece and then sprinkle on herbs and freshly ground pepper. Sprinkle on crushed red pepper flakes, if desired. Spread onion over herbs and cover top of pizza with tomato slices. Lightly salt. Bake for 15 to 17 minutes or until crust is nicely browned.

This makes a drier rather than a wet, juicy pizza because it has no sauce. Amounts of above ingredients may be varied according to individual taste. This pizza can be served with Kristin's Pizza (see recipe, page 184) for nice variety at a gathering.

John Miller
Parent, Kristin Miller '87 and Patrick Miller '93

Spinach Risotto I

Serves 4

INGREDIENTS:

1 tablespoon olive oil
1 cup chopped onion
2 garlic cloves, minced
1 cup Arborio rice
4 cups chicken broth, heat to boil, then simmer
2 cups chopped fresh spinach

3 tablespoons chopped fresh chives
1 tablespoon chopped fresh thyme
Salt and pepper to taste
1/2 cup grated Parmesan cheese

PROCEDURE:

Heat oil in a 4-quart heavy saucepan over moderate heat. Add onion and garlic and sauté until translucent. Add the rice, stirring with a wooden spoon and cook 3 minutes more, being sure nothing is browning. Add heated broth, 1/2 cup at a time, stirring each portion until completely absorbed. When 2 cups broth have been absorbed, add the spinach and herbs. Then continue to add the broth. It will take about 25 minutes to complete. Stir in salt, pepper and Parmesan just before serving.

This is a delicious, light risotto.

Bonnie Sipe
Parent, Brian Sipe '88 and Kevin Sipe '92

Spinach Risotto II

Serves 4 to 6

INGREDIENTS:

2 tablespoons olive oil
1 tablespoon butter
1 yellow onion, finely diced
2 cups Italian Arborio rice
4 to 6 cups chicken stock, preferably homemade
1 large bunch fresh spinach, washed, stemmed and finely chopped

4 ounces freshly grated Parmesan cheese (preferably Reggiano-Parmigiano)
Salt and pepper to taste
Additional Parmesan cheese for table

PROCEDURE:

Heat olive oil and butter over medium heat in a heavy-bottomed deep pan (cast iron is best). When butter foams, add finely diced onion. Sauté until onion begins to color. Add rice and sauté for 2 to 3 minutes over medium-high heat, but do not allow rice to color. Add 2 ladles of chicken stock, stirring constantly with a wooden spoon. When rice absorbs stock, add another ladle of broth and continue stirring. Keep stirring and adding stock slowly until rice is cooked al dente (cooked but still firm to the bite). This will take 20 to 30 minutes. When rice is nearly done, add spinach. When rice is done, remove from heat and stir in grated Parmesan. Add salt and pepper to taste. Serve immediately with additional Parmesan available at the table.

This dish requires about 10 minutes prep time and 30 cooking time (during which it must be stirred constantly). This risotto with a big salad makes a delicious and healthy dinner. Frozen spinach can be substituted for fresh. If canned chicken stock is used, be sure to use low salt type or the risotto will be too salty.

Sonya Eakley Grant '79

Risotto with Mushrooms and Green Vegetables

Serves 3 to 4 as main dish or
6 to 8 as side dish

INGREDIENTS:

2 tablespoons olive oil
1 medium onion, chopped
3 garlic cloves, minced
1 pound fresh mushrooms, cleaned and thickly sliced
4 cups (1 quart) homemade chicken broth (or 4 15-ounce cans)
1 1/2 cups Italian Arborio rice
1/2 teaspoon dried thyme leaves

1 teaspoon chopped fresh rosemary (or 1/2 teaspoon dried)
1/2 cup white wine
1 tablespoon soy sauce
1 1/2 cups broccoli flowerets (small)
1/3 cup fresh or frozen peas
2 tablespoons chopped fresh parsley
1/4 cup freshly grated Parmesan cheese
Salt and pepper
Freshly grated Parmesan cheese for table

PROCEDURE:

Heat oil in a heavy bottomed large pot and sauté onion and garlic until tender. Add sliced mushrooms and sauté over medium heat for 3 to 5 minutes. Heat chicken stock in separate pan while mushrooms are cooking. To the onion/mushroom mixture, add the rice, thyme and rosemary and sauté until grains of rice are coated with oil and mushroom liquid. Add the wine and soy sauce and stir until most of the liquid is absorbed. Stir frequently to avoid sticking. When the wine has just evaporated, stir in 1 or 2 ladles of hot chicken broth. (It should just cover rice.) Cook slowly until it is just absorbed, then add another ladle or 2 of broth, continuing to cook and stir. Continue adding broth until rice is just cooked, about 30 to 35 minutes. About 5 minutes before the rice is ready, stir in raw broccoli flowerets so they barely cook. When finished, add an extra ladle of broth so rice is not too dry. (You may not have to use entire quart of broth.) Stir in peas, parsley and grated Parmesan. Season with freshly ground pepper and salt to taste. Serve extra Parmesan on the side.

This is filling and can be a meal in itself. However, it may also be served with chicken if desired. A green salad is also a nice accompaniment.

John Miller
Parent, Kristin Miller '87 and Patrick Miller '93

Risotto

Serves 4 to 6

INGREDIENTS:

1 medium onion
2 tablespoons butter
2 handfuls (1 cup) Italian Arborio rice
2 cups (1 pint) chicken stock

1/4 cup white wine
1/3 cup grated Parmesan cheese
Freshly ground pepper to taste

PROCEDURE:

Chop onion and sauté in 1 tablespoon of the butter in a large heavy-bottomed pot with a lid. Cook over medium heat, stirring occasionally, until onion is limp, 1 or 2 minutes. Add rice and stir over low heat until translucent. In another saucepan, heat stock to boiling. Add boiling stock and wine to rice and stir to mix. Bring the mixture to a boil, then immediately cut heat back to simmer. Cover and cook for 17 to 20 minutes. Stir in the other tablespoon of butter, Parmesan cheese and pepper and serve immediately.

Easy, tasty meal with salad and bread. For variety, 5 minutes before rice is finished, add herbs, shrimp and/or chopped vegetables of your choice.

Nancy Minton
Parent, Jennifer Minton '96 and Laura Minton '96

Mushroom Risotto

Serves 4 to 8

INGREDIENTS:

2 cups shiitake, oyster
   or Portobello
   mushrooms
1 cup white mushrooms
5 tablespoons butter
   Salt and freshly grated
   pepper
1 tablespoon olive oil
1/3 cup minced onion
1 1/2 cups Arborio rice
1/2 cup white wine

5 cups chicken broth,
   heat to boil, then
   simmer
1/4 cup heavy cream
1/4 cup grated Parmesan
   cheese
2 tablespoons chopped
   fresh parsley

PROCEDURE:

Wash mushrooms in cold water and dry on paper towels. Remove stems and
slice. Cook the mushrooms until soft over moderate heat in a skillet containing
3 tablespoons butter. Salt and pepper to taste and set aside. Heat 2
tablespoons butter and the olive oil in a 4-quart heavy saucepan over moderate
heat. Add onion and sauté until translucent. Add the rice, stirring with a
wooden spoon. Add wine and stir until completely absorbed. Add heated broth,
1/2 cup at a time, stirring each portion until completely absorbed. It is de
rigueur to make risotto at the last minute, but one could stop here and reheat
before adding the mushrooms, cream, cheese and parsley.

*This will serve 4 when it is the main course or 8 as an accompaniment. You can
have family and guests stirring if you choose to make it just before eating. Leftovers
are great!*

Bonnie Sipe
Parent, Brian Sipe '88 and Kevin Sipe '92

Seafood

Trout Almondine

Serves 6

INGREDIENTS:

6 trout fillets (or 3
   pounds fresh fish
   fillets)
1 cup milk
6 tablespoons (3/4 stick)
   butter

1 1/2 cups sliced almonds
   Salt and pepper to
   taste
   Flour for coating
   fillets

PROCEDURE:

Preheat oven to 450°. Soak fillets in milk in a shallow pan for at least 15 minutes. Melt 2 tablespoons of the butter in another shallow pan in the oven. When melted, add almonds and stir until coated with butter. Cook until almonds are lightly brown. Stir occasionally and watch carefully to prevent burning. When brown, remove from oven and set aside. Place the remaining 4 tablespoons of butter in an ovenproof pan large enough to hold fish in a single layer and place pan in oven until butter melts. Take fish fillets out of milk; salt and pepper them and cover them with a light coating of flour. Place fillets skin side up in the preheated pan of melted butter. (Can roll both sides in butter.) Cook in oven for 5 minutes. Turn over and bake for approximately 10 more minutes or until done. Remove fish and place on serving plate. Cover with browned almonds and serve immediately.

Our family traditionally prepares this dish with speckled trout we catch in the Gulf of Mexico. You may substitute any white-flesh fish fillets. Adjust cooking time to thickness of fillets.

James H. Branard, Jr.
Grandparent, Elizabeth Vale '92 and Susannah Vale '95

Wine Poached Fish

Serves 2 to 4

INGREDIENTS:

1 pound fish steaks
(shark, halibut, etc.)
1/2 cup dry white wine
1/4 cup lemon juice

Salt and pepper to
taste
1/2 cup chopped scallions
1 tablespoon butter

PROCEDURE:

Preheat oven to 350°. Place fish in baking dish which is large enough to hold fish in 1 layer and which can also be used on burner on top of stove. Pour wine and lemon juice over fish. Season with a little salt and pepper as desired. Then cover and bake 20 to 25 minutes, until fish is opaque. Remove fish from baking dish and keep warm on separate plate. Place baking dish with wine and lemon juice over fire or burner. Add scallions and butter. Heat until liquid boils and has reduced. Then pour over fish and serve.

Great low cal, healthy dish. Easy to prepare. I always use shark.

Missy Agnew Looney '82

Baked Fish à la Dorothy Steinle

Serves 2 to 3

INGREDIENTS:

1 pound fish fillets (cod,
flounder or haddock)
Seasonings: Cracked
pepper, Lawry
seasoned salt, dried
parsley (to taste)

1/2 cup Triscuit crackers,
pulverized
1/4 cup chopped onions
1/3 pound mushrooms,
sliced
Dabs of butter or
margarine for top

PROCEDURE:

Preheat oven to 450°. Spray a glass pan large enough to lay fillets side by side in 1 layer with non-stick cooking oil. Place fish in pan. Sprinkle top with seasonings. Sprinkle pulverized Triscuits on top of fillets to create light coating. Distribute onions and mushrooms over Triscuits. Place a few of dabs of butter or margarine on top. Bake 15 minutes or until fish is done and Triscuits are brown.

E. Ron Weiner
Husband, Suzanne Baral Weiner, Director of Public Relations

Baked Fish with Infused Oil

Serves 6

INGREDIENTS:

Infused oil:
1 cup olive oil
1 to 2 sprigs rosemary (or herb of your choice)
1 clove garlic, minced
1 3-pound firm fish fillet

Fresh chopped herb of your choice for sprinkling on top
Salt and freshly ground pepper to taste

PROCEDURE:

Infused oil: In a saucepan heat olive oil, rosemary and garlic until hot, then simmer for about 3 minutes. Remove from heat, strain and store in a bottle.

Place a pan of water on lower shelf of oven and preheat to 350°. Cut the fish fillet into serving sizes. Place in an oiled (use infused oil) baking dish. Brush the top of each piece of fish with the infused oil and sprinkle with a fresh chopped herb. Season with salt and pepper to taste. Place pan on middle shelf of oven and bake for about 12 to 18 minutes depending on thickness and preference. Serve on top of a bed of ratatouille (see recipe, page 339).

Anne Otterson
Parent, Eric Otterson '87 and Helen Otterson '89

Swordfish with Niçoise Vinaigrette

Serves 2

INGREDIENTS:

5 tablespoons olive oil
2 1" swordfish steaks
1/4 cup finely chopped
   pitted Kalamata black
   olives
1/4 cup finely chopped
   bottled roasted red
   pepper
3 tablespoons finely
   chopped fresh parsley
1 tablespoon capers
1 flat anchovy fillet
   minced

3 garlic cloves mashed
   to a paste with 1/4
   teaspoon salt
2 tablespoons minced
   scallions
1 1/2 tablespoons balsamic
   or red wine vinegar
Salt and pepper to
   taste
Lemon wedges as an
   accompaniment

PROCEDURE:

In a skillet, preferably non-stick, heat 1 1/2 tablespoons of the oil over moderately high heat until it is hot but not smoking. Pat the swordfish steaks dry and sauté for 4 to 5 minutes on each side, or until they are just cooked through. While the fish is cooking, in a small bowl stir together the olives, roasted red pepper, parsley, capers, anchovy, garlic paste, scallions, vinegar, the remaining 3 1/2 tablespoons oil, salt and pepper to taste. Transfer the swordfish to plates, spoon the sauce over it and serve it with the lemon wedges.

You can also grill the fish.

Susie Spanos
Parent, John Spanos '98

Marinated Swordfish

Serves 8

INGREDIENTS:

8 swordfish steaks
1/2 cup salad oil
1/3 cup soy sauce

1 tablespoon grated
   lemon peel
1 garlic clove, crushed

194

| 2 teaspoons Dijon | 8 lemon slices |
| mustard | 1/4 cup chopped parsley |

PROCEDURE:

Combine and blend all ingredients except lemon slices and parsley. Pour over swordfish and refrigerate 1 to 3 hours. Barbecue swordfish for 5 to 6 minutes on each side over moderate coals. Serve with garnish of lemon slices and parsley.

Quick, easy and great for company.

Sheryl Durkin
Parent, Kimberly Durkin '96 and Kristin Durkin '98

Grilled Marinated Swordfish Steaks

Serves 4

INGREDIENTS:

- 4 center cut swordfish steaks, 6 to 8 ounces each, 1" thick
- Salt and freshly ground pepper to taste
- 3 tablespoons olive oil
- 2 teaspoons soy sauce
- 1 tablespoon red wine vinegar

- 4 sprigs fresh rosemary (or 1 teaspoon dried)
- 1 teaspoon ground cumin
- 1 teaspoon grated lemon peel
- 1 tablespoon finely chopped garlic

PROCEDURE:

Sprinkle fish with salt and pepper on both sides. Place olive oil and remaining ingredients in shallow pan. Blend well. Place swordfish steaks in marinade. Coat well on both sides. Cover pan with plastic wrap and let stand for at least 1/2 hour.

Preheat a charcoal grill or oven broiler. Cook fish on grill 3 to 4 minutes on each side, (or longer, if desired, and depending on the heat of the fire). If cooked under broiler, cook 3 to 4 minutes on each side.

I usually serve with wild and white rice (combined) or small cooked red potatoes and green or spinach salad.

Patty Allen
Grandparent, Ashley Walker '98

Grilled Swordfish

Serves 6

INGREDIENTS:

3 pounds fresh swordfish steaks (each approximately 1" thick, 1/2 pound in weight)
1 cup safflower oil
1/3 cup virgin olive oil
2 teaspoons minced fresh cilantro (or 1 tablespoon minced fresh parsley)

2 teaspoons minced fresh oregano (or 1 teaspoon dried)
1/4 teaspoon puréed garlic
1/4 teaspoon salt
1/4 teaspoon freshly cracked black pepper

Lemon and lime wedges to accompany

PROCEDURE:

Place the swordfish steaks in a shallow container. Mix together all other ingredients (except lemon and lime wedges) and pour over fish. Cover and refrigerate several hours. Turn fish occasionally.

Grill fish 4" to 6" above a hot mesquite or charcoal briquette fire. Baste with marinade for flavor and to prevent the fish from sticking to the grill.

As a general rule, grill the fish 10 minutes per inch of thickness, but watch the timing carefully. Overcooking swordfish results in dryness. The goal is to grill it just until it's done, leaving it still slightly moist. Serve with lemon and lime wedges.

Judith Lanphier Strada '63X
Parent, Nick Strada '92 and Catherine Strada '95

Lemon Swordfish with Avocado Butter

Serves 8

INGREDIENTS:

Marinade:
1/3 cup soy sauce
1/3 cup fresh lemon juice
1 garlic clove, crushed
2 teaspoons Dijon
mustard
1/2 cup olive oil

8 swordfish steaks
(Thresher shark is an
excellent substitute)

Avocado butter:
1/2 cup (1 stick) butter,
softened
1/2 cup ripe mashed
avocado
5 tablespoons fresh
lemon or lime juice
3 tablespoons chopped
fresh cilantro
1 clove garlic, crushed

Lemon or lime wedges
and chopped cilantro
for garnish

PROCEDURE:

Whisk together all marinade ingredients. Place fish in a shallow glass dish and pour marinade over all. (Or another quick trick is to place fish in large, freezer type ziploc baggie, pour marinade in and carefully lock top.) Marinate about 1 hour, (no more than 5 hours). Remove fish from marinade and grill over coals or under broiler for 5 to 6 minutes per side. Do not overcook. Serve fish garnished with lemon or lime wedges, chopped cilantro, topped with avocado butter.

Avocado butter: Whip butter in small mixing bowl until fluffy. Beat in remaining avocado butter ingredients.

This is a wonderful summer entrée. Serve with wheat pilaf, zucchini, red pepper, mushroom sauté.

Heidi Dorris
Parent, Ashley Dorris '96 and Taylor Dorris '98

Grilled Fresh Tuna Steaks
with Lemon Sauce

Serves 6

INGREDIENTS:

Marinade:
1/3 cup mustard
1/3 cup lemon juice
  2 cloves garlic, peeled
    and minced
  3 tablespoons fresh
    rosemary, minced (or
    3 teaspoons dried)
1 1/3 cups olive oil
  2 teaspoons salt
  1 teaspoon ground black
    pepper

  3 pounds fresh tuna, cut
    into 3/4" steaks

Sauce:
  4 tablespoons olive oil
  3 tablespoons
    unbleached white
    flour
1 1/2 cups chicken stock
1/2 cup heavy cream (or
    nonfat evaporated
    milk)
1/2 teaspoon salt
1/2 teaspoon ground black
    pepper

Garnish:
Rosemary sprigs
1 lemon, sliced

PROCEDURE:

Marinade: Combine all the marinade ingredients in the bowl of a food processor fitted with a metal blade and purée for 30 seconds, or until smooth and creamy. Pour the marinade into a glass or stainless steel casserole. Place the tuna steaks in the marinade, pushing them down to make sure they are completely covered with sauce. Marinate at room temperature for 1 hour.

Preheat a grill or broiler until very hot. Preheat oven to 200°.
Take the tuna from the casserole dish, reserving the marinade for the sauce. Grill the steaks over hot coals until done. It should take about 4 minutes on each side, depending on how hot the coals are. (If using a broiler, the time is about the same.) Arrange the grilled fish on a warm platter and place inside the preheated warm oven while you prepare the sauce.

Sauce: Heat the olive oil in a heavy saucepan. Add the flour. Simmer, stirring for about 1 minute. Add the chicken stock, stirring constantly until the sauce begins to bubble. Add the cream, salt and pepper. Bring to a bubbling boil again. Remove from heat. Add the marinade and stir.

Cover the fish lightly with the sauce. Serve the rest on the side. Garnish the platter with rosemary sprigs and lemon slices.

Sara Sweet
Staff, Director of Food Service

Barbecued Butterflied Salmon

Serves 8

INGREDIENTS:

1 fresh salmon,
butterflied, skin on

Sauce:
(I usually double the
sauce for 1 whole
salmon.)
2 tablespoons Dijon
mustard

1 cup (2 sticks) butter
1 clove garlic, chopped
4 tablespoons soy sauce
1 teaspoon Worcester-
shire sauce
2 teaspoons ketchup

PROCEDURE:

Start barbecue grill.
Combine all sauce ingredients. Melt over <u>very</u> low heat so as not to separate the butter, stirring constantly.

Use <u>flat</u> fish cooker for barbecue. Oil cooker with vegetable oil on paper towel. Place washed and dried salmon on cooker and baste with sauce on both sides. When coals are hot and covered with grey ash, place cooker with salmon, flesh side down on barbecue grill over coals. Cooking time is extremely important and will vary according to charcoal heat. Cook flesh side down for approximately 15 minutes and skin side down for 5 minutes. Do not overcook! Fish should be very moist. Serve with warmed sauce.

Pasta pesto and sautéed cherry tomatoes are great with this. Always a request.
Several Bishop's friends have enjoyed this salmon. Always use fresh salmon.
Leftovers reheat nicely in microwave, with sauce heated separately.

Bobbie Kohn Bouillon '62

Salmon North by Northwest

Serves 6

INGREDIENTS:

6 salmon servings
   (steaks or fillets),
   1" thick

Sauce:
1 cup (2 sticks) butter
1/2 cup soy sauce

3 tablespoons ketchup
4 teaspoons dry mustard
5 cloves garlic, crushed
   Lots of freshly ground
   pepper
1/4 cup finely chopped
   parsley

PROCEDURE:

Combine all sauce ingredients in a small saucepan over low heat, stirring with each addition. Cook for 10 minutes. Remove from heat and set aside. With heavy duty aluminum foil, make 6 pans slightly larger than individual pieces of salmon (by folding up edges of foil about 1/2" high). Spread 2 tablespoons sauce on bottom of each pan. Put a salmon serving in each pan. Put 2 tablespoons sauce on top of each salmon. Cook on a barbecue or broil in oven 6" away from heat for about 10 minutes. Spoon on more sauce at about 5 minutes.

This is wonderful with rice or potatoes and a salad. Do not let heat get too hot or ketchup (in sauce) will burn. Enjoy.

Bruce Burgener '61

Grilled Salmon Steaks with Tomato, Cucumber and Lemon Sauce

Serves 4

INGREDIENTS:

4 3/4" thick salmon
  steaks

Sauce:
3/4 cup fresh chopped
  tomato or cherry
  tomatoes
1/2 cup very thinly sliced
  cucumbers
2 tablespoons chopped
  red onions
1 to 2 garlic cloves, crushed
  or minced

1 hot marinated
  jalapeño pepper,
  chopped
1/4 cup olive oil
2 tablespoons lemon
  juice
1/2 teaspoon dry oregano
  leaves
  Salt and pepper to
  taste

PROCEDURE:

Prepare sauce first. Combine all sauce ingredients; stir well. Season with salt
and pepper. Refrigerate until ready to use.

Prepare barbecue grill. When coals are hot, place rack 4" from hot coals. Brush
grill lightly with oil and place salmon on rack. Grill about 6 to 8 minutes on
each side, turning once until cooked. Place salmon on serving plate. Serve
sauce in bowl on side. Spoon sauce over salmon at table.

*This is good with new potatoes and a green salad. This recipe is delicious and the
sauce can be made with a minimum of oil and salt for people on special diets. Also
good with halibut steaks.*

John Miller
Parent, Kristin Miller '87 and Patrick Miller '93

Salmon Soufflé

Serves 6

INGREDIENTS:

1 teaspoon butter
1 tablespoon grated
    Parmesan cheese
4 tablespoons minced
    green onions
4 tablespoons butter
4 tablespoons flour
1 1/2 cup boiling liquid
    (juice from canned
    salmon plus milk)
1/2 teaspoon salt
1/4 teaspoon white pepper
1 teaspoon oregano or
    marjoram (dried)

4 teaspoons tomato
    paste
1/2 cup Eggbeaters (or 5
    egg yolks)
3/4 cup grated Swiss
    cheese
1 cup canned salmon,
    drained and finely
    chopped
6 egg whites, beaten
    until stiff

PROCEDURE:

Preheat oven to 400°. Butter a 2-quart soufflé dish and sprinkle with Parmesan cheese. In a large heavy pot cook the onions in the 4 tablespoons butter for 2 minutes. Add the flour and cook another 2 minutes. Remove the pan from the heat and whisk in the boiling liquid. Add the seasonings and tomato paste. Bring to a boil and cook for 1 minute, stirring constantly. Remove from heat and stir in the Eggbeaters or egg yolks and the cheese. Stir in the salmon. Stir 1/4 of the beaten egg whites into the salmon mixture, then fold the salmon mixture into the remaining egg whites. Turn into the prepared soufflé dish.

Reset oven to 375° and bake soufflé for 40 minutes in the middle level of the oven.

By replacing the egg yolks with the Eggbeaters or a similar egg yolk substitute, the cholesterol level of this recipe is reduced considerably.

Molly Hannan
Parent, Mimi Hannan '92

Parmesan and Herb Shrimp

Serves 12

INGREDIENTS:

4 pounds large shrimp, shelled and cleaned
3/4 cup fresh parsley
1/2 cup fresh cilantro
1/4 cup mint leaves
1 tablespoon tarragon
4 garlic cloves
3 tablespoons Worcestershire sauce
2 tablespoons soy sauce

2 tablespoons cognac or brandy
1 tablespoon mustard
1/8 cup lemon juice
1 cup Parmesan cheese
1/2 cup (1 stick) butter (or margarine), melted
1 teaspoon pepper
Salt to taste

PROCEDURE:

Preheat oven to 375°. Cook shrimp in 12 cups of boiling water for about 5 minutes or until pink. Do not overcook. Drain immediately and place them in an ovenproof serving dish. In a food processor or blender mix all the remaining ingredients thoroughly and spread mixture over the cooked shrimp evenly. Cook in the oven for 15 minutes or until cheese is melted.

Serve with rice or pasta.

Dolores Landa
Parent, Enrique Landa '97 and Fernando Landa '99

Shrimp Etouffé

Serves 4

INGREDIENTS:

1 pound fresh or frozen
   shrimp, peeled
2 cups onion, chopped
1 cup celery, finely
   chopped
2 cloves garlic, minced
3 tablespoons cooking
   oil or butter
4 teaspoons cornstarch

1/2 cup tomato sauce
1 cup water
Salt and freshly
   ground pepper to
   taste
1/4 teaspoon ground red
   pepper (or to taste)
Hot cooked rice for 4

PROCEDURE:

Thaw shrimp if frozen. In a large saucepan cook onion, celery and garlic, covered, in cooking oil (or butter) for 10 minutes or until tender. Stir in cornstarch. Add tomato sauce, water, salt, black pepper and red pepper. Cook and stir until bubbly. Add shrimp. Return to boiling and reduce heat. Simmer, uncovered for 4 to 5 minutes or until shrimp turns pink. Season to taste. Serve over rice.

Can substitute crayfish if available. This is my husband Larry's specialty.

Joan Canby Mugg '66

Shrimp and Cheese Casserole

Serves 4

INGREDIENTS:

6 slices bread (white or
   sourdough)
1/2 pound Old English (or
   extra sharp cheddar)
   cheese, sliced
1 pound cooked shrimp
   (shells and tails
   removed)

1/4 cup (1/2 stick) butter,
   melted
3 eggs, beaten
1/2 teaspoon dry mustard
2 cups (1 pint) milk
Salt to taste

PROCEDURE:

Grease a 9" x 13" casserole. Break bread and cheese into bite size pieces. Arrange 1/2 the shrimp, followed by 1/2 the bread and 1/2 the cheese in casserole. Repeat layers. Pour melted butter over the layers. Add mustard and salt to beaten eggs. Then add milk. Mix together and pour over ingredients in casserole. Let stand a minimum of 3 hours, covered, in refrigerator; overnight, if possible.

Preheat oven to 350°. Bake covered for exactly 1 hour.

Serve with green salad made with red onions, tomatoes and Italian dressing or fruit salad and dinner rolls.

Barbara Young Beebe '55

Baked Shrimp

Serves 2 to 3

INGREDIENTS:

- **1 pound raw shrimp, shelled and deveined**
- **1 cup (2 sticks) butter**
- **3 cloves garlic, crushed**
- **2 cups plain bread crumbs**

PROCEDURE:

Preheat oven to 400°. Butter a shallow baking dish which is large enough to hold shrimp in a single layer. Prepare shrimp. Arrange the raw shrimp on bottom of baking dish. Mix together the melted butter, crushed garlic and bread crumbs. Cover shrimp with bread crumb mixture. Bake for 20 to 25 minutes.

Do not add other seasonings.

Marlene Teitelman
Wife, Headmaster Michael Teitelman and
Parent, Mark Teitelman '88 and Jeffrey Teitelman '90

Corn Crêpes with Shrimp

Serves 8

INGREDIENTS:

Sauce:
4 tomatoes, roasted (broil in oven until brown), peeled and seeded, saving the juices
1/2 medium onion
1/2 cup cilantro
Dash cayenne pepper
Salt

Crêpes:
1 1/3 cups corn meal
2 1/3 cups nonfat or low fat milk
1/2 cup flour
2 whole eggs plus 2 egg whites
1/2 cup packed chopped cilantro
1 tablespoon finely chopped chives

1/4 teaspoon salt
1 tablespoon peanut or corn oil

Filling:
1/2 pound raw shrimp, shelled, deveined and chopped (crabs, scallops or any fish may be substituted)
1 clove garlic, finely chopped
1 teaspoon oil
6 scallions with half of the greens, chopped
1 avocado, chopped
1 serrano chile (amount used determined by taste)
Juice of 1 lime

PROCEDURE:

Sauce: Place ingredients in food processor and process until sauce is finely blended. Set aside until needed.

Crêpes: Two hours in advance, place corn meal in a bowl. Heat milk and pour over corn meal. Stir and set aside. When sauce is prepared and all other ingredients for the filling and crêpes are measured, continue preparing the crêpes. Pour the flour into a sifter and sift into corn meal mixture stirring well. In a separate bowl, beat the eggs and egg whites and add to flour mixture. Add the herbs and salt. Heat griddle, brush with oil and pour about 1/4 cup batter for each crêpe. Cook the crêpes and keep warm. Occasionally stir the batter to mix well before pouring onto the griddle. A little more milk may be added to the batter if the flour swells and thickens the batter too much.

When the crêpes are ready, quickly cook the filling (according to instructions below). Stuff each crêpe with a large tablespoon of filling, roll up and arrange attractively on serving plate. Pour the sauce over the crêpes and serve. The batter and filling yield about 16 crêpes.

Filling: Prepare all ingredients. When the crêpes are cooked, quickly sauté the shrimp and garlic in the oil for about a minute or until the moment they turn pink. Add the scallions, avocado, chile and lime juice. Cook 1/2 minute and use to stuff crêpes as described above.

The crêpes may be prepared ahead and heated in the oven, not microwave. They can be served as a first course or as an entrée for a luncheon.

Anne Otterson
Parent, Eric Otterson '87 and Helen Otterson '89

Thai Shrimp

Serves 4

INGREDIENTS:

1 **pound jumbo shrimp**	1/4 **cup white wine**
1 **clove garlic, minced**	1/8 **cup water**
1 **1" piece fresh ginger,**	1 **tablespoon olive oil**
peeled and minced	1 **small hot red pepper,**
1/4 **cup light soy sauce**	**broken**

PROCEDURE:

Remove legs from shrimp (leave shell on or remove as you prefer) and slightly butterfly to clean. Make a marinade by mixing all remaining ingredients together and marinate shrimp for 1 hour. Barbecue shrimp 2 minutes on each side. You may thread on skewers, if desired, to keep the shrimp from curling up while cooking.

Quick and easy.

Mimi Lee Bulkley '64X

207

Padd Thai

Serves 2

INGREDIENTS:

3 tablespoons cooking oil
1 tablespoon chopped garlic
1/2 cup finely diced baked bean curd
2 eggs
1/2 pound jumbo shrimp, shelled and cleaned
1/2 pound (dry weight) Chantaboon rice noodles (soak in warm water until soft, drain)
2 tablespoons sugar

4 tablespoons fish sauce
3 tablespoons vinegar
1 teaspoon paprika
1 tablespoon coarsely crushed roasted peanuts
1/4 teaspoon ground dried red chile
3 green onions, cut into 1" lengths
6 ounces bean sprouts
1 fresh lime, sliced

PROCEDURE:

Heat oil in a large frying pan on medium heat. Sauté garlic and bean curd for 1 minute. Then add eggs and stir well. Add shrimp and noodles and toss. Add sugar, fish sauce, vinegar, paprika and half the peanuts. Keep tossing for 10 more minutes. Add ground chile, green onion and approximately 2/3 of the bean sprouts. Serve with the remaining peanuts sprinkled on top, the rest of the bean sprouts and sliced lime on the side.

Suthisiri Tilakamonkul,
Parent, Pongsiri Prachyarata-Nawooti '98

Scallops Florentine

Serves 4 to 6

INGREDIENTS:

20 ounces fresh spinach, washed and dried thoroughly

1/2 cup (1 stick) unsalted butter

3 large cloves garlic, finely minced

1 cup (1/2 pint) whipping cream

1 teaspoon freshly ground nutmeg

1/2 teaspoon freshly ground white pepper

1 1/4 pounds bay scallops

8 ounces pasta, cooked

3 ounces Parmesan cheese, freshly grated

1 teaspoon salt

PROCEDURE:

Preheat oven to 425°. Cut stems from spinach leaves and finely mince stems. Melt butter in a heavy 12" skillet over medium-low heat. Stir in minced garlic, spinach stems and salt. Sauté until stems are soft (about 8 minutes). Add whipping cream and simmer until reduced by half (about 5 minutes). Coarsely chop spinach leaves in batches, using On/Off turns in food processor. Add to cream mixture with nutmeg and pepper. Increase heat to high and cook until spinach is heated through (about 3 minutes). Remove from heat. Stir in scallops and pasta. Transfer to shallow 4-quart baking dish. Sprinkle Parmesan cheese on top. Bake until scallops are just opaque (approximately 10 to 12 minutes). Serve immediately.

Great for elegant "ladies luncheon" or buffet.

Valerie Willis
Parent, Stephanie Alyson Willis '89 and Matthew Willis '92

Southern Crab Cakes

Serves 4 or 5 (8 cakes)

INGREDIENTS:

6 slices white bread
1/4 cup olive oil
3 eggs, separated
1/2 teaspoon dry mustard
1/4 teaspoon salt
2 teaspoons Worcester-
shire sauce

1 pound fresh crab meat
or 2 cans of best
quality crab, drained
Paprika
3 tablespoons butter

PROCEDURE:

Trim crusts from bread and cut into small cubes. Pour oil over cubes, tossing with a fork until all are evenly saturated. Combine egg yolks with mustard, salt and Worcestershire sauce and beat lightly with a fork. Stir in bread cubes and crab meat. In a separate bowl, beat egg whites until they form a peak and then gently fold into crab mixture. Heat butter in a large non-stick skillet over medium-high heat. Spoon in mixture to form cakes. Sprinkle with paprika and cook until golden brown. Turn over, sprinkle with more paprika and cook until second side is golden brown (approximately 10 minutes total). Serve at once.

These do need to be cooked just before serving. The recipe halves nicely. Very good with tartar sauce.

Sue Hughes
Grandparent, Adrienne Hoehn '97

Shrimp and Sausage Jambalaya

Serves 4

INGREDIENTS:

1 ham hock
2 bay leaves
1 yellow onion, diced
1/2 green pepper, diced
2 cloves garlic, chopped
1 tablespoon olive oil
2 teaspoons tomato
    paste
1/2 teaspoon thyme
1/2 teaspoon pepper
    Dash cayenne pepper

Dash ground cloves
1 8-ounce smoked
    sausage, sliced 1/4"
    thick
1 cup white rice
1/2 pound medium shrimp
    in shell
1 14-ounce can stewed
    tomatoes, drained
    and chopped
2 tablespoons parsley

PROCEDURE:

In a large pot bring to boil 5 cups of water and the ham hock. Pour water out once it comes to a boil but reserve ham hock. In same pot bring another 5 cups of water to boil with ham hock and bay leaves. Once boiling, turn temperature down and simmer 1 hour. Discard ham hock after the hour but reserve the broth.

In large skillet sauté onion, green pepper and garlic in olive oil for 4 minutes. Turn heat down and blend in tomato paste, thyme, pepper, cayenne and ground cloves. Push mixture to 1 side of skillet and cook sausage on the other side until browned. Then blend onion mixture into sausage. Set aside.

In a saucepan over low heat add 1 cup white rice to 2 1/3 cups ham hock broth. Simmer 30 minutes or until broth is absorbed. In another saucepan bring to boil 4 cups water. Add shrimp and boil 4 minutes. Drain shrimp and immerse in cold water. Peel shrimp and cut in half. Add shrimp to sausage mixture. Stir in stewed tomatoes and parsley. Fold in rice. Serve hot.

To save time substitute beef or chicken broth for the ham hock broth.

Julie Jones Smitherman '82

Gumbo

Serves 6 to 8

INGREDIENTS:

2 tablespoons vegetable
   shortening
2 tablespoons flour
1 10-ounce box frozen
   sliced okra
3 stalks celery, chopped
1 large onion, chopped
1 16-ounce can
   tomatoes
1 8-ounce can tomato
   sauce
1/4 teaspoon Tabasco
3 cups chicken stock
1 clove garlic, crushed
1 teaspoon salt
1/2 teaspoon pepper

1/4 teaspoon crushed
   thyme
1/2 teaspoon crushed
   oregano
2 bay leaves

1 1/2 cups chicken, cooked
   and diced
1 1/2 cups ham, cooked and
   diced
1 1/2 cups whole small (or
   chopped large)
   shrimp, cleaned and
   cooked
Cooked rice for 6 to 8

PROCEDURE:

In a large pan, melt shortening. Add flour and brown. Add next 13 ingredients. (Break tomatoes into pieces with your hands as you add them.) Simmer for 2 hours, covered. Add chicken, ham and shrimp. Simmer uncovered 30 minutes longer. Serve over rice.

Flavor improves with age. Have yet to meet a teenager that doesn't love this soup.

Mary Sloan Mozingo '59

Shrimp Gumbo

Serves 8

INGREDIENTS:

1/2 cup chopped onion
3 tablespoons oil
1/4 cup flour
1 16-ounce can
    tomatoes, chopped
4 cups water
1 10-ounce package
    frozen sliced okra
1 teaspoon salt
1/4 teaspoon cayenne
    pepper
1/4 teaspoon black pepper

Pinch of each of the
    following tied in
    cheesecloth:
    Marjoram, savory,
    basil, thyme, sage,
    rosemary and oregano
1 pound shrimp, shelled
    and cleaned
1 3/4-ounce package
    dried shrimp
1 tablespoon filé
    (powdered sassafras
    leaves used in Creole
    cooking)
Cooked rice to serve 8

PROCEDURE:

Sauté onions in oil in saucepan. Blend in flour. Cook until browned, stirring constantly. Add the tomatoes, water, okra, seasonings and herbs tied in cheesecloth. Mix well. Cook, covered for 30 minutes. Stir in raw and dried shrimp. Cook for 10 minutes longer or until raw shrimp are pink. Remove seasoning bag. Stir in filé just before serving. Serve with rice.

Very good on a cold winter night.

Tempe Pell
Aunt, Elizabeth Vale '92 and Susannah Vale '95

Paella de Mariscos (Seafood Paella)

Serves 6 to 7

INGREDIENTS:

3 cups white rice
Pinch saffron
6 cups warm water
2 artichokes
2 tomatoes
1 green pepper
1 Spanish onion
5 to 6 tablespoons olive oil
4 to 5 cloves garlic
Pinch parsley
1/2 cup white sherry wine
6 prawns
6 shrimp

1/4 pound squid
1/4 pound small clams
1/4 pound mussels
1/4 pound scallops
1/4 pound lobster
(optional)
1 14-ounce can peas
4 lemons, quartered
1 4-ounce jar red
pimento strips
Salt and pepper to
taste

PROCEDURE:

Soak rice and saffron in the warm water in a large pot. Cut artichokes into quarters and remove choke from center. Slice remaining vegetables. Pour the olive oil into an ovenproof large frying pan (12" diameter by 2" depth) or a paella pan. Sauté vegetables in olive oil over medium heat for about 3 minutes, until onions are slightly limp. In a mortar crush garlic and parsley and add sherry to it. Once vegetables are sautéed, strain rice (save the water). Put rice in frying pan with vegetables. Then add garlic/parsley/wine mixture and stir with wooden spoon while cooking over medium heat for 6 to 8 minutes. Add the seafood and peas stirring constantly over medium heat. Pour the reserved saffron/water over the vegetable/seafood mixture until ingredients are covered. Let rice and seafood cook slowly on medium heat. Add a little more saffron/water if all liquid evaporates before rice is cooked.

Preheat oven to 350°. When rice is cooked, cover pan with aluminum foil and put it in the oven for 5 minutes. After 5 minutes or so, turn off oven and let the paella "hang" in the oven for 10 to 15 minutes. This will allow you to get table and guests ready. Take paella out of the oven after 10 to 15 minutes and garnish with quartered lemons and red pimento strips. Add salt and pepper to taste.

Serve with bread and lots of red (or white) wine. Cold paella is also delicious!! Patience is a very important ingredient when you make paella. Paella also allows for many different variations.

Rafael Moyano
Faculty, Foreign Languages Department

Shellfish Paella

Serves 8

INGREDIENTS:

- 8 clams, scrubbed and cleaned
- 2 tablespoons extra virgin olive oil
- 4 cloves garlic, minced
- 2 medium onions, chopped
- 2 small red and yellow bell peppers cut in strips
- 2 cups uncooked brown rice
- 1/2 cup finely chopped parsley
- 2 cups clam juice
- 2 cups water
- 1 cup tomato sauce
- 2 tablespoons sodium reduced soy sauce
- 1/4 cup freshly squeezed lemon juice
- 1/2 teaspoon saffron
- 1 pound bay scallops
- 1 cup frozen peas, thawed
- 2 4-ounce jars sliced pimiento, undrained
- 8 large raw shrimp, shelled and cleaned with tails left on

PROCEDURE:

To clean clams, place in a large bowl and cover with cold water which has been mixed with 2 tablespoons of salt. Sprinkle 2 tablespoons cornmeal over the top. Refrigerate for 3 to 12 hours. Drain and rinse well with clean water. (This procedure will whiten the shells, remove the sand and cause the clams to eject the black material in their stomachs.)

Preheat oven to 350°. Heat oil in a large ovenproof skillet or paella pan. Add garlic, onion and bell pepper and sauté over medium heat for 5 minutes. Add rice and parsley and stir until the rice is well coated with oil. Add clam juice, water, tomato sauce, soy sauce, lemon juice and saffron. Mix well and bring to a boil. Cover and place in the preheated oven and bake for 1 hour and 15 minutes, or until all of the liquid is absorbed. Remove from oven and stir in raw scallops, peas and pimiento. Turn oven off and return paella to oven to keep warm while cooking the shrimp and clams. Do not leave in the oven more than 5 minutes. Steam the clams and shrimp until the clams open and shrimp turn from translucent to opaque, about 2 to 3 minutes. If clams do not open, discard them. To serve, add the shrimp and clams to the rice mixture in the paella pan and place it in the center of the table.

I like to double the number of shrimp. This dish is a beautiful centerpiece in itself.

Joan Black
Faculty, History Department Chair

Muquéca de Peixe
(Brazilian Seafood with Rice)

Serves 8 to 10

INGREDIENTS:

1/4 cup olive oil
2 1/2 large onions, chopped coarsely
5 cloves garlic, sliced
1 leek, cleaned well and sliced
1 1/2 medium green peppers, chopped
2 large tomatoes, chopped coarsely
Salt to taste
Several dashes Tabasco to taste (don't skimp)

1 1/2 pounds fish (halibut or shark) cut into bite size pieces
1 1/2 pounds crab (artificial OK), shrimp and/or lobster, precooked
1 1/2 cups canned coconut milk
1/2 cup chopped parsley
Cooked white rice for 8 to 10 servings

PROCEDURE:

Sauté onion in oil in 8-quart pot. Add garlic and leek. Cover and simmer until tender (approximately 5 minutes). Add peppers and tomatoes. Cover and simmer 5 minutes. Add salt and Tabasco to taste. Add fish. Simmer until cooked (approximately 5 minutes). Add crab, shrimp and/or lobster. Add coconut milk. Heat but do not boil. Sprinkle with parsley. Serve over or with white rice.

Very nice company dinner. Serve with side vegetables and/or salad.

Maria Elena Pires Martins
A.F.S. "Aunt", Justin Shaw '89 and Maiya Shaw '92

Poultry & Game

Mediterranean Chicken

Serves 6 to 8

INGREDIENTS:

Salt and freshly
  ground pepper to
  taste
2/3 cup olive oil
  6 half chicken breasts
  6 chicken legs
  6 chicken thighs
1 1/2 cups dry white wine

1 pound fresh
  mushrooms,
  quartered
1/3 cup finely chopped
  shallots
1 10-ounce box frozen
  artichokes (optional)
1 1/2 cups pitted ripe olives
  3 cups chopped fresh
  tomatoes (or canned)

PROCEDURE:

Preheat oven to 375°. Lightly salt and pepper the chicken. In a large skillet heat the olive oil and brown the chicken. Do not crowd the pan. Cook the chicken in batches if necessary. When the chicken is browned, place in a casserole large enough to hold chicken (in 1 layer) and vegetables. Pour off oil from the skillet and reserve it. Deglaze the pan with the white wine and pour over the chicken in the casserole. Return the oil to the skillet and sauté the mushrooms, shallots and optional artichokes. When these are slightly browned, add to the casserole along with the olives and tomatoes. Cover the casserole and bake for 45 minutes.

Serve with rice and a big green salad and crusty bread. I have used this when I am waiting for house guests who have gone to the zoo and am not sure when they are coming back or how hungry they will be. If you don't eat it all, it makes a great reheated meal the next day.

Chris Young
Parent, Dana Young '87 and David Young '96

217

Sautéed Chicken Breasts
with Lemon and Parsley

Serves 4

INGREDIENTS:

6 boned and skinned
  chicken breast halves
2 tablespoons olive oil
4 tablespoons
  (1/2 stick) unsalted
  butter
Salt and freshly
  ground pepper to
  taste

Juice of 1 lemon
1/2 cup vermouth
3 tablespoons flat leaf
  Italian parsley
1 lemon, thinly sliced for
  garnish

PROCEDURE:

Place breasts between 2 sheets of waxed paper and pound with a mallet until about 1/8" thick. Heat the oil and 2 tablespoons of the butter in a skillet over medium-high heat. Sauté the breasts on both sides briefly (5 minutes). Remove breasts to a warm platter and add salt and pepper. Add lemon juice and vermouth to skillet and turn heat to medium. With a wooden spoon or wire whisk, loosen all residue (browned bits) from bottom of pan. Add parsley and remaining 2 tablespoons of butter to cooking juices. Lower heat. Add chicken breasts, turn them over once in the sauce and then, immediately, transfer them to a warm serving platter. Pour sauce from skillet over them. Garnish with lemon slices.

This is a light, quick and delicious recipe. Serve with risotto with dried wild mushrooms or sautéed mushrooms with garlic.

Heidi Dorris
Parent, Ashley Dorris '96 and Taylor Dorris '98

Chicken Breasts
in Hampshire Sauce

Serves 4

INGREDIENTS:

4 chicken breasts,
    halved, skinned and
    boned
Salt and freshly
    ground pepper to
    taste
1/2 medium onion, finely
    chopped

1/4 cup (1 stick) butter
1/2 cup dry white wine
1 cup (1/2 pint) sour
    cream
1/3 cup pitted medium
    size black olives
1/3 cup chopped fresh
    chives

PROCEDURE:

Sprinkle the chicken with salt and pepper. In a large skillet sauté chicken and onion in melted butter until golden brown. Add wine, cover and simmer for 20 minutes or until chicken is done. Remove chicken to platter and keep warm. Add sour cream and olives to skillet. Heat gently and stir to blend. DO NOT BOIL. Stir chives into sauce and then pour sauce over chicken. Serve immediately.

Serve over hot noodles or rice. A family favorite that is very quick and easy.

Angel Kleinbub
Parent, Christian Kleinbub '95 and Eric Kleinbub '95

Chicken Breasts Florentine

Serves 6

INGREDIENTS:

6 chicken breasts,
   boneless and skinless
1/2 cup flour
1/2 cup (1 stick) butter or
   margarine
3/4 cup chicken broth
2 tablespoons onion,
   finely chopped
1/2 teaspoon salt
1/8 teaspoon pepper
   Dash nutmeg

1 1/2 cups milk
1/2 cup light cream
1 egg yolk
1/2 cup Parmesan cheese,
   grated
2 10-ounce packages of
   frozen chopped
   spinach
2 tablespoons Swiss or
   Parmesan cheese,
   grated

PROCEDURE:

Lightly coat chicken breasts on both sides with 1/4 cup of the flour. Heat 1/4 cup of the butter (or margarine) in medium size skillet over medium heat. Sauté chicken 10 minutes on each side. Add chicken broth. Simmer, covered, over low heat about 10 minutes or until tender.

In a heavy, medium size saucepan melt the remaining 1/4 cup butter (or margarine). Sauté onion, stirring until golden brown (about 5 minutes). Remove from heat. Add the remaining 1/4 cup of the flour, the salt, pepper and nutmeg. Stir until smooth. A little at a time, add milk, then cream, stirring after each addition. Return to heat. Over medium heat, bring to boil, stirring constantly, then reduce heat and simmer 3 minutes, stirring. In small bowl, beat egg yolk with fork. Stir 3/4 cup of the hot white sauce into egg bowl. Mix well. Return egg yolk mixture to saucepan along with the 1/2 cup Parmesan cheese, stirring constantly. Cook, stirring, over low heat just until thickened and cheese is melted. Do not boil. To keep sauce warm, cover saucepan and place over hot water.

Cook spinach according to package directions. Drain in a sieve. Place spinach in a saucepan with 1 cup of the cheese sauce. Cover to keep warm. Layer spinach in the bottom of a buttered 2-quart shallow baking dish. Arrange chicken breasts in a single layer on top of spinach. Cover with remaining sauce.

Sprinkle with the 2 tablespoons grated Swiss or Parmesan cheese. Broil 6" from heat for 4 to 5 minutes or until lightly browned.

I thaw the frozen spinach in the microwave while simultaneously making sauce and browning chicken. I layer in a glass baking dish (looks very pretty). I generally make this ahead of time. Can be refrigerated (layered in covered dish) for 1 or 2 days. Then, instead of broiling, I bake or microwave until heated through . Use FRESH Parmesan. I am generous with the Parmesan and the nutmeg. Experiment. Even people who say they hate spinach will love this dish.

Dottie Engel
Parent, Carly Engel '99

Cayman Island Chicken

Serves 4

INGREDIENTS:

- 4 **boneless chicken breasts**
- 1 **tablespoon extra virgin olive oil**
- 1 **large yellow onion, sliced lengthwise**
- 3 **cloves garlic, finely chopped**

- 2 **ounces lemon juice**
- 4 **ounces dry white wine**
- 1 **teaspoon cracked pepper**
  Enough cooked rice for 4 people

PROCEDURE:

Cut chicken breasts into bite size pieces. Use a tiny amount of oil to moisten skillet and sauté chicken until slightly browned. Add onion, garlic, lemon juice and wine. Add pepper and sauté until the sauce is reduced by half, approximately 15 minutes. Serve over steamed rice.

This is a quick and easy variation of boring old chicken. It's low in calories and fat but still has enough flavor that your body remembers it ate something.

Gail Lichter
Parent, Kris Lichter '89 and Kerrie Lichter '93

Cheesey Stuffed Chicken Breasts

Serves 8 to 10

INGREDIENTS:

**5 to 6 slices of multi-grained
bread**
**1/4 cup dried parsley
flakes**
1/4 cup dried onion flakes
**10 large (or 12 small)
chicken breasts,
boned and skinned**

2 eggs, well-beaten
**1 envelope Italian salad
dressing mix**
**1/4 cup (1/2 stick) butter,
melted**
**1/2 cup grated Swiss
cheese**

PROCEDURE:

Preheat oven to 350°. Using a blender or food processor make fresh bread crumbs from the bread slices. Combine the fresh bread crumbs, parsley flakes and onion flakes in a bowl, mixing well. Dip each chicken breast in the beaten egg and then in the bread crumb mixture, coating each piece generously with crumbs. Place an extra amount of crumb mixture in the center of each breast. Roll breast and place seam side down in an ovenproof casserole. Continue until all breasts are coated. Combine salad dressing mix with melted butter and drizzle over the chicken breasts. Bake for 30 minutes. Remove and sprinkle grated cheese over all. Return to oven for 20 minutes.

Serve leftovers cold, sliced thinly, with a dab of mustard and/or mayonnaise.

Nancy Esenwein Nolan '48

Lemon Herb Chicken

Serves 6

INGREDIENTS:

Marinade:
2 tablespoons finely chopped lemon peel
1/2 cup lemon juice
2 tablespoons oil
1/4 cup finely chopped fresh herbs: Any combination of rosemary, thyme, parsley, basil and oregano
1/2 cup dry white wine
1 teaspoon honey
1/2 teaspoon salt
1/4 teaspoon coarsely cracked pepper

4 whole large chicken breasts, skinned, boned and halved

4 tablespoons olive oil
6 tablespoons whipping cream (or canned nonfat evaporated milk), if desired, to thicken the sauce
Salt and coarsely cracked black pepper to taste
2 tablespoons finely chopped parsley

Garnish:
1 bunch fresh watercress
1 lemon, sliced
2 tablespoons finely chopped parsley

PROCEDURE:

Combine marinade ingredients in small bowl. Whisk until blended. In large shallow (non-aluminum) dish, arrange chicken pieces in a single layer and pour marinade over. Let marinate for 4 hours in refrigerator. Remove chicken pieces and pat dry. Reserve marinade.

Melt oil in large skillet or sauté pan over medium-high heat. Add chicken breasts and sauté for 5 to 7 minutes on each side until tender and brown. Remove to a dish. Remove excess oil. Add reserved marinade to pan and boil until reduced to about 1/2 cup. Add cream (or nonfat evaporated milk) and boil for about 3 more minutes. Season with salt and pepper to taste. Add chopped parsley. Return chicken breasts to sauce and allow to heat through. Place chicken breasts on a platter and surround with fresh watercress, lemon slices and chopped parsley.

This dish is also delicious served cold.

Sara Sweet
Staff, Director of Food Service

Sour Cream Chicken

Serves 4

INGREDIENTS:

- 2 cups (1 pint) sour cream
- 2 tablespoons lemon juice
- 1 3-ounce package slivered almonds
- 1 cup Pepperidge Farm bread stuffing (original style)
- 1/2 teaspoon Lawry's seasoned salt (optional)
- 4 chicken breasts, skinned

PROCEDURE:

Preheat oven to 350°. Mix together sour cream, lemon juice, almonds, stuffing and optional seasoned salt. Stir until well-mixed. Wash and dry chicken breasts. Coat each breast top and bottom with sour cream mixture. Place on baking sheet. Bake in oven for approximately 45 minutes or until chicken is thoroughly cooked. Sour cream topping will appear browned. Serve immediately.

This is a quick and easy recipe which has an elegant taste. Sour cream ingredients may be varied: Dijon mustard is one possibility.

Annellen Simpkins
Parent, Alura Simpkins '90 and Alex Simpkins '96

Sautéed Chicken Breasts
with Mustard Sauce

Serves 4

INGREDIENTS:

4 skinless, boneless
   chicken breast halves
   Salt and freshly
   ground pepper
1 tablespoon olive oil
3/4 cup dry white wine
1 tablespoon fresh lemon
   juice

2 teaspoons Dijon
   mustard
2 tablespoons unsalted
   butter, cut into small
   pieces (or olive oil)

PROCEDURE:

Pound each chicken breast half between sheets of wax paper until flattened to about 1/4". Season with salt and pepper. In a large, heavy, nonreactive skillet heat 1/2 tablespoon of the oil. Add 2 of the breast halves and sauté over medium-high heat until golden brown and just cooked through, about 1 1/2 minutes per side. Transfer to a platter and keep warm. Sauté the remaining breast halves in the remaining 1/2 tablespoon oil. Transfer to serving platter.

Add the wine and lemon juice to the skillet and cook over high heat, scraping up any browned bits, until the wine is reduced by half, about 2 minutes. Whisk in the mustard. Remove the pan from the heat and whisk in the butter, a few pieces at a time (or use olive oil). Add any accumulated juices from the chicken to the sauce and season with salt and pepper. Spoon the sauce over the chicken and serve hot.

A popular dish served at many of our luncheon meetings in the Private Dining Room. Great for home cooking too, because it is easy and quick.

Sara Sweet
Staff, Director of Food Service

Chicken Jane

Serves 6 to 8

INGREDIENTS:

2 frying chickens, cut
   into pieces
1 cup flour
   Salt and pepper
4 tablespoons butter (or
   margarine)

4 tablespoons olive oil
1 large onion, chopped
2 cups sherry
1/2 cup mayonnaise
3 tablespoons chopped
   parsley

PROCEDURE:

Shake chicken pieces in bag with flour seasoned with salt and pepper. Heat butter (or margarine) and oil in electric fry pan to 400°. (You can use frying pan but it tends to spatter.) Brown the chicken pieces, turning to brown both sides. Remove pieces when brown and put in a frying pan. Add the onion and sherry. Simmer over medium heat uncovered for 40 minutes, rotating pieces occasionally to cook evenly. Remove chicken to warm platter. Add mayonnaise to juices in pan. Be careful to merely warm while stirring constantly. If left to boil it will separate. Pour gravy over chicken. Sprinkle with parsley and serve.

This can be served with potatoes, noodles or rice. Can be made ahead and reheated. It is also good cold.

Jane Trevor Fetter '54

Chicken Scaloppine with Hazelnuts

Serves 6

INGREDIENTS:

1 cup hazelnuts
4 tablespoons (1/2 stick)
  butter
1 tablespoon vegetable
  oil
6 chicken breasts,
  boneless, skinless and
  pounded very thin

1 cup flour
2/3 cup dry white wine
  Salt and freshly
  ground black pepper
1 tablespoon balsamic
  vinegar

PROCEDURE:

Put the hazelnuts in a skillet, turn the heat to high and toast, turning frequently. Remove from the pan and if you are using unpeeled hazelnuts, squeeze most of their skin off with your finger tips (when you can handle them). While the hazelnuts are still warm, chop them, not too fine. The largest piece should be the size of a rice kernel.

Put 3 tablespoons of butter and all the oil in the skillet and turn heat to high. Dredge the pounded chicken in flour on both sides and sauté in skillet. Do not place more chicken in pan than will fit loosely. Transfer to platter and do next batch. When all chicken is cooked, put wine in pan, scraping loose residue from the bottom. Add the hazelnuts, letting the wine bubble away until it has evaporated completely. Stir in the remaining 1 tablespoon of butter. (May be prepared ahead to this point.)

Just before serving, sprinkle scaloppine with salt and pepper and return to pan, including juice from bottom of the platter. Turn them 2 to 3 times. Turn off heat. Pour the balsamic vinegar over the scaloppine. Turn them once or twice, then transfer to warm serving dish with all the pan juices. Serve at once.

Heather Gallagher
Parent, Kielty Gallagher '94

Lone Star Chicken

Serves 4

INGREDIENTS:

1 28-ounce can
  tomatoes, undrained
1 medium onion,
  chopped
4 cloves garlic, minced
2 bay leaves
2 teaspoons ground
  cumin
2 teaspoons dried
  oregano, crumbled

2 tablespoons red wine
  vinegar
Salt and pepper to
  taste
1 3-pound chicken, cut
  into pieces (or 4
  chicken breasts)

PROCEDURE:

Put the tomatoes with their juice into a large ovenproof casserole which can also be heated on top of stove. Break tomatoes into bits. Add onion, garlic, bay leaves, cumin, oregano and vinegar. Stir to blend. Add salt and pepper. Simmer sauce on top of stove stirring occasionally for 30 minutes.

Preheat oven to 350°. Add chicken pieces to sauce, pushing them down into the sauce.

Cover casserole and bake for 1 hour (less time if using all breasts).

Quick and easy for family. Serve sauce over rice or pasta.

Valerie Willis
Parent, Stephanie Willis '89 and Matthew Willis '92

Chicken alla Aussie Linda Brown

Serves 6

INGREDIENTS:

4 pounds chicken parts
1 onion, diced
1 green pepper, coarsely
   chopped
2 stalks celery, coarsely
   chopped
   Garlic (to taste),
   minced
   Canola oil for sautéing

1 28-ounce can chopped
   tomatoes with juice
6 tablespoons tomato
   paste
1/2 pound mushrooms,
   sliced in large pieces
2 small zucchini, cut in
   1" pieces
1/2 cup white wine

PROCEDURE:

Microwave chicken pieces until almost done (about 15 minutes). While chicken is cooking, sauté onion, green pepper, celery and garlic in oil in large, heavy pot until soft (about 10 minutes). Add chopped tomatoes with juice. Cook sauce until heated. Add tomato paste and mix well. Add drained chicken pieces. Cover and simmer about 45 minutes until chicken is cooked through. Approximately 15 minutes before completion, add mushrooms, zucchini and white wine.

Serve with wide noodles. It's hard to overcook this dish, so be sure chicken is cooked through before adding mushrooms, zucchini and wine. May add herbs of your choice (basil, oregano, etc.) for additional seasoning.

E. Ron Weiner
Husband, Suzanne Baral Weiner, Director of Public Relations

Honey Chicken

Serves 8

INGREDIENTS:

1 10-ounce bottle Lea and Perrins White Wine
   Worcestershire sauce
1 cup honey
8 chicken breasts, boneless and skinless

PROCEDURE:

Combine the honey and Worcestershire sauce and mix well. Marinate chicken in this mixture <u>overnight</u>. Remove chicken from marinade and cook on barbecue grill.

May vary amounts of honey and Worcestershire to taste. Originally a Navy wife's recipe. Easy. Everyone loves this.

Dee Jerge
Parent, Kari Jerge '98

Anne's Famous Mustard Chicken

Serves 4

INGREDIENTS:

- 8 tablespoons Dijon mustard
- 1 tablespoon minced green peppers
- 2 tablespoons minced parsley
- 2 tablespoons minced fresh basil
- 1 tablespoon minced fresh thyme
- 1 tablespoon minced fresh rosemary

- 5 minced garlic cloves
- 1 tablespoon minced capers

- 1 3-pound broiler/fryer chicken (quartered)
- 1 /2 cups dry white wine
- 2 tablespoons heavy cream or crème fraîche (optional)

PROCEDURE:

Preheat oven to 325°. Combine all ingredients except chicken, wine and cream in a small bowl. Lift skin carefully and smear mustard mixture under it and all over both sides of chicken quarter. Use all of the mixture. Place chicken skin side up in a 9" x 13" baking dish. Pour wine over chicken. Bake 1 hour, basting frequently with juices. Remove chicken to a platter. Pour juices into small saucepan. Remove excess fat if necessary and reduce by boiling about 5 minutes. Thicken with 2 tablespoons cream or crème fraîche if desired. Pour sauce over chicken and serve.

Serve with buttered noodles or angel hair pasta, tossed green salad and crusty bread. Can be prepared ahead up to pouring the wine oven; refrigerate covered.

Anne Ricchiuti
Parent, Michael Ricchiuti '96

Chicken with Olives and Prunes

Serves 10 to 12

INGREDIENTS:

Marinade:
1 head garlic, peeled and puréed
1/4 cup dried oregano
1/2 cup red wine vinegar
1/2 cup olive oil
1 cup pitted Spanish olives
1 cup pitted prunes

1/2 cup capers
6 bay leaves

3 chickens, quartered
1 cup brown sugar
1 cup white wine
3/4 cup fresh coriander, finely chopped

PROCEDURE:

Marinade: In a large bowl combine chicken, garlic, oregano, vinegar, olive oil, olives, prunes, capers, bay leaves and marinate in refrigerator <u>overnight</u>.

Preheat oven to 350°. Arrange chicken in single layer in ovenproof pans and spoon marinade over it evenly. Sprinkle with brown sugar and pour white wine around. Bake 50 minutes to 1 hour. Remove chicken with slotted spoon to a serving platter. Arrange olives, prunes and capers around meat. Spoon pan juices over meat.

Can also be served at room temperature. Absolutely outstanding.

Peggy Preuss
Parent, Peter Preuss '97

Chicken Elizabeth

Serves 4 to 6

INGREDIENTS:

2 tablespoons olive oil
1 tablespoon onion, chopped
1 clove garlic, diced
1 dessert spoon curry powder/paste (or more if desired)
1/2 cup tomato sauce
Salt and pepper to taste
1 or 2 teaspoons lemon juice
2 tablespoons apricot jam

1/2 cup mayonnaise
1 chicken, cooked and cut into bite size pieces (or 2 breasts, halved and boned)
Cooked rice for 4 to 6 (1/2 white mixed with 1/2 brown or wild)
Green peas and chopped pimentos to add to rice for color

PROCEDURE:

Heat oil in large, heavy pot. Soften onion and garlic in oil. Add curry and cook a few minutes. Add tomato sauce. Simmer about 10 minutes. Add salt and pepper, a little lemon juice and stir in jam. Cool slightly and add mayonnaise, then chicken. Heat thoroughly over low heat. Do not bring to a simmer as the mayonnaise will separate if too hot. Serve over rice. To add color, serve a mixture of white and brown or wild rice with added peas and pimentos.

The recipe was served to Queen Elizabeth at her coronation, thus the name. Easy to make for 4 or 100.

Marilyn Ott
Parent, Carter Ott '94

Broccoli Chicken Casserole

Serves 4

INGREDIENTS:

1 cup cooked chicken,
  cubed or shredded
1 cup raw rice, cooked
1/3 cup onion, chopped
1/2 cup celery, chopped
3 tablespoons oil
1 10-ounce package
  frozen broccoli,
  thawed

1 10-ounce can cream of
  mushroom soup
1 soup can milk
1 8-ounce jar Cheez
  Whiz (original or
  Mexican)

PROCEDURE:

Preheat oven to 350°. Prepare chicken. While chicken is cooking, prepare rice according to package directions. Sauté onion and celery in the oil until tender. In a large bowl mix chicken, rice, celery, onion, broccoli, soup, milk and Cheez Whiz. Pour mixture into a greased casserole dish. Bake 40 minutes covered. Uncover and cook an additional 10 to 15 minutes.

Freezes well.

Mary Eikel
Parent, Catherine Eikel '97

Broccoli Walnut Chicken Casserole

Serves 6

INGREDIENTS:

- 1 cup coarsely chopped walnuts
- 3 tablespoons oil or margarine
- 1 medium onion, sliced
- 1/2 pound mushrooms, sliced
- 3 cups broccoli flowerets
- 1/2 cup sliced water chestnuts
- 1 clove garlic, minced
- 1 tablespoon soy sauce
- 1/2 cup (1/4 pint) plain nonfat yogurt
- 2 cups cooked rice or rice pilaf
- 3 chicken breasts, cooked, boned and sliced
- 1/4 pound Monterey jack cheese, shredded
- 1/4 pound cheddar cheese, shredded

PROCEDURE:

Brown walnuts in oil or margarine in a heavy skillet over medium heat, being careful not to burn. Remove, drain and save oil. Add onion and mushrooms to oil; cook for 1 or 2 minutes to soften. Add broccoli; cook until tender. Add water chestnuts and garlic. Remove from heat. Add walnuts, soy sauce and yogurt. Stir until well-mixed.

Preheat oven to 400°. Line a 9" x 13" casserole dish with the cooked rice. Place sliced chicken breasts on rice. Cover with vegetable mixture, top with cheeses. Bake in oven for 15 minutes.

I use olive oil and have substituted the yogurt in place of sour cream, to cut down on fat in the dish.

Erin Barber '79

Chicken Artichoke Casserole

Serves 6 to 8

INGREDIENTS:

4 to 6 chicken breasts, skinned
1 or 2 celery stalks, roughly chopped
1 carrot, peeled and roughly chopped
1 medium onion, roughly chopped
Dash cayenne pepper
1 box Uncle Ben's Long Grain and Wild Rice

1 14-ounce can artichoke hearts, in water
1 10-ounce can cream of mushroom soup
1 10-ounce can cream of chicken soup
1/2 cup mayonnaise
1 tablespoon curry powder
1 cup grated cheddar cheese

PROCEDURE:

Place chicken breasts in large saucepan with celery stalks, carrots, onion and cayenne pepper to taste. Cover with water and simmer until chicken is tender, about 20 minutes. Debone and cut chicken into 1" cubes and set aside.

Preheat oven to 350°. Cook rice according to package directions and place in 9" x 13" baking dish. Cut up artichoke hearts and place on top of rice. Then add chicken. Mix soups, mayonnaise and curry powder and pour on top of rice/artichoke/chicken layers until all is covered. Sprinkle with grated cheddar cheese and cover with foil. Bake for 45 minutes to 1 hour (until bubbly). Remove foil for last 15 minutes of cooking so cheese is golden brown.

I usually serve with a lettuce salad or Waldorf salad. Men (as well as women) love this recipe.

Nancy Mann VanDervoort '32

Chicken and Wild Rice Casserole

Serves 8 to 10

INGREDIENTS:

6 pounds chicken breasts (bone in)
4 cups water
2 cups dry sherry
1 1/2 teaspoons salt
1/2 teaspoon curry powder
1/2 cup chopped celery
1 medium onion, chopped
1 pound fresh mushrooms, sliced

1/4 cup (1/2 stick) butter
2 6-ounce boxes long grain and wild rice
1 10-ounce can condensed cream of mushroom soup
1 cup (1/2 pint) sour cream
Pepper to taste

PROCEDURE:

Simmer chicken in water, sherry, salt, curry powder, celery and onion for 1 hour. Remove chicken, strain and save liquid. Remove bone and skin from chicken and tear meat into small pieces. May be prepared ahead to this point.

Preheat oven to 350°. Sauté mushrooms in butter. Cook rice as directed, using reserved broth from chicken. Blend mushrooms into rice, saving a few for garnish. Blend soup and sour cream together. Add chicken pieces and mix well. Place rice mixture in a large casserole. Place chicken mixture on top. Garnish with reserved mushrooms and bake 1 hour.

Great company casserole. Freezes well. You can use low fat sour cream and a little less butter to reduce fat. People love this.

Galen Cooper
Parent, Tyler Cooper '96X and Megan Cooper '98

Chicken and Noodles Casserole

Serves 8

INGREDIENTS:

1 8-ounce package noodles (thin green noodles or egg noodles)
1 cup (1/2 pint) sour cream
1 cup mayonnaise
2 teaspoons Dijon mustard
1 10-ounce can cream of mushroom soup
1 tablespoon chopped chives (or 4 tablespoons green onions)
6 tablespoons sherry
6 to 8 chicken breasts, cooked, skinned, boned and diced
2 cups grated Cheddar cheese

PROCEDURE:

Preheat oven to 350°. Cook noodles according to package directions. Drain noodles and pour into 9" x 13" casserole dish. Mix together the sour cream, mayonnaise, mustard, mushroom soup, chives and sherry and pour 1/3 of this mixture over the noodles. Then layer chicken over noodles. Pour the rest of the sauce over the chicken and top with cheese. Bake, covered, for about 1 hour.

Better if made a day ahead and refrigerated to allow flavors to blend.

Gayle Stephenson
Parent, William Stephenson '95 and Jill Stephenson '96

Helen's Chicken Noodle Casserole with Green Olives

Serves 6 to 8

INGREDIENTS:

- 1 3-pound chicken fryer
- 2 tablespoons margarine
- 2 tablespoons flour
- 1 tablespoon lemon juice
  Salt and pepper to
  taste
- 1 12-ounce package
  extra wide egg
  noodles
- 1 cup pimento stuffed
  olives, cut in half
- 1 cup grated longhorn
  cheddar cheese

PROCEDURE:

Place fryer, breast side down, in a large pot with just enough lightly salted water to cover. Bring to a boil, then simmer slowly, partially covered, until tender, about 1 hour. (You may refrigerate stock and chicken at this point to defat, if desired.)

Preheat oven to 350°. Remove chicken from pot, reserving the stock. When chicken is cool enough to handle, remove meat from bones and cut into bite size pieces. Melt the margarine in a large saucepan, add the flour and stir over medium heat until lightly brown, about 1 minute. While continuing to stir, gradually add 4 cups of the reserved chicken stock, lemon juice, salt and pepper. Cook until thickened. Boil the noodles according to package directions until tender. Drain and place noodles in a large mixing bowl. Add the chicken pieces, olives and thickened chicken stock. Stir to blend. Correct seasoning. Pour into a lightly greased 10" x 13" casserole. Place in oven and cook for about 30 minutes. Top with the grated cheese and continue cooking for 10 or 15 minutes, until cheese is melted.

Can be made ahead and refrigerated or frozen until cooked. Or you can cook half now and freeze half for later. An old family standby.

Alliene Vale
Grandparent, Elizabeth Vale '92 and Susannah Vale '95

Chicken and Rice Casserole I

Serves 8

INGREDIENTS:

1 cup rice, uncooked
2 cups sliced celery
2 cups finely chopped carrots
1 cup chopped onion
1 cup sliced fresh mushrooms
1 10-ounce can cream of mushroom soup

3/4 cup mayonnaise
3/4 cup water
1/2 cup dry white wine
2 teaspoons curry powder
8 chicken breast halves, skinned and boned
Paprika

PROCEDURE:

Preheat oven to 350°. Place rice in greased 8" x 12" glass baking pan. Combine vegetables and put over rice. In a blender mix well soup, mayonnaise, water, wine and curry powder. Pour half of soup mixture over rice and vegetables. Place chicken breasts on top and cover with remaining soup mixture. Sprinkle with paprika. Cover and bake for 30 minutes. Remove cover and bake another 30 minutes or until bubbly. If it seems dry, add a little more wine or water.

May be made a day ahead.

Patty Poe Kable
Parent, Lucy Kable Means Borsenberger '69
Grandparent, Artie Means '94 and Christopher Means '96

Chicken and Rice Casserole II

Serves 6 to 8

INGREDIENTS:

1 1/2 cups long grain white rice
1/4 cup (1/2 stick) butter or margarine, melted
2 10-ounce cans condensed cream of chicken soup
1 10-ounce can condensed cream of celery soup

1 10-ounce can condensed cream of mushroom soup
1 soup can filled with water
3 to 4 pounds of skinless, boneless chicken breasts or thighs

PROCEDURE:

Preheat oven to 350°. In a bowl mix rice and melted butter. In a separate bowl mix the soups (undiluted) together. Add 3/4 of the soup mixture and the soup can of water to rice and stir. Pour mixture into a greased 10" x 14" casserole dish. Spread evenly. Place chicken on top of rice. Spread remaining 1/4 of the soup mixture over chicken. Bake uncovered for 1 hour.

Quick and easy. Serve with vegetable or salad and you have a complete meal.

Diane Shockley
Parent, Tre Shockley '96 and Tristan Schockley '98

Sister's Chicken Casserole

Serves 6 to 8

INGREDIENTS:

2 whole chicken breasts
(or 4 halves with ribs)

1 cup cooked rice

1 10-ounce can of cream
of chicken soup (do
not dilute)

2 tablespoons minced
onion

2 tablespoons lemon
juice

1/2 cup mayonnaise

Topping:

1/4 cup (1/2 stick) butter
or margarine, melted

1/2 cup crushed
cornflakes

1/2 cup slivered almonds

PROCEDURE:

Simmer, poach or microwave the chicken breasts until tender. When cool
enough to handle, remove skin, bones and any fat/gristle and cut or tear the
meat into bite size pieces. This should yield approximately 2 cups of meat. Cook
rice according to package directions. Pour soup into a large bowl. Add the
minced onion and the lemon juice. With a rubber spatula or wooden spoon,
blend the mixture until it is well-mixed. Add the rice and the chicken to the
soup mixture and mix well. (Note: If the mixture seems very stiff, gradually add
1/4 to 1/2 cup water as needed.) Gently fold in the mayonnaise. Spread the
mixture into a 2-quart baking dish that has been greased lightly or treated with
a vegetable oil spray. Refrigerate overnight or at least 3 to 4 hours.

To bake, preheat the oven to 300°. Remove casserole from refrigerator and pour
the melted butter (or margarine) over the top of the chicken mixture. Combine
the cornflakes and almonds and sprinkle evenly over the butter. Bake casserole
for 1 hour. Serve while hot.

*This is the "company" version and is great for luncheons or buffet suppers because,
except for the topping, it all can be prepared ahead. I like to serve it with an aspic
salad, a hot fruit compote or a green vegetable. It is also a good way to use up a leftover chicken or turkey. Just substitute 2 cups of leftover white or dark meat for the
chicken breasts.*

Jean Spargur Perin '36

242

Easy Chicken or Turkey Casserole

Serves 4 to 5

INGREDIENTS:

2 cups turkey or chicken, cooked and chopped
1 cup cooked rice
1 7-ounce package sliced almonds
1 cup celery, chopped
1 8-ounce can sliced water chestnuts
1 10-ounce can cream of chicken soup
3/4 cup mayonnaise
Salt and pepper to taste
1/2 cup butter (or margarine)
1/2 cup corn flakes

PROCEDURE:

Preheat oven to 350°. Mix all ingredients except for butter (or margarine) and corn flakes and place in ovenproof casserole. Melt the butter (margarine). Crush the corn flakes slightly and add to melted butter (margarine). Let this mixture sit a few minutes, then spoon onto top of casserole. Bake for 45 minutes.

Can be made 24 hours in advance. Also freezes well.

Mrs. Franklin Wright, Jr.
Grandmother, Courtney Wright '98

Chicken with Bulgur, Spinach and Mushrooms

Serves 6

INGREDIENTS:

1 14-ounce can chicken broth
1 cup bulgur wheat
1 cup cooked diced chicken
Olive oil, for sautéing
Salt and pepper to taste
1 cup chopped onion
1 clove garlic, minced

2 bunches fresh (or 10 ounces frozen) spinach, chopped
12 medium mushrooms, sliced
1/4 cup toasted pine nuts
2 tomatoes, diced
1 tablespoon fresh oregano leaves (or 1/2 teaspoon dried)
1/3 cup crumbled feta cheese (or to taste)

PROCEDURE:

Preheat oven to 350°. Heat broth to broiling and mix with bulgur in large bowl. Cover with towel and set aside 30 minutes.

Sauté diced chicken in large skillet with a little oil and season with a little salt and pepper. Remove chicken and set aside. Add a little more oil to the skillet. Add onion and garlic and sauté a few minutes. Stir in the spinach and the mushrooms. Cook until the mushrooms just begin to soften. To the bulgur, add the spinach mixture, pine nuts, tomatoes, chicken and oregano. Toss to mix well. Season with salt and pepper.

Place in lightly oiled 9" x 13" ovenproof casserole. Bake in oven for 20 minutes. Sprinkle with feta cheese and cook 5 or 10 minutes longer until heated through.

This a favorite of our teenagers. A very flexible dish which may be easily expanded by increasing quantities or varied by substituting different types of meat (beef or pork) or other kinds of nuts and vegetables. Leftovers are great right out of the refrigerator.

Silvia Berchtold
Parent, Christophe Berchtold '85 and Nicole Berchtold '87

Chicken Tetrazzini alla Anne

Serves 6

INGREDIENTS:

1/2 pound spaghetti,
    broken in half
5 tablespoons butter
1 onion, chopped
3 garlic cloves, minced
8 ounces fresh
    mushrooms, sliced
1/4 cup flour
1 cup (1/2 pint) milk
1 1/2 cups chicken stock

1/2 teaspoon cayenne
    pepper (or more or
    less to taste)
Salt to taste
2 cups chicken, chopped
    and cooked
1 8-ounce can sliced
    water chestnuts
1/2 cup dry sherry
1 cup freshly grated
    Parmesan cheese
Paprika

PROCEDURE:

In large pot of boiling water cook spaghetti 8 minutes (al dente), then drain and set aside. Melt 1 tablespoon of the butter in large skillet. Sauté the onion, garlic and mushrooms over medium heat until tender. Remove from pan and set aside. In a medium saucepan melt the remaining 4 tablespoons of butter. Add the flour and stir over medium heat 2 minutes. Whisk in the milk, chicken stock, cayenne pepper and salt. Cook over low heat stirring for 3 minutes until thickened. In a large bowl combine the sauce with the mushroom mixture, chicken, water chestnuts and sherry. Stir to blend.

Preheat oven to 400°. In a greased 2-quart baking dish arrange a layer of 1/2 the spaghetti, then a layer of 1/2 the chicken mixture. Sprinkle with 1/2 the cheese and paprika. Repeat layers until mixture is all used. Bake 30 minutes.

Can also be microwaved. Easy to make ahead and freeze. Serve with crusty bread and green salad. I use extra cayenne as my family likes it spicy.

Anne Ricchiuti
Parent, Michael Ricchiuti '96

Chicken Stew with Dumplings

Serves 4 to 6

INGREDIENTS:

Stew:
1 frying chicken, cut in pieces
3 tablespoons butter
1 stalk celery, diced
1 medium onion, chopped
6 cloves garlic, peeled and chopped
1 bay leaf
2 teaspoons cumin
3 cups water
1 tablespoon flour blended with 1/4 cup cold water
Freshly ground pepper (or cayenne) and salt to taste

Dumplings:
1 cup flour
1 teaspoon baking powder
1/2 teaspoon poultry seasoning
1 tablespoon butter
1 tablespoon fresh or dried chopped parsley
3 tablespoons milk
1 egg

PROCEDURE:

Stew: In a large, heavy skillet (or pot) with tightly fitting cover, brown chicken in butter. Add celery, onion and garlic. Add bay leaf, cumin and water. Bring to boil and simmer 1 hour or until chicken is tender. While chicken is cooking, make dumpling batter.

Dumplings: In a large bowl mix flour, baking powder and poultry seasoning. Cut in butter with 2 knives. Add parsley. With a fork beat egg with milk in a small bowl. Add to flour mixture and blend. Set aside.

When chicken is done, blend flour with a little cold water and add to pot to thicken broth. Correct seasoning with freshly ground pepper or cayenne and salt to taste. Drop dumpling batter by spoonfuls onto chicken pieces. Cover and steam 10 minutes or until dumplings test clean with a toothpick.

Judith Combs
Parent, Portia Edwards '96

Acapulco Enchilada Baskets

Serves 6

INGREDIENTS:

6 flour tortillas, medium size
Oil for frying
2 cups diced cooked chicken or turkey
1/2 cup chopped ripe olives
1 cup slivered or chopped almonds

1 cup (or less) canned enchilada sauce or red Mexican chile sauce
2 cups (1 pint) sour cream
1 1/2 cups shredded sharp cheddar cheese
4 tablespoons green onions, chopped
2 medium tomatoes, chopped

PROCEDURE:

Tortilla cups: May be made the day before serving. Fry each tortilla in small amount of oil, just to soften. Preheat oven to 250°. Form tortillas into basket shapes in ovenproof bowls. Bake 1 hour.

Filling: In large mixing bowl combine chicken, olives, almonds and enough sauce and sour cream to moisten and flavor, reserving remaining sour cream for garnish.

Fill tortilla baskets with filling. Top with cheese. Reheat to melt cheese and heat through. Top each with rest of sour cream, chopped green onions and tomatoes.

This is a festive, prepare-in-advance dinner. Nice with an avocado/Mandarin orange/red onion, butter lettuce green salad.

Mariel Bradley
Grandparent, Justin Shaw '89 and Maiya Shaw '92

Arizona Chicken Enchilada Casserole

Serves 6

INGREDIENTS:

1 large chicken
1/2 teaspoon salt
1 large onion, minced
2 tablespoons cooking
  oil or butter
1 4-ounce can diced
  green chiles
2 10-ounce cans cream
  of chicken soup
1 cup reserved chicken
  broth

Pepper to taste
1 dozen corn tortillas,
  quartered
Grated cheddar and
  Monterey jack cheese
  as desired.
Sliced green olives or
  chopped black olives
  for garnish

PROCEDURE:

Place chicken in a large pot. Add water just to cover chicken. Add 1/2 teaspoon salt to water. Bring water to a boil over high heat, then turn heat down, cover pot and simmer until chicken is done (approximately 1 hour). When chicken is done, remove to a cutting board to cool. Reserve broth. In a large skillet, sauté onion in a little oil or butter. Add the chiles, soup and 1 cup of reserved broth and mix well. Add pepper to taste. Remove skin and bones from chicken and cut into medium size pieces. Add to soup mixture and heat.

Preheat oven to 350˚. Put a layer of tortillas in bottom of a lightly greased 3-quart round or oblong baking dish. Add a layer of the soup and chicken mixture and a layer of cheese. Repeat the layers until all is used, ending with cheese. Sprinkle with sliced green or chopped black olives, if desired. Bake for 30 minutes.

Enjoy with big tossed salad and French bread. For spicier taste add more chiles.

Bunny Smith Garrett '60

Chicken Enchiladas

Serves 6 to 8

INGREDIENTS:

3 whole chicken breasts
1 cup (1/2 pint) sour
   cream
1 10-ounce can cream of
   chicken soup
6 green onions, chopped
1 4-ounce can diced
   green chiles

1 clove garlic, minced
Dash oregano
1 dozen flour tortillas
   Oil for cooking
    tortillas
   Grated cheddar
    cheese, for topping

PROCEDURE:

Cook the chicken breasts and dice the meat. Mix chicken with sour cream, soup, green onions, chiles, garlic and oregano.

Preheat oven to 350°. In a skillet cook tortillas in small amount of oil to soften. Place approximately 1/4 cup of the chicken mixture in each tortilla. Roll and place close together with seam side down in a lightly greased 9" x 13" rectangular casserole. Top with cheddar cheese. Bake for 20 minutes.

Serve with salsa, apple sauce and green salad.

Anne Gilchrist
Parent, Jennifer Gilchrist '94

Chicken Enchilada Suiza

Serves 6 to 8

INGREDIENTS:

- 1 12.5-ounce can white chicken
- 1 10-ounce jar salsa verde (tomatillo sauce)
- 1 10-ounce jar salsa autentica (red salsa)
- 1 10-ounce can chicken broth
- 3 tablespoons orange juice concentrate

- 4 ounces Monterey jack cheese, cubed
- 1 cup (1/2 pint) sour cream (low fat optional)
- 2 tablespoons flour
- 8 corn tortillas

PROCEDURE:

Preheat oven to 350°. Mix chicken with 1/2 the tomatillo sauce. In a saucepan (large enough to fit tortilla for dipping) add the rest of the tomatillo sauce, 1/4 jar salsa autentica, chicken broth, orange juice, cheese, sour cream and flour. Heat until cheese is melted and stir to blend. Place tortilla into heated sauce and remove immediately. Leave in sauce only long enough to moisten (too long and tortilla will become mushy). Put 1/4 cup chicken mixture across diameter of tortilla and roll up. Place rolled tortilla seam side down in 10" x 13" baking dish that has been sprayed with vegetable oil. Continue until all tortillas are in pan and then pour sauce over top. Bake 20 minutes. Place under broiler for 5 minutes just before serving.

Delicious white sauce enchilada.

Michele Petrie
Friend

Santa Cruz Enchilada Pie

Serves 6

INGREDIENTS:

1 tablespoon flour
1 tablespoon oil
1 15-ounce jar Santa
  Cruz Chili Paste*
2 cups chicken broth
  Minced garlic to taste
  Salt and pepper to
  taste
1/2 cup oil
1 dozen corn tortillas

1 pound longhorn
  cheese, grated
3 chicken breasts,
  cooked and shredded
1/2 onion, finely chopped
1 cup sliced black olives
1 15-ounce can whole
  kernel corn, drained
1 cup (1/2 pint)
  whipping cream

PROCEDURE:

Preheat oven to 350°. Brown flour in 1 tablespoon oil in frying pan, then stir in chili paste, chicken broth, garlic, salt and pepper until smooth. Heat 1/4 cup oil in small pan (large enough to hold tortilla for dipping). Dip tortillas, 1 at a time, into hot oil to soften. Add more oil as needed. Arrange 6 tortillas (overlapping) in the bottom of a lightly greased 10" x 13" casserole. Pour 1/2 of the chili sauce over tortillas, then cover with 1/2 of the cheese, all of the chicken, onions, olives, corn and whipping cream. Cover with the rest of tortillas and top with the remaining chili sauce and cheese. Bake for 30 minutes.

*Santa Cruz Chili Paste is a unique mild chili blend available in Arizona and in specialty shops in other areas. If you substitute another type of chili paste or powder, quantity will depend on "hotness" of chili blend you use.

Jean England Neubauer '67

Chicken in Flour Tortilla

Serves 8

INGREDIENTS:

4 chicken breast halves, boned and skinned (1 1/2 pounds)
8 8" flour tortillas
1 4-ounce can green chiles, cut in strips
1 pound Monterey jack cheese, cut into finger size strips
Salt and pepper, to taste
1 tablespoon dried basil

2 10-ounce cans cream of chicken soup
1/3 cup white wine or sherry
1 cup (1/2 pint) sour cream
1/2 cup grated Monterey jack cheese
Chopped avocado, salsa and sour cream for toppings

PROCEDURE:

Preheat oven to 350˚. Cut each chicken breast in half, then cut each half into 2 or 3 strips. Place 2 or 3 strips in middle of tortilla. Place 2 or 3 chile strips and cheese strips on top of chicken. Sprinkle with salt, pepper and lightly with basil. Roll up and place close together in a lightly greased 9" x 13" pan with the seam side down.

In a medium size bowl mix together cream of chicken soup, wine (or sherry) and sour cream. Pour this sauce over rolled tortillas, covering all edges. Bake covered for 1 hour. Uncover and sprinkle with grated cheese and bake 15 minutes more. Serve with chopped avocado, sour cream and salsa.

Can be made in the morning and cooked before dinner. These lift out perfectly. No messy enchilada.

Marilyn Royle Brucker '48

Chicken Olé Simplicitas

Serves 6

INGREDIENTS:

4 large chicken breasts
1 dozen fresh corn
  tortillas
1 10-ounce can cream of
  chicken soup
1 10-ounce can cream of
  mushroom soup
1 cup low fat milk

1 medium onion, finely
  chopped
1 1/2 8-ounce cans green
  chile salsa
6 ounces cheddar
  cheese, grated
6 ounces Monterey jack
  cheese, grated

PROCEDURE:

Cover chicken breasts with lightly salted water in a saucepan and simmer until tender. Cool, remove meat from bones and cut into small pieces. Save and refrigerate the broth until cooking time (following day). Cut tortillas into small pieces (1 1/2" "squares" or 1" strips). Combine soups, milk, onion and salsa in a large bowl and mix well. Add chicken, tortilla chunks and 1/2 of each of the grated cheeses. Stir to mix. Pour into buttered casserole (either 9" x 13" oblong or your favorite deep round one) and refrigerate for 24 hours or <u>overnight</u>.

Remove from refrigerator and bring to room temperature. Preheat oven to 350°. Sprinkle remaining grated cheese over the top and bake for 1 hour. If it becomes dry, add a little of the chicken broth you saved yesterday or cover with aluminum foil during baking.

Our kids love this one and so do their friends. Can be successfully doubled and it's good the next day. A green salad with oil and vinegar dressing goes well on the side.

Pinkie Wornham
Staff, Associate in Admission and
Parent, Wendy Wornham '72, Cynthia Wornham '73,
Thomas Wornham '78, JoAnn Bivin Wornham '81

Mexican Chicken

Serves 4

INGREDIENTS:

1 10-ounce can cream of
   chicken soup
1/2 soup can water
1 tablespoon onion
   flakes
4 ounces diced green
   chiles

4 chicken breasts,
   cooked, skinned,
   boned and cut into
   small pieces
2 fresh tomatoes, cut
   into small pieces
1 cup grated cheddar
   cheese
1 6-ounce package corn
   chips

PROCEDURE:

Mix soup, water, onion flakes and chiles in a small bowl. In a larger bowl mix chicken, tomatoes and cheese. Add soup mixture to chicken mixture and stir to blend. Pour into microwave cooking dish. Cook in microwave oven on high for 15 minutes. Crumble chips over top before serving.

Quick and easy.

Dana Stringfield
Grandparent, Matthew Lewis '95

Fiesta Lasagne

Serves 8 to 10

INGREDIENTS:

3 16-ounce cans
  chicken broth
12 chicken breast halves,
  skinned
1 14-ounce can ready
  cut tomatoes, with
  juice
1 2.25-ounce can sliced
  black olives
1 16-ounce container
  fresh, mild tomato
  salsa (found in
  refrigerator section)

8 flour tortillas
2 cups (1 pint) sour
  cream
1 1/2 pounds Monterey jack
  cheese, grated

Garnish:
Salsa
Avocado slices
Sour cream

PROCEDURE:

In a large pot bring chicken broth to a boil. Place chicken breast halves into boiling broth. Bring broth back to a simmer and cook chicken for 5 minutes, turn off heat, cover and let sit in broth another 20 to 30 minutes. Remove chicken and shred meat.

Preheat oven to 325°. Combine tomatoes, olives and salsa. Spread thin layer of tomato mixture in bottom of lightly greased 9" x 13" baking dish. Cover with 4 flour tortillas overlapping as needed to cover tomato mixture. Layer 1/2 of remaining tomato mixture and 1/2 of chicken. Spread 1/2 of sour cream and 1/2 of cheese. Repeat layers ending with cheese. Bake for 35 to 45 minutes. Serve with extra salsa, avocado slices and sour cream.

This is great. It freezes well. Always receives lots of compliments.

Susan Oliver
Parent, Josh Oliver '96 and Hunter Oliver '98

Chicken Maple Curry

Serves 6 to 8

INGREDIENTS:

8 pieces of chicken (thighs or boneless breast meat)
3/4 cup maple syrup
1/4 cup vinegar
2 teaspoons soy sauce
1 1/2 cups tomato sauce
2 teaspoons curry powder
4 cloves

2 tablespoons sherry
Salt and pepper
4 stalks celery, diced
1 green pepper, coarsely chopped
6 to 8 mushrooms, quartered
2 ounces raisins
2 ounces slivered almonds

PROCEDURE:

Put chicken in a large bowl or flat baking pan. In another bowl mix together maple syrup, vinegar, soy sauce, tomato sauce, curry powder, cloves, sherry, salt and pepper and pour over chicken. Marinate for 4 hours, covered, in the refrigerator.

Preheat oven to 325°. Put the chicken and sauce into a large flat baking pan. Add celery, green peppers and mushrooms. Bake for 45 to 60 minutes (deboned chicken takes less time). Add raisins and almonds before serving.

Serve over white rice. Good party dish.

Susanna Smith
Parent, Troy Smith '97 and Adam Smith '98

Curried Chicken (or Turkey) Crêpes

Yields 10 to 12 crêpes

INGREDIENTS:

Crêpes:
3/4 cup low fat or nonfat milk
3/4 cup water
3 egg whites

1 teaspoon sugar
1 tablespoon brandy
1 1/2 cups presifted flour
2 tablespoons oil
Extra oil for cooking

Filling:
2 onions, chopped
3 to 4 cloves garlic, minced
2 tablespoons olive oil
4 tablespoons flour
1 1/2 tablespoons curry powder (or to taste)
1 to 2 cups chicken broth
1 apple, peeled and chopped
2 tablespoons chutney (Major Gray's mango)
3 to 4 tablespoon golden raisins
1 tablespoon honey or corn syrup
3 to 4 cups chicken or turkey, cooked and chopped

PROCEDURE:

Crêpes: Place all ingredients (except for extra oil) in blender jar in order listed. Cover and blend for about 1 minute at top speed. Stop and scrape flour off sides with rubber scraper. Blend a few seconds more. Pour into bowl. Cover and refrigerate 1 to 2 hours.

Brush oil on 7" skillet (using 2 crêpe pans or skillets works better and goes faster). Pour crêpe batter on hot skillet in thin layer, barely covering surface. Cook at medium heat about 1 1/2 minutes or until lightly golden, then turn over. Cook on second side about 30 seconds until crêpes turn golden on that side as well. Remove from heat. Stack on plate and keep covered until ready to use.

Filling: Preheat oven to 350°. In a medium saucepan sauté onion and garlic in oil. When cooked, stir in flour and curry powder. Slowly add chicken broth, stirring well until thickened. Add apple, chutney and raisins and continue to cook until apple is tender (about 10 to 15 minutes). Stir in honey or corn syrup. Pour about half of this sauce onto chicken or turkey in a bowl and stir to blend. Fill crêpe with this mixture, putting several tablespoons in each and roll up. Place filled and rolled crêpes in oiled baking dish. Spread extra sauce over top of crêpes. Bake for 10 to 15 minutes until crêpes are hot and bubbly.

Crêpes and filling can both be make a day ahead, stored separately in refrigerator and assembled the day you are using them. Or, crêpes can be completely assembled the day before and covered and refrigerated until baking time. A nice accompaniment to these crêpes is a spinach crêpe with a Mornay sauce and a green salad.

This very low fat, no cholesterol version of crêpes is easy and tastes the same as richer versions. The crêpes can be filled with fruit for dessert or meat or vegetables as a main course.

Pat and John Miller
Parents, Kristen Miller '87 and Patrick Miller '93

Bombay Curry Puff Pie

Serves 6

INGREDIENTS:

Pie Filling:
3 tablespoons butter
3 cups diced onions
2 cups diced uncooked
   chicken (optional)
4 cups diced mixed
   vegetables (fresh
   steamed, canned or
   frozen) potatoes, peas
   plus any others
   (carrots, corn, green
   beans, lima beans,
   etc.)
2 cloves garlic, minced
3 tablespoons curry
   powder

3 tablespoons chutney
1/2 cup golden raisins
   Salt and pepper, to
   taste

Pie Crust:
Your favorite pastry
   recipe which yields
   double crust for 9" pie
1 tablespoon cumin seed
   (to add to pastry)
1 to 2 tablespoons milk (to
   glaze top)

PROCEDURE:

Pie Filling: Preheat oven to 400°. Melt butter in large skillet, add onions and sauté slowly for 15 minutes until translucent but not burned. Add meat if using. Continue to cook slowly and add vegetables, garlic, curry powder, chutney and raisins. Add salt and pepper to taste.

Pie Crust: Make your favorite pie pastry, adding the cumin seed with the flour. Roll out pastry for bottom shell and place in 9" pie plate. Add filling (which should mound very high on the plate, 3" to 3 1/2" in the center). Roll out pastry top and place on top of filling. Trim and pinch edges to seal. Make 5 knife slits in the top and brush lightly with milk. Bake until medium brown, 45 to 60 minutes. Serve hot or cold.

Christopher's English great-grandfather served in a British turn of the century regiment in India. Great-grandmother raised four children and adapted Indian flavors to English recipes. Ingredients depended on what was at hand: Left-over lamb or beef then. Now we are practically vegetarian. Butter has been reduced but peas and potatoes are essential. Cooks can fiddle with all ingredients except with the ratio of onion to butter because it binds and thickens the vegetables. This is our family's favorite dinner; it goes cold to the Pops or beach picnic, or warms a chilly evening. Biryani rice and green salad, Italian breads and chutneys, peanuts, coconut and avocado work well as accompaniments. Fiddling with the flavor and ingredients is essential.

Paddi Arthur
Parent, Christopher Arthur '99

Chicken Curry

Serves 4

INGREDIENTS:

2 tablespoons canola oil
1 medium onion, chopped
1 level tablespoon Bolst mild curry powder
4 chicken breasts, skinned, boned and cut into 1 1/2" cubes

2 cloves garlic, chopped
1 14-ounce can chopped tomatoes, undrained
1 green apple, peeled, cored and chopped
1 tablespoon seedless raisins
1/2 cup chicken broth (optional)

PROCEDURE:

Heat the oil in a large thick-bottomed pan. Add the onion and cook gently until transparent (5 to 10 minutes over low heat). Add curry powder and mix well. Continue cooking for 5 minutes, being careful not to burn the curry powder. Add the chicken pieces and stir to cook the outside until all the pieces have just turned white. Add the garlic, tomatoes, apple and raisins. Cover and simmer gently for about 40 minutes. Add a little chicken broth if sauce seems too thick during cooking.

Serve with plain boiled rice, poppadums and mango chutney. Bolst is the best curry powder, but others will do. Amount of curry powder used may be adjusted to taste.

Jane Lamb
Parent, Catherine Lamb '88 and William Lamb '94

Burmese Chicken Curry

Serves 4 to 6

INGREDIENTS:

3 tablespoons vegetable oil
1 cup chopped onion
2 tablespoons finely chopped garlic
1 tablespoon finely chopped ginger
1 teaspoon salt
2 tablespoons ground turmeric

1 tablespoon paprika
1/2 teaspoon red chili powder
2 to 3 pounds chicken pieces (breasts, thighs, legs)
1 tablespoon fresh coriander
1 teaspoon cinnamon

PROCEDURE:

Heat oil in a heavy saucepan large enough to hold all the ingredients. Add onions, garlic and ginger. Sauté until light brown. Stir in salt, turmeric, paprika and chili powder. Cook on low heat and stir for 2 to 3 minutes to keep from browning. You want spices to heat up, to release flavor, but not to burn. Add chicken pieces, stirring until meat is well-coated. Cover and simmer for 35 to 40 minutes. Chicken should be tender. Do not add water as the juices from the chicken will be sufficient. Stir occasionally to keep from sticking. By the end of the cooking time, most of liquid will have evaporated and oil will have formed a gravy and floated to the top. Stir in coriander and cinnamon and cover for a few minutes.

Serve with steamed white rice or jasmine rice and fresh vegetables. This is even better when made a day ahead.

Nancy Minus
Grandparent, Dana Young '87 and David Young '96

Chinese Chilled Noodles

Serves 2, as main course

INGREDIENTS:

8 ounces chicken breast
fillet
1/2 cup peeled, seeded and
julienned* cucumber
1/2 cup julienned* ham

* Julienne strips should
be very thin (only
slightly thicker than
the noodles) and 2"
long

Sauce:
1/2 cup chicken stock
5 tablespoons soy sauce
2 tablespoons vinegar
3/4 teaspoon sugar
1 tablespoon chili oil
4 tablespoons finely
chopped leek

8 ounces dried Chinese
noodles
2 tablespoons sesame oil
2 tablespoons salt

PROCEDURE:

Simmer the chicken breast in lightly salted water for 12 minutes. Drain and cool, then julienne same size as cucumber and ham. Set aside. Mix the sauce ingredients and put in a serving bowl and refrigerate. Put noodles in large pot of salted boiling water. When water comes to a boil again, add 1 cup cold water. When water boils again, drain noodles. Spread drained noodles in serving dish and sprinkle sesame oil over noodles to keep from sticking. Arrange the chicken, cucumber and ham in three sections over noodles. At the table, pour sauce over, toss gently to mix and serve immediately.

The chicken, cucumber and ham may be julienned the day before and refrigerated so it's very easy to complete the preparation and assemble just prior to serving.

Irene Ma
Parent, Marisa Ma '91 and Jonathon Ma '95

261

Edie's Chicken

Serves 6 to 8

INGREDIENTS:

3 tablespoons Hoisin
   Sauce (Plum Sauce)
2 tablespoons honey
1/4 cup soy sauce (or more
   to taste)
1 tablespoon fresh
   ginger, peeled and
   chopped fine

4 cloves garlic, chopped
   fine
3 tablespoons sherry
16 pieces of chicken
   (thighs, drumsticks,
   breasts)
Cooked rice as an
   accompaniment

PROCEDURE:

In a medium size bowl mix all ingredients (except chicken and rice) together as a marinade. Place chicken in an ovenproof casserole. Pour marinade over chicken pieces and let stand for 1 hour.

Preheat oven to 350°. Bake chicken for 1 hour, turning pieces after 30 minutes. Serve with rice. You can use the marinade as a sauce for the rice and chicken.

This recipe, as far as I know, is completely original to my friend Edie, who was born in Korea and calls this dish "Korean Plum Chicken", though her kids call it "Mother's Chicken".

Lois Case
Parent, Robert Case '99

Shoyu Chicken

Serves 4 to 6

INGREDIENTS:

4 tablespoons oil
1/2 cup shoyu (soy sauce)
4 tablespoons honey
1 1/2 cups water
3 to 4 pieces (cloves) star anise
1 teaspoon Chinese Five Spice powder
3 to 4 pounds fresh chicken (wings, drumettes, thighs and/or chopped small breasts), skin removed if desired

1/4 cup cornstarch mixed with 3 tablespoons water
1/4 cup sherry
Chopped Chinese parsley (cilantro) for garnish

PROCEDURE:

Place oil, shoyu, honey, water, star anise and Five Spice in a large 2 to 3-quart pan. Bring to a boil and stir to blend. Add chicken and simmer 30 minutes or until tender. Remove chicken from stock and set aside. Stir cornstarch mixture into stock and bring to boil. Stir in sherry and boil for 1 minute. Return chicken to stock and simmer 10 to 15 minutes to glaze chicken. Serve chicken and gravy glaze over brown or white rice. Garnish with Chinese parsley (cilantro).

Star anise is available at Asian markets. It comes in clusters; break off pieces that are partially open with seed visible. Prick open seeds with sharp pointed knife. (Keep unused clusters in airtight container for future use.) Can omit cornstarch if desired. Can be made a day ahead, refrigerated and heated the next day.

Virginia W. Westgate '46

Rosemary Roast Chicken

Serves 4

INGREDIENTS:

1 whole chicken (about
  3 1/2 pounds)
3 tablespoons olive oil
  Salt and pepper to
  taste

1 lemon, quartered
1 to 2 onions, roughly
  chopped
6 to 8 cloves garlic
2 to 4 sprigs rosemary

PROCEDURE:

Preheat oven to 450˚. Wash and pat dry the chicken inside and out. Trim off excess fat. Rub the skin and cavity with the olive oil and sprinkle with salt and pepper. Squeeze lemon over the inside and outside of the chicken. Stuff the cavity with most of the onions, lemon (after squeezing), 1/2 the garlic and 1/2 of the rosemary sprigs. Place the chicken breast side down in a glass baking dish lined with foil. Put the remainder of the onions, garlic and rosemary in the pan around the chicken. Place in oven and cook for 30 minutes. Turn the chicken over and roast another 40 minutes. Total cooking time should be 20 to 25 minutes per pound. Remove chicken from oven and let stand for 10 minutes to "set".

This is my favorite way to roast chicken. The high heat crisps the outside and the inside stays firm and moist, not steamed like chicken cooked at the usual recommended 350˚. You can add a little chicken broth (or water) and white wine to the roasted garlic and onion residue in the pan and cook down to make a wonderful sauce if you like. The very best part of this recipe is the way it perfumes the house while it is cooking. The rosemary roasting in the pan is so wonderful. If you like, sprinkle chicken with fresh chopped oregano and rosemary before roasting.

Chris Young
Parent, Dana Young '87 and David Young '96

Mama's Delicious Chicken

Serves 4

INGREDIENTS:

1 4-pound chicken
1 10-ounce can chicken
  broth
2 tablespoons butter
1 large onion, chopped

2 matzos, placed in
  water
Salt and pepper
2 cloves garlic
Paprika

PROCEDURE:

Clean chicken thoroughly under warm water. Remove neck, gizzard and liver and place them in saucepan with the chicken broth. Simmer for about 30 minutes until done. Remove chicken parts from broth and set aside.

Melt butter in a frying pan and sauté onion over medium-high heat, stirring to prevent burning. Cook onions until limp, approximately 10 minutes. Wring out matzos and place with cooked onions, gizzard and liver in chopping bowl. Strip all meat from neck and add to chopping bowl and mix all ingredients together. Chop all ingredients. Season to taste with salt and pepper.

Preheat oven to 350°. Peel garlic cloves and put through garlic press. Rub chicken, inside and out, with the garlic. Sprinkle a little salt, pepper and paprika inside and out. Lift skin of chicken and place chopped stuffing mixture underneath; place leftover stuffing inside. Bake for 1 1/2 hours or until done.

This is so delicious and really quite easy. You can serve with baked potatoes and salad.

Phyllis Z. Leive
Grandparent, Joshua Zetumer '99

265

Chicken Barbecue

Serves 2 to 4

INGREDIENTS:

6 chicken drumsticks
1 bunch cilantro leaves
4 to 8 Jalapeño peppers (to taste)
1 teaspoon red pepper (to taste)
1 3" piece ginger

1 1/2 cups (3/4 pint) plain yogurt
Salt to taste
2 fresh limes

PROCEDURE:

Skin and wash chicken, then pierce meat with fork several times. Place cilantro (leaves and stems may be used), jalapeño peppers, red pepper and ginger in the jar of a blender and blend into a paste. May add few spoons of yogurt to assist in blending. Add remainder of yogurt to paste and mix well. Season with salt to taste. Place chicken in a large bowl and cover with the yogurt mixture. Marinate at least 6 hours, although overnight is better. Grill on barbecue, turning over as needed. Squeeze on fresh lime just before eating.

Nisha Goyal
Parent, Rocky Goyal '94, Shilpi Goyal '97, Vishal Goyal '98

Jerk Chicken

Serves 4

INGREDIENTS:

1 whole chicken with or without skin
1/4 cup soy sauce
1 clove garlic

2 tablespoons brown sugar
2 tablespoons Jerk Seasoning

PROCEDURE:

Preheat oven to 350°. Rub ingredients over chicken and marinate overnight. You may also bake without marinating. Place in ovenproof pan and bake for 1 to 1 1/2 hours basting every 20 minutes.

You can buy Jerk Seasoning in specialty stores. If Walkerswood brand is available, it is the best. Chicken drumsticks and wings go well with this sauce and makes a good hors d'oeuvre dish.

Christine Galan '80

Katie T.'s Chicken Sandwiches

Serves 8

INGREDIENTS:

8 boneless chicken breasts	1/4 cup relish
1 cup Wishbone Italian salad dressing	Salt and pepper
1 1/2 cups mayonnaise	3 garlic cloves, pressed
1/2 cups ketchup	1 teaspoon lemon juice
	Good soft Italian bread, sliced

PROCEDURE:

Place boneless chicken breasts in a shallow pan with about 1 cup of Wishbone Italian dressing. Marinate covered in refrigerator for at least 6 hours. (Breasts may be marinated a day ahead.) Remove chicken from refrigerator and bring to room temperature 1 hour before cooking.

Sauce: Mix together the mayonnaise, ketchup, relish, salt, pepper and garlic. Squeeze a little fresh lemon juice into sauce too. This adds to the flavor. Refrigerate for at least 6 hours. May be done a day ahead.

Grill chicken over medium-hot coals about 4 minutes per side or until done. Slice chicken breasts into strips. Spread sauce on the 8 slices of bread. Place chicken on top of each slice.

Kids love these sandwiches. A great dinner served with a green salad and French fries topped with fresh Parmesan cheese.

Shannon Turner
Parent, Katie Turner '95 and Annie Turner '97X

Hot Chicken Salad Pie

Serves 4 to 6

INGREDIENTS:

2 cups diced cooked chicken
1 1/2 cups diced celery
1 teaspoon grated onion
Salt to taste
1/4 teaspoon white pepper
1 teaspoon lemon juice
1/3 cup chopped pecans

3/4 cup mayonnaise
3/4 cup plain yogurt
1 9" baked pie shell
1 cup finely crushed potato chips
1/2 cup grated cheddar cheese

PROCEDURE:

Preheat oven to 350˚. In a large mixing bowl combine chicken, celery, grated onion, salt, white pepper, lemon juice, pecans, mayonnaise and yogurt and mix lightly but thoroughly. Place all into the baked pie shell. Top with potato chips and cheese. Bake for 20 to 25 minutes. Serve hot.

Always a success. Looks pretty on the plate and it's delicious.

Kathy Renner
Parent, Bailey Renner '99

Turkey Tetrazzini

Serves 10 to 12 adults
or 5 to 6 male teenagers

INGREDIENTS:

5 cups dry, broken
  spaghetti
1/2 cup safflower oil
2 teaspoons dried
  parsley
1 teaspoon dried basil
3 teaspoons dried chives
Few rosemary sprigs
  (optional), leaves
  finely chopped
2 tablespoons solid
  chicken base
1 cup flour

4 cups (1 quart) nonfat
  yogurt
4 cups (1 quart) nonfat
  milk
4 10-ounce cans white
  turkey
1/2 cup water (to rinse out
  turkey cans)
1 16-ounce bag frozen
  peas (optional)

PROCEDURE:

Cook spaghetti in boiling water for 10 to 15 minutes in a 4-quart container. Rinse in colander. Drain. Set aside.

Make white sauce: Heat oil in heavy 8-quart container on medium heat. Add herbs and chicken base. Stir until hot. Add flour and mix until all lumps are gone. Add yogurt and mix well. Add 1/2 cup of the milk and stir well. Add another 1/2 cup milk and stir until well-blended. Add last 2 cups of milk, continuing to stir. When sauce is smooth, add turkey and mix. Use water to rinse out cans from the turkey and add to sauce. Stir until heated completely. Add spaghetti and optional peas. Mix well and heat. Stir frequently while heating to prevent scorching. Serve.

Refrigerates very well. Microwave 2 cups on a plate for 3 minutes on high (covered with wax paper) for an easy snack for hungry teens. Variations: 1.) Fill 9" x 11" glass dish, garnish with pulverized cornflakes and bake at 325° for 20 to 30 minutes or until bubbly. If starting with cold tetrazzini, bake 40 to 50 minutes at 325°; 2.) add curry to vary the flavor; 3.) use as filling for crêpes (without the spaghetti).

Gwen Foss
Parent, Sandy Foss '92X and Lynn Foss '95

Turkey Stew

Serves 8

INGREDIENTS:

1 onion, finely chopped
2 garlic cloves, finely
   chopped
1/4 cup raisins
1/2 cup fresh cilantro,
   chopped
1/4 cup smooth peanut
   butter
1 tablespoon Angostura
   bitters

1 1/2 teaspoons sugar
1/8 cup chili powder
1 teaspoon cinnamon
1/2 teaspoon cumin
3 cups defatted chicken
   stock
2 pounds cooked turkey,
   skin removed and cut
   into strips

PROCEDURE:

In a large heavy pot combine all ingredients except for turkey and chicken stock. Mix well and cook uncovered over medium heat, stirring frequently for about 10 minutes. In a saucepan bring chicken stock to a boil and add to sauce. Cook over very low heat stirring occasionally for 30 minutes. Add turkey strips and cook 15 minutes longer.

Low in fat and cholesterol.

Terry Lakenan Rismon '73X

Turkey Taco Casserole

Serves 6

INGREDIENTS:

- 1 tablespoon oil or butter
- 1 medium onion, chopped
- 1 stalk celery, chopped
- 1 large carrot, chopped
- 1 pound ground turkey
- 1 tomato chopped (or 1 14-ounce can of ready-cut tomatoes)
- 1 package taco seasoning mix
- 1 cup uncooked pasta (elbow macaroni or your favorite)
- 1 10-ounce can chicken broth
- 1 cup grated cheddar cheese

PROCEDURE:

In a large covered saucepan, heat oil and sauté onion, celery and carrot over medium heat. When vegetables are soft, add ground turkey. Continue cooking mixture until all pink is gone from meat (breaking up turkey into small bits). Add chopped tomato (or ready-cut tomatoes), taco seasoning mix, pasta and chicken broth. Mix thoroughly. Bring to boil, reduce heat to low and cover pan. Cook, stirring occasionally, 15 minutes or until pasta has absorbed liquid. Add cheese, mix thoroughly and cover again for a few minutes until cheese is melted.

Good family dinner; kids like it; provides balanced meal if served with fruit. Can add any chopped vegetables that your family likes (mushrooms, zucchini, etc.)

Candy Cassidy Pagano '73

Ground Turkey German Meatballs

Serves 4

INGREDIENTS:

1 1/2 pounds ground turkey
1 large onion, finely
  chopped
2 eggs
1 1/2 teaspoons salt
Pepper to taste
3/4 cup Progresso Italian
  dried bread crumbs

Dash nutmeg
  (optional)
2 tablespoons butter or
  margarine
1/2 cup water
1 tablespoon all purpose
  flour
1/4 cup warm water

PROCEDURE:

In a large bowl mix together all ingredients except butter, flour and water. Form mixture into meatballs with a diameter of a half dollar. Melt butter in frying pan and brown meatballs on all sides. Add 1/2 cup water to pan, cover tightly, let meatballs simmer over medium heat for about 20 minutes. Remove meatballs from pan and put aside. In measuring cup, add flour to 1/4 cup warm water. Mix until smooth and add to drippings in pan. Stir until a smooth, thickened gravy is formed. Put meatballs back in pan, simmer covered over low heat for another 5 minutes and then serve.

Quick and easy on a school night. Kids love 'em.

Kimberly Miller
Parent, Camden Miller '94X, Trent Miller '96, Derek Miller '98

Thanksgiving Turkey

Serves 18 to 22

INGREDIENTS:

1/4 cup olive oil
1 tablespoon paprika
1 teaspoon garlic salt

1 18 to 22-pound fresh turkey

PROCEDURE:

Preheat oven to 450°. Mix olive oil, paprika and garlic salt together and rub the turkey with the mixture. Place turkey on a rack in a large roasting pan and cook, uncovered, for 15 minutes.

Reduce oven temperature to 325° and cover turkey loosely with aluminum foil. For stuffed turkey, cook for 18 to 24 minutes per pound. For unstuffed turkey, cook for 15 to 18 minutes per pound. One hour before turkey will be done, remove foil. Baste frequently until done.

This recipe was given to two of our five sons many years ago by an Italian grocer in New York City, when our youngest son, a college student at that time, spent Thanksgiving with our second son and his wife. When the boys went to buy a turkey, the grocer saw how young they were and told them to cook the turkey this way and they did. That Christmas, Wink, our youngest, shared the recipe with us and we, all Faulkners, have been doing it "Wink's" way ever since.

Patricia Williams Faulkner '42

Turkey Breast
with Orange and Ginger

Serves 4 to 6

INGREDIENTS:

2 1/2 pounds turkey breast
1/2 teaspoon paprika
1 medium onion, sliced
1/2 cup orange juice
    concentrate
2 tablespoons chopped
    parsley

2 teaspoons soy sauce
2 tablespoons brown
    sugar, packed
1/2 teaspoon ground
    ginger
1/3 cup water

PROCEDURE:

Rinse turkey; pat dry. Place turkey breast in a 9" x 13" roasting pan and place under broiler to brown. Remove and preheat oven to 400°. Sprinkle turkey breast with paprika. Arrange onion slices over turkey.

In a medium size bowl combine juice concentrate, parsley, soy sauce, brown sugar, ginger and water and stir well to mix. Pour over turkey. Bake, lightly covered, for 1 hour, basting once or twice with pan juices.

Easy, fast, low fat dish with a gourmet taste. Also, all ingredients are easy to store in advance for those sudden last minute dinner guests.

Cheryle Gaillard Tkach '65

Stuffed Cornish Game Hens, Mexican Style

Serves 2

INGREDIENTS:

- 2 frozen Cornish game hens
- 1 16-ounce roll frozen sausage
- 1 4-ounce can diced green chiles

- 20 soda crackers (Saltines)
- 2 tablespoons butter

PROCEDURE:

Preheat oven to 375˚. Thaw the hens and the sausage at room temperature. Mix the chiles with the sausage. Crumble the crackers into small pieces or crumbs and mix these with the sausage and chile mixture. Stuff the hens with this mixture. Place hens in an ovenproof pan. Put 1 tablespoon of butter on top of each hen. Bake hens for 1 hour and 15 minutes. Baste with butter and pan juices occasionally.

A romantic dinner for two. My boyfriend invented this recipe 16 years ago and we have enjoyed cooking it together ever since.

Patricia Barsotti '66

Josh's Quail on the Trail

Serves ?? (depends on your luck)

INGREDIENTS:

Quail breast filets
Jalapeños, cut into
strips

Bacon, 1 slice per
breast
Toothpick
Cajun spices

PROCEDURE:

Make slit on each side of breast fillet and put jalapeño strip into slit. Wrap breast and pepper with bacon strip. Secure with toothpick. Place breasts in a shallow pan and coat with Cajun spices. Barbecue over hot coals until bacon is crisp and breast is cooked through.

Be prepared to cool your mouth with drinks. Excellent! Easy at home or in camp.

Josh Oliver '96

Meat

Killer Fillet of Beef

Serves 6

INGREDIENTS:

1 3-pound beef fillet
Salt and pepper to
taste
2 tablespoons butter

1 14-ounce can beef
consommé
1/2 cup (1 stick) butter
3/4 bunch parsley
2 cloves garlic, minced

PROCEDURE:

Preheat oven to 425°. <u>Day before</u>: In a heavy pan which can be used on top of stove and in oven, brown fillet (after patting with salt and pepper) in the butter. Do this quickly over medium-high heat, turning fillet to brown all sides. When brown, remove fillet from pan, pour out excess fat. Return fillet to pan, place pan in oven. After 5 minutes, pour the consommé into the bottom of pan. Cook for 20 minutes more. Take out. Baste meat occasionally as it cools. Refrigerate when cool.

When chilled, remove meat to a cutting board and cut into 1/4" slices. Mix butter, parsley and garlic in food processor. Place 1 teaspoon of mixture between each slice of meat, then squeeze meat back together firmly so that it looks untouched. Return fillet to pan with the consommé, baste and refrigerate until the next day.

Two hours before serving, take fillet out of refrigerator and warm to room temperature. Preheat oven to 450° and heat meat in oven for 10 minutes. Serve immediately.

Medium rare, mouth watering and well worth the preparation time.

Heather Gallagher
Parent, Kielty Gallagher '94

Stuffed Flank Steak

Serves 6

INGREDIENTS:

2 cups stuffing mix
1 3/4 pounds tenderized
   flank steak
Flour
Salt and pepper to
   taste
Oil

Sauce:
1 10-ounce can chopped
   Ro-tel tomatoes with
   chiles
2 dashes ketchup
3 green onions, sliced
5 fresh mushrooms,
   sliced

PROCEDURE:

Preheat oven to 350°. Prepare stuffing as directed. Roll stuffing in steak (jelly roll fashion) and secure with toothpicks. Dredge lightly in flour with salt and pepper. In a heavy ovenproof pot with a lid, brown in oil, on all sides. Pour off excess oil. Mix sauce ingredients together. Pour sauce over meat. Cover and bake for about 2 hours basting once or twice. Slice to serve.

Cynthia Sawyer Hart '48

Adams' Family Salsa Beef

Serves 6

INGREDIENTS:

1 4-pound beef brisket
   (or London broil)
1 12-ounce can beer
1 16-ounce jar salsa

12 flour tortillas
1 cup sour cream
1/2 cup fresh cilantro
   leaves

PROCEDURE:

Preheat oven to 325°. Place beef in a 3 or 4-quart casserole with a lid. Pour beer and salsa over meat. Cover and bake for about 3 to 4 hours or until meat pulls apart easily. Serve with warm tortillas and garnish with sour cream and fresh cilantro.

A family favorite that's easy for college kids to cook and serve to friends.

Karen Adams
Parent, Jane Adams '87, Charlie Adams '91, Russell Adams '94

Brandy Roast Beef
with Porcini Mushrooms

Serves 4 to 6

INGREDIENTS:

- 1/4 cup plus 2 tablespoons olive oil
- 4 to 5 cloves garlic
- 1 tablespoon chopped fresh rosemary (or 1 teaspoon dried)
- 2 or 3 bay leaves
- 1 2-pound beef tenderloin
- 1 tablespoon flour plus extra to flour meat
- 1 cup brandy
- 2 cups beef broth
- 4 Porcini mushrooms (or brown mushrooms with large fleshy caps)
- 1/2 cup chopped parsley
- 1/2 cup chopped walnuts

PROCEDURE:

In a heavy covered sauté pan (large enough to hold tenderloin) with a lid, place 2 tablespoons olive oil and 3 to 4 cloves of sliced garlic. Place pan over medium/high heat. When garlic has turned to pale gold, add rosemary and bay leaves cut in halves. Lightly flour the meat, put in the pan and brown on all sides over medium-high heat. When the meat is browned, pour in brandy and 1 cup of broth; turn the heat to low, cover the pan with lid slightly ajar and cook for 45 minutes or until the meat is tender. While the meat is cooking, wash the mushrooms in cold water to remove the grit. Cut into 1/2" slices. In a frying pan, place 1/4 cup olive oil, 1 clove of chopped garlic and 1 tablespoon of flour. Cook over medium heat, stirring frequently, to obtain a creamy mixture. Add mushroom slices, 1/4 cup of the parsley, walnuts, 1 cup of broth (either a light beef broth or the gravy from the meat) and cook slowly for 10 minutes. When the meat is done, remove it and let it rest for 10 minutes. Cut meat in slices of medium thickness and place on a serving platter. Spoon mushroom sauce on top and garnish with fresh parsley. May serve the extra gravy on the side.

When, tired of death and destruction, I finally went home after WWII and I found a new person living with my family, a lady in her sixties, beautiful and aristocratic, the sister of Maestro Mascagni, the well-known composer of Cavalleria Rusticana. It was this lady who, together with my mother, introduced me to Roast Beef with Brandy. I do love the arias of Cavalleria ("Gli aranci olezzano..."), but, since then, I have equally loved this dish. Buon appetito!

Otto Mower
Faculty, Foreign Languages Department Chair
and
Anita Chaffee-Mower
Faculty, Mathematics Department

Authentic German Sauerbraten

Serves 6

INGREDIENTS:

3 to 4 **pounds eye of round roast**

Marinade:
2 1/2 **cups red wine vinegar**
1 1/2 **cups water**
1 **large onion, quartered**
1 **stalk celery (with top), sliced**
1 **carrot, sliced**
1 to 2 **whole bay leaves**

1 **teaspoon whole cloves**
1 **teaspoon peppercorns**
1 to 2 **sprigs fresh parsley**
1 **cup red table wine**

Gravy:
8 **ginger snap cookies**
4 **tablespoons flour**
3/4 **cup water**
1/2 **cup sour cream**

PROCEDURE:

To prepare marinade: Place all marinade ingredients <u>except red table wine</u> in a medium saucepan and bring to a boil. Allow marinade to cool completely. Place meat in a large mixing bowl. (In selecting marinating dish, keep in mind that you want the liquid to cover as much of the meat as possible. You can cut the roast up into 2 to 4 pieces if necessary to insure that the marinade reaches as much of the meat as possible.) Pour marinade and red table wine over meat, covering as much of the surface of the meat as possible. Marinate in refrigerator for at least <u>24 hours</u> (3 to 5 days recommended).

To cook roast: Pat the meat dry with paper towels. Brown roast on all sides in 1/4 cup hot butter in a large Dutch oven (the more attention you take to browning the meat, the richer the color of the gravy). Pour marinade over the meat. Add whole ginger snap cookies and simmer covered over low heat until meat is tender (approximately 2 to 2 1/2 hours). (Note: Meat will be very tender, but very dry and must be served with <u>plenty</u> of gravy.) Remove meat from Dutch oven. Strain off the vegetables, reserving the liquid. Return strained liquid to Dutch oven. Mix together the flour and water and stir into the liquid. Simmer, stirring constantly, until gravy thickens. When thick, turn down the heat and add sour cream.

(Note: Sour cream will not blend well into gravy if gravy is not thick enough.) The above measurements for flour and water may vary depending on how much liquid you have to start. It will appear to be a lot of gravy, but the gravy is the best part.

This is an old authentic German recipe of my mother's. My mother marinates the meat for up to 7 days. Serve with homemade German spaetzle.

Dottie Engel
Parent, Carly Engel '99

Sherried Beef

Serves 6

INGREDIENTS:

2 pounds stewing beef
1 10-ounce can cream of
   mushroom soup
1 package dry onion
   soup mix
1 cup dry sherry

1 teaspoon parsley,
   chopped
1 teaspoon black pepper
   Cooked rice or wide
   noodles for 6

PROCEDURE:

Preheat oven to 325°. Trim fat from stewing beef and cut into bite size pieces. Mix all ingredients together and place in a covered 2 to 3-quart baking dish. Cook in oven for 2 1/2 to 3 hours. Do not let liquid evaporate too much or meat will dry out. Add a little water to the sauce if it gets too thick. Serve with rice or wide noodles.

This is one of those dishes that you prepare during winter exams. It's cold and dark outside, your home will smell delicious and your students will feel like someone truly cares about them; and it's all so easy.

Marilyn Bilger
Parent, Lauren Bilger '93 and Whitney Bilger '96

New Orleans Pot Roast

Serves 8

INGREDIENTS:

1/2 teaspoon each:
   pepper, ground cloves,
   mace, allspice
   Salt to taste
1 4-pound pot roast
1 large onion, chopped
1 clove garlic, chopped
1/4 cup vegetable oil
2 tablespoons lemon
   juice
1 tablespoon vinegar
   Flour to coat meat
   Oil to seal meat

2 cups tomato juice or
   canned tomatoes
1 1/2 cups beef stock
2 or 3 bay leaves
4 large carrots, peeled
   and cut into 2" pieces
4 onions, cut into
   quarters
4 potatoes, peeled and
   cut into quarters
   Flour to thicken
   gravy, if desired

PROCEDURE:

Mix together the pepper, cloves, mace, allspice and salt and rub into surface of the meat. In a bowl large enough to hold the meat, mix together the chopped onion, chopped garlic, vegetable oil, lemon juice and vinegar. Place meat in bowl, cover and allow to marinate for 5 hours in refrigerator. Turn occasionally. Remove meat from marinade. Sprinkle with flour and sear in oil in a heavy pot. Turn meat over with wooden spoon to sear all sides. Pour off oil. Add marinade to pot, the tomato juice (or canned tomatoes with their liquid), beef stock and bay leaves. Cover and simmer for 3 hours. Add carrots, onions and potatoes 45 minutes before roast is done. Thicken stock with flour, if desired, and serve as gravy.

You may shorten marinating time (or skip) if you are in a rush. Our family loves the aroma of this dish cooking. Even better as leftovers the next day.

Mildred Branard
Grandparent, Elizabeth Vale '92 and Susannah Vale '95

282

Cidered Beef

Serves 10 to 12

INGREDIENTS:

7 strips bacon
3 pounds lean beef, cubed
1/2 cup flour
  Salt and pepper to taste
2 tablespoons butter
1 medium onion, chopped
1 large carrot, sliced
1 clove garlic, minced
1 small bay leaf
1/2 ounce unsweetened chocolate, grated
2 tablespoons tomato paste

1 cup stock (beef or vegetable)
2 cups fresh apple cider
4 tablespoons cider vinegar
1/2 teaspoon dried thyme
1/2 teaspoon dried oregano
1 pound fresh mushrooms
  Cornstarch mixed with water to thicken sauce, if desired

PROCEDURE:

Preheat oven to 325°. Cut bacon into bits and fry until crisp. Drain on paper towels leaving 2 to 4 tablespoons of fat in large fry pan. Dust the beef cubes in flour, salt and pepper and brown in bacon fat. Remove beef cubes and put in an ovenproof casserole dish. Put 1 tablespoon of the butter in the same frying pan used to brown the beef. Add the onions and carrots. Cook until lightly browned. Add these to casserole along with crisp bacon, garlic, bay leaf, grated chocolate, tomato paste, stock, apple cider and enough cider vinegar to keep sauce from tasting sweet. Sprinkle with herbs (thyme and oregano), mix well, cover and cook in oven for about 3 hours until the meat is very tender. Cut mushrooms in thick slices and sauté in the remaining 1 tablespoon of butter, briefly. When meat is tender, check seasonings and add the mushrooms. Mix well. (You can mix a little corn starch in some water and add if you want a thicker sauce.)

Your kitchen will smell wonderful while this is cooking. Serve with homemade mashed potatoes or spaetzle. Enjoy. This is a recipe from my friend, Dricka Campbell, in Manchester, Vermont.

Jeanne Smith
Parent, Jenner Smith '99

Carbonnade of Beef with Croutons

Serves 4 to 6

INGREDIENTS:

2 pounds chuck steak,
  cut into 1" cubes
2 tablespoons olive oil or
  beef drippings
4 onions, chopped
1 1/2 tablespoons flour
1 12-ounce bottle
  Guiness Stout
2 garlic cloves
1/2 teaspoon thyme
1 bay leaf

2 teaspoons red wine
  vinegar
1/2 teaspoon salt
2 tablespoons butter,
  softened
French Dijon style
  mustard
4 to 6 thick slices of French
  bread (1 per person)
Pepper to taste

PROCEDURE:

Preheat oven to 325°. Dry the meat cubes with paper towels. In a heavy frying pan, heat the oil or beef fat and brown the meat over a medium-high heat. Remove the meat with a slotted spoon to a 2 1/2-quart ovenproof casserole. Lower the heat slightly. In the remaining oil (add a bit more if needed), brown the onions taking care not to burn them. Sprinkle the flour over them and stir until the flour turns to a golden color. Scrape the onions and flour into the casserole. To the casserole, add the Guiness, 1 of the garlic cloves, herbs, 1 teaspoon of the vinegar and the salt. Cover and cook in oven for 2 to 2 1/2 hours, until the beef is very tender.

For the croutons, place the softened butter on a plate and squeeze in 1 clove of garlic with a press. Add 1/2 teaspoon French mustard and mix the seasoned butter with a fork. (Omit the garlic here if you are not a garlic fancier.) Just before you are ready to serve, toast the bread on both sides under the broiler. Spread 1 side with the seasoned butter and broil for a few more seconds.

To serve, season the carbonnade to taste with pepper, the remaining 1 teaspoon wine vinegar and 1 to 3 teaspoons French mustard. Place a crouton on each plate and pour the carbonnade over it.

Carbonade de boeuf (carbonnade of beef) is to Belgium what boeuf bourguignon is to Burgundy. The two preparations are actually quite similar. The French use red Burgundy wine where the Belgians employ beer. Because of its sugar and malt, the beer lends a special richness of flavor to the stew. My favorite cooking beer is Guiness stout. This is a savory and flavorful dish. Mashed or boiled parslied potatoes and a simple vegetable such as buttered carrots or zucchini are good accompaniments. Beer or a full-bodied red wine could be offered with the meal.

Marianne Engle
Parent, Lindsey Engle '94 and Jordan Engle '98

Mother's Rechauffé

Serves 4 to 5

INGREDIENTS:

2 pounds round steak, cubed
1 large onion, chopped
1 garlic clove, minced
1/2 cup mushrooms, washed and sliced
1 cup (1/2 pint) sour cream

1 8-ounce can tomato sauce
1 tablespoon Worcester- shire sauce
1 teaspoon salt
1/8 teaspoon pepper
1/2 cup sherry, port, claret or Burgundy wine

PROCEDURE:

Brown steak, onion and garlic in a large, deep fry pan in some fat (there may be enough on the steak to brown steak sufficiently without adding fat). Add mushrooms, sour cream, tomato sauce, Worcestershire sauce, salt and pepper. Cook slowly for 1 and 1/2 hours on top of stove until meat is tender. Add wine just before serving. Can be made in the morning or the day before.

Good over steamed rice or noodles. As the name "Rechauffé" (reheated) implies, this tastes better the second day.

Melissa Renaud Markey '69

Ian's "Super" Beef Stew

Serves 6 to 8

INGREDIENTS:

2 pounds stew meat, cut into 1" cubes
Salt and pepper to taste
3 tablespoons butter
1 15-ounce can tomato juice
1 30-ounce can tomatoes (drained), coarsely chopped
5 stalks celery, leaves as well, roughly chopped
2 carrots, peeled and roughly chopped

3 garlic cloves, finely chopped
3 potatoes, peeled and roughly chopped
6 tablespoons barley
5 beef bouillon cubes
1 15-ounce can corn
3 tablespoons Worcestershire sauce
3 cups water
2 bay leaves
1/2 teaspoon thyme
1 10-ounce package frozen okra

PROCEDURE:

Season the beef cubes lightly with salt and pepper. In a 4 1/2-quart stew pot, sauté the meat cubes in butter until they are browned on all sides (about 5 minutes). Add the remaining ingredients (except for okra) in the order listed. (More water may be added at any time throughout the cooking as desired.) Bring the stew to a boil, lower heat, partially cover and simmer for at least 6 hours. (Cooking very slowly allows the carrots and potatoes to stay intact and firm.) Add okra 30 minutes before end of cooking time. Stir occasionally and taste for seasoning. A little cayenne pepper may be added for a hotter bite.

This is the most incredibly delicious slow simmering stew. It is so good that it should be shared with family and friends and is wonderful to serve in front of the TV on Super Bowl Sunday, but any time is just fine. A family favorite with French bread.

Jane and Ian Jones
Parents, Victoria Jones '97 and Andra Jones '99

Boeuf Bourguignon
(Burgundy Beef)

Serves 6

INGREDIENTS:

1/4 cup shortening or oil
3 pounds lean stewing
  beef or a chuck roast,
  cut into cubes
3 tablespoon flour
  Salt to taste
1/2 teaspoon pepper
1/2 teaspoon dried thyme

1 cup canned condensed
  beef broth, undiluted
1 cup dry red wine
12 small white boiling
  onions
1/2 pound fresh
  mushrooms (or 1
  4-ounce can sliced
  mushrooms)

PROCEDURE:

Preheat oven to 325° about 4 hours before dinner. Heat shortening or oil in large skillet and brown meat cubes. Stir in flour, salt, pepper and thyme, scraping bottom of skillet well. Turn all into 2-quart casserole. Pour in beef broth and wine. Cover casserole and bake for 2 hours. At end of 2 hours, add onions and mushrooms. If mixture seems dry, pour in equal amounts of wine and beef broth. Continue baking about 1 to 1 1/2 hours or until meat is fork tender. Remove from oven, skim any fat.

Serve right from casserole with mashed potatoes or rice.

Carol Gable
Grandparent, Michael Gable '99

Lauren's Cholent

Serves 4 to 6

INGREDIENTS:

1 1/2 pounds flanken (stew meat or short ribs), cut into 1" cubes

1 2-ounce package onion soup mix (Telma is a good Kosher brand)

1 8-ounce can tomato sauce

1 1/4 cup great northern beans, washed and drained

1 1/4 cup pearl barley, washed and drained

6 cups water

1 kishka (found in Kosher markets), frozen

PROCEDURE:

Wash the meat. Place the meat in the bottom of a large crockpot. Pour the onion soup mix over the meat. Pour the tomato sauce over the meat and soup mix. Add the beans and the barley to the pot. Pour the water over all the above. Unwrap the frozen kishka, removing both the outer wrap and the next layer. Double wrap the kishka in foil and set it in the top of the crockpot (it will float). (It should still be frozen when you add it to the pot.) Put the lid on the crockpot. Set the temperature to low and cook <u>overnight</u>. The cholent will be ready for lunch the next day.

Cholent is the traditional hot dish served on Shabbat day for lunch. Because of the custom of eating a hot, cooked meal on Shabbat, many people serve a cholent, a tasty stew or soup that includes meat, potatoes, beans and/or rice in a variety of combinations.

Lauren Izner Ramenofsky '72X
Parent, David Ramenofsky '99

Swahili Stew

Serves 8 to 10

INGREDIENTS:

1 2-pound beef chuck roast
2 cups flour, sifted
1 teaspoon garlic salt
1 teaspoon black pepper
1 teaspoon chopped dill weed
1 teaspoon chopped oregano
1 cup vegetable oil
1/2 cup red wine or red wine vinegar
3 cups beef broth

2 1/2 pounds white rose potatoes, washed and quartered but not peeled
1 2-pound bag new baby carrots, cleaned and peeled
3 large yellow onions, chopped
1 bunch celery, washed and coarsely chopped or sliced
1 bay leaf
1 1-pound bag frozen green peas

PROCEDURE:

Cut the chuck roast into 1" cubes, making sure to remove the tough connective tissue you will encounter in the process (but you can leave the fat on). Mix the flour, garlic salt, black pepper, dill weed and oregano and dredge the beef cubes in this mixture until all cubes are completely dusted. Shake off the excess flour. In a large frying pan, heat 1/4" of oil over medium-high heat. Pan fry the beef cubes until well-browned. Do not try to cook more than 1 layer of beef at a time. Using a 10" frying pan, you will probably need to do at least two batches. After the last batch, use the wine (or vinegar) to de-glaze the frying pan. Save the drippings to add to the crock pot. The flour from the meat will thicken the juice. Using a large crock pot (10-quart or larger), heat the beef broth to a boil. Add the quartered potatoes, carrots, onions, celery, bay leaf, browned meat and pan drippings. Cook for 1 hour at 220°. Lower the heat to simmer and cook at least 2 additional hours, stirring occasionally. Add the frozen peas 15 to 30 minutes before serving. Season to taste and serve.

There's nothing like a hot bowl of hearty stew on a cold, winter's night with fresh biscuits. And this simple recipe is fun because as long as you follow the basic procedure, there is no limit to the way you can improvise to get different tastes. Stewed tomatoes can be added for variety or you can substitute a different vegetable for the peas. By the way, Swahili was my nickname at San Miguel/Bishop's, hence the name for the recipe.

Tom Sayer '77

Teriyaki Burgers

Yields 6 burgers

INGREDIENTS:

1 1/2 pounds ground beef
1 1/2 cups soft bread crumbs
 1/4 cup finely chopped
      onion
    2 eggs, slightly beaten

2 tablespoons sugar
3 tablespoons soy sauce
1/4 cup water, scant
1 clove garlic, crushed
  Dash ground ginger

PROCEDURE:

Combine ground beef with remaining ingredients. Mix well, shape into 6 patties and barbecue.

I barbecue them in a hamburger basket so they don't fall apart. These are always juicy and a hit with the teenagers.

Lucy Kable Means Borsenberger '69
Parent, Artie Means '94 and Chris Means '96

Texas Beef Brisket Barbecue

Serves 12 to 16

INGREDIENTS:

3 to 4 cups mesquite or
        hickory chips
    1 5 to 6-pound beef
        brisket
    1 recipe Texas Barbecue
        Sauce

        Texas Barbecue Sauce:
        (2 cups)
    1 cup tomato juice
  1/4 cup vinegar

1/4 cup ketchup
1/4 cup Worcestershire
     sauce
  2 tablespoons brown
     sugar
  2 teaspoons dry mustard
1 1/2 teaspoons onion salt
  1/2 teaspoon pepper
      Several dashes bottled
         hot pepper sauce

PROCEDURE:

About an hour before cooking time, soak mesquite or hickory chips in enough water to cover. In covered charcoal grill arrange *hot* coals on both sides of a foil drip pan. Drain chips. Sprinkle the coals with some of the chips. Place the brisket atop grill over drip pan. Brush with some of the Texas Barbecue Sauce. Lower hood. Grill 1 hour, adding additional coals and chips as needed. Turn brisket, brushing both sides with additional barbecue sauce. Lower grill hood again; grill 50 to 55 minutes more or until meat is well-done, adding more coals and chips as needed. Brush with sauce during the last 20 minutes of cooking. Heat remaining barbecue sauce to pass with brisket.

Texas Barbecue Sauce: In a 1-quart saucepan combine all sauce ingredients. Simmer, covered, 5 minutes.

Mimi King
Aunt, Elizabeth Vale '92 and Susannah Vale '95

Barbecued Flank Steaks

Serves 4 to 6

INGREDIENTS:

Marinade:
1/4 **cup soy sauce**
3 **tablespoons honey**
3 **tablespoons red wine vinegar**
1 1/2 **teaspoons garlic powder**

1 1/2 **teaspoons ginger powder**
3/4 **cup salad oil**
1/2 **teaspoon onion powder**

3 to 4 **pounds flank steak**

PROCEDURE:

Mix marinade ingredients together. Place flank steak in a pan with the marinade. Marinate meat for at least 4 hours turning several times. Remove meat from pan and place on grill over hot charcoal. Cook approximately 4 to 5 minutes per side for rare. To serve, slice diagonally across grain.

I usually serve with rice, tossed green salad and fresh fruit. Great for family barbecue or any casual gathering.

Alice Saunders
Parent, Paul Saunders '96 and Carl Saunders '98

Rocky Mountain Brisket

Serves 6

INGREDIENTS:

1 4-pound beef brisket
2 tablespoons Liquid Smoke
1 teaspoon salt
1 1/2 teaspoons pepper
2 tablespoons chili powder
1 teaspoon crushed bay leaves

Barbecue sauce:
3 tablespoons brown sugar
1 14-ounce bottle ketchup
1/2 cup dark beer
2 tablespoons Liquid Smoke
Salt and pepper to taste
4 tablespoons Worcestershire sauce
3 teaspoons Colman's dry mustard
2 teaspoons celery seeds
6 tablespoons butter

PROCEDURE:

Preheat oven to 325°. Rub meat completely with Liquid Smoke. Place meat fat side up in a large roasting pan. Combine salt, pepper, chili powder and crushed bay leaves. Sprinkle dry seasoning mixture on top. Cover tightly. Bake for 4 hours. Scrape seasoning off meat and cut in very thin slices across the grain. Serve with barbecue sauce.

Barbecue sauce: Combine all ingredients. Bring to a boil, stirring occasionally. Cook for 10 minutes. Serve with sliced brisket.

Serve with crusty French bread, green salad and mashed potatoes for a wintry evening meal. It is also excellent served on onion rolls the next day. I often double this so I will be sure to have leftovers.

Heidi Dorris
Parent, Ashley Dorris '96 and Taylor Dorris '98

Southwestern Chili Verde de Ortiz

Serves 4 to 6

INGREDIENTS:

1 pound diced pork steaks, stew beef or diced chicken

1 large yellow onion, sliced

1 bunch green onion, chopped

2 tablespoons olive oil

2 roasted* jalapeño peppers (optional)

1/2 pound roasted* Anaheim green chiles

2 Guerito (yellow) peppers

1 tablespoon minced garlic

1 large tomato, diced

1 teaspoon ground cumin

1 teaspoon ground coriander

Salt and pepper to taste

1 14-ounce can seasoned tomato sauce

1 bunch cilantro, chopped

PROCEDURE:

*To roast chiles, lay chiles on broiling pan and broil until skins blister and blacken slightly. Turn them over and roast other side. Peel the skins under running water and remove seeds. Preroasted chiles may be purchased in Mexican mercados or canned roasted chiles may be used.

Preheat large frying pan to medium heat. Add olive oil and sauté meat and onions for 3 to 5 minutes or until meat is browned and onions are soft. Dice all roasted chiles, garlic and tomato and add to pan, stirring to mix ingredients. Add cumin, coriander, salt and pepper. Then stir in tomato sauce. Reduce heat to low and simmer for 10 to 15 minutes or until liquid has evaporated. Stir in chopped cilantro and serve.

Should be served with warm flour tortillas, frijoles (refried beans), shredded cheese and salsa on the side. Freezes well and is great wrapped in a tortilla as a burrito for leftovers. Meat may be deleted from this recipe for a great vegetarian dish. Also good with tofu as a meat substitute.

Alysun Kayser-Ortiz '79

Chili Con Carne Cordon Bleu

Yields 6 servings with beans, 4 without

INGREDIENTS:

1/4 pound kidney suet, broken up (any friendly butcher will give you a piece)
2 pounds beef, diced
4 cloves garlic, minced
2 medium white or yellow onions, chopped
Salt and black pepper to taste
5 tablespoons chili powder, at least

3 palmfuls whole cumin seed, at least
1 teaspoon dried oregano, no more
2 8-ounce cans tomato sauce
2 8-ounce cans tap water, at least
2 15-ounce cans pinto beans, if desired

PROCEDURE:

Render suet in medium-hot large skillet. Discard solid remains. Add meat, garlic and 1 1/2 chopped onions. Salt and pepper lightly. Sauté until meat is well-browned and onion translucent. Transfer to cooking pot and add remaining ingredients except for beans. Bring to a boil, reduce heat so chili simmers with lid ajar for 1 1/2 hours, stirring about every 20 minutes. Add more water if chili is too thick and more tomato sauce to adjust red color. Add beans now, if you wish, and continue simmering another 1/2 hour. If you like your chili with slightly more authority, carefully add more chili powder. Be generous with cumin seed. Skim off any excess grease and stir in a bit more chili powder just before serving to enhance rich aroma. Offer remainder of chopped onion as garnish.

This old, handed-down family recipe for Texas-style chili has been praised by chili heads, or connoisseurs, far and wide. In 1976, it received the coveted Cordon Bleu Award of The Wine and Food Society of London, La Jolla Chapter. For really world-class chili, a few secrets must be shared: Buy the least expensive cut of beef, e.g., shoulder or neck or chuck; dice, (don't grind) into small pieces about half the size of the first joint of your little finger; brown in rendered kidney suet in which you also sauté the garlic and onion; instead of ground cumin powder, use whole cumin seeds rubbed between the palms of your hands; allow freshly crushed seeds to fall into pot and when you think you have used enough cumin, add some more. The rest is a cinch. Chili is even better when refrigerated overnight and reheated but it may be necessary to reconstitute with a little water.

William Black
Parent, Alexandra Black Narasin '86

Pap Pap's Chili for 500!

Serves 500

INGREDIENTS:

18 pounds dried cooked pinto beans, or 120 cans
1 cup salt
9 pounds oil for browning
100 pounds chopped lean meat
6 pounds flour
1 1/2 cups salt

48 pounds onions, chopped
90 cloves garlic, minced
8 1/2 cups chili powder
6 ounces comino powder
48 15-ounce cans Ro-tel tomatoes and chiles
4 gallons tomato paste

PROCEDURE:

If using dried beans, cook beans with 1 cup salt in a very large pot of water (or several pots). When done, drain beans and reserve. Heat the oil in the pot(s) and brown the meat. Skim off the excess oil. Add the flour and the 1 1/2 cups salt and stir well. Add the onions and garlic and cook until both are limp. Add remainder of ingredients (including beans). Simmer 6 hours.

One year our school needed to raise funds for several projects which were in danger. My parents had the idea that if volunteers would come together and cook for a week, a Saturday night chili dinner would save the day. And so they came. Wednesday night they chopped and chopped, Thursday night they sautéed, Friday night they fried the meat and opened the cans. All night Friday and Saturday they stirred and stirred! By dinnertime on Saturday everything was ready and hauled into the school gym. What a successful fund raiser. The love that went into that chili. My parents knew that the success of our education rested on their participation in any way they could. With fond and devoted memories, I submit this recipe in hopes there will always be chili dinners for good causes.

Submitted in loving memory of my father, Dr. Richard A. Martin.

Lynn Martin Gaylord
Parent, Charlie Gaylord '96

Marilyn's Meatballs

Serves 6

INGREDIENTS:

1 pound lean ground
  beef
2 tablespoons chopped
  parsley
2 slices bread soaked in
  water, squeezed dry
2 eggs
1 15-ounce can spinach
  squeezed dry and
  chopped
2 cloves garlic, minced
  Salt and pepper to
  taste

Flour for coating
  meatballs
Olive oil for sautéing
2 onions, finely chopped
1 tablespoon chili
  powder
1 tablespoon flour
1/4 pound fresh
  mushrooms, sliced
2 8-ounce cans tomato
  sauce

PROCEDURE:

Preheat oven to 400°. Mix together (with your hands) the beef, parsley, bread, eggs, spinach, garlic, salt and pepper and shape lightly into golf size balls. Roll lightly in flour and brown in hot olive oil in a frying pan. Put cooked balls into a 3 to 4-quart casserole. In the same frying pan sauté the onions with the chili powder that has been mixed with the 1 tablespoon flour. Cook over medium heat, stirring occasionally until onions are translucent. Then add the sliced mushrooms, 2 cans tomato sauce and 2 cans water. Mix well, heat to a simmer and pour sauce over meat balls. Bake for 30 minutes. Serve over cooked rice.

I make this a day ahead as I feel the flavors blend better.

Pat Warner Mitchell '45

Meatballs with Beer Sauce

Serves 4 to 6

INGREDIENTS:

1/4 cup olive oil
1 package onion soup
   mix
1 12-ounce can beer
1 cup (1/2 pint) sour
   cream
   Brown rice for 4 to 6

Meatballs:
2 pounds ground beef
1/2 cup bread crumbs
1 clove chopped garlic
1 teaspoon Worcester-
   shire sauce
1/2 teaspoon pepper
2 tablespoons chopped
   onion

PROCEDURE:

Combine meatball ingredients, mix well and form into about 30 meatballs. Heat olive oil in electric frying pan at 325°. Add meatballs and brown, turning often. Drain off fat. Sprinkle onion soup mix over meatballs, add the beer, cover and simmer 10 minutes. Remove the meatballs to a bowl. Add sour cream to frying pan and heat until blended. Serve the meatballs and the beer sauce over the brown rice.

This recipe was given to me back in the late 1950's by Ann Irvine Lounsberry who is now deceased. She was student body president 1950-51 and my dear friend.

Shirley Nash '51

Swedish Meatballs

Serves 4

INGREDIENTS:

1 cup fine dry bread
   crumbs
1 cup milk
1 onion, finely grated
1 teaspoon salt
1/8 teaspoon nutmeg
1/8 teaspoon ginger
1/4 teaspoon pepper

1 egg
1 1/2 pounds ground beef
   Oil for frying
1 10-ounce can tomato
   soup
1 14-ounce can beef
   bouillon

PROCEDURE:

To make bread crumbs: Dry sliced bread in oven turned to lowest setting until thoroughly dry (several hours or overnight). Grind finely.

Preheat oven to 325°. Mix bread crumbs and milk. Add onion, seasonings and egg. Mix with meat and shape into medium size balls. Brown in oil (1/8" deep in frying pan) and remove to casserole. Mix the tomato soup with the beef bouillon. Pour over meatballs. Cover and bake for 30 minutes. Uncover and continue cooking for 30 minutes more.

You may use prepared bread crumbs but I prefer to make my own. (It is best to make them the day before.)

Lucy Kable Means Borsenberger '69
Parent, Artie Means '94 and Chris Means '96

Hamburger Stroganoff

Serves 6

INGREDIENTS:

2 tablespoons cooking
oil
1 pound ground beef
1/2 cup chopped onions
1/2 teaspoon salt
1/4 teaspoon pepper

1 8-ounce can
mushrooms (stems
and pieces) with
liquid
2 tablespoons flour
1 10-ounce can cream of
mushroom soup
1 cup (1/2 pint) sour
cream

PROCEDURE:

Heat the cooking oil in a frying pan. Add ground beef (crumbled in small pieces) and chopped onion. Cook until well-browned, adding more oil to prevent sticking. Add salt, pepper and mushrooms (with liquid). Stir in flour and cream of mushroom soup. Mix thoroughly. Cook slowly for 20 minutes. Add sour cream. Heat and serve.

Serve on cooked rice or mashed potatoes. Can be made ahead and heated.

Mrs. Frances L. Thompson
Grandparent, Summer Thompson '97

Johnny Wamsutta

Serves 6 to 8

INGREDIENTS:

1 pound ground
  hamburger meat
4 large yellow onions,
  chopped
3 10-ounce cans tomato
  soup
1 1/2 tablespoons Worcestershire sauce
3 to 4 dashes Tabasco sauce

6 ounces very thin
  noodles
1/2 pound American or
  mild cheddar cheese,
  grated
Grated Parmesan
  cheese to sprinkle on
  top, if desired

PROCEDURE:

Preheat oven to 350°. In a large heavy pot brown ground meat; drain off excess fat. Add chopped onions and let simmer 30 minutes. Add tomato soup, Worcestershire sauce and Tabasco. Let mixture simmer 1 hour. Cook noodles in 6 cups lightly salted water until tender. Add to hamburger mixture. Then add cheese. Place in 9" x 13" pan. Bake for 30 minutes, covered. Remove cover at end of baking time and sprinkle with Parmesan cheese. Allow to finish cooking until bubbly.

This can be made ahead and frozen. I usually serve with a lettuce salad and garlic bread. Great for football parties.

Nancy Mann VanDervoort '32

Hamburger Casserole

Serves 4

INGREDIENTS:

1 1/2 pounds ground beef
1/2 cup onion, chopped
8 ounces tomato sauce
2 teaspoons chili powder
Garlic salt (to taste)
Spray cooking oil

1 8-ounce can
buttermilk biscuits
(10 to 12)
2 cups cheddar cheese,
shredded
1/2 cup sour cream
1 egg, beaten

PROCEDURE:

Preheat oven to 375°. Brown beef and onion over medium heat in frying pan. Drain fat from pan. Add tomato sauce, chili powder and garlic salt. Simmer this mixture over low heat, stirring occasionally. Spray a 9" x 9" casserole dish with cooking oil. Open biscuits and separate into halves. Place bottom halves of biscuits on bottom of dish leaving top halves for later. Combine 1 cup of the cheese with the sour cream and egg in a bowl and mix well. Stir this mixture in with the beef until cheese starts melting over very low heat. Spoon beef mixture over biscuits in dish. Place the rest of biscuits on top to cover beef. Sprinkle the remaining 1 cup of cheese over the biscuits. Bake for 30 minutes or until biscuits are light brown.

You should mince onions finely if serving to children. They love this dish. And it's easy to make.

Alexandra Helm '71

301

Daddy's Favorite Casserole

Serves 4

INGREDIENTS:

1 pound ground beef
1 small onion, chopped (optional)
4 ounces noodles
1 10-ounce can cream of mushroom soup
1 8-ounce can whole kernel corn

1 2.25-ounce can chopped ripe olives (optional)
12 Ritz crackers, crumbled
1/2 cup grated cheddar cheese (optional)

PROCEDURE:

Preheat oven to 350°. Brown ground meat and onion together. At the same time cook noodles according to package directions. Layer in 1 1/2-quart casserole dish: Noodles, 1/2 the meat, mushroom soup, corn (drained), chopped olives, remaining meat and crumbled crackers. Bake for 1 hour. Sprinkle grated cheese on top after removing from oven.

Freezes well. When freezing, I bake it for 30 minutes, cool and freeze. On thawing, bake for another 30 to 45 minutes.

Virginia Eikel
Grandparent, Catherine Eikel '97

Johnny Marzetti

Serves 8 to 10

INGREDIENTS:

1/2 pound mushrooms, sliced
2 onions, finely chopped
1 green pepper, finely chopped
1 stalk celery, finely chopped
1 pound lean ground beef
1 pound lean ground pork

1 28-ounce can tomatoes
1 6-ounce can tomato paste
1 10-ounce can tomato soup
1 pound fresh fettucini noodles
3/4 pound New York sharp cheddar cheese, grated

PROCEDURE:

Preheat oven to 325°. Sauté mushrooms, onions, pepper and celery. Add meat and brown. Then add tomatoes, tomato paste and tomato soup. Stir to blend well, then turn off heat. Boil noodles according to package directions, then drain. Combine noodles, meat mixture and the cheese, saving some cheese for garnishing on top. Pour mixture into 10" x 14" casserole dish and sprinkle reserved cheese on top. Bake for 1 hour.

Great Midwestern dish. Perfect with a salad and crusty bread on a cold night. Freezes well.

Galen Cooper
Parent, Tyler Cooper '96X and Megan Cooper '98

Mexican Casserole

Serves 6

INGREDIENTS:

- **1 pound ground beef or turkey**
- **1 10-ounce can "hot" enchilada sauce (milder sauce may be used to suit individual taste)**
- **1 package dry spicy taco seasoning**

- **1/2 pound cheddar cheese, diced**
- **1 16-ounce can refried beans**
- **Tortilla chips or tortillas, shredded lettuce, chopped tomatoes and avocados**

PROCEDURE:

Brown ground beef or turkey in saucepan. Drain off any fat. Add enchilada sauce and taco seasoning. Blend well. Add cheese and refried beans. Stir frequently over low heat to avoid scorching while cheese melts. Can be served over tortilla chips topped with shredded lettuce and chopped tomatoes and avocados. Or use as a filling in corn or flour tortillas that can be rolled burrito style.

This dish was popular in my home because it was simple and the ingredients could be kept on hand, so my boys could make it easily. Leftovers microwave well.

Suzanne Baral Weiner
Staff, Director of Public Relations and Marketing

303

Haystacks

Serves 4

INGREDIENTS:

1 pound hamburger
1/2 onion, diced
1 clove garlic, minced
1 6-ounce can tomato
    paste
1 teaspoon chili powder
    Salt to taste
1 teaspoon oregano
1 teaspoon cumin
1 15-ounce can tomato
    sauce

1 cup water
2 teaspoons sugar

1 medium package
    tortilla or corn chips
    Optional toppings:
    Grated cheese, olives,
    avocado, tomato, sour
    cream

PROCEDURE:

In a large skillet brown the hamburger meat. Add onion and garlic and sauté with the meat. Add the next 8 ingredients and simmer 1/2 hour. If it looks too dry, add a little more water, but the mixture should be thick.

To serve, spoon mixture over chips. Serve with your choice of toppings.

Your kids will love this. My kids choose this for birthday dinners every year.

Betsy Gill Sherman '65

Cornish Pasties

Serves 6

INGREDIENTS:

Pie dough (homemade
or frozen), enough for
12 6" circles
36 1" cubes of sirloin
    steak
1 1/2 cups finely chopped
    raw potatoes
1 1/2 cups finely chopped
    carrots

1 1/2 cups finely chopped
    onions
3 tablespoons butter
    Salt and pepper to
    taste
6 teaspoons water

PROCEDURE:

Preheat oven to 350°. Roll out enough pie dough to make 6 6" circles. Fill half of each circle with 6 small cubes of steak, 1/4 cup each of potatoes, carrots and onions. Cover with 1/2 teaspoon butter. Sprinkle with salt and pepper as desired. Sprinkle with 1 teaspoon of water. Roll out the remaining pie dough and cut 6 more 6" circles. Cover the filled circles and seal edges with fork moistened with water. Prick top of each to let out steam. Bake on greased cookie sheet for 30 to 35 minutes or until pie crust is golden brown.

Served with tossed green salad.

Mary Barkalow Joyce '34

Marinade for Leg of Lamb

Yields marinade for 4 to 5 pounds leg of lamb

INGREDIENTS:

1 4 to 5-pound leg of lamb, boned and butterflied	1/2 teaspoon ginger
	1/4 teaspoon pepper
1 clove garlic, split	2 tablespoons chutney
1 1/2 teaspoons salt	1/3 cup fresh lemon juice
1 teaspoon curry powder	2/3 cup salad oil

PROCEDURE:

Lay lamb out flat and rub cut garlic all over surface (reserving garlic). Mix together all spices (salt, curry, reserved ginger and pepper). Rub spices into lamb. Place lamb in a shallow pan. Chop solid pieces of chutney, crush garlic and combine with lemon juice and salad oil. Pour over lamb. Cover lamb and marinate <u>overnight</u> in refrigerator, turning when the spirit moves you. Grill lamb on barbecue. Heat any remaining marinade and pour over the lamb before serving.

Because of the unevenness of a butterflied lamb, you will end up with pink to well-done slices. Slice on the diagonal in 1/4" to 1/2" cuts and pour marinade over meat prior to presentation.

Gordon R. "Zeke" Knight
Staff, Director of Development

Lamb

Serves 8

INGREDIENTS:

**4 to 5 pound lamb rump half
(part without bone)
Margarine to rub over
lamb
Flour
Thyme**

**1 10-ounce can cream of
mushroom soup or
cream of celery soup
1 10-ounce can jellied
consommé
1/2 teaspoon curry powder
1 clove garlic, diced
1/2 cup red wine**

PROCEDURE:

Preheat oven to 300°. Wash lamb and dry with paper towels. Rub lamb thoroughly with margarine then pat (top and bottom) with flour and thyme. In a bowl mix the cream of mushroom soup (or cream of celery soup), consommé, curry powder, garlic and wine. Put lamb in a deep casserole dish with a tight fitting lid (can add foil around edges of pan so lid is tight). Pour mixture over the lamb, then cover and bake for 2 1/2 to 3 hours. Serve over rice or noodles.

Lamb and Zucchini Casserole (see recipe, page 335) go well together.

Suzy Comer McFall '72

Chili Leg of Lamb

Serves 8

INGREDIENTS:

1 6 to 7-pound leg of
   lamb (American)
2 tablespoons flour
2 to 4 tablespoons red chili
   powder (New Mexico
   Chimayo or Hatch,
   preferred)
1 teaspoon salt

Gravy:
Flour and water to
  thicken
Salt and pepper

PROCEDURE:

Preheat oven to 325°. Mix flour, chili powder and salt together and rub half on 1 side of leg of lamb. Insert meat thermometer into fleshiest part of leg, making certain it does not touch bone. Place the lamb, coated side up, into on open roasting pan. (Some people use a rack to hold the lamb; it's your choice.) Pour about 1" of water into the pan. Cook for 1 hour, then turn lamb over and rub remaining mix on other side and finish roasting (about 30 minutes more). Add water as needed to keep level at 1/2" to 1". Cook until thermometer reads 170° for well-done, 150° for medium-rare. Or, cook 13 to 15 minutes per pound for well-done, 10 to 12 minutes per pound for medium-rare.

Remove lamb and make stove top chili gravy in the pan. Thicken "leavin's" with flour and water. Stir over medium-high heat until gravy cooks down and thickens to desired consistency. (Gravy should not be too thick.) Season to taste with salt and pepper.

This New Mexico recipe is a family special and is at least 100 years old. Serve with rice (a great combination).

G. Williams Rutherford
Former Trustee and
Parent, Amanda Rutherford May '68, Tim Rutherford '71 (San Miguel),
George Rutherford '70 (San Miguel)
Grandparent, Anna Gwyn May '95, Ryan Paros '95,
Christopher Rutherford '98, Abigail Rutherford '00

Pennsylvania Sauerkraut and Pork

Serves 4

INGREDIENTS:

  1 3-pound pork loin
    roast
32 ounces sauerkraut
1/2 cup water
  1 apple, pared and thinly
    sliced

PROCEDURE:

Preheat oven to 350°. Place pork in medium size roasting pan. Lightly rinse sauerkraut to get rid of some of the brine. Place sauerkraut and water around pork in pan. Place pared thinly sliced apple over sauerkraut. Cover and bake in oven for 3 1/2 to 4 hours.

Serve with mashed potatoes and applesauce. Great for family dinner on a cool evening.

Mary B. Delhamer
Grandparent, Brent Delhamer '98

Crown Roast of Pork

Serves 16 to 24

INGREDIENTS:

1 crown roast pork (16
   to 24 ribs)
Salt and pepper

Stuffing:
1 cup chopped onions
1/2 cup chopped celery
   (optional)
1/3 cup butter, melted
3 cups peeled and
   chopped apples

1 cup yellow raisins,
   soaked in warm water
   for 15 minutes
2/3 pound lean sausage,
   crumbled and cooked
6 cups pulled bread
   crumbs
1 teaspoon each
   cinnamon, thyme,
   nutmeg and mace
1 teaspoon salt

PROCEDURE:

Have butcher trim a rack of pork and prepare in a crown. The size may vary from 16 ribs to 24. The latter makes a beautiful presentation for a holiday party and serves 24.

Preheat oven to 450°. Cover bone ends to prevent from burning. Rub with salt and pepper. Place pork crown on a foil-lined pan to enable transfer to platter for serving. Put in 450° oven and reduce to 350°. Roast 20 minutes per pound or until interior temperature is 150° (for medium-rare). Prepare stuffing (see instructions below) while roasting, then remove roast from oven, stuff center and continue roasting. Usual roasting time is 2 to 2 1/2 hours. Baste a few times. Extra stuffing can be placed in covered casserole and heated 1/2 hour.

Stuffing: In a skillet sauté onion and celery lightly in 3 tablespoons of the butter. Place apples, raisins, sausage and bread crumbs in a large mixing bowl. Add sautéed onion/celery mixture, seasonings and remaining butter and toss to combine. Taste for seasonings. Follow instructions above for cooking.

Anne Otterson
Parent, Eric Otterson '87 and Helen Otterson '89

Ham 'n Turkey Pastry Puff

Serves 4 to 6

INGREDIENTS:

1 1/2 cups cubed cooked
    turkey
   1 4-ounce package
    sliced ham
   1 cup grated Swiss
    cheese
1/4 cup green onion
1/4 cup mayonnaise
1/2 teaspoon dry mustard

1 teaspoon garlic salt
1/2 teaspoon Worcester-
    shire sauce
1 17-ounce package
    frozen puff pastry
Egg wash prepared
    with 1 egg mixed
    with 1 teaspoon
    water

PROCEDURE:

Preheat oven to 450°. In blender or food processor, mince turkey and ham. Place in medium bowl with grated Swiss cheese and green onion. Blend with mayonnaise, mustard, garlic salt and Worcestershire sauce; set aside.

Thaw pastry dough for 20 minutes; unfold sheets. On lightly floured board, roll dough to remove creases. Using a 9" cake pan as a guide, cut circles from each sheet of dough.

Place 1 circle on ungreased cookie sheet; prick with fork. Mound turkey mixture in center of dough, leaving 1 1/2" of dough showing at edge of circle. Place other circle of pastry dough on top, stretching gently to cover turkey mixture and to meet edges at bottom. Seal edges together with light brushing of cold water. Poke hole in the top of center of mound to let steam escape during cooking.

To decorate: Scallop outer edges of circle with a sharp knife. Brush top of entire pastry puff with egg wash. Do not seal edges at bottom with egg mix or pastry will not puff as well. Allow to set briefly and repeat the egg wash. Avoiding cutting all the way through the dough, with sharp knife lightly score mound with 7 lines starting in center and going to edges in spoke fashion.

Bake for 15 minutes. Turn oven down to 400° and continue cooking another 15 minutes. Allow to cool for 10 minutes before serving.

This is a wonderful party recipe that looks difficult but is easy. I serve hot gravy and a Caesar salad with it. I usually make ahead and freeze and then add egg wash and put holes in top just before baking.

Joan Kibbey Taylor '40

Ham and Cheese Turnovers

Serves 35

INGREDIENTS:

Crust:
2 1/2 tablespoons yeast
5 cups warm water
3 tablespoons sugar
2 1/2 tablespoons salt
7 1/2 cups white flour
7 1/2 cups wheat flour
Oil

Filling:
Prepared pizza sauce
2 1/2 pounds ham, thinly
sliced
2 1/2 pounds, mozzarella
cheese, thinly sliced

Egg wash:
1 egg
1/4 cup milk

PROCEDURE:

In a 20-quart mixing bowl, combine yeast, water and sugar. Using a dough hook, add salt, white and wheat flours. Beat for 7 to 10 minutes. Place dough in an oiled bowl and let rise until doubled, about 1 hour. Roll out dough about 1/4" thick. Cut into 6" rounds. Place 1 tablespoon sauce, 1 ounce ham and 1 ounce cheese on 1 side of each round. Fold each round in half, pressing edges together to seal. Place turnovers on greased sheet pans and let rest for 30 minutes or until ready to bake.

Preheat oven to 450°. Combine the egg and milk for the egg wash. Brush over turnovers. Bake until browned.

This recipe won First Prize in the 1984 California Milk Advisory Board's school food service achievement awards competition.

Sara Sweet
Staff, Director of Food Service

Vegetarian Main Courses

Two-tone Luncheon Cheesecake

Serves 10

INGREDIENTS:

1 1/3 cups bread crumbs
5 tablespoons butter, melted
3 8-ounce packages of cream cheese, softened
1/4 cup heavy cream
1/2 teaspoon salt
1/4 teaspoon nutmeg
1/4 teaspoon cayenne pepper
4 eggs
1 cup shredded Swiss cheese

1 10-ounce package frozen chopped spinach, thawed and squeezed dry
2 1/2 tablespoons minced green onions
3 tablespoons butter
1 pound mushrooms, finely chopped
Salt and pepper to taste

PROCEDURE:

Preheat oven to 350°. Mix the bread crumbs and butter and press into the bottom and sides of a 9" spring form pan. Bake for 10 minutes. Cool.

Reset oven to 325°. Beat the cream cheese, cream, salt, nutmeg and cayenne together until smooth. Beat in the eggs, 1 at a time. Divide the cream cheese mixture between two bowls. Stir the Swiss cheese into 1 bowl and the spinach and green onions into the other. Pour the spinach filling into the cooled crust. Sauté the mushrooms in the butter for a few minutes until their moisture has evaporated. Spoon over the spinach filling. Pour the cheese filling over the mushrooms.

Bake the cheesecake for 1 1/4 hours. Turn the oven off and cool in the oven with the door ajar for 1 hour. Serve at room temperature.

The wedges of cheesecake may be served with a little fresh tomato sauce to add color. This is an impressive dish to offer at a picnic, too.

Molly Hannan
Parent, Mimi Hannan '92

Hearty Vegetarian Casserole

Serves 6 to 8

INGREDIENTS:

2 tablespoons butter
4 cloves garlic, crushed
1 cup chopped onion
1 cup sliced mushrooms
4 potatoes, boiled and mashed
1/2 medium cabbage, sliced and steamed lightly
1 cup cooked chick peas (garbanzo beans)
1 cup (1/2 pint) yogurt

2 tablespoons poppy seeds
1 tablespoon dill seeds
1 tablespoon celery seeds
1/4 cup chopped fresh parsley
1/2 teaspoon salt
1/2 teaspoon pepper
3/4 cup grated cheddar cheese

PROCEDURE:

Preheat oven to 350°. Grease a 3-quart casserole. Melt the butter in a skillet over medium-high heat and sauté garlic, onion and mushrooms. In a large bowl mix potatoes and cabbage. Stir in chick peas and garlic/mushroom/onion mixture. Stir in yogurt, then add seeds, parsley, salt and pepper and turn into casserole. Sprinkle cheese on top and bake for 30 minutes or until cheese is bubbly and casserole sizzles.

This is delicious and filling; good as leftovers, too. There are many good taste contrasts in this recipe.

Natasha Halpert
Aunt, Alura Simpkins '90 and Alex Simpkins '96

Eggplant Veggie Casserole

Serves 8

INGREDIENTS:

1 medium eggplant,
  cubed
3 green peppers, cubed
3 large tomatoes, cut up
1 large or 2 medium
  onions, coarsely
  chopped

1 teaspoon sugar
Salt and pepper to
  taste
Herb seasonings (your
  favorite)
8 ounces cheddar or
  Monterey jack cheese

PROCEDURE:

Preheat oven to 400°. Layer vegetables in order listed in a 10" x 14" casserole dish. Sprinkle with sugar and seasonings. Cube the cheese and layer on top. Cover casserole and bake for 30 minutes. Uncover casserole and lower oven to 350°. Bake another 30 minutes or until done. A golden sauce forms on the bottom.

Eggplant is the base, but this can also be made with zucchini or crookneck squash. Avoid mushrooms as they contain too much liquid. Can use canned tomatoes in a pinch.

Karin F. Donaldson
Parent, Christopher Donaldson, '93 and Leslie Donaldson '95

Linguine with Spinach and Beans

Serves 6

INGREDIENTS:

8 ounces uncooked
   linguine
1/4 cup olive oil
1/2 cup chopped onion
2 cloves garlic, minced
1/4 teaspoon red pepper
   flakes
1/4 cup water
1/4 teaspoon chicken
   bouillon granules

1 10-ounce box frozen
   spinach (thawed and
   squeezed dry)
1 15-ounce can Mexi-
   beans
1/4 cup grated Parmesan
   cheese

PROCEDURE:

Cook linguine according to package instructions. In a large skillet heat oil over medium heat. Add onion, garlic and red pepper flakes. Cook, stirring often, until onion is softened. Add water and bouillon granules stirring until bouillon is dissolved. Add spinach and beans. Stir and cook for 3 to 4 minutes to heat through. Toss with hot drained linguine. Sprinkle with Parmesan cheese.

A great way to get kids to eat greens. One can red kidney beans, drained, can be substituted for Mexi-beans.

Keggie Gillmor Mallett '63

Puja's Rumbledethumbs

Serves 8 to 10

INGREDIENTS:

4 large potatoes, cooked
  with skins on and
  mashed
1 cabbage, coarsely
  chopped and cooked
  until just tender
1 cup milk
1/4 cup butter or
  margarine, softened
1 large onion, chopped

1 cup cottage cheese
2 to 3 cups grated cheddar
  cheese
2 teaspoons dried
  parsley
1 teaspoon pepper
1 tablespoon caraway
  seeds
2 tablespoons
  horseradish

PROCEDURE:

Preheat oven to 350°. Grease a 2-quart casserole. Reserving half the grated
cheese for the top, mix all the ingredients together and place in the casserole.
Sprinkle the cheese on top and bake for 30 to 40 minutes. You will know when
it is done because it will be bubbling and the cheese will be melted and crispy
around the edges. Should it brown too fast, cover it.

*Originally a Scottish dish, this has counterparts in every folk tradition. It's delicious
and will please even those who don't like cabbage much.*

*Natasha Halpert
Aunt, Alura Simpkins '90 and Alex Simpkins '96*

Herbed Tomatoes, Swiss Chard and Potatoes Parmigiano

Serves 8

INGREDIENTS:

1 to 2 potatoes (3/4 pound)
1 tablespoon extra virgin olive oil
4 cloves garlic, finely minced
1/2 teaspoon crushed red pepper
1/2 teaspoon dried oregano

1 28-ounce can whole Italian plum tomatoes, with liquid
2 pounds Swiss chard (red or white)
2 to 4 tablespoons freshly grated Parmigiano-Reggiano

PROCEDURE:

Scrub potatoes, leave skins on and cut into 1" cubes. Steam potatoes for about 25 minutes or until tender. Pour the olive oil into a large sauté pan. Add garlic and crushed red pepper and cook over low heat for 10 minutes, stirring occasionally to prevent burning. Do not turn the heat up too high. Be patient! Add oregano and tomatoes, with liquid, breaking the tomatoes apart with your fingers as you go. Cook over medium-high heat until thickened, about 10 minutes. Wash Swiss chard well. Cut off the main stems and discard. Chop the leaves into bite size pieces. When the tomato sauce is thickened, add Swiss chard and potatoes. Cover pan and simmer 10 minutes. Check a few times and stir. Sprinkle the cheese over the vegetables. Cover so the cheese will melt. Serve immediately.

Lesa Heebner
Friend, Summer Thompson '97

318

Swift Summer Squash Casserole

Serves 4

INGREDIENTS:

- 2 pounds summer squash (young and thin)
- 2 cups large curd cottage cheese
- 1 tablespoon dried basil (or 1/4 cup chopped fresh)

- 2 tablespoons dried parsley (or 1/4 cup chopped fresh)
- Salt and pepper to taste
- 2 cups grated cheddar or Swiss cheese
- 1 tablespoon paprika

PROCEDURE:

Preheat oven to 350° (if cooking immediately). Grease a 2-quart casserole.
Lightly steam summer squash. Slice lengthwise in 1/4" to 1/2" slices. Then cut
at 3" intervals. Layer half of squash in greased casserole. Add cottage cheese
and spread evenly. Top with remaining squash, basil and parsley. Season with
salt and pepper. Cover with grated cheese and sprinkle paprika on top. Bake for
20 to 30 minutes or refrigerate to bake later, allowing some extra time if casserole
is cold when it goes into the oven.

*Easy to make and can be prepared ahead and held uncooked until needed. For a
tasty "non-meat" dinner, you might like this with a salad and a quick bread.*

Natasha Halpert
Aunt, Alura Simpkins '90 and Alex Simpkins '96

Vegetarian Chili I

Serves 6

INGREDIENTS:

2 tablespoons olive or cooking oil
1 1/2 cups chopped celery
1 1/2 cups chopped green peppers
1 cup chopped onion
3 cloves garlic, minced

2 28-ounce cans cut up tomatoes, undrained
3 16-ounce cans red kidney beans, rinsed and drained
1/2 cup raisins
1/4 cup red wine vinegar
1 tablespoon chili powder
1 tablespoon snipped parsley

2 teaspoons salt
1 1/2 teaspoons dried basil, crushed
1 1/2 teaspoons dried oregano, crushed
1 1/2 teaspoons ground cumin
1 teaspoon ground allspice
1/4 teaspoon pepper
1 bay leaf
1 12-ounce can beer
3/4 cup cashews
1 cup shredded Swiss, mozzarella or cheddar cheese

PROCEDURE:

Heat oil in a 4 1/2-quart pot. Add celery, green pepper, onion and garlic. Cook covered until vegetables are tender, but not browned. Stir in undrained tomatoes, drained beans, raisins, vinegar, chili powder, parsley, salt, basil, oregano, cumin, allspice, pepper and bay leaf. Bring to boil. Reduce heat and simmer, covered, for 1 1/2 hours. Stir in beer and cashews. Return to boil. Simmer on low heat for 30 minutes or until chili is desired consistency. Remove bay leaf. Sprinkle cheese on top of each serving.

Serve with cornbread during a Sunday N.F.L. game.

Susanna Smith
Parent, Troy Smith '97 and Adam Smith '98

Vegetarian Chili II

Serves 8

INGREDIENTS:

2 tablespoons corn oil
2 cups chopped onions
3 cloves garlic, chopped
2 tablespoons chili powder
1 teaspoon ground cumin
1 cup diced carrots
1 green pepper, diced
2 14-ounce cans chopped tomatoes, undrained

1 15-ounce can garbanzo beans, drained
1 15-ounce can kidney beans, drained
1 11-ounce can corn niblets, drained
A few drops Tabasco or hot pepper sauce

PROCEDURE:

In a 5-quart saucepan, heat oil and cook onions, garlic, chili powder and cumin for 2 to 3 minutes, stirring well. Add carrots and green peppers; sauté for 2 minutes. Add tomatoes, garbanzo beans, kidney beans, corn and Tabasco or hot pepper sauce. Bring to boil. Reduce heat and simmer, covered, stirring occasionally, for 30 to 40 minutes.

Serve with crackers, over rice or in pita pockets. Makes a good meal with a tossed green salad. Freezes well.

Nancy Minus
Grandparent, Dana Young '87 and David Young '96

Lentil Chili

Serves 4

INGREDIENTS:

2 tablespoons canola oil
2 onions, chopped
2 celery sticks, sliced
2 cloves garlic, chopped
1 teaspoon paprika
1/4 teaspoon chili powder
  (or more to taste)
6 ounces green lentils
1 6-ounce can tomato
  paste

1 14-ounce can chopped
  tomatoes
2 cups water
1 red bell pepper, seeded
  and chopped
Salt to taste
1 15-ounce can red
  kidney beans, drained
2 tablespoons chopped
  parsley, plus extra for
  garnish

PROCEDURE:

Heat oil in a large pan and gently sauté the onion and celery until softened. Add the garlic, paprika and chili powder and continue to cook for 1 more minute. Add the lentils, tomato paste, tomatoes, water and red pepper with salt to taste. Cover and simmer gently for about 50 minutes. Add the drained kidney beans and parsley and cook for another 10 minutes or until lentils are tender. Sprinkle with parsley and serve.

Brown rice or French rolls are good accompaniments. A vegetarian dish we all enjoy.

Jane Lamb
Parent, Catherine Lamb '88 and William Lamb '94

"Chaco Chili"
(New Mexican Vegetable Stew)

Serves 3 to 5

INGREDIENTS:

3 to 4 tablespoons canola oil
1 large onion, chopped
1 green bell pepper,
    chopped
1 red bell pepper,
    chopped
4 to 6 cloves garlic, minced
2 small zucchini, sliced
2 small yellow squash,
    sliced
2 small carrots, sliced
2 teaspoons cumin
    powder (or more to
    taste)
2 tablespoons red chili
    powder (or more to
    taste)

1/2 teaspoon oregano
1 28-ounce can (3 cups)
    whole tomatoes,
    undrained
2 cups cooked garbanzo
    or kidney beans
2 cups fresh or frozen
    corn

    Fresh cornbread or hot
    brown rice
    Grated cheddar cheese
    Sour cream for
    topping

PROCEDURE:

Heat oil in a large, heavy pot over medium heat and sauté onion, peppers, garlic,
squashes and carrots in oil until colors deepen, 5 minutes or so. Add seasonings
(cumin, chili powder and oregano) and allow to "cook in", stirring for 2 to 3
minutes. Add tomatoes with their liquid (break up with spoon). Add beans and
corn and simmer for 30 minutes over low heat. Adjust seasonings. Serve over
hot corn bread or brown rice, with grated cheese and a dollop of sour cream on
top.

*Keeps well in refrigerator for a week or so. Reheat and serve as suggested. Quick
and easy, but flavor does improve overnight.*

Roberta Susanna Young '63

Flat (Mimidaddy) Enchiladas

Serves 4

INGREDIENTS:

2 to 4 cups prepared
    enchilada sauce
2 tablespoons chili
    powder
1/2 teaspoon salt
1/2 teaspoon pepper
1 teaspoon garlic powder
1/2 teaspoon cumin

1 onion, chopped
1/2 head lettuce
2 to 4 cups grated sharp
    cheddar cheese
4 tablespoons oil
4 eggs
12 corn tortillas

PROCEDURE:

Make enchilada sauce: Pour the enchilada sauce into saucepan and heat. Spice up canned sauce with chili, salt, pepper, garlic powder and cumin. (Use other spices if you want.)

Chop onion and lettuce and put on separate plates. Grate cheese and put on another plate. Heat 2 tablespoons of oil in 2 frying pans (1 for tortillas and 1 to fry eggs).

Construct enchilada as follows: (All may be cooked just before the meal by the cook or each person eating can cook his own.) Heat 1 tortilla in oil for 30 seconds, dip in enchilada sauce and put on plate. Top each tortilla with onion, lettuce and cheese. Repeat until you have 3 layers of tortilla, onion, lettuce and cheese. Fry egg and put on top. Pour 2 to 3 tablespoons of sauce over the egg. Smaller portions can be made by reducing the number of layers.

This was my grandmother's "authentic" New Mexico recipe which she short cut by using prepared sauce. You can make your own sauce from scratch if you want. Great for teenagers and their friends for a quick party dinner.

Timothy Rutherford '71 San Miguel
Parent, Ryan Paros '95, Christopher Rutherford '98, Abigail Rutherford '00

Tofu Enchiladas

Serves 4 to 5

INGREDIENTS:

1 medium onion,
  chopped
18 ounces tofu
1/2 teaspoon garlic powder
  (more or less to taste)

1 1-pound can enchilada
  sauce
1 pound Monterey jack
  cheese
1 dozen flour tortillas

PROCEDURE:

Preheat oven to 350°. Mash together onion and tofu. Add garlic powder to taste. Mix 1/2 cup of enchilada sauce into tofu mixture. Grate or slice cheese. Grease a 10" x 14" baking pan generously. Hold each tortilla in hand while spooning in 2 tablespoons tofu mixture and cheese. Roll up tortilla and arrange in pan until all tortillas are packed in neatly and close. Pour remainder of enchilada sauce over rolls, making sure to allow sauce to reach between pan and tortillas. Cover with aluminum foil. Bake 1 hour.

This is a great favorite. I serve with salad. Very inexpensive too!

Linda Lyerly Shackelford '64X

Quesadillas

Yields 4

INGREDIENTS:

Spray cooking oil for
    sautéing
2 cups mushrooms,
    chopped
4 ounces Muenster
    cheese, shredded
1/4 cup scallions, chopped

1/4 cup fresh cilantro,
    chopped
1 tablespoon canned
    chopped mild green
    chiles
4 small (6") flour tortillas

PROCEDURE:

Spray large skillet with oil. Sauté mushrooms until lightly browned. Remove and wipe skillet. In small bowl combine mushrooms, cheese, scallions, cilantro and chiles. Divide mixture among 4 tortillas, spreading almost to edges. Fold in half. Spray skillet and sauté filled tortillas until brown. Turn and cook other side.

Yum Yum!

Betty Harrington Dickinson '39

Chiles Rellenos Casserole

Serves 8 to 12

INGREDIENTS:

1 28-ounce can whole
    green chiles
16 ounces Monterey jack
    cheese, grated
16 ounces sharp cheddar
    cheese, grated

5 eggs
1 16-ounce can
    evaporated milk
8 ounces tomato sauce
    or mild salsa

PROCEDURE:

Preheat oven to 350°. Split and layer 1/2 of the chiles in a greased 10" x 14" casserole dish. Sprinkle 1/2 the cheese over chiles. Repeat layers. Beat together the eggs and milk; pour over chiles and cheese. Bake for 30 minutes. Spoon tomato sauce or salsa on top and bake 10 more minutes.

Quick and easy! Great for potlucks.

Lynette Giovanazzi Blakney '64

Easy Baked Chiles Rellenos

Serves 6 to 8

INGREDIENTS:

Butter or margarine
(or vegetable oil
spray) to grease pan
1 7-ounce can whole
green chiles or 3
4-ounce cans chopped
green chiles
2 cups grated cheddar
cheese

6 well-beaten eggs
3/4 cup milk
1/2 cup flour
1/2 teaspoon baking
powder
1/4 teaspoon salt
Sour cream for
topping (optional)

PROCEDURE:

Preheat oven to 450°. Grease (or spray with vegetable oil) a 8" x 12" x 2" baking pan. Place green chiles in layers. Sprinkle cheese on top. Beat eggs, milk, flour, baking powder and salt until well-blended. Pour mixture over cheese and chiles. Bake for 15 to 20 minutes or until puffy and golden brown. Top with cheese or sour cream as desired. Serve hot and enjoy.

Serve with green salad and Mexican corn bread. Quick and easy.

Beverly Harmon Harker '42

Vegetarian Pecan Patties

Yields 12 patties

INGREDIENTS:

6 eggs
2 cups grated American
  or cheddar cheese
1 cup pecans, coarsely
  chopped
1 large onion, finely
  chopped
1/4 teaspoon thyme
1/2 teaspoon sage
1 cup OroWheat
  Seasoned Bread
  Dressing mix

Lawry's Seasoning Salt
  to taste
Pepper to taste
1/2 cup vegetable oil for
  frying

26 ounces prepared
  tomato sauce,
  mushroom gravy or
  Creole sauce

PROCEDURE:

Beat eggs thoroughly and set aside. Grate cheese. Mix eggs, cheese, pecans and onion in a bowl. Add seasonings and mix well. Form into medium size patties. Heat oil in a 12" frying pan. Cook patties over medium-high heat until brown. Add more oil as needed. Drain on paper towels.

Preheat oven to 325°. Place patties in a lightly oiled, shallow 10" x 14" casserole. Cover with tomato sauce, mushroom gravy or Creole sauce. Heat in oven for approximately 20 minutes, until sauce is bubbling.

Freezes well. I serve with baked potatoes and salad.

Mable Olson
Grandparent, Tiffany Hodgens '99

Vegetables & Side Dishes

Sassy Asparagus

Serves 6 to 8

INGREDIENTS:

2 pounds asparagus,
    washed, with bottom
    tough end of stems
    removed
1/3 cup white wine
    vinegar

1/4 cup water
1/3 cup sugar
1/4 teaspoon celery seeds
1 cinnamon stick
3 whole cloves

PROCEDURE:

Steam asparagus until just tender. Blanche in cold water. Drain and place in serving dish. Heat all remaining ingredients in saucepan until sugar dissolves. Pour over drained asparagus. Let stand 2 or 3 hours.

This is a wonderful, easy vegetable dish for the Easter season or for a ladies' luncheon.

Lynn Cassidy
Parent, Tom Cassidy '94

Artichoke Casserole

Serves 6 to 8

INGREDIENTS:

2 15-ounce cans
   artichoke hearts
   (5 to 8 per can)
1 to 2 tablespoons butter
1 onion, peeled and
   chopped
1 8-ounce can
   mushrooms, drained

2 carrots, peeled and
   sliced
1/4 cup chopped fresh
   parsley
   Lawry's Seasoned Salt
   to taste
1 medium size box garlic
   and cheese croutons

PROCEDURE:

Preheat oven to 350°. Cut up artichokes into 4 pieces. Place all vegetables into a buttered 9" x 13" baking dish. Dot with the remaining butter. Sprinkle with fresh parsley. Sprinkle with Lawry's salt and croutons. Bake for 30 minutes or until croutons brown.

Carol Alessio
Parent, Michael Alessio '97 and Annie Alessio '98

Broccoli Cheese Bake

Serves 6 to 8

INGREDIENTS:

1 egg
2/3 cup mayonnaise
1 10-ounce can
   mushroom soup
2 10-ounce packages of
   frozen chopped
   broccoli, thawed and
   drained

1 medium onion, finely
   chopped
1 cup grated Swiss
   cheese
1/2 cup canned French
   fried onions

PROCEDURE:

Preheat oven to 350°. Beat egg slightly. Add mayonnaise and soup and blend. Stir in broccoli, onions and cheese. Pour into a 1 1/2-quart casserole dish. Sprinkle with French fried onions. Bake for about 35 minutes.

Karin F. Donaldson
Parent, Chris Donaldson '93 and Leslie Donaldson '95

Purple Cabbage Sauté

Serves 6

INGREDIENTS:

1 large purple onion, chopped
2 to 6 tablespoons butter
1 large head purple cabbage

1/3 cup balsamic vinegar
1/4 cup brown sugar
Salt and pepper

PROCEDURE:

In a large pan, gently cook onions in 2 tablespoons butter for 5 minutes. Slice cabbage thinly, add to onions and continue cooking for 5 more minutes, stirring occasionally. Add more butter, if desired. Mix vinegar and sugar together and add to cabbage. Cover and simmer for 25 minutes. Taste for flavor and add salt and pepper if desired.

Anne Otterson
Parent, Eric Otterson '87 and Helen Otterson '89

Chili Peas

Serves 6 to 8

INGREDIENTS:

2 slices bacon
3 tablespoons finely
   chopped onion
1 clove garlic, finely
   chopped

1 17-ounce can small
   green peas with liquid
1/2 cup chili sauce
   Pinch oregano
   Pinch cumin

PROCEDURE:

Fry bacon until crisp. Remove from pan, reserving grease and break into small pieces. Sauté onion and garlic in bacon grease. When onion and garlic are browned, place in a medium saucepan with bacon pieces and peas with their liquid. Add chili sauce, oregano and cumin. Let cook slowly about 10 minutes to heat through.

Great complement to meat or fish dinners.

Mary Martin
Grandparent, Jenner Smith '99

Copper Penny Carrots

Serves 8

INGREDIENTS:

2 pounds carrots, peeled
   and thinly sliced
1 small green pepper,
   finely chopped
1 medium onion, finely
   chopped
1 10-ounce can tomato
   soup
1/2 cup sugar

1/2 cup apple cider
   vinegar
1 teaspoon prepared
   mustard
1 teaspoon
   Worcestershire sauce
   Salt and pepper to
   taste

PROCEDURE:

Cook carrots in salted water until medium done. Rinse. Put carrots, green pepper and onions in a bowl. Combine remaining ingredients in a saucepan. Bring to a boil, stirring until well-blended. Pour over carrots and refrigerate overnight. Heat to serve.

Anna Louise Whitehouse White '33

Spinach Casserole

Serves 8

INGREDIENTS:

- 2 10-ounce packages frozen chopped spinach, thawed and well-drained
- 2 cups Pepperidge Farm Stuffing
- 1 large onion, chopped
- 4 eggs, beaten

- 1/2 cup (1 stick) butter or margarine, melted
- 1 teaspoon pepper
- 1/4 teaspoon thyme
- 1/2 cup grated Parmesan cheese
- 1/2 tablespoon garlic salt
- Dash nutmeg

PROCEDURE:

Preheat oven to 350°. Mix together all ingredients (except for nutmeg) until well-combined. Put this mixture in a greased 3 to 4-quart casserole. Sprinkle grated nutmeg over top. Bake for 30 minutes, uncovered.

This recipe can be made ahead. Just increase cooking time if refrigerated. This recipe is a hit, especially with men!

Pat Warner Mitchell '45

Yellow Squash Casserole

Serves 8

INGREDIENTS:

2 1/2 pounds yellow or white
    squash
1 medium onion, thinly
    sliced
2 hard-boiled eggs,
    chopped

1/2 cup butter or
    margarine, softened
1/4 cup half and half
    Salt and pepper to
    taste
15 soda crackers

PROCEDURE:

Preheat oven to 350°. Wash and slice squash. Cook with thinly sliced onion in boiling water until tender. Drain well. Cream squash, onion, eggs, 1/4 cup of the butter and the half and half. Add salt and pepper to taste. Spoon into greased round (7" or 8" diameter) soufflé-type casserole dish. Crumble crackers and mix with remaining 1/4 cup of butter. Sprinkle over top of squash mixture. Bake for 30 to 35 minutes.

Mary Eikel
Parent, Catherine Eikel '97

Thanksgiving Onions

Serves 6

INGREDIENTS:

3 16-ounce cans small
    white onions, drained
1 10-ounce can cream of
    mushroom soup
1/3 cup dry sherry

1 cup (1/2 pint) sour
    cream
1/2 teaspoon Fines Herbes
1/2 pound cheddar cheese,
    grated

PROCEDURE:

Preheat oven to 325°. Place drained onions in a deep 2 or 2 1/2-quart baking dish. Mix together the cream of mushroom soup, sherry, sour cream and Fines Herbes. Pour this mixture over the onions. Top with grated cheddar cheese. Bake for 30 minutes. Then broil for 5 minutes, or until cheese is bubbly and slightly browned.

Very quick and easy. This is a wonderful accompaniment to a traditional Thanksgiving feast.

Wendy Walker
Parent, Ashley Walker '98

Zucchini Casserole

Serves 8

INGREDIENTS:

2 cups (1 pint) sour cream
6 zucchini, sliced
2 small onions (or 1 medium), sliced in rings or diced

8 ounces Monterey jack cheese, shredded
Grated Parmesan cheese to sprinkle on top

PROCEDURE:

Preheat oven to 325°. Mix all ingredients together thoroughly. Pour into a lightly greased 9" x 13" casserole. Sprinkle Parmesan cheese generously on top. Cook uncovered for 1 hour.

Gay McFall Wells '69

Sweet and Sour Zucchini

Serves 6

INGREDIENTS:

2 tablespoons dehydrated chopped onions
1/8 cup white wine vinegar
1/3 cup vegetable oil
3/4 cup sugar
1 teaspoon salt

1/2 teaspoon pepper
2/3 cup cider vinegar
1/2 cup chopped green pepper
1/2 cup chopped celery
5 to 6 unpeeled zucchini, thinly sliced

PROCEDURE:

Soak onions in wine vinegar. In a large bowl mix together all other ingredients. Pour onion mix over vegetables and mix well. Chill before serving.

Keeps well for several days. I often use this dish instead of a salad.

Edith Stevens Haney '34

Green and Gold Casserole

Serves 6 to 8

INGREDIENTS:

1 pound zucchini, sliced
1 16-ounce can corn
1 1/2 cups farmer style
cottage cheese
2 tablespoons sour
cream
2 tablespoons flour
1 teaspoon salt
Dash pepper

2 to 4 dashes Tabasco sauce
2 eggs
1 4-ounce can diced
green chiles
3/4 cup grated cheddar
cheese
1/2 cup bread crumbs
1 tablespoon butter,
melted (optional)*

PROCEDURE:

Preheat oven to 350°. Butter a 2 1/2-quart casserole. Cook zucchini in boiling, salted water just until tender. Drain. Drain corn. In mixing bowl or blender jar combine cottage cheese, sour cream, flour, seasonings and eggs. Beat or blend until smooth. Fold zucchini and corn into cottage cheese mixture and add chiles. Taste to correct seasonings. Pour into casserole. Sprinkle cheese and bread crumbs over top. Bake 45 minutes. Can be prepared ahead or day before. Cover with foil and refrigerate if not cooking immediately.

*To make buttered bread crumbs, crumble dried out bread (bread may be dried out in oven on "low" or "warm" setting) and mix with melted butter.

I serve with ham or sliced turkey and salad. Great for an informal dinner.

Margaret E. Arthur
Grandparent, Douglas Arthur '99

Prize-winning Zucchini Pie

Serves 12

INGREDIENTS:

8 medium zucchini
  squash
1 large onion
2 tablespoons butter or
  margarine
1 pound mozzarella
  cheese

2 eggs
2 tablespoons oregano
  Garlic powder to taste
  Grated Parmesan
  cheese (to sprinkle on
  top)

PROCEDURE:

Preheat oven to 350°. Slice zucchini and onions and sauté in a large frying pan in butter or margarine for 10 minutes, or until limp. Drain off excess liquid. Grate mozzarella cheese. In a bowl, beat eggs and add cheese and mix together. Stir into cooked vegetables along with the oregano and garlic powder to taste. Pour into a 9" x 13" pan. Sprinkle top with enough Parmesan cheese to cover. Bake for 30 minutes, or until bubbly and top is nicely browned. To serve, cut into squares.

Quick and easy, especially if you have a food processor for slicing and grating. Excellent either hot or cold. A good substitute to take to a party if you are asked to bring a salad. Makes a nice cold hors d'oeuvre, too. Also, try a combination of summer and yellow squash instead of zucchini.

Jill Thurston See '62

Ratatouille

Serves 6 to 8

INGREDIENTS:

1 red bell pepper,
   charred, skinned and
   diced
1 eggplant or 1 1/2
   pounds Japanese
   eggplant
1 teaspoon salt
5 zucchini
1 large red onion,
   chopped
3 large cloves garlic,
   chopped
4 tablespoons olive oil
1/4 cup dried currants

1 pound fresh tomatoes,
   peeled, seeded and
   chopped or 1 1-pound
   box of Pomo tomatoes
   or ready-cut canned
   tomatoes
1/2 teaspoon thyme
1 teaspoon each fresh
   basil and summer
   savory
1 tablespoon chopped
   parsley
Pinch cayenne
Salt and pepper

PROCEDURE:

Preheat oven to 350°. Prepare red pepper by charring over a flame or under a grill. When thoroughly charred, pop in a plastic bag for 16 minutes, then peel and dice. Check skin of eggplant for bitterness. If bitter, peel. If not bitter, retain the skin and cut into 1/2" cubes. Sprinkle with 1/2 teaspoon salt and set aside. Repeat with the zucchini.

Slowly cook the chopped onion and garlic in 2 tablespoons of the olive oil in a large sauté pan until soft and aromatic. Transfer from pan to a bowl. Pat eggplant and zucchini dry. Turn up the heat under the sauté pan adding 1 tablespoon olive oil. When pan is hot, add zucchini and sauté until lightly browned. Transfer to bowl with onion mixture. Repeat with eggplant adding another tablespoon olive oil.

Lower heat and transfer vegetable and onion mixture to saucepan. Add diced peppers, currants, tomatoes, herbs, cayenne and pepper. Mix thoroughly and bring to a simmer. Taste for salt.

At this point, you may transfer ingredients to a baking dish. Cover first with wax paper at the surface and then with cover. Place in oven and cook for 1 hour. Serve as a bed for baked fish (see recipe, page 193), or as a hot or cold vegetable, summer or winter.

Anne Otterson
Parent, Eric Otterson '87 and Helen Otterson '89

Grandma's Vegetable Medley

Serves 6 to 8

INGREDIENTS:

6 zucchini
2 carrots, peeled
2 celery stalks
1 potato, peeled
1 onion
1 14-ounce can Italian-
   style stewed tomatoes

1 to 2 tablespoons olive oil
1 clove garlic
1 tablespoon chopped
   parsley
Salt and pepper

PROCEDURE:

Cut zucchini, carrots, celery stalks and potato into bite size pieces. Dice onion. Chop stewed tomatoes for a few seconds in blender. Coat a large pot with olive oil. Add vegetables, garlic, parsley and stewed tomatoes. Salt and pepper lightly. Cook covered for 45 minutes (or until veggies are tender) over low heat, stirring occasionally. Remove garlic before serving.

Variation: Brown chopped meat in olive oil before adding vegetables. This makes a wonderful meal with French bread. This is a family favorite handed down from my grandmother, Carmen Salomone.

Jennifer Lauer '94

Vegetable Collage

Serves 8 to 10

INGREDIENTS:

1 cup cooked black
  beans*
1 yellow onion for
  cooking beans
1 tablespoon oil
1 purple onion, chopped
1 cup cubed zucchini
1 red bell pepper, cut in
  1/4" cubes
1 yellow or purple bell
  pepper, cut in 1/4"
  cubes

4 ears of fresh corn,
  kernels removed from
  the ear (if corn is not
  in season, substitute
  1 yellow summer
  squash cut into 1/4"
  cubes)
1/4 cup chopped cilantro
1 tablespoon chopped
  Italian parsley

PROCEDURE:

Prepare all ingredients. (See bean preparation instruction below.) Sauté the purple onion in oil with 2 tablespoons water. (Sautéing in the oil releases the essences and the water prevents burning.) Add the zucchini and peppers and sauté, stirring over high heat. After a few minutes, add the corn (or summer squash) and continue cooking for another 2 minutes. Stir in the beans and herbs and remove from heat. Serve.

*The beans can be prepared by cooking 1 package of dried black beans in water with 2 quarters of an onion for an hour or more. Just as they are barely tender, remove 1 cup and rinse. Set aside for the collage.

To make a wonderful soup with the remaining beans (not used in collage recipe): Add the remaining onion, chopped, a good dash of cayenne pepper and 1/2 teaspoon salt. Cook another 15 to 30 minutes until beans are soft. With a slotted spoon, remove 2/3 of the beans and purée with 2 cups water. Return to pot and mix well. Heat and serve as a healthy, low fat soup.

Anne Otterson
Parent, Eric Otterson '87 and Helen Otterson '89

Great Baked Beans

Serves 12

INGREDIENTS:

1 pound bacon, cooked
   and chopped
2 onions, chopped
7 pounds canned baked
   pork and beans,
   drained

1 pound hot Italian
   sausage, cooked and
   sliced
3 Granny Smith apples,
   chopped
2 cups barbecue sauce

PROCEDURE:

After frying the bacon, drain off all but 2 tablespoons of the bacon grease and sauté the onions. In a large pot or pan, combine all the ingredients and simmer on top of stove, stirring occasionally (or bake in a 350° oven) for 45 minutes.

Apples need not be cooked all the way. They add a wonderful crunch and complement to the beans. Feel free to add more meat or apples to your liking. It's impossible to ruin these wonderful beans!

Lynn Martin Gaylord
Parent, Charlie Gaylord '96

Jeff and Jere's Favorite Baked Beans

Serves 20

INGREDIENTS:

- 1 12-ounce package light (low fat) sausage
- 2 large onions, finely chopped
- 1 1/2 cups lightly packed brown sugar
- 2 3-pound cans B&M Baked Beans
- 2 tablespoons Dijon mustard
- 1 tablespoon Worcestershire sauce

PROCEDURE:

Preheat oven to 350°. Place sausage in a 4-quart heavy pot or casserole which can be used on top of stove and in oven. Cook over medium heat while stirring and breaking sausage into small pieces. Add onion and cook for about 5 minutes. Add brown sugar and simmer 5 more minutes. Remove the pork chunk from each can of beans and discard. Add the beans to the sausage and onion mixture. Add the Dijon mustard and Worcestershire sauce and mix well. Place in oven and bake for 40 minutes. Stir 2 or 3 times while baking.

Can't have a picnic without these beans!

Ward Wyatt Deems
Parent, Jeff Deems '91 and Jeremy Deems '94

Vestry Dinner Calico Beans

Serves 8 to 10

INGREDIENTS:

1/2 pound bacon, cooked, drained and cut into 1/2" pieces
3 tablespoons bacon drippings
3 onions, chopped
1/4 cup packed brown sugar
1/4 teaspoon garlic salt

1/4 teaspoon dry mustard
1/2 cup ketchup
1/4 cup vinegar
1 15-ounce can, drained, each: Green lima beans, butter beans, kidney beans
1 15-ounce can pork 'n beans, undrained

PROCEDURE:

Sauté the onions in the bacon drippings until translucent. In a large ovenproof pot, combine the onions with the bacon, brown sugar, garlic salt, dry mustard, ketchup and vinegar. Place over medium-high heat. Bring to a simmer. Lower heat and cook gently for 20 minutes.

Preheat oven to 350°. Add the beans to the onion mixture and stir to mix. Cover pot and place in the oven and bake for 1 hour or longer.

Great for large groups as recipe can be doubled easily. Freezes well and is very easy to make. Fabulous taste with a barbecue meal.

Lenore Hughes
Wife of The Rt. Rev. Gethin B. Hughes, Chairman, Board of Trustees

Beans for a Crowd

Serves 20 to 30

INGREDIENTS:

1 pound bacon, cut in
   pieces
1 onion, chopped
1 green pepper, chopped
2 15-ounce cans pork
   and beans
2 15-ounce cans kidney
   beans, drained
2 15-ounce cans lima
   beans with ham

2 15-ounce cans whole
   onions, drained
2 16-ounce cans
   pineapple tidbits,
   drained
1 cup ketchup
3 tablespoons molasses
1 cup brown sugar
4 to 6 tablespoons Worcestershire sauce

PROCEDURE:

Preheat oven to 325°. Sauté together the bacon, onion and green pepper until the bacon is done. In a large bowl combine the remaining ingredients. With a slotted spoon, remove the sautéed bacon, onion and green pepper from the bacon drippings and add to other ingredients in bowl. Mix well and pour into a 10" x 14" baking dish. Bake 1 1/2 to 2 hours.

This recipe is great for any get-together or pot-luck supper. It serves 20 to 30 but can be easily cut down. It can be frozen. You can also leave out one type of bean and add more of another to suit your taste.

Barbara Riggs
Aunt, Chris Donaldson '93 and Leslie Donaldson '95

"Hoppin' John"

Serves 6 to 8

INGREDIENTS:

6 slices thick bacon
1 large onion, coarsely chopped
2 15-ounce cans black-eyed peas
1 cup cooked white rice

2 15-ounce cans stewed tomatoes
2 slices white bread, toasted, buttered and cubed
Butter for toast

PROCEDURE:

In a large frying pan, fry bacon until crisp. Drain on paper towels and set aside. Sauté the onion in the bacon drippings over medium heat until transparent, about 5 minutes. Add the black-eyed peas (undrained). Cook 30 minutes over medium-low heat. Cut bacon into 1/4" pieces and add to black-eyed peas. Add the cooked rice and stir to blend well. Top with the heated tomatoes and then the cubed toast.

Old Southern tradition to serve on New Year's Day. Guaranteed to bring good luck for the upcoming year. Great with corn bread.

Judy and Bob Ackerly, Trustee
Parents, Nelson Ackerly '92 and Brien Ackerly '94

Red Beans and Rice (New Orleans Style)

Serves 6

INGREDIENTS:

12 slices bacon, cut into 1" pieces
1 large onion, diced
1 large green bell pepper, seeded and diced

2 15-ounce cans red kidney beans, undrained
Salt and pepper to taste
Tabasco sauce to taste
Rice for 6 servings

PROCEDURE:

In a large skillet fry bacon pieces until brown. Pour off rendered fat, leaving bacon in pan. Add onion and pepper and continue frying, stirring occasionally, until vegetables are tender and lightly browned. Add beans (with all their liquid) and salt and pepper to taste. Toss in 2 or 3 good shakes of Tobasco; stir to mix. Bring mixture back to a simmer, cover pan, turn heat to low and simmer gently for about 20 to 30 minutes while you cook rice according to package directions. Serve beans over rice in generous quantity.

Serve as a main dish with a green salad and French bread.

Dorothy Anne Williams
Headmistress, 1975-83

Vegetable Rice Pilaf

Serves 4 to 6

INGREDIENTS:

1 cup Basmati rice or long grain rice
2 cups cold water
2 tablespoons butter (or oil)
1 small onion, thinly sliced
1 small potato, peeled and diced in 1/2" cubes
1/3 cup frozen green peas
1/3 cup cauliflower pieces

(may substitute any vegetables: Carrots, zucchini, green beans, etc.)

Spices:
1 teaspoon salt
2 bay leaves
3 whole cloves
1 1/2 " stick cinnamon
2 pieces green cardamons

PROCEDURE:

Wash and soak rice for 30 minutes in cold water. In 5-quart non-stick pot heat butter (or oil) and sauté onion on medium heat until soft and lightly brown. Add spices and cook 2 to 3 minutes to allow the spices to release flavor. Add all vegetables, stir well and cook on low to medium heat, covered, until vegetables are tender (10 to 15 minutes). Drain water from soaking rice. Add rice to pot. Add a fresh 2 cups of cold water. Cover pot and cook on high until water boils. Turn heat to low. Cook until water evaporates (10 to 15 minutes). Remove from heat and set aside with cover on pot 10 to 15 minutes to allow the steam to cook the vegetables and rice slightly more. Gently fluff pilaf with fork. Serve on platter lined with fresh green leaves of any variety of lettuce.

Basmati rice is available in gourmet section of most grocery stores.

Nisha R. Goyal
Parent, Rocky Goyal '94, Shilpi Goyal '97, Vishal Goyal '98

Rice Pilaf

Serves 4

INGREDIENTS:

4 tablespoons (1/2 stick)
    unsalted butter
1/4 cup finely chopped
    onion
1 medium garlic clove,
    finely chopped
1/4 cup fine noodles,
    broken into 1 1/2"
    pieces

1 cup rice
2 cups chicken stock
    (homemade is best)
    Parsley, finely chopped
    Salt and pepper to
    taste

PROCEDURE:

Melt butter. Sauté onion and garlic in butter for 1 minute. Add noodles and sauté 1 more minute. Add rice and sauté another minute or so. Bring chicken broth to a boil, add to rice mixture, cover and cook over low heat for 25 minutes. Turn heat off and leave cover on for 5 more minutes. Add plenty of finely chopped parsley and salt and pepper to taste.

This recipe goes well with anything and can easily be doubled.

Gretl Malnic Mulder '53

Rice Mallorca

Serves 8

INGREDIENTS:

Butter or oil to grease
    casserole
3 cups cooked white rice
3 cups (1 1/2 pints)
    sour cream
1 6-ounce can chopped
    green chiles (drained)

3/4 pound Monterey jack
    cheese (in strips)
    Salt and pepper to
    taste
1 cup grated cheddar
    cheese

PROCEDURE:

Preheat oven to 350°. Butter sides and bottom of a 1 1/2-quart casserole. Put 1/3 of the rice in a layer on the bottom. Mix together the sour cream and chiles. Spread 1/2 the sour cream mixture on the rice. Then lay 1/2 the jack cheese strips over this mixture. Repeat with 1/3 of the rice, remaining sour cream and chiles and remaining jack cheese. Top with last 1/3 rice and season with salt and pepper. Cover with the grated cheddar cheese. Bake for 30 minutes.

Good with ham, roast pork, broiled or barbecued chicken. Transports well.

Melody Pourade Fleetwood '56

Chile Rice Cheese Bake

Serves 6 to 8

INGREDIENTS:

1 cup long grain rice
2 1/2 cups water
1 teaspoon salt
2 tablespoons butter
1/2 cup minced onion or 3/4 cup chopped onion
Salt to taste
1 cup (1/2 pint) light cream

1 4-ounce can diced green chiles
1/2 pound Monterey jack cheese, cubed
2 cups (1 pint) sour cream
Paprika

PROCEDURE:

Preheat oven to 325°. Simmer rice in salted water in uncovered saucepan 15 to 20 minutes or until tender. Melt butter in skillet and sauté onions until transparent. Remove from heat and stir in salt and cream. Set aside.

In a 2-quart casserole, alternate layers of rice, diced green chiles, cubed cheese, onion/cream sauce and sour cream. Sprinkle with paprika. Bake for 35 minutes or so until bubbly hot.

This can be made a day ahead. It is a great side dish with meat or fish.

Gretchen Simpson
Parent, Kelly Simpson '92 and Kristy Simpson '96

Arroz con Chiles Rellenos

Serves 8

INGREDIENTS:

2 cups uncooked rice
1/2 cup oil
6 white onions, finely chopped
6 green chiles, canned

1/2 pound Monterey jack cheese, grated, or cream cheese
1/4 cup (1/2 stick) butter
4 cups beef stock
Salt and pepper to taste

PROCEDURE:

Fry rice in oil, but do not brown. Set aside to cool. When cool, place a layer of rice in a large saucepan with a tight cover. Add a layer of onion, then a layer of chiles which have been stuffed with the cheese. Repeat this procedure until all of these ingredients are used, making the last layer rice. Dot top of rice with butter. Place the beef stock in a saucepan, season with salt and pepper and bring to a boil. Pour boiling stock over all. Cover tightly and cook slowly on top of the stove for 1/2 hour.

Liz Crowell '82

Grits Soufflé

Serves 12

INGREDIENTS:

1 1/2 cups quick-cooking hominy grits
1/2 cup (1 stick) butter
1/2 pound sharp New York cheese or 1 stick extra-sharp Cracker Barrel cheese, grated

1 teaspoon salt
3 teaspoons Lawry's seasoned salt
3 eggs, beaten
Butter or oil to grease casserole dish

350

PROCEDURE:

Preheat oven to 300°. Cook hominy grits in 6 cups boiling water for about 2 minutes. While hot, stir in butter and grated cheese. Blend, cool a little, then add salt and seasoned salt. Stir in eggs and mix well. Pour the grits mixture into a lightly greased 9" x 13" casserole dish. Bake for about 1 hour.

My mother always took this dish to church suppers in my Missouri hometown. Delicious served with hot biscuits and strawberry jam, plus iced-tea with mint sprigs from the garden.

Brynell Somerville '72

Corn Pudding

Serves 6 to 8

INGREDIENTS:

1 15-ounce can creamed corn
1 15-ounce can whole kernel corn, drained
4 tablespoons sugar
4 tablespoons flour
4 eggs, slightly beaten
2 cups milk
1/2 cup (1 stick) butter, melted

PROCEDURE:

Preheat oven to 325°. Mix first 6 ingredients together. (Be sure to drain whole kernel corn.) Stir in the melted butter and blend well. Pour mixture into a greased 8" x 11" casserole dish. Bake for 1 hour. When done, knife inserted in center should come out clean.

A good vegetable side dish that is quick and easy.

Diane Shockley
Parent, Tre Shockley '96 and Tristan Shockley '98

Liboria's Polenta

Serves 6 to 8

INGREDIENTS:

1 medium onion
2 cloves garlic
1/2 cup (1 stick) butter
8 ears of corn

1 1/2 cups chicken broth
1 1/2 cups polenta
1/2 cup grated Parmesan
cheese

PROCEDURE:

Finely dice onion and garlic. Melt butter in a large heavy pan. Sauté onion and garlic in butter over medium-high heat, stirring constantly for 1 or 2 minutes. Cut corn kernels off cob and add to onion and garlic. Sauté, stirring for 2 more minutes. Add broth and polenta. Heat, stirring, until mixture thickens enough to hold up a wooden spoon. Add the grated Parmesan cheese. Mix thoroughly and serve.

Quick and easy. Polenta is available in cornmeal section of grocery store.

Nancy Minton
Parent, Jennifer Minton '96 and Laura Minton '96

Roasted Potatoes with Garlic, Rosemary and Sage

Serves 4

INGREDIENTS:

4 large russet (or 8
medium red) potatoes
1/3 cup extra virgin olive
oil
5 garlic cloves, unpeeled

5 4" sprigs fresh
rosemary
8 sage leaves
Salt and freshly
ground pepper, to
taste

PROCEDURE:

Preheat oven to 400°. Peel and cut the potatoes into 3/4" cubes. Keep potatoes in water until ready to use. In a large skillet, heat the oil until almost smoking. Drain the potatoes thoroughly and blot with paper towels. Place them in the hot oil. Sear until golden (being careful not to burn), stirring occasionally. This step generally takes about 10 to 15 minutes. Remove and place in a single layer in an 8" x 10" ovenproof casserole dish. Distribute garlic, rosemary and sage on top of the potatoes. Salt and pepper to taste. Then bake for 20 minutes or until potatoes are done.

This is a great party recipe that goes well with grilled lamb or beef. All but the baking can be done ahead of time, which allows the cook to enjoy her guests!

Gail Lichter
Parent, Kris Lichter '89 and Kerrie Lichter '93

Gratin of Potatoes

Serves 6

INGREDIENTS:

1 1/2 cups milk
2 1/2 cups heavy cream
   2 cloves garlic, minced
    Salt and white pepper
   1 pound russet potatoes

1 pound white rose
   potatoes
1 pound sweet potatoes
1/4 cup fresh grated
   Parmesan cheese

PROCEDURE:

Preheat oven to 350°. Put milk, cream, garlic, salt and pepper into a large bowl. Have a lightly greased or oiled 10" x 14" gratin dish ready. Peel and slice (1/4" thick) each type of potato separately, putting them into the milk mixture separately. Layer each type in the gratin dish so that the sweet potato is in the middle layer. Pour over the remaining milk mixture and sprinkle cheese over the top. Bake for 1 to 1 1/2 hours.

Anne Otterson
Parent, Eric Otterson '87 and Helen Otterson '89

Spanish Potato Omelet
(Tortilla de Patatas)

Serves 4 to 6

INGREDIENTS:

1/2 cup olive oil for frying
4 medium potatoes,
    peeled and cut in
    1/2" cubes
1 medium onion,
    chopped

2 cloves garlic, chopped
6 eggs
1/2 teaspoon salt
1/8 teaspoon pepper

PROCEDURE:

Heat all but 2 tablespoons of the oil in 8" skillet over medium heat until hot.
Add potatoes, onion and garlic and stir until tender and golden brown. Drain
excess oil from potato mixture. In a bowl, beat eggs with salt and pepper. Add
hot potato mixture to eggs and stir well. Heat the remaining 2 tablespoons of oil
in same skillet over medium heat until hot. Pour potato/egg mixture into skillet
and cook at low heat uncovered until eggs are set, about 5 to 10 minutes.
Loosen edge and turn omelet over by using a plate and covering skillet. Cook
over medium heat until other side is brown and slip onto serving plate. Cut like
a pie into wedges and serve hot or cold as an appetizer or side dish.

*Be creative. To the potato mixture you can also add cheese, shrimp, tomatoes,
peppers, peas, ham, etc.*

*Valerie Benito,
Parent, Edward Benito-Nedel '95*

Aunt Jean's Potatoes

Serves 6

INGREDIENTS:

- 6 medium potatoes
- 2 tablespoons butter or margarine
- 1 10-ounce can cream of chicken soup
- 1 cup (1/2 pint) sour cream (nonfat OK)

- 1/3 cup chopped green onion
- 1 1/2 cups grated cheddar cheese (nonfat OK)
- 1 cup crushed corn flakes
- 2 tablespoons butter or margarine, melted

PROCEDURE:

Preheat oven to 400°. Bake the potatoes until just tender. Reset oven to 350°. Cool, peel and grate the potatoes. Heat 2 tablespoons butter (or margarine) with the soup. Blend in the sour cream, onion and cheese. Stir in potatoes. Put mixture into a greased 2 1/2-quart shallow casserole. Mix corn flakes with the 2 tablespoons melted butter and sprinkle over top. Bake for 45 minutes.

Sharon Flood
Parent, Johanna Flood '99

Yummy Potatoes

Serves 8

INGREDIENTS:

6 medium boiling
   potatoes (White Rose)
1 1/2 cups (3/4 pint) sour
   cream
1 teaspoon salt
3 to 4 green onions, sliced

1 1/2 cups grated cheddar
   cheese (sharp or
   longhorn)
Bread crumbs or
   paprika to sprinkle on
   top

PROCEDURE:

Peel and boil potatoes whole until just tender. Cool slightly. Preheat oven to 350°. Grate potatoes with coarse grater into mixing bowl. Mix together sour cream, salt, green onions and grated cheese. Fold this mixture into potatoes. Put potato mixture into greased casserole dish. (Use a round deep one like a soufflé dish, 7" to 8" diameter.) Sprinkle lightly with bread crumbs or paprika. Bake for 30 minutes or until bubbling. If made ahead and refrigerated, bake 45 minutes.

Mary Ruyle
Parent, Chad Ruyle '96

K. P.'s Potato Decadence

Serves 6

INGREDIENTS:

5 to 6 medium potatoes
1 10-ounce can cream of
   chicken soup
2 cups (1 pint) nonfat
   yogurt
1/2 teaspoon onion powder
1/2 teaspoon garlic powder

1/2 teaspoon white ground
   pepper
1 tablespoon olive oil
1 cup corn flake crumbs
   (or other crispy cereal
   favorite)
1 cup grated cheddar
   cheese

PROCEDURE:

Preheat oven to 350°. Peel and boil potatoes in a large pot of lightly salted water until tender. (When pierced with fork, potato should be firm but not hard in center.) Drain potatoes and cool. (I place potatoes in a bowl and put in freezer for 20 minutes.) While potatoes are cooling, combine the soup, yogurt, onion powder, garlic powder and pepper in the pot the potatoes were in. Warm up mixture on low heat, then remove from heat. In a shallow dish, drizzle the olive oil onto the cornflake crumbs and stir to coat evenly. Grate potatoes. Add potatoes and cheese to pan containing soup/yogurt mixture. Stir to mix well. Place potato mixture in a lightly greased 9" x 13" baking dish and sprinkle corn flakes over top. Bake for 45 minutes.

A great dish to prepare ahead of time for a dinner party.

Kathleen Parnell Steele '80

Sweet Potato Casserole

Serves 6

INGREDIENTS:

1 **28-ounce can sweet**
   potatoes, undrained
4 **tablespoons butter**
1/2 **cup brown sugar**
1/4 **teaspoon nutmeg**

2 **eggs**
1 **8-ounce can crushed**
   pineapple

Marshmallows for top

PROCEDURE:

Preheat oven to 350°. Heat sweet potatoes in juice. When hot, discard most of the juice. Beat potatoes with all other ingredients except marshmallows using hand-held electric mixer. Pour into buttered 9" x 13" casserole dish. Bake 30 to 45 minutes or until set. Remove from oven, place marshmallows on top, return to oven until marshmallows brown.

Chopped pecans may be added to recipe.

Virginia Eikel
Grandparent, Catherine Eikel '97

Holiday Sweet Potatoes

Serves 12

INGREDIENTS:

4 large sweet potatoes
2 eggs
1/2 cup (1 stick) butter
1/3 cup sugar
1 tablespoon cinnamon
1 teaspoon nutmeg

Topping:
3/4 cup brown sugar
4 tablespoons flour
4 tablespoons butter
3/4 cup chopped pecans

PROCEDURE:

Preheat oven to 350°. Cut sweet potatoes in quarters and boil until tender. Peel off skin. While still hot, beat with a mixer until creamy. Add eggs, butter, sugar, cinnamon and nutmeg. Mix well and pour into a greased 10" x 14" casserole.

Combine the topping ingredients, cutting the butter into the flour with a pastry blender or fork. Sprinkle topping over the sweet potato mixture. Bake for 30 to 40 minutes.

In the South sweet potatoes are a "must" for Thanksgiving and Christmas dinners. They also go well with pork. The casserole may be made a day or two ahead.

Sue S. Hughes
Grandparent, Adrienne Hoehn '97

Sweet Potatoes and Mandarin Oranges

Serves 6

INGREDIENTS:

- 6 medium sweet potatoes
- 4 tablespoons (1/2 stick) butter, melted
- 6 tablespoons brown sugar
- 3 tablespoons Myer's Dark Rum

- 1/2 teaspoon salt
- 1/4 teaspoon pepper
- 2 11-ounce cans Mandarin oranges, drained
- 3 tablespoons chopped pecans

PROCEDURE:

Preheat oven to 425°. Bake sweet potatoes for 30 minutes to 1 hour, depending on their size. After 15 minutes, pierce in several places with a fork to keep the skins from exploding. Test for doneness with a fork; it should go in easily.

Lower oven to 375°. Mash the potatoes and mix with 2 tablespoons of the butter, 4 tablespoons of the brown sugar, the rum, salt and pepper. Fold in 1 of the drained cans of Mandarin oranges. Butter well a 10" x 14", ovenproof casserole (or one of equivalent size that can be used as a serving dish) and add the potatoes. Arrange the other can of Mandarin oranges in a pattern on top of the potato mixture. Sprinkle with the remaining sugar, butter and pecans. Bake for 30 minutes.

This can be assembled a day or two ahead and heated before serving.

Cary Tremblay
Parent, Maurile Tremblay '88 and Sean Tremblay '98

Sweet Potato and Carrot Purée

Serves 6

INGREDIENTS:

4 large sweet potatoes
1 pound carrots, peeled
    and cut into 2" pieces
2 1/2 cups water
1 tablespoon sugar

1/4 cup (1/2 stick) butter
1/2 cup lite sour cream
1/2 teaspoon grated
    nutmeg

PROCEDURE:

Punch holes with a fork in potatoes and microwave on high for approximately 15 minutes. In a saucepan, cover carrots with water, add sugar and 2 tablespoons of the butter. Boil until water evaporates and carrots begin to sizzle in butter (about 30 minutes). Do not let carrots burn. Scrape out flesh of sweet potatoes and add to carrots in food processor fitted with steel blade. Add remaining butter, sour cream, nutmeg and process until very smooth. To reheat, put in ovenproof pan and cover with foil. Heat at 350° for 25 minutes.

Freezes well. Leftovers make great soup with addition of chicken stock.

Peggy Preuss
Parent, Peter Preuss '97

Quiche, Cheese & Eggs

Tomato, Basil and Cheese Tart

Serves 6

INGREDIENTS:

Shell:
1 1/2 cups flour
6 tablespoons (3/4 stick) cold butter, cut into bits
2 tablespoons cold vegetable shortening
1/4 pound sliced bacon, cooked, drained and crumbled
3 to 4 tablespoons ice water
Raw rice for weighting the shell

Filling:
1 cup firmly packed fresh basil leaves
1/2 cup plus 2 tablespoons whole milk ricotta cheese
2 large eggs
1/4 pound mozzarella cheese, grated
1/2 cups grated Parmesan cheese
4 large (2 pounds) firm ripe tomatoes, sliced 1/3" thick, drained on paper towels, lightly salted
Vegetable oil for brushing tomatoes

PROCEDURE:

Shell: Blend flour, butter, shortening and bacon until mixture resembles coarse meal. Add 3 to 4 tablespoons ice water to form a dough. Knead briefly, form into ball, flatten slightly, dust with flour and refrigerate for 1 hour.

Roll dough 1/8 " thick to fit 9" tart pan with removable bottom. Prick bottom of shell and refrigerate 30 minutes. Preheat oven to 425°. Line shell with foil, add rice and bake for 15 minutes. Remove rice and foil and bake 3 minutes longer. Turn oven down to 350°.

Filling: In food processor, purée basil leaves, ricotta and eggs. Add cheeses and blend briefly. Pat tomato slices dry. Line shell with tomato end pieces and spoon cheese mixture over slices. Arrange remaining tomato slices in overlapping circular pattern over the cheese mixture. Brush lightly with oil. Bake for 40 to 50 minutes. Let stand 10 minutes.

Serve hot or room temperature. My favorite version of quiche.

Peggy Preuss
Parent, Peter Preuss '97

Cheese Pie

Yields 9" pie

INGREDIENTS:

Dough:
1/2 cup (1 stick) unsalted
    butter, chilled
1 cup flour
3 tablespoons ice water
Pinch salt

Cheese filling:
1 1/2 pounds Gruyere
    cheese, grated (or
    only 1 pound, if
    desired)
1/2 cup milk
    Pinch white or black
    pepper
3 large eggs, separated
    (whites must be
    beaten immediately
    prior to use)

PROCEDURE:

Dough: Mix butter with flour until it has the consistency of sand. You may use a pastry blender or a food processor fitted with a steel knife. Add the water and salt. Mix briefly until dough is formed. Form into ball, wrap in plastic and let rest 1 hour at room temperature. Roll out dough and fit into a 9" pie pan.

Preheat oven to 375°.
Cheese filling: In a bowl, mix the grated Gruyere with the milk and pepper. Lightly beat egg yolks and add to cheese mixture and mix well. Beat the egg whites until stiff. Gently fold egg whites into cheese mixture. Pour mixture into pie pan lined with dough. Cook 40 to 45 minutes.

Tastes great with romaine lettuce salad.

Catherine Rivier
Parent, Lauraine Rivier '93 and Cedric Rivier '96X

Tomato Pie

Serves 6 to 8

INGREDIENTS:

1 frozen 8" pie shell
3 to 4 large firm, vine-ripened tomatoes, cut in 1/2" thick slices
Salt and pepper
1 cup mayonnaise
1 cup grated cheddar cheese

1/2 cup chopped green onion
2 to 3 tablespoons chopped fresh basil and/or oregano

PROCEDURE:

Preheat oven to 350°. Precook the frozen pie shell according to package instructions. Layer the tomato slices in the shell. Salt and pepper the tomatoes to taste. Mix the mayonnaise, cheese, onion, basil and oregano together in a bowl. Spread this cheese mixture over the tomatoes. Bake in oven for 35 minutes until the cheese has melted and the top of the pie has browned slightly (not too brown or it will be dry).

My mother-in-law adds cooked bacon and/or potatoes to this pie to make it even heartier. This pie is excellent served with any type of meat. Best made with firm (not overly ripe) tomatoes.

Lolly Smyth Freese '68X

Quiche Bombay

INGREDIENTS:

1 9" unbaked pie shell
1 pound bulk pork sausage
1/4 cup grated (or finely minced) onion
1 cup grated sharp cheddar cheese
1 tablespoon flour
1 medium tomato, sliced

2 eggs
1 12-ounce can evaporated milk
Dash salt
1 1/2 teaspoons curry powder
1 tablespoon chopped parsley

PROCEDURE:

Preheat oven to 350°. Brown sausage. Drain fat. Add onion and cook until tender. Pour mixture into pie shell. Sprinkle grated cheese and flour on top. Arrange sliced tomatoes on the cheese. Beat eggs, milk, salt and curry powder. Pour over the mixture in pie shell. Sprinkle parsley on top. Bake for 45 minutes, until set. Let stand for 15 minutes before serving. Serve warm.

Makes a wonderful luncheon dish. Serve with white wine and a tossed salad. Tastes great even when cold from the refrigerator.

Fay Ferreira Wallace '64

Spinach Quiche

Serves 8 to 10

INGREDIENTS:

1 unbaked deep 9" pastry shell

1 10-ounce package frozen chopped spinach

8 ounces mozzarella cheese, grated

2 tablespoons all-purpose flour

1 cup milk

3 eggs, beaten

1/2 teaspoon salt

1/8 teaspoon pepper

Dash ground nutmeg

PROCEDURE:

Preheat oven to 425°. Prick bottom and sides of pastry shell with fork and bake for 6 to 8 minutes. Set aside.

Lower oven to 350°. Cook spinach according to package directions, drain well and let cool. Combine cheese and flour in a bowl; set aside. Combine milk, eggs, salt, pepper and nutmeg. Mix well. Stir in spinach and cheese. Pour mixture into partially baked pastry shell. Bake for 50 to 60 minutes. Cool slightly before serving.

To freeze: Bake only 40 minutes, cool, wrap tightly in aluminum foil and freeze. Before serving, thaw and bake 15 to 20 minutes.

Good and easy. Especially tasty as leftovers, if you have any. Can substitute broccoli or mixed vegetables for spinach. Add more cheese for cheesier quiche.

Barbara Barnard Proctor '70

Holiday Egg Casserole

Serves 4 to 6

INGREDIENTS:

8 hard cooked eggs
1/4 cup butter, softened
1/2 teaspoon minced
parsley
1 tablespoon grated
onion
1/3 cup finely grated
boiled ham
American or cheddar
cheese

Béchamel sauce:
3 tablespoons butter
4 tablespoons flour
1 bouillon cube (beef),
dissolved in water
1 cup boiling water
salt, pepper and
paprika
3/4 cup half and half
cream

PROCEDURE:

Preheat oven to 300°.

Béchamel Sauce: In a medium saucepan, combine butter and flour. Stir continuously over medium heat until butter is melted and bubbly. Do not brown. Add remaining ingredients and cook, stirring continuously until thick and smooth. Remove from heat and set aside to cool before pouring over eggs.

Halve eggs and remove yolks. Blend mashed yolks with butter, parsley, onion and ham. Generously stuff egg whites with the above (like deviled eggs) and put into greased chafing or casserole dish. Cover eggs with béchamel sauce and sprinkle generously with cheese. Heat in oven for 25 minutes.

Serve with blueberry muffins and fruit of your choice. This can be made in advance and refrigerated until heated in oven. Do not freeze; eggs become tough. Wonderful for Christmas or New Year's morning buffet. Recipe easily doubled to serve more.

Carolyn Coverdale '60

Sauce, Relish & Pickles

Mango Salsa

Serves 4

INGREDIENTS:

1 large mango, peeled
and diced
1/2 cup diced jicama

2 tablespoons chopped
fresh mint leaves
1 tablespoon lime juice

PROCEDURE:

Mix all ingredients and chill.

Serve with grilled chicken or fish or as a salsa for a different accompaniment to Mexican food.

Susan McClellan
Parent, Ryan McClellan '96

Salsa Chunky

Yields 2 cups

INGREDIENTS:

1 14-ounce can
ready-cut tomatoes,
slightly drained
1 firm ripe tomato,
chopped and drained
1 4-ounce can diced
green chiles
1 8-ounce can green
tomatillos (optional),
finely chopped and
well-drained

1/2 cup finely chopped
onion
4 tablespoons red wine
vinegar
2 tablespoons olive oil
1 teaspoon garlic salt
1/4 teaspoon pepper
1 teaspoon oregano
1/2 cup chopped cilantro
leaves

PROCEDURE:

Combine all ingredients and refrigerate until ready to use. Serve with tortilla chips.

Good stuff. Use it on tacos, tostadas, quesadillas and omelets. Add a jar of prepared mild or medium hot salsa to extend the recipe and still have a fresh taste.

Jeff Deems '91 and Jeremy Deems '94

Tomato Basil Beurre Blanc

Yields 1 1/2 cup

INGREDIENTS:

1 cup (2 sticks) unsalted
    butter
12 large fresh basil leaves
1 medium tomato
1/4 cup white wine
    vinegar
1/4 cup white wine

2 shallots, finely
    chopped
Salt and pepper to
    taste

PROCEDURE:

Cut butter into 1/4" slices. Remove the stems from the basil leaves and julienne the leaves, (i.e., stack 4 or 5 leaves; roll them from the point to the base; with a thin-bladed knife, cut the basil crosswise into very thin strips). Peel and seed the tomato and cut into 1/2" cubes.

In a medium size, heavy, non-aluminum saucepan, reduce the wine vinegar, wine and shallots to 1 tablespoon. With the pan over medium-high heat, whisk in 1 or 2 slices of butter. When the butter is creamy but not melted, beat in another 2 slices. Turn the heat to low and, whisking constantly, continue to add more butter, 2 slices at a time. It is very important to add more butter only when the previous addition has become creamy and thick. (Turn the heat up a little, if butter is not melting. Do not turn it too high because if the sauce becomes too hot, it will separate; if this happens, remove pan from heat for a moment, add more butter, continue to whisk and return to heat when smooth again.) When all the butter has been whisked in, remove from heat, stir in the salt, pepper, tomato cubes and the strips of basil. Scrape the sauce into a small serving bowl and set in a warm but not hot place until ready to serve.

Especially good served over individual servings of salmon fillets which have been grilled, sautéed or baked in oven according to method described in recipe on page 193. Also wonderful with sautéed or steamed scallops.

Anne Otterson
Parent, Eric Otterson '87 and Helen Otterson '89

Mustard Dill Sauce

Yields approximately 1 1/2 cups

INGREDIENTS:

1/2 cup Dijon mustard
2 teaspoons powdered
   mustard
5 tablespoons sugar
1/4 cup white wine
   vinegar

1/3 cup vegetable oil
1/3 cup olive oil
1/2 cup chopped fresh dill
   leaves
Salt to taste

PROCEDURE:

Combine the mustard, mustard powder and sugar in mixing bowl. Using a wire whisk, stir in the vinegar. Gradually add the oils, stirring rapidly with the whisk. Add the dill and salt. Taste and correct the flavors by gradually adding more sugar, vinegar or salt.

Easy, great tasting sauce for fish!

Sara Sweet
Staff, Director of Food Service

Remoulade Sauce

Yields 2 cups

INGREDIENTS:

4 tablespoons Dijon
   mustard
1/2 cup tarragon vinegar
2 tablespoons ketchup
1 tablespoon paprika
1/2 teaspoon cayenne
   pepper

1 teaspoon salt
1 clove garlic
1 cup salad oil
1/2 cup minced green
   onions with tops
1/2 cup finely minced
   celery

PROCEDURE:

Combine all ingredients in a blender and purée. Pour into bowl, cover and place in refrigerator to chill. Use as sauce for chilled, cooked shrimp. To make shrimp extra delicious, marinate shrimp in sauce in refrigerator 4 to 5 hours.

Cecile Reed Renaudin '64
Parent, Reed Renaudin '93 and Claire Renaudin '98

Dark Sweet and Sour Sauce

Serves 4

INGREDIENTS:

2 small cloves garlic (or 1 large), chopped
2 slices fresh ginger, peeled and finely chopped
1 or 2 tablespoons vegetable or peanut oil

4 tablespoons vinegar
2 tablespoons corn flour
5 tablespoons sugar
4 tablespoons soy sauce
1 cup water
1/8 teaspoon red pepper flakes (optional)

PROCEDURE:

Sauté garlic and ginger in oil over moderately low heat. Meanwhile, mix together vinegar, corn flour, sugar, soy sauce, optional red pepper flakes and water. Add to oil mixture and stir constantly until sauce darkens and thickens.

This sauce is not the same color as the pinkish sweet-sour sauces you see in Chinese restaurants, but we have come to enjoy this darker version. I usually serve it with farmer-style spareribs which I've boiled for an hour or so, cooled and then fried until just a little crispy in a light vegetable oil. You can reheat the ribs in the sauce after it's thickened. (I add the red pepper flakes when I don't need to accommodate the sensitive palates of children.)

Lois Case,
Parent, Robert Case '99

Midwest Cranberry Sauce

Serves 12

INGREDIENTS:

1 pound raw cranberries, washed
1 1/2 cups water

2 cups sugar
1 16-ounce can sour red cherries

PROCEDURE:

Combine cranberries and water, bring water to a boil and cook cranberries until soft (approximately 10 minutes). Press cranberries through a colander or sieve over a bowl to catch the juice. To cranberry juice add the sugar and the sour red cherries with juice. Simmer until the sugar is melted. Do not boil. Cool and refrigerate.

Will keep 2 or 3 weeks in the refrigerator. Delicious when served with fowl or any kind of meat dish.

Mary Jane Norris
Grandparent, Keller Norris '90, Matt Norris '92, Reggie Norris '94

Peg's Homemade Apple Sauce

Serves 8

INGREDIENTS:

4 large or 5 medium Macintosh apples
1/3 cup granulated sugar

1 cup water
3 shakes cinnamon powder

PROCEDURE:

Core and quarter apples. Do not peel (as the more reddish the color of the apple skin, the prettier the look of the final sauce). Place apples in a covered saucepan with the sugar, water and cinnamon and cook over medium heat until mushy, approximately 30 minutes. Press apple mixture through an old-fashioned type sieve into a glass bowl. Cool to room temperature, then cover and refrigerate.

Will keep in refrigerator for 1 week.

Peg Andrews Barnard '38

Cranberry Sauce

Serves 6 to 8

INGREDIENTS:

1 orange
1 pound cranberries,
fresh

2 pippin apples, peeled
and cored
2 cups sugar

PROCEDURE:

Peel orange, saving peel. Remove white membrane from orange. Put orange peel, orange, cranberries and apples through coarse blade on food grinder. Stir in sugar and refrigerate for at least 24 hours. Still better if allowed to meld for 3 days.

This sauce can be kept in the refrigerator for 3 to 4 weeks. It freezes very well. This easy to make dish has been the hit of our family Thanksgiving dinner for years. Because no cooking is involved, it's fun for young children to make.

Linda Morefield
Parent, Michael Morefield '97

Cranberry Relish

Yields 6 cups

INGREDIENTS:

3 tart apples (Granny Smith or pippin), peeled, cored and diced

2 slightly ripe pears, peeled, cored and diced

2 pounds fresh cranberries

1 cup golden raisins

2 cups sugar

1 cup freshly squeezed orange juice

2 tablespoons grated orange rind

2 teaspoons cinnamon

1/4 teaspoon nutmeg

1/2 cup Grand Marnier or other orange liqueur

PROCEDURE:

Mix together all the ingredients except for the Grand Marnier in a saucepan. Bring to a slow boil. Then reduce the heat to low and simmer, uncovered, for 45 minutes, until thick. Remove from the heat and stir in Grand Marnier. Let cool to room temperature. Refrigerate, covered, until serving time.

Easy. Can make ahead of time. Freezes well. Great with turkey dinners.

Arline Greene
Parent, Cheryl Greene '98

The Best Hot Fudge Sauce

Yields 2 cups

INGREDIENTS:

3 ounces good quality
    bittersweet chocolate
1 1/3 sticks unsalted butter
1/2 cup Dutch process
    unsweetened cocoa
    powder
1/2 cup brown sugar,
    packed

1/2 cup granulated sugar
1 teaspoon instant
    coffee powder
2/3 cup whipping cream
1 teaspoon vanilla

PROCEDURE:

Put all ingredients (except vanilla) in double boiler and, stirring occasionally, heat for approximately 25 to 30 minutes, until all ingredients are melted and sauce is slightly thickened. Remove from heat and stir in vanilla. Sauce may be used immediately or stored in refrigerator for up to 1 month. Reheat sauce in double boiler or microwave on low heat for approximately 1 minute.

Although not for the cholesterol conscious, this is a wonderful sauce and it reheats beautifully (without formation of sugar crystals). It is great over vanilla ice cream, poached pears, etc.

Elaine Muchmore
Parent, Mary Beth Muchmore '96X

Amadio's Hot Fudge Sauce

Yields 2 cups

INGREDIENTS:

6 squares unsweetened
   baker's chocolate
3 cups powdered sugar,
   sifted (more to taste)

1 5-ounce can
   evaporated milk
   (more if desired)
1/2 cup (1 stick) butter

PROCEDURE:

Melt chocolate in top of double boiler over simmering water. When melted, add sifted powdered sugar. Stir until thoroughly mixed. Add milk gradually, while stirring. Add the stick of butter and continue stirring while it melts, blending melted butter into sauce. Continue stirring until all the butter is melted and the sauce is well-blended and smooth. If too thick, add more milk. You may add more powdered sugar to taste. Serve warm over ice cream.

This is the recipe for the decadent hot fudge sauce made on Sundays and birthdays by Amadio Gasmen, beloved member of the school's Filipino kitchen staff. All boarders during the 50s and 60s will have fond, mouth-watering memories of this sauce. In Amadio's words, "My own recipe for hot fudge sauce that all my friends that graduated always talk about". Amadio had a special way with chocolate and was also famous for the large solid chocolate rabbits which he made in his own molds and placed in the center of the tables in the Scripps Hall dining room every Easter. The lovely, luscious centerpieces were eagerly devoured by appreciative boarders.

Amadio Gasmen
Former Kitchen Staff

Peach Chutney

Yields 8 12-ounce jars

INGREDIENTS:

1 No. 10 can (12 to 13 cups) sliced peaches
1/2 tablespoon salt
4 ounces ginger (1/2 preserved and 1/2 fresh root)
4 tablespoons syrup from bottle of preserved ginger
3 1/2 cups sugar
1 1/2 cups vinegar

4 tablespoons Worcestershire sauce
3 large cloves garlic, minced
1 cup chopped onion
3/4 cup bottled lime juice
3/4 teaspoon ginger powder
1 pod chile pepper, finely chopped
1 cup golden raisins

PROCEDURE:

Drain peaches. (Note: You may reserve juice and use for sweetening when you make apple sauce.) Slice each peach piece in half, place in a large bowl and add the salt. Mix all ingredients except raisins and peaches in a large kettle and bring to boil. When onions are soft, add peaches and raisins. Boil for a few minutes. Put into sterilized jars and seal. If there seems to be too much liquid, save it for another can of peaches.

I prefer not to use this chutney until it has stood for a year. Letting it stand for a time, maybe a month or so is OK, but the longer it stands in sealed jars, the better it tastes. If you like it "hotter", you can use more chile pods, but I prefer it with only 1 pod.

Ruth Jenkins,
Headmistress Emeritus, 1963-71

Onion Confit

Yields 2 to 3 cups

INGREDIENTS:

3 tablespoons butter
2 pounds onions, peeled
and sliced
1/2 teaspoon salt
Pepper to taste

1/4 cup sugar
1/2 cup sherry vinegar
2/3 cups red wine vinegar
2 tablespoons grenadine

PROCEDURE:

Melt butter in a sauté pan and add onion, salt, pepper and sugar. Cover pan and cook over low fire for 30 minutes; stirring from time to time. Then add the remaining vinegars and grenadine and cook 30 minutes, uncovered, stirring as necessary. Mixture should thicken like a marmalade.

You may store refrigerated in jars for gifts or serve with red meat roasts or wild game as a condiment.

Anne Otterson
Parent, Eric Otterson '87 and Helen Otterson '89

Old South Cucumber Lime Pickles

Yields 6 to 8 pints

INGREDIENTS:

7 pounds cucumbers,
  sliced crosswise
2 gallons water
1 cup Mrs. Wages
  Pickling Lime
8 cups distilled white
  vinegar, 5% acidity

8 cups sugar
1 tablespoon salt
  (optional)
2 teaspoons mixed
  pickling spices

PROCEDURE:

Soak clean cucumbers in water and lime mixture in crockery or enamel ware for 12 hours or overnight. Do not use aluminum ware. Remove sliced cucumbers from lime water. Rinse 4 times in fresh ice water. Combine vinegar, sugar, salt and mixed pickling spices in a large pot. Bring to a low boil, stirring until sugar dissolves. Remove syrup from heat and add sliced cucumbers. Soak 6 to 7 hours or overnight.

Boil slices in the syrup 40 minutes. Fill sterilized canning jars with hot slices. Pour hot syrup over the slices, leaving 1/2" between top of syrup and top of jar. Cap each jar when filled. Process pints 10 minutes (quarts 15 minutes) in a boiling water bath canner. Test jars for airtight seals according to manufacturer's instructions. Refrigerate unsealed jars.

My Aunt Johnnie has been making these pickles for years. Once you taste them, you won't be able to eat another store bought pickle. Mrs. Wages Pickling Lime is available in Tupelo, Mississippi and sometimes in grocery and/or hardware stores in other areas.

Jeanne Smith
Parent, Jenner Smith '99

Beverages

Holiday Punch

Yields 3 quarts

INGREDIENTS:

2 cups water
1 cup sugar
4 cups (1 quart) plain
   iced tea
1 cup freshly squeezed
   lemon juice

1 46-ounce can
   cranberry juice
1/2 teaspoon cinnamon
   Dash cloves

PROCEDURE:

Boil the water in a large pot and dissolve the sugar in it. Remove from heat and mix in remaining ingredients. Chill.

Sara Sweet
Staff, Director of Food Service

Fruit Punch

Yields approximately 2 gallons

INGREDIENTS:

16 oranges
16 lemons
2 46-ounce cans
   unsweetened
   pineapple juice
3 cups sugar
2 cups water

6 29-ounce bottles
   ginger ale
1 large block of ice
1 bunch mint
1 pint strawberries,
   washed and stemmed
2 oranges, sliced

PROCEDURE:

Squeeze juice from oranges and lemons into a large bowl. Add pineapple juice. In a saucepan, mix sugar and water and bring to a boil, stirring until sugar is dissolved. Cool and add to juices. Pour into a large punch bowl and add ginger ale. Add a large block of ice, mint leaves, strawberries and sliced oranges.

My mother's favorite punch recipe. It's wonderful!

Kristen Druker
Faculty, History Department and
Parent, Mara Druker '99

Hot Cider

Yields 1 gallon

INGREDIENTS:

2 tablespoons whole
cloves
3 oranges
1 gallon apple cider
1 cup brown sugar

1 teaspoon whole cloves
2 to 3 cinnamon sticks
2 teaspoons whole
allspice

PROCEDURE:

Preheat oven to 325°. Stick the cloves into the oranges. Place in baking dish, add a small amount of water to bottom of pan, cover and bake for 1 hour. When the oranges are done, place them along with the remaining ingredients into a 6-quart or larger saucepan. Bring to a boil and simmer uncovered 20 minutes. Serve.

We like to simmer and serve this cider throughout December. You'll find the whole house smells wonderful.

Cathy Menifee Petre '61

Russian Tea

Yields approximately 2 1/2 cups
of powdered concentrate

INGREDIENTS:

1 cup Tang powdered
mix
1 cup instant tea
powdered mix

1/3 cup sugar (or the
equivalent in sugar
substitute)
1/2 package Kool Aid
Lemonade powdered
mix (or Gatorade Mix)

PROCEDURE:

Mix all ingredients together. Store in an airtight jar. To serve, mix 2 to 3 teaspoons of tea concentrate per cup of hot water.

Amounts of all ingredients may be adjusted to suit individual tastes. Wonderful drink for cold weather or anytime you are "under the weather" with a cold.

Chris Young
Parent, Dana Young '87 and David Young '96

Hot Toddy

Yields 1 toddy

INGREDIENTS:

Pinch superfine sugar
1 strip lemon peel stuck
  with 1 whole clove
Pinch cinnamon
  (or 1" piece cinnamon
  stick)

3 ounces bourbon or
  blended whiskey
Boiling water

PROCEDURE:

Warm a mug or glass under hot water. Dry the mug. Place a silver spoon in mug to prevent breaking. Place sugar, lemon peel, cinnamon and whiskey in mug. Pour in boiling water to fill. Stir. Enjoy!

A wonderful remedy for a cold and a perfect drink to enjoy with a book and warm fire.

Liz Armstrong
Parent, Mac Armstrong '93 and Annie Armstrong '96

Refreshing White Wine
Citrus Punch

Yields 1 1/2 quarts

INGREDIENTS:

**3 1/2 cups freshly squeezed
orange juice
2 cups dry white wine
1/2 cup Cointreau**

**Thinly cut orange and
lemon slices**

PROCEDURE:

In a large glass pitcher combine orange juice, wine and Cointreau. Stir together.
Cover pitcher with clear wrap and refrigerate until well-chilled. Just before
serving, add several slices of orange and lemon to the pitcher. Stir again and
serve.

*This punch looks pretty in the pitcher and goes well with many brunch and
luncheon menus.*

*Marilyn Bilger
Parent, Lauren Bilger '93 and Whitney Bilger '96*

Desserts

Miss Cummins' Cookies

Yields 6 dozen

INGREDIENTS:

- 1 cup (2 sticks) margarine
- 1 cup granulated sugar
- 1 cup powdered sugar
- 1 cup vegetable oil
- 2 eggs, lightly beaten

- 1 teaspoon vanilla (or almond) extract
- 4 cups flour
- 1 teaspoon soda
- 1 teaspoon cream of tartar
- 1/2 teaspoon salt

PROCEDURE:

In a mixing bowl cream margarine and sugars until very smooth. Add vegetable oil, eggs and vanilla (or almond) extract, 1 at a time, beating well after each addition. Sift dry ingredients together and add to the wet. Mix well. Cover bowl and refrigerate dough overnight.

In the morning, preheat oven to 350°. Make small balls with the dough, place on lightly greased cookie sheets and press down with a fork, or with a nut or candied cherry. Bake for 8 to 10 minutes.

Ruth Jenkins, Headmistress Emeritus, kindly provided this recipe from Miss Cummins. Ruth describes these cookies as being light, rich and simply delicious!

Miss Caroline Seely Cummins
Headmistress, 1921-53

Aunt Polly's Sugar Cookies

Yields 42 cookies

INGREDIENTS:

1/2 cup shortening
1/2 teaspoon salt
1/2 teaspoon grated lemon
    peel
1/2 teaspoon nutmeg
  1 cup sugar
  2 eggs, well-beaten

2 tablespoons milk
2 cups all-purpose flour
1 teaspoon baking
    powder
1/2 teaspoon baking soda
    Sugar for sprinkling
    on top

PROCEDURE:

Preheat oven to 375°. Combine shortening, salt, lemon peel and nutmeg with an electric mixer and blend well. Add sugar gradually and cream well. Add beaten eggs and milk and mix well. Sift flour with baking powder and soda. Add to creamed mixture, blending well. Drop from teaspoon onto lightly greased baking sheets. Leave generous space between as cookies will spread. Let stand a few minutes, then flatten cookies by stamping with a glass covered with a damp cloth. Sprinkle with sugar. Bake for 8 to 12 minutes.

Mimi King
Aunt, Elizabeth Vale '92 and Susannah Vale '95

Sand Dollar Cookies

Yields 3 to 4 dozen

INGREDIENTS:

1/2 cup (1 stick) butter,
    softened
1/2 cup granulated sugar
1/2 cup powdered sugar
1/2 cup vegetable oil
  1 egg
  1 teaspoon vanilla

2 cups + 2 tablespoons
    flour
1/2 teaspoon cream of
    tartar
1/2 teaspoon baking soda
1/2 teaspoon salt
  3 tablespoons granulated
    sugar

PROCEDURE:

Preheat oven to 350°. Cream together the softened butter and the granulated sugar. Blend well. Add the powdered sugar, oil and egg and blend well. Add vanilla and blend well. Next add the flour, cream of tartar, baking soda and salt. Mix into a ball and refrigerate. After the dough is well-chilled, roll dough into walnut-size balls. Sprinkle with sugar and flatten with the bottom of a cut crystal glass which has a star pattern in the bottom. Bake 8 to 10 minutes. Do not let them get too brown or they will be too crispy.

Molly Crabtree
Parent, Scott Crabtree '96 and Adrienne Crabtree '98

Spritz

Yields 6 to 8 dozen

INGREDIENTS:

3 cups (6 sticks) butter	3 egg yolks
2 1/4 cups sugar	6 cups flour
3 tablespoons orange juice	

PROCEDURE:

Preheat oven to 350°. Cream butter and sugar well. Add orange juice and egg yolks and mix well. Add flour 1 to 2 cups at a time, mixing very well after each addition. Fill cookie press with dough. Press out on ungreased cookie sheet. Bake for 11 to 12 minutes. Remove immediately and cool on cookie rack.

Can add food coloring to parts of dough. May need to add flour to restore consistency to dough. Cookies store well in an airtight container. (Separate layers with wax paper.) Also freeze well if stored as described above.

Gwen Foss
Parent, Sandy Foss '92X and Lynne Foss '95

Sugar Cookies

Yields 3 dozen

INGREDIENTS:

Cookies:
1 cup (2 sticks) unsalted
   butter, at room
   temperature
1 1/4 cup sugar
1 egg
1 teaspoon vanilla
1/2 cup all-purpose flour
1/2 teaspoon baking
   powder
1/2 teaspoon salt

Royal Icing:
1 egg white
1/8 teaspoon cream of
   tartar
1 1/4 cups sifted
   confectioners' sugar

PROCEDURE:

Cookies: Cream butter and sugar on medium speed until light and fluffy. Beat in egg and vanilla. Sift together dry ingredients, add to wet ingredients and mix until blended. Divide the dough into 3 balls, wrap and refrigerate 3 to 4 hours before rolling out. (The dough may be frozen.)

Preheat oven to 375°. Lightly butter cookie sheets. Remove 1 ball of dough from the refrigerator; roll it out 1/8" thick and cut with cookie cutters. Sprinkle with sugar, if desired. Place on greased sheets and bake 8 to 10 minutes until cooked through. While the first cookies bake, remove the second ball of dough, roll and cut as with the first. The same with the third. If you choose to use fancy or complicated cutters that make transferring raw cookies to baking sheets difficult, try rolling dough out directly onto the lightly buttered baking sheets. Cut out shapes, lift off dough scraps between them. Scrap dough may be rerolled and cut, but only once. After two rollings, the dough becomes too tough to be palatable.

Cool cookies on wire racks. Once cool, they can be left plain or decorated dozens of ways: Sift cocoa or powdered sugar over them; drizzle over melted chocolate, or pipe chocolate into specific designs; glaze with powdered sugar that's been smoothed out with a touch of milk; glaze, then sprinkle with candies, chopped nuts, colored sugars; pipe or spread with durable Royal Icing.

Royal Icing: Beat egg white and cream of tartar until frothy. Gradually beat in sugar, until the icing is thick and smooth. Spread thinly over cool cookies, add colored sprinkles, or pipe designs in various colors using pastry bag. If icing stiffens too much to pipe, thin with few drops of lemon juice. This frosting dries very hard.

Cookies freeze beautifully. Whether presented plain, with just a sparkle of sugar or gaily decorated, these classic sugar cookies will please the kid in all of us. Want to hang them on the Christmas tree? Simply poke them with a wide straw before baking.

Judith Lanphier Strada '63X
Parent, Nick Strada '92 and Catherine Strada '95

Best Roll Out Cookie Dough

Yields 3 dozen

INGREDIENTS:

1/2 cup (1 stick) butter, softened
1 cup sugar
1 egg, beaten

1 teaspoon vanilla
1 3/4 cups flour
1 teaspoon baking powder

PROCEDURE:

Mix butter and sugar until creamy. Add egg and vanilla and mix. Sift together the flour and baking powder and add to butter mixture. If mixture is too stiff, add 1 teaspoon water. Refrigerate dough for 1 hour.

Preheat oven to 375°. Roll dough out 1/8" thick on floured board. Cut out cookies with your favorite shape cutters. Decorate with sprinkles. Bake 8 to 10 minutes on ungreased cookie sheet. Remove immediately to cool.

Carol Guess
Parent, Graham Guess '90, Garrett Guess '93, Gillian Guess '95X,
Gaylen Guess '98

White Cookies...Finnish
(For Valentine's Day, Easter, Christmas)

Yields 5 dozen

INGREDIENTS:

1 cup white sugar
1 cup (2 sticks) butter
2 eggs
3 tablespoons cream
1 teaspoon vanilla

3 cups flour, sifted
1/4 teaspoon salt
1 teaspoon baking soda
1/2 teaspoon cream of
   tartar

PROCEDURE:

Blend the sugar and butter together until creamy. Add the eggs, cream and vanilla and mix well. Add the sifted flour, salt, baking soda and cream of tartar. Mix well. Chill dough in refrigerator at least 1 hour before rolling out.

Preheat oven to 375˚. Remove dough from refrigerator and roll out thin on floured board. Using Valentine, Easter or Christmas cookie cutters, cut out cookies. Place on lightly greased cookie sheet and bake for 7 to 10 minutes.

This is a typical Finnish cookie; can be decorated with Valentine hearts for Valentine's Day or frosting for Easter and Christmas. We eat them plain. They are very good with cider or coffee.

Joan Canby Mugg '66

Mailanderli
(Swiss Christmas Cookies)

Yields 30 to 40 small cookies

INGREDIENTS:

1/2 cup (1 stick) salted
   butter
1/2 cup granulated sugar
1 egg
   Grated peel of 1 lemon

1 2/3 cups sifted flour

Glaze:
1 egg yolk plus few drops
   water

PROCEDURE:

Preheat oven to 350°. Cream butter and sugar until fluffy, then add egg and lemon peel and mix well. Add sifted flour and stir until well-blended. Cover and let dough rest in refrigerator about 1 hour. Roll out on lightly floured board to 1/4" thickness and cut into small desired shapes. Place on greased cookie sheets and brush glaze twice on cookies. Bake for about 15 minutes or until golden.

This is the most popular Christmas cookie in Switzerland as well as with our family. These cookies keep 3 to 4 weeks in an airtight container and also freeze well.

Silvia Berchtold
Parent, Christophe Berchtold '85 and Nicole Berchtold '87

Shortbread Cookies

Yields 2 1/2 dozen

INGREDIENTS:

1 cup (2 sticks) butter or margarine, softened
1/2 cup sugar
2 cups flour

2 tablespoons caraway seeds or sugar to sprinkle on top

PROCEDURE:

Preheat oven to 350°. Cream butter (or margarine) and sugar. Add flour and mix until blended. Roll into a ball. Roll or pat out a third of the dough at a time on a bread board until 1/4" thick. Cut into small squares. Place on an ungreased cookie sheet and sprinkle lightly with caraway seeds or sugar. Bake for 12 to 15 minutes.

Lucy Kable Means Borsenberger '69
Parent, Artie Means '94 and Chris Means '96

Sand Tarts
(Christmas Cookies)

Yields 80 to 100

INGREDIENTS:

1 cup (2 sticks) softened
  butter
2 cups granulated sugar
2 eggs
3 cups presifted flour

Decorations:
1 teaspoon cinnamon
1/2 cup sugar
Almonds (about 50),
  whole, raw, sliced in
  half along their
  length

PROCEDURE:

Preheat oven to 400°. Beat butter, then add sugar and beat until well-mixed. Separate 1 of the eggs and reserve the white. Add the yolk and the other whole egg to the butter/sugar mixture. Beat to mix well. Then add flour and mix well. If dough is too stiff, mix in a few drops of water to help soften. Chill dough covered in refrigerator at least 1 hour. Roll thin (approximately 1/8") on floured board and cut into 2" rounds. Place on greased cookie sheet; brush with unbeaten egg white. Mix together the cinnamon and sugar. Sprinkle cookies with cinnamon/sugar mixture and press half an almond in the middle (outside up). Note: Cinnamon/sugar best sprinkled from a shaker, like a salt shaker. Bake for 6 to 8 minutes or until golden or very lightly brown.

This is a family heirloom from my Aunt Kit who made them every Christmas as I grew up and I have carried on the tradition. These cookies should be thin *and crisp. They keep well for weeks in an airtight container.*

Pat Miller
Parent, Kristin Miller '87 and Patrick Miller '93

Walnut Crescents or Horns

Yields 18 to 22 medium crescents

INGREDIENTS:

Dough:
1/2 cup (1 stick) butter or
　　margarine, softened
1/2 cup cottage cheese
　　(small curd)
1 teaspoon vanilla
1 cup flour

Topping:
2/3 cup granulated sugar
1/2+ teaspoon cinnamon
2/3 cups walnuts, finely
　　chopped (in nut mill)
1 egg yolk with 1
　　teaspoon water
Extra granulated sugar
　　for tops

PROCEDURE:

Blend softened butter with cottage cheese and vanilla. Add flour and mix until smooth (using hands if necessary). Pat into ball. Cover and chill 1 hour or more. Meanwhile combine sugar, cinnamon and walnuts.

Preheat oven to 375°. Divide dough in half and roll out on floured board or between sheets of wax paper. Roll dough into a rectangle about 1/8" thick (fairly thin). Cut into 3" squares and place about 1 teaspoon of nut mixture in center of each square. Roll from 1 corner to the opposite corner and curve slightly to form crescent or horn. Place on greased cookie sheet, lining up and making 2 vertical rows. Roll out rest of dough and repeat process. You should have between 18 to 22 crescents. (Put a few in the middle of sheet if rows are crowded.) Brush tops with beaten egg mixed with water. Sprinkle tops with extra granulated sugar. Bake for about 20 minutes or until brown and puffy. (You may want to rotate cookie sheets a few minutes before end of cooking time to insure even browning.) Remove from sheet to rack to cool.

This is a delicious pastry (similar to rugulach), very crispy and light. These are best served hot or baked fresh the day you serve them. They will keep in an airtight tin for 3 to 5 days.

Pat Miller
Parent, Kristin Miller '87 and Patrick Miller '93

Vanilla Crescents

Yields about 30 cookies

INGREDIENTS:

1 1/4 cups flour
1/2 cup (1 stick) butter, softened
1/3 cup confectioners' sugar

1/2 cup blanched almonds, ground or chopped very finely (almost to a paste)
2 teaspoons vanilla
Optional for dipping: Ghirardelli's semisweet chocolate

PROCEDURE:

Preheat oven to 325°. Put all ingredients except chocolate in a bowl and mix by hand until you have a well-mixed soft dough. Pinch off pieces about the size of a walnut and roll between hands into a thick sausage. Bend into a crescent shape and place on ungreased cookie sheet. Bake for 20 to 25 minutes. Cookies will be light brown. Remove from baking sheet onto another cold baking sheet and let cool. For a special treat melt semisweet Ghirardelli chocolate and with a spatula cover half of each crescent (top and bottom) with chocolate. Place on a cookie sheet covered with waxpaper and refrigerate for at least 1/2 hour or until the chocolate is hard. These should always be kept refrigerated.

You can also refrigerate the dough and when chilled, roll it out and cut it into cookie shapes. Be sure you don't underbake these, but once they begin to turn brown they become dark fairly quickly. Cookies will keep for weeks stored in refrigerator in covered container. They also freeze well.

Christiane Knauer Creighton '43.

Mexican Wedding Cakes

Yields 3 to 4 dozen

INGREDIENTS:

1 cup (2 sticks) butter or margarine
1/2 cup powdered sugar
1/2 teaspoon salt
1 teaspoon vanilla extract

2 cups sifted flour
2 cups walnuts, finely chopped
Powdered sugar (approximately 2 cups for topping)

PROCEDURE:

Preheat oven to 325°. Cream butter and sugar for 2 to 3 minutes until very smooth. Add salt, vanilla and flour and mix well. Add walnuts and mix. Shape into 1" balls. Place on ungreased cookie sheet. Flatten with tumbler dipped in flour. Bake for 12 minutes. While warm, sift powdered sugar over cookies.

Lucy Kable Means Borsenberger '69
Parent, Artie Means '94 and Chris Means '96

"Sandies"

Yields about 3 dozen

INGREDIENTS:

3/4 cup softened butter
   (margarine will do)
1 teaspoon vanilla
1 tablespoon water
1/3 cup sugar
1/8 teaspoon salt
2 cups sifted cake flour
   (if you use all-purpose
   flour, take out 2
   tablespoons)

1 cup coarsely chopped
   walnuts
1 cup semisweet
   chocolate morsels
1 cup granulated sugar
   (approximately)

PROCEDURE:

Preheat oven to 300°. Combine butter, vanilla, water, sugar and salt and blend well. Stir in flour. Add the walnuts and chocolate morsels. Form into 1" balls. Place on ungreased cookie sheet. Bake for 20 to 25 minutes. While still warm, roll in granulated sugar.

These cookies are just delicious and have become a tradition in our family at Christmas time. They were passed on to us by my grandmother.

Jennifer Lauer '94

Chocolate Chip Cookies

Yields 36 very large cookies

INGREDIENTS:

1 cup (2 sticks)
  margarine
1 cup solid vegetable
  shortening
1 1/2 cups sugar
1 1/2 cups brown sugar,
  packed
3 eggs

3 teaspoons vanilla
5 cups flour
1 teaspoon salt
1 1/2 teaspoons baking soda
24 ounces chocolate
  chips
1 cup chopped nuts
  (optional)

PROCEDURE:

Preheat oven to 375°. Combine margarine and vegetable shortening. Add sugars and beat until creamy. Add eggs and vanilla and beat until light and fluffy. Add flour, salt and baking soda and mix until well-blended. Stir in chocolate chips and nuts (if desired). Drop 1/4 cup or 1/3 cup of batter for each cookie onto lightly greased cookie sheets. Press down to flatten. (These cookies are large!) Bake for 12 to 14 minutes or until golden brown. Time may vary depending on oven.

If you underbake slightly, cookies will be soft. The soccer team loves these!

Diane Shockley
Parent, Tre Shockley '96 and Tristan Shockley '98

Chocolatey Chippies

Yields 3 to 4 dozen

INGREDIENTS:

2 1/2 ounces unsweetened
  baking chocolate
1/2 cup (1 stick) butter
1 cup white sugar (or
  1/2 white, 1/2
  brown, packed)
2 teaspoons vanilla
1 egg
1/2 cup milk or light
  cream (may be sour)

1 teaspoon baking soda
1 1/2 cups flour (may be 1
  cup white, 1/2 cup
  whole wheat)
Pinch salt
1 cup chopped nuts
  (walnuts or pecans)
6 ounces chocolate
  chips

PROCEDURE:

Preheat oven to 350°. Melt baking chocolate and butter together in the top of a double boiler. Cool slightly and pour into the bowl of an electric mixer. Mix in sugar and vanilla. In a small bowl beat egg and milk; add baking soda, stir. Mix flour with salt and add flour mixture in thirds to chocolate mixture, alternating with liquid ingredients, beginning and ending with flour mixture, mixing after each addition. Stir in nuts and chocolate chips. Drop batter onto baking sheets by tablespoons and bake 8 to 10 minutes, or until just dry and firm to the touch. These have a brownie-like texture and must not be overbaked.

Recipe doubles nicely. Makes about 3 dozen, depending on size.

Natasha Halpert
Aunt, Alura Simpkins '90 and Alex Simpkins '96

Super Chocolate Chip Cookies

Yields 5 dozen

INGREDIENTS:

3/4 cup shortening (or margarine)
1/2 cup (1 stick) butter
1 cup sugar
1 cup packed brown sugar
3 eggs
1 tablespoon vanilla
1 teaspoon lemon juice

2 teaspoons baking soda
1 teaspoon salt
1/2 teaspoon cinnamon
1/2 cup oatmeal
3 cups flour
14 ounces semisweet chocolate chips
2 cups chopped walnuts (optional)

PROCEDURE:

Preheat oven to 350°. In large bowl, beat together shortening, butter and sugars until light and fluffy. Beat in eggs, 1 at a time, beating well after each addition. Beat in vanilla and lemon juice. Mix in dry ingredients until well-combined. Stir in chocolate chips and nuts. Drop by large spoonfuls 3" apart on ungreased baking sheets. Bake 14 to 18 minutes.

Jeannette Ruchlewicz
Parent, Brian Ruchlewicz '97

Colossal Cookies

Yields 4 dozen

INGREDIENTS:

1/2 cup (1 stick) butter
1 1/2 cups sugar
1 1/2 cups brown sugar, packed
4 large eggs
1 teaspoon vanilla
1 18-ounce jar chunky peanut butter

1 18-ounce box rolled oats
6 ounces semisweet chocolate chips
2 1/2 teaspoons baking soda

PROCEDURE:

Preheat oven to 350°. In a large bowl, beat together butter and sugars. Blend in eggs and vanilla. Add peanut butter and mix well. Stir in oats, chocolate chips and baking soda and mix well. Drop by scant 1/4 cup, about 4" apart on ungreased cookie sheet. Flatten with fork to 2 1/2" diameter. Bake 10 to 12 minutes. Cool 1 minute on baking sheet, then remove to wire rack to cool completely.

Store in tightly covered container.

JoAnn Vasil
Parent, Stephen Vasil '93 and Stacy Vasil '95X

Chocolate Chip Macaroon Cookies

Yields 24 to 36 small cookies

INGREDIENTS:

1/3 cup flour
1/4 teaspoon baking
   powder
1/8 teaspoon salt
  1 tablespoon butter
  2 large eggs
3/4 cup granulated sugar
1 1/2 teaspoons vanilla

16 ounces shredded
   coconut
12 ounces semisweet
   chocolate chips

Frosting:
1 cup semisweet mint
   chocolate chips

PROCEDURE:

Preheat oven to 325°. Line 2 cookie sheets with aluminum foil and spray with vegetable oil. Sift together flour, baking powder and salt into small bowl. Melt butter in microwave, set aside (not to harden). Place eggs in bowl of electric mixer and beat until well-mixed. Gradually add sugar while continuing to beat for 5 minutes until fluffy and light yellow. Add the butter and vanilla and mix well. Add the flour mixture and mix until blended. Fold in coconut and chocolate chips. Drop well-rounded teaspoons of mixture on cookie sheet, 1 1/2" apart. Bake for 8 to 9 minutes or until cookies begin to brown slightly around the edges.

Frosting: Melt mint chips in double boiler or microwave. Remove cookies from cookie sheets and place upside down on paper towels to cool slightly. Then spread mint chocolate mixture with knife on bottoms of cookies. Place cookies chocolate side up on wax paper and chill in refrigerator until chocolate is hard.

I have colored the coconut for holidays to make more festive.

Kristina Starkey '68X

Best Guess Cookies

Yield 5 to 6 dozen

INGREDIENTS:

1 cup brown sugar
1 cup white sugar
1 cup (2 sticks) butter, softened
1 cup oil
3 1/2 cups flour
1 teaspoon salt
1 teaspoon soda
1 teaspoon cream of tartar

1 egg, beaten
2 teaspoons vanilla
1 cup coconut
1 cup oats
1 cup Rice Krispies
6 ounces chocolate chips
6 ounces butterscotch chips

PROCEDURE:

Preheat oven to 350°. With an electric mixer, cream brown and white sugars with softened butter. Add oil and mix well. Sift together flour, salt, soda and cream of tartar and add to butter mixture. Mix well. Add beaten egg and vanilla and mix until well-blended. Add coconut, oats, Rice Krispies, chocolate chips and butterscotch chips and mix on low speed or stir in by hand. Drop by teaspoonfuls onto greased cookie sheet. Bake for 13 minutes. Cool 5 minutes. Remove from cookie sheets.

Carol Guess
Parent, Graham Guess '90, Garrett Guess '93, Gillian Guess '95X, Gaylen Guess '98

"Crackle"

Serves 15+

INGREDIENTS:

Non-stick cooking spray
Soda crackers to line a 10" x 14" pan
1/2 cup (1 stick) margarine
1/2 cup (1 stick) butter

3/4 cup sugar
10 ounces Reeses peanut butter chips
12 ounces semisweet chocolate (or milk chocolate) chips

PROCEDURE:

Preheat oven to 350°. Spray a 10" x 14" jelly roll pan or cookie sheet with 1" sides with nonstick cooking spray. Line the pan with a single layer of soda crackers. In a saucepan combine the margarine, butter and sugar. Bring to a slow boil, stirring until all ingredients dissolve, 3 to 4 minutes. Pour this butter/sugar mixture evenly over the soda crackers. Bake for 6 to 7 minutes. Sprinkle the 2 bags of chips over the buttery crackers. Return to oven for 1 to 2 minutes more, then remove and immediately spread melted chips evenly over entire bed of crackers. Cool in refrigerator until solid. Cut or break into squares.

Quick to make. Best if stored frozen or chilled.

Barbara Murfey
Parent, Scott Murfey '95

Double Chocolate Cookies

Yields 3 dozen

INGREDIENTS:

5 ounces semisweet chocolate, broken in pieces	2 teaspoons vanilla
1/2 cup packed brown sugar	1 cup minus 2 tablespoons flour
1/2 cup (1 stick) butter	1/2 teaspoon baking soda
1 egg	1/2 (or 1) cup chocolate chips
	1/2 cup nuts (optional)

PROCEDURE:

Preheat oven to 350°. In the bowl of a food processor fitted with a steel knife, combine chocolate and sugar. Process until chocolate is fine as sugar. (If using a mixer, melt chocolate and add to creamed butter and sugar.) Add butter, blend 30 seconds, then add egg and vanilla. Add flour and soda, then top with chocolate chips (and optional nuts). Process just to mix; do not pulverize chocolate chips. This will take 2 On/Off turns of the food processor. Drop dough by teaspoons onto lightly greased baking sheet. Bake 10 minutes.

These very rich cookies are fragile when they are hot out of the oven; transfer from cookie sheet very carefully so they don't fall apart. May prepare with electric mixer.

Virginia Thomas
Parent, Brad Thomas '84

Chocolate Charlies

Yields 16 large cookies

INGREDIENTS:

2 ounces unsweetened
   chocolate
6 ounces semisweet
   chocolate
2 tablespoons unsalted
   butter
1/4 cup all-purpose flour
1/4 teaspoon baking
   powder
1/8 teaspoon salt

2 eggs
3/4 cup sugar
2 teaspoons instant
   coffee
1/2 teaspoon vanilla
6 ounces semisweet
   chocolate chips
8 ounces chopped
   walnuts or pecans

PROCEDURE:

Preheat oven to 350°. Melt unsweetened chocolate, semisweet chocolate and butter in a small, heavy saucepan over very low heat, stirring slowly but constantly. When smooth, remove from heat and let cool. Sift the flour, baking powder and salt into a small bowl. Beat the eggs, sugar, coffee and vanilla in a large bowl on medium-high speed for 1 or 2 minutes to thicken slightly. Then lower speed and beat in the cooled, melted chocolate and flour mixture. Stir in chocolate chips and nuts. Drop heaping tablespoons of batter onto foil-lined cookie sheets. Bake until cookies look shiny outside and still moist, but not gooey inside, approximately 10 minutes for large cookies, less for smaller ones. Cool completely before trying to take the cookies off the foil.

These cookies have a crisp, chocolate, meringue-like exterior and a soft, fudge-like interior, irresistible to chocolate lovers.

Judith Lanphier Strada '63X
Parent, Nick Strada '92 and Catherine Strada '95

No-Egg Chocolate Cookies

Yields 4 to 5 dozen

INGREDIENTS:

1/2 cup (1 stick) butter or
     margarine
12 ounces chocolate
     chips

1 14-ounce can
     sweetened condensed
     milk
1 cup flour
1 cup chopped nuts
1 1/2 teaspoons vanilla

PROCEDURE:

Preheat oven to 350°. Heat the butter, chocolate and condensed milk in top of a double boiler until chocolate is thoroughly melted. Stir to blend well. Pour chocolate mixture into a mixing bowl and let cool slightly. Add remaining ingredients and mix well. Drop by teaspoonfuls onto a foil-lined, lightly greased cookie sheet. Bake 7 minutes. Remove carefully from foil with a spatula and let cool.

Caroline Duncombe Pelz '36

Lace Cookies

Yields 2 dozen 2" cookies

INGREDIENTS:

1/2 cup white sugar
1/2 cup brown sugar
1 cup quick-cooking
   oatmeal

1/2 teaspoon salt
1 tablespoon flour
1 egg, well-beaten
1/2 teaspoon vanilla

PROCEDURE:

Preheat oven to 325°. Place the sugars, oatmeal, salt and flour in the bowl of an electric mixer. Beat together the egg and vanilla in a small bowl. Add to mixing bowl and beat at medium speed until ingredients are well-mixed. Put foil on cookie sheet. Drop cookie dough by teaspoon onto foil. Do not put cookies too close together as they will spread. Press down a bit. Bake until golden brown, approximately 10 minutes. Cool, then peel cookies from the foil. Store in a tin to keep crisp.

Rosamond Larmour Loomis
Headmistress, 1953-62

Crispy Oatmeal Coconut Cremes

Yields 7 dozen

INGREDIENTS:

1 cup shortening
1 cup sugar
1 cup brown sugar,
   firmly packed
2 eggs
1 teaspoon vanilla
   extract
2 cups all-purpose flour

1 teaspoon baking soda
1/2 teaspoon salt
1/2 teaspoon baking
   powder
2 cups crisp rice cereal
2 cups regular oats
1 cup flaked coconut

PROCEDURE:

Preheat oven to 350˚. Beat shortening and sugars at medium speed with a mixer until blended. Add eggs and vanilla and beat well. Combine flour and next 3 ingredients. Then add to shortening mixture. Mix well. Stir in rice cereal, oats and coconut. Shape into 1" balls. Place 2" apart on lightly greased cookie sheets. Flatten slightly with fork. Bake for 10 to 12 minutes. Transfer to wire racks to cool.

Tommy King
Cousin, Elizabeth Vale '92 and Susannah Vale '95

Oatmeal Crispies

Yields 5 dozen

INGREDIENTS:

1 1/2 cups sifted all-purpose
    flour
1 teaspoon salt
1 teaspoon baking soda
3 cups quick cooking
    oatmeal
1 cup chopped walnuts

1 cup (2 sticks) butter*
1 cup brown sugar, well
    packed
1 cup sugar
2 eggs, well-beaten
1 teaspoon vanilla

PROCEDURE:

Sift together flour, salt and baking soda. Add oatmeal and nuts. In another bowl cream butter. Gradually add sugars and cream thoroughly. Add eggs and vanilla. Beat well. Add flour mixture to butter mixture and mix well. Shape into log rolls (1 1/2" to 2" diameter) and chill thoroughly.

When ready to bake, preheat oven to 350˚. Slice log rolls into 1/4" thick rounds. Bake on ungreased cookie sheet 8 to 10 minutes.

*Note: May substitute margarine for butter but cookies will be more chewy and less crispy.

As an option, 1/2 cup raisins or dates may be added. It's very handy to have a couple of these log rolls in the freezer for unexpected guests.

Carolyn Yorston
Headmaster's Advisory Council and
Parent, Wendy Yorston Stevens '75

Oatmeal Crisps

Yields 4 dozen

INGREDIENTS:

1 cup brown sugar,
   packed
1/2 cup shortening
1/4 cup (1/2 stick) butter
1 egg, room temperature

1/2 teaspoon soda
1/4 teaspoon salt
2 cups rolled oats
1 cup raisins (or nuts)

PROCEDURE:

Preheat oven to 375°. Combine brown sugar, shortening and butter in a saucepan and melt over low heat, stirring. Remove from heat and cool slightly. Add 1 well-beaten egg, soda, salt, oats and raisins (nuts). Mix well. Drop by teaspoons on a well-greased and floured cookie sheet. Bake for about 7 minutes. Cool slightly before removing from cookie sheet.

Ellin Todd '68

Oatmeal Cinnamon Drops

Yields 6 dozen

INGREDIENTS:

1 cup (2 sticks) butter
2 cups granulated sugar
2 eggs
1 tablespoon molasses
2 teaspoons vanilla
2 cups all-purpose flour

2 teaspoons cinnamon
1 1/2 teaspoons baking soda
2 cups quick oats
2/3 cup raisins
1 cup nuts
1/2 cup chocolate chips

PROCEDURE:

Preheat oven to 350°. Cream together butter and sugar. Add eggs, molasses and vanilla and mix well. Combine flour, cinnamon and soda and gradually add to creamed mixture while mixing. Stir in oats, raisins, nuts and chocolate chips. Drop by rounded teaspoons onto ungreased cookie sheet. Bake for 12 minutes or until light brown.

Freeze well. Can use margarine in place of butter.

Elsie Lee Collier Smith '34

Grandma Gollmer's Oatmeal Cookies

Yields 4 dozen

INGREDIENTS:

1/2 cup raisins
1 cup water
1 cup sugar
1 cup (2 sticks) margarine

2 eggs, well-beaten
2 cups flour
1 teaspoon baking soda
1/2 cup walnuts
2 cups oatmeal

PROCEDURE:

Preheat oven to 375°. Simmer raisins in the water for approximately 5 minutes. Drain, saving water. Beat sugar and margarine together well. Add the eggs to the sugar/margarine mixture. Beat. Add 1/2 cup raisin water, beat. Add flour and soda and mix well. Fold in walnuts, oatmeal and the cooked raisins. Mix well. Drop batter by spoonfuls onto greased cookie sheet. Bake 7 to 9 minutes until a little brown around the edges. Cool on wax paper.

Lila I. Gollmer
Grandparent, Kimberly Durkin '96 and Kristin Durkin '98

Butterscotch Crisps

Yields 24

INGREDIENTS:

1 12-ounce package butterscotch chips
1/2 cup smooth peanut butter
3 cups Special K cereal

1 cup walnuts or pecans
1 cup sweetened, flaked coconut, lightly browned in butter

PROCEDURE:

Melt butterscotch chips and peanut butter together in microwave. Add cereal, chopped nuts and the coconut and stir to mix. Drop mixture by teaspoons onto cookie sheet. (Be sure to leave space between cookies as they will spread. They will be flat, like pralines.) Place in refrigerator and serve after they have cooled. Store in refrigerator.

Gray Kristofferson
Parent, Cannon Kristofferson '90X and Karen Kristofferson '93

Auntie Phoebe's Christmas Hermit Cookies

Yields 4 dozen

INGREDIENTS:

1 cup (2 sticks) butter
2 cups brown sugar
3 eggs
1/2 teaspoon baking soda
1 teaspoon cinnamon
1 teaspoon cloves
1/4 teaspoon nutmeg
1/2 teaspoon salt

3 1/2 cups flour
1/2 cup milk
1 cup raisins
1 cup chopped walnuts
Several small pieces of
maple sugar candy
per cookie

PROCEDURE:

Preheat oven to 350°. Cream butter and sugar well. Beat in eggs, 1 at a time. Combine dry ingredients and add alternately with milk, mixing well after each addition. Fold in raisins and walnuts. Shape into 1 1/2" size balls and place on lightly greased cookie sheet. Flatten into 3" circles. On the top of each cookie place a few pieces of the maple sugar candy. Bake for about 12 minutes.

As a young bride I remember receiving a shoebox filled with cookies from my husband's great aunt. As I soon learned, she shared these special cookies with all her loved ones, never once revealing the recipe or allowing anyone to be present when she baked them. Over the years since her death we have conferred and experimented to try to duplicate these wonderful treats. We almost have it, except for the maple sugar candy which somehow only slightly melts and should be gooey to the taste. Any help will be much appreciated! Submitted in loving memory of Auntie Phoebe Gaylord from Hamilton, New York.

Lynn Martin Gaylord
Parent, Charlie Gaylord '96

Gramma Betty's Ginger Cookies

Yields 4 to 5 dozen

INGREDIENTS:

- 4 cups flour
- 1 tablespoon baking soda
- 1 teaspoon ginger
- 1 teaspoon cinnamon
- 1 teaspoon salt

- 1 cup sugar
- 1 cup shortening
- 3 eggs
- 1 cup molasses

PROCEDURE:

Preheat oven to 325°. Sift together flour, baking soda, spices and salt. Set aside. Cream sugar and shortening together until well-blended. Beat in eggs. Alternately blend in flour mixture and molasses. Batter will be thick. Drop by rounded spoonfuls onto nonstick cookie sheet. Bake for 10 to 15 minutes. Remove from cookie sheets and let cool, turning over after a few minutes. Store in airtight container.

An old family recipe. Enjoy.

Carol Ann Lattimer
Faculty, Math Department and
Parent, Heather Lattimer '89

Graham Cracker Cookies

Yields 4 dozen

INGREDIENTS:

24 graham cracker
    squares broken on
    dividing line, making
    48 rectangular pieces
1/2 cup (1 stick) plus 1
    tablespoon butter

1 cup plus 2 tablespoons
    brown sugar, packed
1 cup chopped walnuts

PROCEDURE:

Preheat oven to 350°. Butter a 10" x 15" jelly roll pan and place graham crackers in pan side by side in 1 layer. Melt butter and sugar in a small saucepan stirring constantly until smooth. Pour over crackers. Cover with chopped nuts. Bake 8 to 10 minutes. Remove to racks and let cool.

Everyone loves these. Can be frozen.

Elizabeth Schutt '22

Ruth's Meringues

Yields 3 to 4 dozen

INGREDIENTS:

4 egg whites at room
    temperature
1/8 teaspoon salt

1 cup sugar
1 teaspoon vanilla

PROCEDURE:

With rack in middle of oven, preheat oven to 275°. Be sure bowl, beaters and other utensils are clean and grease-free. Cut brown paper grocery bags to line tops of 2 cookie sheets. In medium bowl, using electric mixer at high speed, beat egg whites and salt until foamy. Continue beating and gradually add sugar and vanilla. Beat until mixture stands in stiff peaks and looks glossy. Drop by rounded teaspoons onto prepared cookie sheets. Bake 30 to 40 minutes. If meringues lift easily off paper, they are done. Allow to cool 5 minutes on cookie sheets before storing in airtight tin.

These small light cookies are delicious with fresh fruit for dessert or on a tea table. They need special care in humid climates. Keep in tightly sealed containers and do not expose to the air for extended periods.

Cindy Ker Elrod '64X

Overnight Meringues

Yields 3 dozen

INGREDIENTS:

2 egg whites
3/4 cup sugar
1/2 teaspoon vanilla

6 ounces semisweet
    chocolate chips
1 cup chopped pecans

PROCEDURE:

Preheat oven to 350°. Beat egg whites with an electric mixer on high speed until stiff. Add sugar gradually while continuing to beat at high speed for 5 minutes. Fold in vanilla, chocolate chips and pecans. Drop from teaspoon onto foil-lined cookie sheets. Put sheets in oven and turn off heat. Leave <u>overnight</u> (or at least 8 hours). Don't peek! Leave oven door closed!

No butter or egg yolks! Store in air tight container. Freeze well.

Mildred Branard
Grandparent, Elizabeth Vale '92 and Susannah Vale '95

Peanut Butter Kiss Cookies

Yields 48 cookies

INGREDIENTS:

1 3/4 cups flour
1 teaspoon baking soda
1/2 teaspoon salt
1/2 cup packed brown
    sugar
1 egg
2 tablespoons milk

1 teaspoon vanilla
1/2 cup shortening
1/2 cup peanut butter
48 chocolate candy
    kisses, unwrapped
1/2 cup sugar

PROCEDURE:

Preheat oven to 375˚. Combine all ingredients except for kisses and sugar. Mix until dough forms. Shape into 48 balls. Roll in sugar. Bake 10 to 12 minutes on ungreased cookie sheet. Immediately after taking cookies out of oven, place 1 kiss on top of each cookie. Press down firmly. Remove cookies from cookie sheet with spatula to cool.

Extra tasty, "killer kookies"! Easy to make.

Marie-Claire Brien '76

Peanut Butter Cookies

Yields 5 dozen

INGREDIENTS:

1 cup solid vegetable
    shortening
1 cup sugar
1 cup brown sugar
2 cups flour

1 teaspoon baking soda
2 eggs, well-beaten
1 cup peanut butter
1/2 teaspoon salt
1 tablespoon milk

PROCEDURE:

Preheat oven to 325°. Cream shortening and sugars. Add flour and baking soda and mix well. Add eggs, peanut butter, salt and milk and mix until well-blended. Drop by teaspoons onto an ungreased cookie sheet and press each down (to approximately 1/4" thick) with a fork. Bake for 15 to 20 minutes.

Susannah Vale '95

Mabel's Date Cookies

Yields 2 dozen

INGREDIENTS:

2 eggs, beaten
1 teaspoon vanilla
1 cup sugar
1 cup flour
1 teaspoon baking
    powder

1/8 teaspoon salt
2 cups chopped pitted
    dates
1 cup chopped walnuts
    Powdered sugar to
    coat bars

PROCEDURE:

Preheat oven to 325°. Beat eggs. Mix in the vanilla. Add sugar, flour, baking powder, salt and mix well. Stir in dates and walnuts. Butter a 9" x 9" pan and cover the bottom with wax paper. Fill pan with the dough. Bake for 25 to 30 minutes. Cookies should be soft to the touch when done. Allow to cool in pan for 10 minutes. Turn the pan over and remove the wax paper. Cut into bars, allow to cool. Roll in powdered sugar.

Secret: Do not overcook!

Mary Lieurance Sease '35

Persimmon Spice Cookies

Yields 2 dozen

INGREDIENTS:

4 ripe persimmons
(approximately
3 cups)
1/2 cup (1 stick) butter
1/2 cup sugar
1 egg
1/2 cup yellow raisins
1 cup crushed walnuts

2 shots (2 ounces)
whiskey (optional)
2 1/4 cups flour
1/4 teaspoon salt
1 teaspoon nutmeg
1 teaspoon cinnamon
1/2 teaspoon ground
cloves
1 teaspoon soda

PROCEDURE:

Preheat oven to 325°. Slice persimmons (with skins on) and mash in a bowl. (Persimmons must be very soft and ripe.) Cream butter and sugar with electric mixer. Add egg and continue beating until light in color and fluffy. Stir in persimmons, raisins, walnuts and optional whiskey. Mix dry ingredients together and mix with wet ingredients until well-blended. Spoon batter onto greased cookie sheets. Bake for 15 minutes.

Great to make in the fall when persimmons are in season (especially if you have access to a persimmon tree)! Chewy cookies are easy to make!

Nina Pellar Le Baron '75

Sour Milk Orange Cakes

Yields 6 dozen 2" cakes

INGREDIENTS:

2 cups granulated sugar
1 cup shortening
2 eggs
1 cup (1/2 pint) sour
   milk*
1 teaspoon soda
4 cups flour
1 teaspoon baking
   powder

Grated peel and juice
   from 1 orange

Frosting:
Grated peel and juice
   from 1 orange
2 cups powdered sugar
   (approximately)
2 tablespoons butter

PROCEDURE:

Preheat oven to 325°. With an electric mixer cream together the sugar and shortening. Add eggs to sugar/shortening mixture and mix well until light yellow and fluffy. Mix together sour milk and soda. Mix together flour and baking powder. With mixer running at medium speed alternately add milk/soda mixture and flour/baking powder mixture to eggs/sugar/shortening mixture. Add the grated orange peel and juice to cookie mixture and mix well. Drop batter by teaspoons onto ungreased cookie sheet. Cook until cake-like in texture, about 10 minutes.

Frosting: Place grated peel and juice from the orange in bowl of electric mixer. Beat in powdered sugar until texture is spreadable. Add butter and continue to blend until smooth.

*Milk must be allowed to sour.

Robin Goss Kishbaugh '72

"Killer" Brownies

Yields 16 brownies

INGREDIENTS:

4 ounces unsweetened
  chocolate
1 cup (2 sticks) butter
  or margarine
3 eggs

2 cups sugar
1 teaspoon vanilla
1 cup sifted flour
1/4 teaspoon salt

PROCEDURE:

Preheat oven to 350°. Melt chocolate and butter (or margarine) over hot water (or in the microwave). Beat eggs, sugar and vanilla together. Beat in chocolate mixture. Sift flour and salt together. Add gradually to chocolate mixture and mix well. Pour into greased 9" square pan. Bake for 30 to 40 minutes. Cool thoroughly and cut into small squares.

These are ultra rich!

Catherine Blair
Parent, Trevor Blair '95 and Peter Blair '97

The Best Brownies

Serves 12

INGREDIENTS:

2 eggs, slightly beaten
1 cup sugar, sifted
1/2 cup flour, sifted
1/2 cup butter (1 stick),
  melted

2 ounces semisweet
  chocolate, melted
1/8 teaspoon salt
1 teaspoon vanilla
1 cup broken pecan nuts
  (optional)

PROCEDURE:

Preheat oven to 350˚. Mix all ingredients together in the order listed and blend well after each addition. Pour into an 8" x 8" pan that is greased or lined with wax paper. Bake for 25 minutes. Cool for approximately 20 to 30 minutes then cut into serving squares (while still warm). Allow to cool completely before removing from pan.

Freezes well. Quick and easy.

Joan M. McKenna
Parent, Mary McKenna '82, Maria McKenna '86,
Christopher McKenna, 88, Sean McKenna '90, Matthew McKenna '98

Brownies

Yields 15 to 20

INGREDIENTS:

4 ounces unsweetened
   chocolate
2 cups sugar
4 eggs
1/2 cup vegetable oil
2 teaspoons vanilla

1/2 teaspoon salt
1 teaspoon baking
   powder
1 1/3 cups sifted flour
1 cup chopped nuts

PROCEDURE:

Preheat oven to 350°. Melt the chocolate in a double boiler or the microwave. Meanwhile, mix the sugar and the eggs together in a mixing bowl and beat until light in color and fluffy. When the chocolate is melted, mix the oil and chocolate together. Cool the chocolate/oil mixture to room temperature and pour into the mixing bowl with the eggs and sugar. Add the vanilla. Blend until mixed. Mix the salt and baking powder in with the flour. Add flour mixture to the mixing bowl. Blend thoroughly. Add the nuts. Blend gently. Pour the dough into a greased 9" x 13" pan. Bake for 25 to 30 minutes, or until a toothpick inserted in the dough comes out clean. Cool and cut into squares.

Sarah Fraser '88

Triple Espresso Brownies

Yields 36 bars

INGREDIENTS:

Brownies:
1 21-ounce package
   brownie mix
1/2 cup water
1/4 cup vegetable oil
1 egg
2 teaspoons instant
   espresso powder
1 teaspoon vanilla

Filling:
1/4 cup butter
1/2 cup brown sugar
1 egg
2 teaspoons instant
   espresso powder
1 teaspoon vanilla

1 cup nuts chopped
8 ounces bittersweet
   chocolate, chopped
   coarsely

Glaze:
3 ounces bittersweet
   chocolate
1 tablespoon butter
1/4 teaspoon instant
   espresso liquid
1 to 2 tablespoons milk
   (the last 2 ingredients
   may be omitted if a
   really good
   bittersweet chocolate
   is used)

PROCEDURE:

Preheat oven to 350˚.
Brownies: (Disregard instructions on the brownie mix box.) Combine the brownie mix with the water, vegetable oil, egg, instant espresso powder and vanilla in a medium bowl and mix until well-blended. Pour batter into an oiled 9" x 13" baking pan. Bake for 20 minutes.

Filling: Cream the butter, sugar and egg. Beat in espresso powder. Add vanilla, nuts and chocolate and mix until blended. Spread over partially baked brownies and return to oven to bake for 15 to 20 minutes more. Brownies should just be set, not over-baked.

Glaze: Melt chocolate with butter, add coffee and milk for spreadability. Drizzle over warm brownies.

Super rich!

Virginia Thomas
Parent, Brad Thomas '84

Caramel Brownies

Yields 2 dozen

INGREDIENTS:

1 box German chocolate
    cake mix
2/3 cup evaporated milk
3/4 cup (1 1/2 sticks)
    margarine, melted

1 cup chopped walnuts
1 14-ounce package
    caramels
1 cup chocolate chips

PROCEDURE:

Preheat oven to 350°. Mix dry cake mix with 1/3 cup of the evaporated milk, margarine and nuts. Press 1/2 of the cake mixture into a 9" x 13" x 2" greased and floured pan and bake exactly 6 minutes. Let cool.

Melt caramels in a double boiler with the remaining 1/3 cup of evaporated milk. Stir occasionally until completely melted and well-blended. Pour caramel mixture over cake mixture in pan.

Mix chocolate chips and remaining cake mixture and crumble over the caramels. Bake 20 minutes. Let cool completely (may chill in refrigerator), then cut into squares.

These freeze well.

Sarah Burton
Parent, Jorie Burton '99

Chocolate Chip Bars

Yields 48 bars

INGREDIENTS:

1/2 cup sugar
1/2 cup loosely packed
　　brown sugar
1/2 cup canola oil
　1 egg or 1/4 cup egg
　　substitute
　1 teaspoon vanilla

3/4 cup unbleached flour
2/3 cup whole wheat flour
1/2 teaspoon baking soda
1/2 teaspoon salt
3/4 cup chocolate chips
1/2 cup nuts (optional)

PROCEDURE:

Preheat oven to 350°. Using an electric mixer, beat sugars and oil together until blended. Add egg and vanilla. Beat until somewhat fluffy. In another bowl combine flours, soda and salt. Add to first mixture and thoroughly blend with a wooden spoon. Spread dough into ungreased 9" x 13" pan. (It takes some patience to get it evenly distributed.) Sprinkle chocolate chips and optional nuts over top and press into dough with back of spoon. Bake for 12 to 15 minutes or until dough starts to darken in color. Do not overbake! Cool on rack and cut into bars.

This is an easier and healthier version of chocolate chip cookies.

Margaret Sottosanti
Parent, Wayne Sottosanti '87, Mark Sottosanti '89, Paul Sottosanti '98

Corn Flake Bars

Yields 20 bars

INGREDIENTS:

7 cups corn flakes
1 cup Planters cocktail
　　peanuts
1 cup (1/2 pint) heavy
　　cream

1 cup white sugar
1 cup Karo syrup, light
　　or dark

PROCEDURE:

Pour corn flakes into a large bowl. Separate peanuts (if stuck together) and sprinkle in with flakes. In a medium size saucepan mix together cream, sugar and syrup and bring to a boil. Boil until syrup forms a soft ball in ice water. (Test at 7 minutes.) Pour hot syrup over flakes and peanuts and stir to moisten all. Pour mixture into a lightly greased 9" x 13" glass dish. Flatten with a fork. When cool, cut in bars. Wrap in foil and store in refrigerator.

Be sure to work quickly when stirring flakes and syrup together so you can pour mixture into pan before syrup hardens.

Elsi Volker
Grandparent, Lori Volker '97

Cheesecake Bars

Yields 24 bars

INGREDIENTS:

1/2 cup (1 stick) butter or margarine
1/2 cup brown sugar, packed
1 1/2 cups unbleached white flour
1/3 cup finely chopped walnuts (optional)
1 1/2 cups cottage cheese

1/2 cup (half of an 8-ounce package) softened cream cheese
2 eggs
1 teaspoon vanilla extract
1/2 teaspoon grated lemon (or orange) peel
1 tablespoon fresh lemon juice

PROCEDURE:

Preheat oven to 350°. Melt butter (or margarine) and place in a bowl with 1/4 cup brown sugar, flour and walnuts (optional). Mix until uniformly combined. Press the mixture firmly into the bottom of an ungreased 8" x 8" baking pan. (You may prebake the crust at this time for 10 minutes, if you like a crispier bottom layer.) Purée the cottage cheese for several minutes in a blender or a food processor fitted with a steel blade. Add remaining ingredients (including remaining brown sugar) and process for a few minutes more. Spread the cheese mixture over the prebaked (or unbaked) crust. Bake for 30 to 40 minutes or until the top feels firm to the touch. Cool before cutting into bars.

Keep beautifully up to a week in an airtight container in the refrigerator.

Eileen Pue
Parent, Sean Pue '93 and Lisa Pue '96

"Smithee Squares"

Yields 4 dozen bars

INGREDIENTS:

1/2 cup (1 stick)
   margarine (not
   butter), melted
1 box yellow cake mix
3 eggs
1 8-ounce package
  cream cheese,
  softened

1 1-pound box powdered
  sugar
1/2 cup flaked coconut
1/2 cup chopped walnuts
  or pecans

PROCEDURE:

Preheat oven to 325°. Combine margarine, cake mix and 1 of the eggs. Stir together until dry ingredients are moistened. Put mixture into bottom of well-greased 10" x 15" jelly roll pan. Beat remaining 2 eggs lightly, then beat in cream cheese and powdered sugar. Stir in coconut and nuts. Pour mixture over batter in jelly roll pan, spreading evenly. Bake 45 to 50 minutes or until golden brown. Cool pan on wire rack to room temperature. When cool, cut into squares.

Use plain cake mix, not the kind with pudding added. Do not use whipped margarine.

Kathleen Johnson '92

Lemon Squares

Yields 2 dozen

INGREDIENTS:

1/2 cup powdered sugar
2 cups flour
1 cup (2 sticks) butter, chilled
Pinch of salt
9 tablespoons flour

9 tablespoons lemon juice
6 eggs
3 cups sugar
Grated peel of 1 lemon
Powdered sugar for dusting top

PROCEDURE:

Preheat oven to 325°. Cut together first 4 ingredients with a pastry blender. Pat into the bottom of a 10" x 14" greased pan. Bake for 15 minutes. Remove from oven.

Reset oven to 350°. Mix together flour, lemon juice, eggs, sugar and lemon peel. Pour over baked bottom (while it is hot) and bake for 25 minutes. Dust with powdered sugar when cool and cut into squares.

Always a hit!

Galen Cooper
Parent, Tyler Cooper '96X and Megan Cooper '98

German Apple Cheese Bars

Yields 24 bars

INGREDIENTS:

Crust:
1 cup (2 sticks) unsalted butter
2 cups flour
1/2 cup sugar
1/8 teaspoon salt

Filling:
8 ounces cream cheese
1/2 cup sugar
1 egg
1/2 teaspoon vanilla

Topping:
3 small tart apples
1 tablespoon cinnamon
1/2 cup sugar

PROCEDURE:

Preheat oven to 375°.
Crust: Mix crust ingredients in a food processor fitted with a steel knife until dough ball begins to form. Remove and pat into bottom of a 9" x 13" glass pan. Bake for 15 minutes until very lightly brown. Set aside and cool.

Filling: Combine the cream cheese and the 1/2 cup sugar and beat until smooth. Add egg and vanilla and mix to blend well. Pour over pastry crust and spread evenly.

Topping: Peel and core apples. Slice very thinly and evenly. Lay overlapping rows from end to end over the filling. (Small apples will make 4 rows and larger, 3 rows.) Mix the cinnamon and sugar together and sprinkle over top. Bake 30 minutes. Cool and refrigerate before cutting. Cut between the 3 or 4 rows of apples to make bars.

Jean Stenstrom
Parent, Kerri Stenstrom '87 and Douglas Stenstrom '91

Taggart's Chocolate Birthday Cake

Serves 10 to 12

INGREDIENTS:

- 1 package chocolate fudge cake mix
- 1 3-ounce package chocolate fudge pudding mix
- 1/2 cup oil
- 1/2 cup water
- 1 cup (1/2 pint) sour cream

- 1 6-ounce bag chocolate chips
- 4 eggs
- 1 12-ounce bag chocolate chips
- 1 10-ounce can milk chocolate frosting

PROCEDURE:

Preheat oven to 350°. Combine first 7 ingredients and beat with a mixer. Grease a bundt pan. Pour half of the batter into the pan. Sprinkle with half of the 12-ounce bag of chips. Pour in the remaining batter and sprinkle with the rest of the chips. (Yes, this was a whole new bag of chips!)

Bake for 45 minutes. Cool in pan for 10 minutes, then turn out on rack to cool completely. Frost with canned milk chocolate frosting. (Canned frosting is MANDATORY for this recipe.)

I make this cake as a birthday gift for my chocoholic friends. They love it!

Dawn Fletcher Matthiesen '64X

Best Ever Chocolate Cake

Serves 8

INGREDIENTS:

Cake:
- 1/2 cup (1 stick) margarine
- 1/2 cup (1 stick) butter
- 4 tablespoons cocoa
- 1 cup water
- 2 cups flour
- 2 cups sugar
- 1 1/2 tablespoons baking soda
- 1/2 tablespoon salt
- 2 eggs, beaten
- 1/2 cup buttermilk

Icing:
- 1/2 cup (1 stick) butter
- 4 tablespoons cocoa
- 6 tablespoons buttermilk
- 1 teaspoon vanilla
- 1 1-pound box powdered sugar

PROCEDURE:

Cake: Preheat oven to 350°. Combine margarine, butter, cocoa and water. Melt in microwave or on the stove. Mix flour, sugar, baking soda and salt. Combine butter mixture and flour mixture. Add eggs and buttermilk and mix well. Pour batter into 9" x 13" pan or 2 round 9" pans. Bake for 30 minutes. Cool before frosting.

Icing: Melt butter and mix in cocoa, buttermilk, vanilla and powdered sugar. Beat until smooth and the right consistency to spread on cake.

Marion Steefel
Summer neighbor, Jessie Amberg '96 and Laurie Amberg '98

Cocoa-Mocha Cake

Serves 10 to 12

INGREDIENTS:

Cake:
2 tablespoons instant
  coffee granules
1 1/2 cups boiling water
1 cup oatmeal
1/2 cup (1 stick) butter
1 cup white sugar
1 cup brown sugar
1 teaspoon vanilla
2 eggs
1 teaspoon baking soda
1/2 teaspoon salt
1 1/3 cups sifted flour

2 tablespoons cocoa,
  sifted

Frosting:
3 tablespoons butter,
  softened
2 cups powdered sugar,
  sifted
Dash salt
1 teaspoon vanilla
2 tablespoons reserved
  coffee liquid

PROCEDURE:

Cake: Preheat oven to 350°. Grease and flour a 9" x 9" pan. Combine coffee and boiling water. (Set aside 2 tablespoons of this for frosting.) Pour remainder of hot coffee mixture over oatmeal and cover for 20 minutes. Beat butter and add sugars and beat until light and fluffy. Blend in vanilla and eggs. Add oatmeal/coffee mixture. Sift soda, salt, flour and cocoa. Add to creamed mixture. Mix well. Pour into greased and floured pan. Bake for 50 minutes. Let cool and frost.

Frosting: Beat butter until smooth. Gradually add sifted powdered sugar and dash of salt while continuing to beat. Add vanilla, then the 2 tablespoons of coffee liquid and mix well.

This is a terrific, rich, moist cake that (I hate to say) my mother says "men love". It lasts a long time and is equally delicious unfrosted.

Liz Armstrong
Parent, Mac Armstrong '93 and Annie Armstrong '96

Kahlúa Cake

Yields 16 thin slices

INGREDIENTS:

1 package devil's food
    pudding cake mix
1/2 cup sugar
1/3 cup vegetable or corn
    oil
3 eggs
3/4 cup water
1/4 cup Wild Turkey
    bourbon
1/2 cup Kahlúa
3/4 cup double strength
    black coffee

2 teaspoons cocoa
Dash vanilla

Icing:
1/2 cup (1 stick) butter
1 cup sugar
1/3 cup evaporated milk
1/2 cup semisweet
    chocolate chips
Dash Kahlúa

PROCEDURE:

Cake: Preheat oven to 350°. Combine all cake ingredients in mixing bowl. Beat for 4 minutes. Pour mixture into a greased and floured bundt pan and bake for 50 minutes. Set pan on a thick towel to cool for 10 minutes. Invert cake onto a serving plate and cool completely.

Icing: Bring icing mixture (minus chocolate chips and Kahlúa) to a boil stirring constantly. Cook for 2 minutes. Remove from heat and add chocolate chips and dash of Kahlúa. Pour over cake immediately.

This is a friend's recipe I have used a lot for music faculty parties and as the finale to after-concert receptions. People always ask for it and, because it is so rich, a little goes a long way.

Elizabeth Snite Edgerton '57

Chocolate Kahlúa Cake

Serves 8 to 10

INGREDIENTS:

1 package devil's food
cake mix
4 eggs
1 cup (1/2 pint) sour
cream
1/2 cup water
1/4 cup Kahlúa
1 3-ounce package
instant chocolate
pudding
1 6-ounce package
Ghirardelli chocolate
chips

Coffee-Kahlúa Creme:
2 cups (1 pint) whipping
cream
2 tablespoons instant
coffee
1/4 cup Kahlúa

Toasted slivered
almonds for topping

PROCEDURE:

Cake: Preheat oven to 350°. Place all cake ingredients except chocolate chips in a large mixing bowl. Mix thoroughly (at least 2 to 3 minutes). Stir in chocolate chips and turn into well-oiled bundt pan. Bake 50 minutes to 1 hour. Let cool 20 minutes and turn out of pan. Serve with the whipped Coffee Kahlúa Creme mixture (instructions below) piled in the center of the bundt cake. Top the creme with lots of toasted slivered almonds.

Coffee Kahlúa Creme: Whip cream and Kahlúa in chilled bowl. Gradually add coffee. Whip until stiff.

This is a most requested birthday celebration dessert at our house.

Heidi Dorris
Parent, Ashley Dorris '96 and Taylor Dorris '98

427

Cinnamon Chocolate Cake

Yields 24 to 36 pieces

INGREDIENTS:

2 cups sugar
2 cups flour
1/2 cup (1 stick) butter
1/2 cup shortening
1 cup water
4 tablespoons cocoa
1/2 cup buttermilk
2 eggs, slightly beaten
1 teaspoon baking soda
1 teaspoon cinnamon
1 teaspoon vanilla

Frosting:
1/2 cup (1 stick) butter
4 tablespoons cocoa
6 tablespoons milk
1 1-pound box powdered
   sugar
1 teaspoon vanilla
1 cup chopped pecans

PROCEDURE:

Preheat oven to 400˚. Combine sugar and flour in a large mixing bowl. In a saucepan, mix butter, shortening, water and cocoa. Bring to a rapid boil. Pour over sugar and flour and stir well. Add buttermilk, eggs, soda, cinnamon and vanilla and mix well. Pour into greased 11" x 16" pan. Bake for 20 to 25 minutes.

Frosting: Begin to make frosting 5 minutes before the cake is done. Melt and bring to a boil butter, cocoa and milk. Add to this mixture the sugar, vanilla and nuts. Mix thoroughly and spread over slightly warm cake.

Makes a wonderful birthday cake.

Heather Lattimer '89

Chocolate Fudge Swirl Cake

Serves 12

INGREDIENTS:

1/2 cup (1 stick) plus 2 tablespoons butter, softened

8 ounces cream cheese, softened

2 1/4 cups sugar

1 tablespoon cornstarch

3 eggs

1 3/4 cups plus 2 tablespoons evaporated milk

1 1/2 teaspoons pure vanilla extract

2 cups flour, sifted

1 teaspoon salt

1 teaspoon baking powder

1/2 teaspoon baking soda

4 ounces semisweet chocolate, melted

Frosting:

1/4 cup evaporated milk

1/4 cup (1/2 stick) butter

6 ounces semisweet chocolate chips

1 teaspoon vanilla extract

2 1/2 cups sifted powdered sugar

PROCEDURE:

Cake: Preheat oven to 350°. In a mixing bowl cream the 2 tablespoons butter with the cream cheese, 1/4 cup of the sugar and the cornstarch with an electric mixer or by hand. Add 1 egg, 2 tablespoons evaporated milk and 1/2 teaspoon vanilla extract. Beat at high speed until smooth and creamy. Set aside. Grease and flour a 9" x 13" pan. In the bowl of an electric mixer, combine the flour with the remaining 2 cups sugar, salt, baking powder and baking soda. Add the 1/2 cup butter and 1 cup evaporated milk. Blend for 2 minutes at low speed. Add the remaining 3/4 cup evaporated milk, 2 eggs, melted chocolate and 1 teaspoon vanilla. Continue beating 2 minutes at low speed. Spread half of this batter in pan. Spoon cream cheese mixture over batter, spreading carefully with a knife to cover. Top with remaining chocolate batter; spread to cover. Bake 50 to 60 minutes until cake springs back in center when lightly touched. Cool and frost.

Frosting: Combine milk and butter in saucepan. Bring to a boil. Remove from heat. Blend in chocolate chips and stir until completely melted. Stir in vanilla and powdered sugar. Beat until spreading consistency. If necessary, thin with a few drops of milk.

Though this fabulous chocolate cake takes a little time, it will receive raves from all those chocolate dessert lovers. It is a definite winner and worth the effort.

Penny Palmer Lumpkin '57

Carrot Cake I

Yields 9" x 13" x 2" cake

INGREDIENTS:

Cake:
- 2 cups sugar
- 2 cups sifted flour
- 1 1/2 cups vegetable oil
- 2 teaspoons baking soda
- 1 teaspoon salt
- 2 teaspoons cinnamon
- 2 teaspoons ginger
- 4 eggs
- 3 cups grated carrots
- 1 cup chopped walnuts

Frosting:
- 8 ounces cream cheese
- 1/4 cup (1/2 stick) butter
- 2 teaspoons vanilla
- 3 cups sifted powdered sugar

PROCEDURE:

Preheat oven to 350°. Mix all cake ingredients except carrots and walnuts with electric mixer. Fold in carrots and walnuts. Pour batter into a greased and floured 9" x 13" x 2" pan. Bake for 1 hour. Mix together frosting ingredients until well-blended. When cake is cool, spread frosting over the top.

Cecile Reed Renaudin '64
Parent, Reed Renaudin '93 and Claire Renaudin '98

Carrot Cake II

Yields 3-layer 9" cake

INGREDIENTS:

2 cups flour
2 teaspoons baking powder
1 1/2 teaspoons baking soda
2 1/2 teaspoons cinnamon
1 teaspoon salt
4 eggs, beaten
1 1/2 cups oil
2 cups sugar
1 8-ounce can crushed pineapple, drained (I usually add another 1/2 can)

2 cups grated carrots, packed

Frosting:
1 8-ounce package cream cheese
1/2 cup (1 stick) butter
1 box powdered sugar
1 teaspoon vanilla

PROCEDURE:

Preheat oven to 350°. Sift together the flour, baking powder, baking soda, cinnamon and salt and set aside. In a large bowl, beat eggs and mix in oil, sugar, pineapple and carrots. Add flour mixture and mix well. Pour batter into 3 greased and floured 9" cake pans. Bake for 35 to 40 minutes. Let cool completely, then frost as a 3-layer cake.

Frosting: Beat together cream cheese and butter. Add powdered sugar and vanilla slowly to cream cheese mixture and beat until well-blended.

One cup of chopped nuts may be added. This recipe will also make a 9" x 13" cake. Use the same cooking time.

Jill Lecoq
Staff, Business Office

Killer Carrot Cake

Yields 9" x 13" cake

INGREDIENTS:

2 cups flour
2 teaspoons baking soda
2 1/2 teaspoons cinnamon
1/2 teaspoon salt
3 eggs
3/4 cup salad oil
3/4 cup buttermilk (or regular milk)
2 teaspoons vanilla
2 cups sugar
2 cups grated carrots
1 cup shredded coconut

1 cup crushed pineapple, well-drained
1 cup chopped nuts (optional)

Frosting:
6 ounces soft cream cheese (low cal OK), softened
4 tablespoons (1/2 stick) butter, softened
1 1/2 cups powdered sugar
1/2 teaspoon vanilla

PROCEDURE:

Preheat oven to 350°. Sift flour, soda, cinnamon and salt together into a bowl. In another bowl beat eggs until slightly fluffy. Add salad oil, buttermilk and vanilla and mix well. Fold flour mixture into egg mixture. Fold in sugar, carrots, coconut, pineapple and nuts. Pour batter into a greased 9" x 13" pan. Bake for 55 minutes (or until toothpick inserted in center comes out clean).

Frosting: After cake has cooled, combine frosting ingredients in bowl of electric mixer. Beat at low speed to mix and then high speed to thoroughly blend. Frost cake.

Great for non-chocolate eaters!

Kristina Starkey '68X

Don't Peel the Apples Cake

Serves 12

INGREDIENTS:

2 eggs, well-beaten
3 cups raw apples,
    chopped but not
    peeled
1 cup chopped nuts,
    preferably pecans
1 cup oil

2 teaspoons vanilla
2 cups sugar
3 cups sifted flour
1/2 teaspoon salt
1 teaspoon baking soda
2 teaspoons cinnamon

PROCEDURE:

Preheat oven to 325°. In large bowl beat eggs with electric mixer. Add chopped apples and nuts to eggs. Add oil and vanilla and mix until well-blended. Add dry ingredients and mix thoroughly until dry ingredients are well-blended with moist ingredients. Put batter in ungreased tube pan. Bake 1 hour and 20 minutes.

Quick and easy. Serve at room temperature or warmed, with ice cream or plain. Great as a cozy fall or winter dessert.

Gail Shaw
Parent, Justin Shaw '89 and Maiya Shaw '92

Applesauce Spice Cake

Yields 1 bundt cake

INGREDIENTS:

2 cups sugar
1 cup (2 sticks)
    margarine
2 eggs
2 teaspoons vanilla
2 cups applesauce
4 cups flour

1 teaspoon salt
2 teaspoons baking soda
1 29-ounce jar
    mincemeat
1 cup chopped nuts
    (optional)

PROCEDURE:

Preheat oven to 350°. Butter and flour a bundt cake pan. In a large mixing bowl, cream sugar and margarine with electric mixer. Add eggs and vanilla. Beat in applesauce. In a separate bowl mix together flour, salt and baking soda. Slowly add flour mixture to applesauce mixture with mixer on slow speed. Fold in mincemeat and nuts. Pour into prepared bundt pan and bake for 1 to 1 1/2 hours.

Serve with rum-flavored hard sauce or whipped cream. Also good as a coffee cake. To give as gifts, bake in 4 8" x 4" foil pans (greased and floured) for about 30 to 40 minutes.

Jane Sinclair Diehl
Grandparent, Jeff Deems '91 and Jeremy Deems '94

Apple Cake

Serves 10 to 12

INGREDIENTS:

Cake:
3 cups flour
1 teaspoon soda
1 teaspoon salt
1 teaspoon cinnamon
1 cup oil
2 cups sugar
2 eggs
1 teaspoon vanilla
3 to 4 cups (5 to 6) medium McIntosh or Granny Smith apples, peeled and cut into large slices

1 cup chopped nuts

Frosting:
1 box powdered sugar
8 ounces cream cheese, softened
1 tablespoon butter
1/2 teaspoon vanilla
1 to 2 teaspoons cream
1/2 cup chopped nuts

PROCEDURE:

Cake: Preheat oven to 300°. Sift together the first 4 dry ingredients and set aside. Mix the oil and sugar together until well-blended. Beat in the eggs and vanilla. Add the dry ingredients and mix well. Fold in the apples and nuts. Batter will be very thick. Pour into greased and floured 9" x 13" pan. Bake 1 hour.

Frosting: Beat all ingredients and spread on cooled cake.

Jeannette Ruchlewicz
Parent, Brian Ruchlewicz '97

Fresh Apple Cake

Serves 18 to 20

INGREDIENTS:

Cake:
2 cups sugar
3 eggs
1 cup cooking oil
1/4 cup orange juice
3 cups plain flour
1/4 teaspoon salt
1 teaspoon baking soda
1/2 teaspoon cinnamon
1/2 teaspoon nutmeg
1 teaspoon vanilla

2 cups finely chopped,
  peeled apples
1 cup flaked coconut
1 cup chopped pecans

Topping:
1/4 cup (1/2 stick) butter
  (or margarine)
1/2 cup sugar
1/4 cup buttermilk

PROCEDURE:

Cake: Preheat oven to 325°. Combine ingredients in order given, mixing well after each addition. Bake in tube pan 1 1/2 hours.

Topping: Place ingredients in a saucepan. Bring to a boil stirring to mix. Continue cooking at a low boil until butter (or margarine) and sugar are melted and sauce is well-blended and smooth. Do not cook too long or sauce will separate. Spoon hot topping over cake as soon you take out of oven. Let cake stay in pan until cool.

Granny Smith apples are best for this cake but any cooking apple is fine.

Jean Ashby
Grandparent, Ryan Ashby '98 and John Ashby '99

Old-fashioned Southern Apple Cake

Serves 12

INGREDIENTS:

3 eggs
1 3/4 cups sugar
1 cup vegetable oil
2 cups sifted flour
1/4 teaspoon salt
1 teaspoon baking soda
1 tablespoon cinnamon
3 green apples, peeled and diced

1 cup chopped nuts

Glaze:
1 cup sugar
1/2 cup (1 stick) butter
1/4 teaspoon vanilla
1 tablespoon light Karo syrup
1/4 cup buttermilk

PROCEDURE:

Preheat oven to 325°. In a large bowl, beat the eggs. Add the sugar slowly and continue beating until light and fluffy. Mix in oil. In a small bowl, mix together dry ingredients. Add dry ingredients to wet and mix until well-blended. Stir in diced apples and nuts. Bake in a 9" x 13" greased pan for 1 hour. Cool in the pan.

Glaze: Combine all ingredients in a medium saucepan over medium-low heat. Bring to a boil, stirring constantly. Remove from heat and cool in the pan. When cooled, but still liquid, pour over cooled cake.

This cake is not for dieters. It's very rich. May be served without the glaze. This recipe was given to me about 1974 by an old Alabama country woman.

Shirley Nash '82

Pioneer Cherry Cake

Serves 12

INGREDIENTS:

Cake:
2 cups flour
2 cups sugar
1 cup canned pitted sour
  cherries (with juice)
1 cup finely chopped
  nuts (pecans or
  walnuts)
1 1/2 teaspoons baking soda

2 eggs

Butter Sauce:
3/4 cup (1 1/2 sticks)
  butter, melted
4 1/2 tablespoons flour
1 1/2 cups sugar
1 1/2 cups milk
1 1/2 teaspoons vanilla

PROCEDURE:

Preheat oven to 350°.
Cake: Mix together all cake ingredients until well-blended. Pour into well greased and floured bundt pan. Bake for 45 minutes. Cool in pan for 15 minutes. Turn out onto rack. When completely cool, turn out on serving plate.

Butter sauce: Combine all sauce ingredients except vanilla in a saucepan or double boiler. Cook over low heat stirring constantly until thick like pudding. Remove from heat and stir in vanilla. Serve warm over cake.

This is so easy to make and very impressive. Sauce could be kept warm in a crockpot or on a hot tray for a buffet.

Marci Gessay
Parent, Brooke Gessay '99

Blueberry Cake

Yields 12 to 16 pieces

INGREDIENTS:

2 1/2 cups all-purpose flour
   1 teaspoon baking
     powder
  1/2 teaspoon baking soda
   1 cup (2 sticks) butter or
     margarine, room
     temperature
1 1/4 cups sugar
   1 teaspoon vanilla
  1/2 teaspoon grated lemon
     peel
   2 large eggs
   1 cup (1/2 pint) sour
     cream

Filling:
2 tablespoons sugar
1 cup blueberries
1/2 cup walnuts, chopped
    medium-fine

Topping:
1 tablespoon sugar
1/2 teaspoon ground
    cinnamon

PROCEDURE:

Preheat oven to 350°. In a mixing bowl, stir together flour, baking powder and soda. Set aside. In large bowl of electric mixer, at medium speed, thoroughly beat together butter, sugar, vanilla and lemon peel. Beat in eggs 1 at a time and then sour cream. At low speed, gradually beat in flour mixture until blended. Spoon about 1/3 of batter into greased and floured 9" or 10" tube pan.

Mix ingredients for blueberry filling and sprinkle half of filling over batter in tube pan. Repeat layers, ending with the third layer of batter.

Mix topping ingredients and sprinkle on cake. Bake on rack below center of oven for 45 to 50 minutes until cake tester inserted in center of cake comes out clean. Do not overbake or it will be dry. Cool 10 minutes, then loosen around edges and turn out on rack. Cool completely before cutting.

Emily R. Gill '62

Banana Cake

Yields 9" x 13" cake

INGREDIENTS:

1 cup (2 sticks) butter
3 cups sugar
2 eggs, beaten
2 cups mashed, ripe
   bananas
2 teaspoons baking soda

**8 tablespoons
   buttermilk
3 cups flour
1 teaspoon salt
2 teaspoons vanilla
1 cup pecans (if desired)

** May substitute 6 tablespoons of sweet milk plus 2 tablespoons of white vinegar for buttermilk.

PROCEDURE:

Preheat oven to 350°. Grease and flour a 9" x 13" pan. Cream butter and sugar. Add beaten eggs and mashed bananas and mix well. Dissolve soda in buttermilk and add alternately with flour, mixing well after each addition. Add salt and vanilla and mix until blended. Stir in pecans if desired. Turn into pan. Bake for 1 hour. Test with toothpick at 45 minutes. Toothpick should come out clean when done.

Freezes well. Very moist.

Kendra Jensen Belfi '64

Rhubarb Upside Down Cake

Yields 9" x 13" cake

INGREDIENTS:

5 cups chopped fresh
   rhubarb
1 cup sugar
1 3-ounce package
   strawberry jello

3 cups white miniature
   marshmallows
1 box white cake mix

PROCEDURE:

Preheat oven to 350°. Chop rhubarb and put into a lightly greased 9" x 13" pan. In a small bowl, mix sugar and strawberry jello (straight from the box) together. Sprinkle over rhubarb. Sprinkle miniature marshmallows over sugar/jello mixture. Prepare the white cake mix according to package directions and pour over marshmallows. Bake for 1 hour. Cool slightly (10 or 15 minutes) and turn upside down on platter. Serve (completely cooled) with whipped cream.

A colorful, yummy break from strawberry shortcake and very easy. This recipe is best made in the spring when fresh rhubarb is readily available.

Roberta Fouke DeWitt '64

White Fruitcake

Yields 6   5 1/2" x 2 1/2" loaf cakes

INGREDIENTS:

1 **4-ounce jar candied orange peel**
1/2 **cup chopped candied red cherries**
1 1/2 **cups chopped candied pineapple**
1 **cup dates, chopped**
1 **cup dried apricots, chopped**
1 **cup golden raisins, chopped**
1/2 **cup apricot brandy**

1 **cup (2 sticks) butter**
5 **eggs**
1/2 **cup dry white wine or unsweetened apple juice**
2 **cups unsifted flour**
1 1/2 **teaspoons baking powder**
1 **teaspoon salt**
2 **cups shredded coconut**
2 **cups sliced almonds**

PROCEDURE:

First soak dried and candied chopped fruits in the apricot brandy <u>overnight</u>.

Preheat oven to 325˚. Beat together butter, eggs and white wine. Slowly add flour, baking powder and salt. Add coconut and almonds to soaked fruit and mix well. Carefully fold fruit mixture into dough. Divide dough between greased and floured loaf pans and bake approximately 1 hour until cake tests done in the middle. Cakes can then be soaked in brandy-soaked cloths for several weeks and served at your convenience.

Good light dessert with coffee.

Kathy Applen
Parent, Ethan Applen '92 and Ellie Applen '99

Lemon Curd Cake

Serves 6 to 8

INGREDIENTS:

Butter to grease
8" cake pan
Bread crumbs to
sprinkle in pan
1 cup all-purpose flour
1 teaspoon baking
powder
1/4 teaspoon salt
2 eggs
2/3 cup sugar

1/2 teaspoon vanilla
1/4 cup milk
4 tablespoons unsalted
butter, melted

1 11-ounce jar
Robertson's Lemon
Curd (or use Lemon
Curd recipe, page
462)

PROCEDURE:

Preheat oven to 350°. Butter and sprinkle with bread crumbs an 8" round cake pan. Sift flour, baking powder and salt together in a mixing bowl. In a large bowl, beat eggs with electric beater until well-blended. Add sugar slowly and continue to beat until mixture falls back into bowl in a lazy ribbon when the beater is lifted out. Mix in vanilla.

With a rubber spatula, gently fold the flour mixture and milk alternately into the eggs and sugar by first adding about 1/3 of the flour, then a little milk, then about 1/3 of the flour, the remaining milk and last the remaining flour. Before the last of the flour has been folded completely into the batter, add the melted butter. As soon as there is no trace of either flour or butter, pour the batter into the prepared pan.

Bake for 30 to 40 minutes or until golden brown. Cool cake in pan for 10 minutes then turn out on rack to cool completely. When cool, slice twice and fill in torte fashion with lemon curd. (Use approximately 1/2 jar or make Lemon Curd recipe, page 462). Sprinkle sifted confectioners' sugar on top if desired.

A nice cake to welcome new neighbors!

Ellie Dillemuth
Parent, Ann Dillemuth '92 and Julie Dillemuth '94

Citrus Cake

Yields 16 to 24 pieces

INGREDIENTS:

1 3-ounce package
   lemon jello
1 box lemon cake mix
4 eggs
3/4 cup oil

3/4 cup water

Glaze:
1 cup powdered sugar
1/3 cup lemon juice

PROCEDURE:

Preheat oven to 350°. Blend the jello, cake mix, eggs, oil and water with an electric mixer at medium speed for 2 minutes. Pour into a lightly greased and floured 9" x 13" x 2" cake pan. Bake for 35 minutes or until toothpick inserted in center comes out clean. While cake is still hot, poke holes in the top of the cake with a fork. Mix the powdered sugar and lemon juice together and pour over cake. Smooth out the glaze so that the entire cake surface is covered. Enjoy!

Kerri Sandstrom Trowbridge '88

Hunter's Lemon Cake

Yields 1 bundt cake

INGREDIENTS:

1 package Duncan Hines
   Lemon Supreme Cake
   mix
4 eggs
3/4 cup oil
3/4 cup milk

Icing:
1/3 cup lemon juice
1 2/3 cups powdered sugar

PROCEDURE:

Preheat oven to 325°. Mix together cake mix, eggs, oil and milk. Beat with hand held electric mixer for at least 2 minutes. Pour into a greased and floured bundt pan. Bake for 50 to 55 minutes. Let cool in pan for 10 minutes. Remove cake from pan and invert on serving plate. Poke at least 50 times with ice pick to make holes all over. Spoon icing (instructions below) slowly over top allowing to sink into cake before adding more.

Icing: Mix lemon juice and powdered sugar in a small saucepan and heat until sugar is dissolved. Set aside until cake is done.

Hunter Oliver '98

Lemon Cake

Serves 12

INGREDIENTS:

3/4 cup (1 1/2 sticks)
   butter or margarine
1 1/2 cups sugar
   3 eggs
2 1/4 cups flour
   1/2 teaspoon salt
   1 teaspoon baking soda

3/4 cup buttermilk
   Peel of 1 lemon, grated

Glaze:
1/2 cup sugar
   Juice of 2 lemons

PROCEDURE:

Preheat oven to 350° (for a metal pan) or 325° (for a glass pan). Grease and flour a 9" x 13" metal or glass pan. Cream butter (or margarine) and sugar. Beat the eggs slightly and add to creamed mixture and mix well. Sift together the flour, salt and baking soda then add to the creamed mixture and beat on medium speed until well-blended. Add buttermilk and lemon peel and continue beating until blended. Pour batter into pan and bake for 35 to 40 minutes.

While cake is baking, make glaze by mixing together the sugar and lemon juice in a small saucepan and heating until sugar melts. When cake is done to your firm touch, remove from oven and use toothpicks or pronged fork to make holes all over cake. Then drizzle the glaze over cake. Leave to cool.

Heather Gallagher
Parent, Kielty Gallagher '94

So Good Orange Cake

Serves 12

INGREDIENTS:

1 3/4 cups flour, sifted
   1/4 teaspoon salt
     6 egg whites, room
        temperature
1 1/2 cups sugar
     6 egg yolks, fresh

6 tablespoons fresh
   orange juice
1 tablespoon grated
   orange peel
Confectioners' sugar

PROCEDURE:

Preheat oven to 350°. Mix flour and salt together in a small bowl. Place the egg whites in a large bowl. With electric mixer beat egg whites until foamy. Gradually add 1/2 cup of the sugar to egg whites, beating well after each addition. Continue beating until stiff. Set aside. With electric mixer beat egg yolks until thick and lemon colored, about 3 minutes. (Do not overbeat.) Gradually add remaining sugar to egg yolks. Beat until smooth. At low speed alternate adding flour mixture and orange juice to egg yolks. Start and end with flour. Add orange peel. With whisk or spatula gently fold yolk mixture into egg whites.

Pour batter into an ungreased 10" x 4 1/2" tube pan without removable bottom or a 9" x 10" x 4" Kugelhopf pan. Bake 35 to 40 minutes in tube pan or 50 to 55 minutes in Kugelhopf, until cake springs back when pressed with finger. Invert over bottle and cool completely. Remove from pan, place on a serving plate and dust with confectioners' sugar.

Use serrated knife to cut; makes an easier job. Very delicate, soft cake.

Dana Dahlbo
Parent, Alison Dahlbo '97

Mertie's Gold Cake

Serves 12

INGREDIENTS:

2 1/2 cups sifted cake flour
2 1/2 teaspoons baking powder
3/4 cup (1 1/2 sticks) butter
1 1/4 cups sugar
8 egg yolks beaten until thick and lemon colored
3/4 cup milk
1/2 teaspoon lemon extract

1 12-ounce jar orange marmalade

Seven Minute Frosting:
2 egg whites
1 1/2 cups sugar
5 tablespoons cold water
1/4 teaspoon cream of tartar
1 teaspoon vanilla

PROCEDURE:

Preheat oven to 350°. Mix sifted cake flour and baking powder and sift together 3 times. With an electric mixer cream butter thoroughly. Add sugar gradually. Continue creaming butter and sugar together until light and fluffy. Add beaten egg yolks and mix well at medium speed. Add flour mixture alternately with milk, a small amount at a time. Beat on low speed after each addition until smooth. Add lemon extract and beat on medium speed until well-mixed.

Bake in 3 greased round 9" layer pans for 20 to 25 minutes or until done. (Check by inserting toothpick in cake. Done when toothpick comes out clean.) Put layers together with orange marmalade and frost top and sides with Seven Minute Frosting.

Seven Minute Frosting: Place egg whites, sugar, water and cream of tartar in the top of a double boiler and beat with a hand-held electric mixer until thoroughly blended. Place pan over rapidly boiling water. Beat egg mixture constantly with the electric mixer for 7 minutes. Remove frosting from heat. Add the vanilla and continue beating until the frosting is the right consistency to be spread.

Cake is also good with chocolate filling and frosting. One of my favorite ways to serve it is with one of the sugar-free raspberry jams as filling and chocolate frosting. This is my great-grandmother's recipe!

Cherie Elaine Haynes '64

Class of '79 Birthday Cake

Serves 8 to 10

INGREDIENTS:

Cake:
1 white cake mix
Food coloring: Blue,
   red, yellow and green

Frosting:
1/2 cup (1 stick)
   margarine, softened
1 1/2 cups powdered sugar
2 heaping tablespoons
   marshmallow creme
1 teaspoon water

PROCEDURE:

Cake: Follow directions on box to make batter. Pour into a 9" x 13" cake pan. Drop 2 drops of each food color evenly spaced on top surface of batter. With spatula slowly swirl in figure 8 motion to spread color throughout cake batter. Don't over swirl. Two figure 8's ought to do it. Follow directions on box for cooking time and temperature. Cool cake before frosting.

Frosting: Combine the margarine, the powdered sugar, marshmallow creme and water. Mix with electric mixer until well-blended. Spread frosting on cool cake.

Quick and easy frosting. Yummy, yummy, yummy.

Charlotte C. Bentley '79

"Let Them Eat Cake" or
The Mighty Golds' Victory Cake!

Serves 16 people on Weight Watchers
or 4 with hearty appetites

INGREDIENTS:

Cake:
1 **box yellow cake mix**
1 **3-ounce box instant**
   vanilla pudding
4 **eggs**
1/2 **cup vegetable oil**
1/2 **cup rum (more or less**
   to taste)
1/2 **cup water**

1/2 **cup chopped nuts**
   (optional)

Sauce:
1/4 **cup water**
1/4 **cup rum**
1/2 **cup (1 stick) butter**
1 **cup sugar**

PROCEDURE:

Cake: Preheat oven to 350°. Mix all cake ingredients (except for nuts) together.
Beat for 2 to 3 minutes until mixture is smooth, moist and GOLDEN. Place
chopped nuts in bottom of a well-greased bundt pan. (This step may be omitted
if you are allergic to nuts or if you are a PURPLE MONKEY.) Pour batter into the
pan. Bake for 50 to 55 minutes.

Sauce: Simmer sauce ingredients on low heat for 2 minutes (PURPLES) or zap
them in the microwave (GOLDS) for 30 seconds to 1 minute until bubbly. Pour
over cake when it emerges from the oven. Let cake stand for 30 minutes before
turning upside down onto a serving platter.

*Be sure to have extra rum on hand to console those Royal Purples after being
trounced by the Mighty Golds!!*

Susie Boughton Ley '65

Custard Cake

Serves 12

INGREDIENTS:

3/4 cup milk
4 large (or 5 small) eggs
1 cup granulated sugar
1 1/2 tablespoons unflavored
gelatine

2 cups (1 pint) whipping
cream
1 small angel food cake
1 7-ounce package
sweetened angel flake
coconut

PROCEDURE:

Put 1/2 cup of the milk in double boiler. Scald as for custard (until milk coats a silver spoon). Break and separate eggs, placing yolks in a small bowl. Add the sugar to yolks while beating. Stir egg yolk mixture into scalded milk in top of double boiler. When custard thickens, remove from stove. Stir in gelatine which has been dissolved in remaining 1/4 cup milk. Whip egg whites until stiff; fold egg whites into custard. Whip 1 cup of the whipping cream until stiff. Just as custard begins to cool (do not let custard cool too much), fold in the whipped cream. Break up the angel food cake and cover bottom of a tube pan. Add 1/2 of custard mixture. Add more cake pieces and more custard, alternating. Finish top with remaining pieces of cake.

Set overnight in refrigerator. Unmold on serving plate and frost with the remaining 1 cup of whipping cream (whipped until stiff). Cover with coconut.

This is a very special dessert. Save for only a few occasions because of its caloric and cholesterol content.

Mrs. W. L. Strong, Sr.
Grandparent, William Strong '99

Easy Coconut Cake

Yields 9" x 13" cake

INGREDIENTS:

1 box yellow cake mix
1 cup (1/2 pint) sour cream
3/4 cup vegetable oil
4 eggs
1 teaspoon vanilla

1/4 cup sugar
3/4 cup milk
8 ounces Cool Whip
7 ounces shredded or flaked coconut

PROCEDURE:

Preheat oven to 350°. (Ignore directions on cake mix box.) Mix first 5 ingredients with electric mixer on medium speed for 3 minutes. Pour into 9" x 13" greased and floured cake pan. Bake 30 minutes. Cool cake completely. Boil sugar and milk stirring to mix well. Pierce cooled cake with meat fork making many holes. Pour hot mixture slowly over cake allowing it to soak in before adding more. Cool completely. Spread Cool Whip over cool cake. Cover with coconut. Refrigerate or freeze.

Freezes beautifully.

Mrs. William. B. Bowie
Grandparent, Erinn Murphy '94X, Meghan Murphy '96X,
Kaitlin Murphy '99

Flop Cake

Serves 6 to 8

INGREDIENTS:

4 eggs
1 box brown sugar
2/3 cup oil
2 cups Bisquick
1 cup shredded coconut

1 12-ounce package
  chocolate chips
1 cup chopped pecans
1 teaspoon vanilla
  Powdered sugar to
  dust (optional)

PROCEDURE:

Preheat oven to 350°. Grease a 9" x 13" pan. Cream eggs and brown sugar together. Add oil and Bisquick. Mix well. Add remaining ingredients (except powdered sugar). Pour into greased pan. Bake 35 to 40 minutes. This cake will puff up in the middle while cooking . When it flops in the middle, it is done. Dust lightly with powdered sugar (optional).

Men love this cake. I never frost it because it is very rich!

Joella Geoffrey Brannon '76

Roz's Rum Bundt Cake

Serves 8 to 10

INGREDIENTS:

1 box yellow cake mix
1 3-ounce package
  French vanilla
  instant pudding
4 eggs
1/2 cup water
1/2 cup canola oil
3/4 cup dark rum

Oil and sugar for bundt
  pan
1/2 cup chopped nuts
  (optional)
Powdered sugar

PROCEDURE:

Preheat oven to 325 °. Blend cake mix, pudding mix, eggs, water, oil and rum with an electric mixer until well-mixed. Oil and sugar a bundt pan, placing (optional) nuts in bottom. Pour cake batter into pan. Bake for 50 to 60 minutes until cake springs back when lightly touched. Cool in pan on rack. When cool, turn out onto serving plate.

Sherry may be substituted for rum. Freezes beautifully.

Judy J. Cater
Parent, Joanne Cater '98

Graham Cracker Cake

Serves 10 to 12

INGREDIENTS:

1 3/4 cups graham cracker crumbs
1/2 cup flour
2 teaspoons baking powder
1/4 teaspoon salt
1 cup sugar
1/2 cup shortening

1 teaspoon vanilla
3 eggs, separated
3/4 cup milk
1/2 cup chopped nuts
Seven Minute Icing (see recipe, page 447)
Mandarin orange sections for garnish

PROCEDURE:

Preheat oven to 375°. Make crumbs by sealing graham crackers in a ziploc bag and crushing with a rolling pin. Sift together flour, baking powder and salt. Set aside. Cream sugar and shortening. Beat until fluffy. Add vanilla and beaten egg yolks and mix thoroughly. Add 1/2 of the graham cracker crumbs and about 1/2 of the milk and mix well. Add remaining crumbs and mix. Then, alternately add the rest of the milk and the dry ingredients. Beat until smooth and stir in chopped nuts. Beat egg whites until stiff and fold into batter. Pour into 2 greased and floured 8" cake pans. Bake for 25 to 30 minutes. Cool in pans on wire racks for 10 minutes, then remove cakes to racks to cool completely. Frost with Seven Minute Icing (see recipe, page 447) and garnish with well-drained Mandarin orange sections.

Traditionally served for my husband's birthday!

Carol Ann Lattimer
Faculty, Math Department and
Parent, Heather Lattimer '89

Nut Torte

Serves 6 to 8

INGREDIENTS:

3 eggs
1 cup sugar
1/2 teaspoon vanilla

1 cup graham cracker
crumbs
1/2 cup chopped walnuts

PROCEDURE:

Preheat oven to 350°. Beat eggs. Add sugar and beat until light yellow and well-blended. Add vanilla and beat until well-mixed. Fold in finely crushed crumbs and nuts. Pour this mixture into a greased 8" round cake pan. Bake for 25 to 30 minutes. When done, top of cake will be a little crusty and the center soft.

Quick and easy. Serve with whipped cream or vanilla ice cream if desired.

Barbara Markstein
Grandparent, Kyle Markstein '99

Viennese Nusstorte

Serves 10 to 12

INGREDIENTS:

7 eggs, separated
1 cup sugar
1 teaspoon vanilla
3 1/2 cups walnuts, finely chopped

Filling:
1 cup (1/2 pint) whipping cream
3 tablespoons sugar
2 tablespoons instant coffee powder
1/2 teaspoon vanilla
1/2 cup walnut halves

PROCEDURE:

Preheat oven to 325°. Beat egg yolks with sugar until smooth and light yellow. Add vanilla and nuts. Beat egg whites until stiff and gently fold 1/4 of egg whites at a time into beaten yolks. Line 2 8" cake pans with wax paper. Pour 1/2 the batter into each pan and bake for about 40 minutes, until a toothpick inserted in the center comes up dry. Let cool in pans about 20 minutes before removing. Frost cake when completely cool.

Filling: Whip cream, then add sugar, coffee and vanilla. Spread whipped cream between the two cake layers, then spread over top and sides. Decorate with walnut halves.

Guten appetit.

Suzanne Angelucci
Parent, Barbara Angelucci Giammona '77

455

Easy Pound Cake

Serves 10

INGREDIENTS:

1 cup (2 sticks) unsalted butter, softened
8 ounces cream cheese, softened
2 cups sugar
2 teaspoons lemon juice
2 teaspoons vanilla extract
6 eggs
2 cups flour
3 teaspoons baking powder
1/2 teaspoon salt
Powdered sugar for garnish

PROCEDURE:

Preheat oven to 350°. Butter and flour a bundt pan. Cream butter, cream cheese and sugar until light and fluffy. Add lemon juice and vanilla and mix well. Beat in eggs 1 at a time. Add sifted dry ingredients and mix well. Pour into prepared pan and bake for 50 to 60 minutes. Cool in pan for 15 minutes. Turn out onto rack and sprinkle powdered sugar on top.

This is a wonderful cake and quite simple to make. It freezes well and smells wonderful.

Mrs. Edna C. Pollak
Grandparent, Lindsay Pollak '97

One Step Pound Cake

Serves 10 to 12

INGREDIENTS:

2 1/4 cups flour
2 cups sugar
1/2 teaspoon salt
1/2 teaspoon soda
3 eggs
1 teaspoon grated lemon peel
1 teaspoon vanilla
1 cup (2 sticks) softened butter
8 ounces orange flavored yogurt
Powdered sugar for garnish

456

PROCEDURE:

Preheat oven to 325°. Combine all ingredients (except powdered sugar) in bowl of electric mixer. Blend at low speed, then beat at medium speed 3 minutes. Pour into greased and floured bundt cake pan and bake for 55 to 60 minutes or until a tester comes out clean. Cool 15 minutes and remove from pan. Sprinkle with powdered sugar.

Serve with fruit, ice cream or whipped cream. Recipe from my friend Chris Dong.

Jeannette Ruchlewicz
Parent, Brian Ruchlewicz '97

Holiday Cheesecake

Yields 10 1/2" cake

INGREDIENTS:

- 1 tablespoon butter
- 1 cup graham cracker crumbs
- 4 cups (2 pints) cream cheese
- 2 cups sugar

- 1 teaspoon vanilla
- 6 large eggs
- 4 cups (2 pints) sour cream

PROCEDURE:

Preheat oven to 375°. Butter a round 10 1/2" spring form pan and coat sides with graham cracker crumbs. (Crumbs may be made by sealing graham crackers in ziploc bag and crushing with rolling pin.) Soften cream cheese in large bowl. Add the sugar and vanilla. Beat until blended. Beat in eggs 1 at a time. Add sour cream, slowly blending. Do not beat. Pour batter into prepared pan. Bake for 45 minutes. Then turn off oven, leaving cake in the oven <u>overnight</u>. Use your favorite topping or serve plain.

I usually make this the evening before. Cake should stay in oven until oven is cool.

Virginia Griffin
Grandparent, Amy Griffin '94 and Robert Griffin '96

Cheesecake

Serves 10 to 12

INGREDIENTS:

1 1/2 cups graham cracker
    crumbs
1 cup sugar
1/4 cup (1/2 stick) butter,
    melted

2 8-ounce packages
    cream cheese
    (or 5 3-ounce
    packages)
3 eggs
2 teaspoons vanilla
2 cups (1 pint) sour
    cream

PROCEDURE:

Preheat oven to 375°.
Crust: Lightly butter sides of a 9" spring form pan and sprinkle with 2 tablespoons of the cracker crumbs. (Crumbs may be made by sealing graham crackers in ziploc bag and crushing with rolling pin.) Set aside 2 tablespoons crumbs for top. Mix remaining crumbs with 1/4 cup of the sugar and the melted butter. Spread evenly over bottom and up sides of pan; press firmly with fingers.

Filling: Beat cream cheese until smooth and fluffy (2 to 3 minutes with mixer at low speed). Gradually beat in 1/2 cup of sugar, 1 teaspoon vanilla and the eggs 1 at a time. Continue to beat until creamy and light. Pour mix over crumbs and bake for 20 minutes. Remove from oven and let stand at room temperature for 15 minutes.

Turn oven to 475°.
Topping: Mix sour cream with the remaining 1/4 cup sugar and 1 teaspoon vanilla. Spoon onto filling. Sprinkle with crumbs. Bake for 10 minutes. Cool to room temperature, then refrigerate to chill thoroughly (2 or 3 hours) before cutting.

Sour cream will be soft when removed from oven. It will harden when chilled.

Katie Wilson '68

Divine Cheese Pie

Serves 10 to 12

INGREDIENTS:

16 graham crackers,
 crushed
1/4 cup (1/2 stick) butter,
 melted
2 8-ounce packages
 cream cheese
2 eggs
1/2 cup sugar
1 teaspoon vanilla

Topping:
1 cup (1/2 pint) sour
 cream
2 tablespoons sugar
1 teaspoon vanilla

PROCEDURE:

Preheat oven to 350°. Mix the graham cracker crumbs and melted butter and press into bottom and sides of a 9" pie pan. Bake 5 minutes. Set aside to cool.

Mix cream cheese, eggs, sugar and vanilla. Pour this mixture into the cool shell. Bake 15 minutes. Cool 5 minutes.

Topping: With an electric mixer, beat the sour cream with the sugar and vanilla. Cover pie with this mixture. Bake 5 minutes more. After cooling, place in refrigerator for 24 hours or not less than 5 hours.

This is the best cheese cake and it is very easy to make. In fact it's so good you may want to make two of them. I really hope you try this cheese pie, it just melts away in your mouth.

Santa Alioto
Grandparent, Melissa Alioto '97

Marble Cheesecake

Serves 10 to 12

INGREDIENTS:

Crust:
1 1/4 cups graham cracker crumbs (or chocolate wafers)
1/2 teaspoon cinnamon
1/4 cup butter (or margarine), melted

Filling:
12 ounces cream cheese, softened
1/2 cup sugar
1 teaspoon grated lemon peel
2 eggs
1/2 cups (3/4 pint) sour cream
8 ounces semisweet chocolate

PROCEDURE:

Preheat oven to 350°. Use a 9" loose bottom, spring form cake pan.

Crust: Make crumbs by sealing graham crackers or chocolate wafers in a ziploc bag and crushing with a rolling pin. Combine all crust ingredients and mix well. With damp fingers, press into bottom and up sides of spring form pan. Chill in refrigerator.

Filling: Combine cream cheese, sugar and lemon peel. Beat until well-blended. Beat in eggs. Beat in sour cream until smooth. Melt chocolate in top of double boiler (or in microwave on medium for 3 minutes or more, as needed). Cool chocolate slightly and add to cream cheese mixture and stir with a fork until marbleized. Pour into crust and bake for 35 to 40 minutes or until set. Chill 2 hours or longer, then remove rim.

Always a favorite.

Lauren Abrams
Parent, Adam Abrams '94

Buttermilk Cupcakes

Yields 33 cupcakes

INGREDIENTS:

Cupcakes:
2 1/2 cups all-purpose flour
2 teaspoons baking soda
1/4 teaspoon salt
2 cups sugar
1/4 cup plus 1 tablespoon
   cocoa
2 eggs
1 cup vegetable oil
1 cup buttermilk
1 cup hot water
1 teaspoon vanilla
   extract

Frosting (2 1/2 cups):
1 16-ounce package
   powdered sugar,
   sifted
1/4 cup cocoa
1/2 cup (1 stick) butter (or
   margarine), melted
1/3 cup buttermilk
1 teaspoon vanilla
   extract

PROCEDURE:

Preheat oven 350°. Combine cupcake ingredients in a large mixing bowl. Beat at low speed with an electric mixer until blended. Beat at high speed for 2 more minutes. Spoon batter into paper-lined muffin pans, filling 2/3 full. Bake for 20 minutes or until a wooden pick inserted into center comes out clean. Remove from pans and let cool completely on wire racks. When cool, spread frosting on top of each cupcake.

Frosting: Combine all ingredients in a mixing bowl; beat at low speed with an electric mixer until smooth.

Everyone seems to love the cupcakes. They are not too sweet and I often use applesauce in place of the vegetable oil to reduce the fat.

Carol M. Yates
Parent, Todd Yates '98 and Scott Yates '99

Lemon Curd

Yields 3 2 1/2-pint jelly jars

INGREDIENTS:

4 large lemons   **4 large eggs**
1/2 cup (1 stick) butter   **1 1/2 cups sugar**

PROCEDURE:

Grate the peel of the lemons and squeeze for juice. Melt the butter in the top of a double boiler. Beat the eggs into the melted butter. Add the sugar, grated lemon peel and juice. Cook over simmering water, stirring constantly, until well thickened . Cool and use as suggested below. Will keep for several days in the refrigerator. When stored in sterile jars, shelf life is 2 months.

Can be used to fill tartlet shells or as a spread on bread or cookies or Lemon Curd Cake, page 443. You may also fold in 1 cup of whipped cream and serve over berries. Sinfully rich and delicious!

Anne Otterson
Parent, Eric Otterson '87 and Helen Otterson '89

Lemon Pudding Cake with Berries

Serves 6

INGREDIENTS:

Lemon cake:
3 large eggs, separated
3/4 cup sugar
2 tablespoons butter
1 tablespoon grated
   lemon peel
1 cup buttermilk
1/3 cup lemon juice
1/4 cup all-purpose flour

Topping:
1 cup fresh berries

Berry Sauce:
2 cups fresh raspberries,
   blueberries or
   strawberries (or a
   combination), rinsed
   and drained (or 1 10-
   ounce package frozen
   fruit in syrup)
3 tablespoons sugar
1 tablespoon berry
   flavored liqueur such
   as Chambord or
   Framboise

PROCEDURE:

Preheat oven to 350°. Place a buttered 5 to 6 cup soufflé (or other straight-sided) baking dish in a larger baking pan (at least 2" deep). Set aside. In a deep bowl, whip egg whites on high speed until foamy. Continue to beat, gradually adding 1/4 cup of the sugar, until whites hold short distinct peaks. Set aside. In another bowl, beat remaining 1/2 cup sugar, butter, lemon peel and egg yolks on high speed until mixture is thick and light in color. Stir in buttermilk, lemon juice and flour. Stir into the batter about 1/4 cup of the egg whites. Gently but thoroughly fold in remaining egg whites. Pour batter into soufflé dish. Set dish in pan on center rack of oven.

Pour boiling water into pan up to level of batter. Bake until pudding is a rich brown on top and feels firm in center when lightly touched (about 1 hour). Serve hot or cool, scooping portions from bottom of dish to get sauce that forms. Serve with berry sauce and fresh berries over the top.

Berry Sauce: In a blender or food processor, purée the fresh raspberries (or thawed frozen raspberries in syrup) with the sugar and berry-flavored liqueur. To remove seeds, rub purée through a fine strainer into a bowl. If making ahead, cover and chill up to 2 days. If using other fruit, use sugar and liqueur to taste as they will not be as tart as raspberries.

Mouth watering, worth the trouble.

Mary Newberry
Staff, Development Office and
Parent, Nancy Newberry '97X

Fruit Terrine with Raspberry Sauce

Serves 8

INGREDIENTS:

2 cups (1 pint) fresh
   strawberries, hulled
2/3 cup sugar
1/4 cup orange juice
2 tablespoons lemon
   juice
2 cups (1 pint) low fat
   yogurt

Raspberry Sauce:
1 pint fresh raspberries
   or 12-ounce package
   unsweetened frozen
   raspberries, thawed
2 tablespoons sugar
1 teaspoon vanilla

**Strawberries or
raspberries for
garnish**

PROCEDURE:

Terrine: Purée the strawberries in a food processor or blender for 30 seconds or
until smooth. In small saucepan over medium-low heat combine sugar, orange
juice and lemon juice. Heat about 3 minutes or until sugar dissolves, stirring
occasionally. Add sugar mixture to purée. Blend until just combined. Stir in
yogurt. Pour mixture into a 9" x 9" metal baking pan. Cover and freeze about 1
hour until partially frozen. Stir to break up ice crystals. Return to freezer 1 hour
longer. Stir again. Transfer to 7" x 4" x 3" loaf pan. Cover and freeze 3 hours or
overnight.

To serve, remove terrine from pan by dipping bottom of pan in warm water.
Loosen sides with knife. Unmold on platter. Slice and serve over raspberry sauce
(instructions below). Garnish with strawberries or raspberries.

Raspberry Sauce: In blender or food processor purée raspberries until smooth.
Place fine mesh strainer over small bowl and press raspberry purée through
strainer with wooden spoon. Discard seeds. Stir sugar and vanilla into strained
sauce.

*This is a pretty, light summer dessert. Light pink terrine over darker rose sauce on
plate.*

*Dana Dahlbo
Parent, Alison Dahlbo '97*

Strawberries Dessert

Serves any number you like

INGREDIENTS:

Strawberries
Pistachio ice cream

Amaretto liqueur

PROCEDURE:

Wash and cut up strawberries to desired size. Serve on individual dessert plates with pistachio ice cream on the side. Sprinkle Amaretto over strawberries and ice cream.

This recipe is ideal for an informal dinner gathering.

Helga Halsey
Parent, Jane Halsey '65, Anne Halsey-Smith '67, Heidi Halsey '92

Fresh Fruit with Pure Maple Syrup and Whipped Cream

Serves 4

INGREDIENTS:

2 cups sliced peaches,
**   strawberries or**
**   blueberries**
1 to 3 tablespoons pure
**   maple syrup**

Sprinkle of salt, if
**   desired**
1 cup (1/2 pint) heavy
**   cream (chilled)**
Mint leaves for garnish

PROCEDURE:

Slice fruit. Add maple syrup to taste (a little goes a long way). Sprinkle on a small amount of salt if desired. Refrigerate in a covered non-aluminum container. Whip cream with an electric mixer until soft peaks are formed. Dish fruit into serving dishes. Top with a dollup of whipped cream and a sprig of mint.

Quick and easy. Whipped cream is not necessary for dieters. This is a family summer favorite and very good after spicy or heavy dinners.

Leslie Collins Cook '81

"Cool and Tasty" Surprise Dessert

Serves 10

INGREDIENTS:

- 1 16-ounce container cottage cheese (small curd)
- 1 8-ounce container whipped topping
- 1 6-ounce box lemon jello
- 1 8-ounce can crushed pineapple (or fruit cocktail), drained

PROCEDURE:

In a large serving bowl, mix together the cottage cheese and whipped topping. Add the powdered jello slowly and mix until well-blended. Blend in fruit. Refrigerate for 1 hour.

For an extra pleasing decoration, top bowl with sliced bananas or strawberries. Recipe can be halved for smaller portions.

Mildred Santeramo
Grandparent, Laura Addario '94

Pear Jello Mold

Serves 8 to 16

INGREDIENTS:

- 1 29-ounce can Bartlett pears
- 3 tablespoons water
- 1 6-ounce box jello (preferably strawberry/banana or lime)
- 8 ounces cream cheese
- 1 cup (1/2 pint) whipping cream

PROCEDURE:

In a saucepan place syrup from Bartlett pears and water and bring to a boil. Remove pan from heat and dissolve jello in the syrup. Thoroughly mix cream cheese and pears in blender or food processor. Slowly combine the 2 mixtures with a wire whisk. Beat whipping cream with electric beater until peaks form. Add whipped cream to the jello mixture, mixing well with a wire whisk. Pour into mold. Refrigerate until set.

Quick and easy. May be made 2 days prior to serving. Serve surrounded with sliced fresh fruits.

Bobbi Susselman
Parent, Jordan Susselman '96, Brandon Susselman '99,
Dalton Susselman '99

Apricot Crêpes

Serves 8

INGREDIENTS:

Your favorite dessert crêpe recipe (for 16 crêpes)

Filling:
8 ounces cream cheese
1/4 cup (1/2 stick) butter
1/4 cup sugar
1 1/2 teaspoons vanilla
1 teaspoon grated lemon

Sauce:
2/3 cup apricot jam
1/2 cup orange juice
2 tablespoons butter
1 tablespoon lemon juice

Garnish:
1/4 cup slivered almonds, toasted

PROCEDURE:

Make 16 dessert crêpes using your favorite recipe. Preheat oven to 350°. Blend filling ingredients until smooth. Fill each crêpe and fold. Place in 10" x 14" baking pan. In a saucepan heat sauce ingredients, stirring to mix well. Pour over filled crêpes. Heat crêpes in oven for 10 minutes. Garnish with almonds.

May be made a day ahead and reheated.

Elaine Morris Miller '64X

Ginger Pancakes
with Lemon Sauce

INGREDIENTS:

2 cups Bisquick
1 egg
1 1/3 cups milk
1 1/2 teaspoons ginger
1 teaspoon cinnamon
1/2 teaspoon ground
    cloves
3/4 cup whipped cream
    cheese

Lemon Sauce:
1/2 cup (1 stick) butter or
    margarine
1 cup sugar
1/4 cup water
1 egg, well-beaten
    Grated peel of 1 lemon
3 tablespoons lemon
    juice

PROCEDURE:

Beat Bisquick, egg, milk, ginger, cinnamon and cloves with hand beater until smooth. Pour scant 1/4 cup batter onto hot, lightly oiled griddle. Cook until pancakes are dry around the edges, turn and cook until golden brown.

Lemon Sauce: Heat all ingredients to boiling over medium heat, stirring constantly.

Fill every 2 pancakes with lemon sauce, garnish with cream cheese and top with lemon sauce.

Adele Weidenkopf Kayser '45
Parent, Robin Kayser '70, Alysun Kayser-Ortiz '79, Wendy Kayser Leslie '79X

Fruit Pizza

Serves 10 to 12

INGREDIENTS:

1 20-ounce roll
   refrigerator sugar
   cookies
1/2 cup sugar
3 tablespoons corn
   starch
2 tablespoons orange
   juice
2 tablespoons lemon
   juice
8 ounces cream cheese

2 tablespoons sugar
1 teaspoon vanilla

Topping:
Sliced fresh fruit such
   as bananas, kiwi,
   grapes, strawberries,
   pineapple, berries

PROCEDURE:

Preheat oven to 350°. Cut cookie dough into 1/4" slices. Lay on 12" pizza pan and pat together and flatten to completely cover bottom. Bake for 12 to 18 minutes or until browned. Cool.

Glaze: In a small saucepan mix together the 1/2 cup sugar, cornstarch and orange juice. Boil until thickened. Remove from heat and stir in lemon juice. Cool.

Filling: Mix together cream cheese, sugar and vanilla. Spread on cooled baked cookie dough.

Cover with sliced fruit. Make decorative patterns. Be creative. Drizzle glaze over fruit. Refrigerate until ready to serve.

Kids love this and so do adults. Great for any occasion.

Marjie Entz Smoot '65

Danish Dessert

Serves 8 to 12

INGREDIENTS:

A:
2 cups flour
1 cup margarine, softened
1/2 cup brown sugar, packed
1/2 cup chopped pecans

B:
2 packages Dream Whip (or 4 cups Cool Whip or whipped cream)

8 ounces cream cheese, softened
1 cup powdered sugar
1 teaspoon vanilla

C:
1 package Danish Dessert (Junket)
1 package frozen raspberries, partially thawed

PROCEDURE:

A: Preheat oven to 350°. Mix first 3 ingredients together until well-blended. Add chopped pecans and mix well. Crumble into 9" x 13" glass pan. Bake 15 to 20 minutes until mixture is a golden brown. Cool. Recrumble. Set aside.

B: Prepare Dream Whip according to package directions. (The 2 packages will yield 4 cups whipped topping.) Mix the prepared Dream Whip (or Cool Whip or whipped cream) with the softened cream cheese, sugar and vanilla until well-blended. Put 1/2 the crumbs from part A in the bottom of an ungreased 9" x 13" pan. Spread filling (part B) over crumb mixture. Then spread remaining crumbs over cream cheese mixture. Refrigerate at least 6 hours.

C: Follow Danish Dessert (Junket) recipe from box. Add berries. Refrigerate.

To serve, spoon sauce (C) over refrigerated individual servings that have been placed on serving plates.

Although this sounds time consuming, it is very easy, incredibly well-received and fool proof. It is best if made in the morning for evening eating or even made the day before. If you cannot find the Junket Danish Dessert, you can use prepared strawberry glaze.

Judy Hamer
Parent, Heidie Hamer '86, Kristie Hamer '88, Jake Hamer '91,
Aimie Hamer '92, Hallie Hamer '94, Cassie Hamer '98

Bride's Hot Cobbler

Serves 6

INGREDIENTS:

1/4 cup (1/2 stick)
unsalted butter
3/4 cup sugar
3/4 cup flour
1 1/2 teaspoons baking
powder

1/2 teaspoon baking soda
Pinch salt
2/3 cup milk
1 16-ounce can sliced
peaches, undrained
Dash nutmeg

PROCEDURE:

Preheat oven to 350°. Put butter in an 8" x 12" x 2" pan and place in oven to melt. Remove from oven and skim off solid fat particles on top of melted butter. In a medium size bowl mix together sugar, flour, baking powder, baking soda, salt and milk. Stir until well-blended. Pour this mixture slowly into pan with the butter. Do not stir. The butter will rise to the top. Top with drained canned peaches. Sprinkle with nutmeg if desired. Bake for 25 to 30 minutes, until golden brown and puffy.

Can use other fruits such as cherries or pineapple. Quick and easy for new cooks (and "old" cooks on a tight schedule).

Alliene Vale
Grandparent, Elizabeth Vale '92 and Susannah Vale '95

471

Apple Crisp

Serves 8 to 10

INGREDIENTS:

5 to 8 large tart apples such as Granny Smith
1/2 teaspoon cinnamon
1/3 cup sugar
1 cup plus 2 tablespoons flour

1/2 cup (1 stick) plus 2 tablespoons butter (or margarine)
1 cup packed brown sugar

PROCEDURE:

Preheat oven to 375°. Spray a 9" x 13" baking pan with vegetable oil. Slice apples and put in pan. Sprinkle to taste with cinnamon. Then sprinkle sugar evenly over apples. Lightly dust apples with 2 tablespoons flour. Then drizzle with 2 tablespoons melted butter (or margarine). Mix 1/2 cup butter (or margarine), 1 cup flour and the brown sugar together, using a fork or your fingers until mixture begins to stick together but is still crumbly. Put crumbled topping over apples and bake for 45 to 55 minutes. Check apples with point of a sharp knife to see if they are soft. Soft apples, bubbly juice and lightly browned topping indicate the dessert is ready.

Suzanne Baral Weiner
Staff, Director of Marketing and Public Relations

Apple Raspberry Crumble

Serves 4

INGREDIENTS:

3 large Granny Smith
    apples
1 tablespoon lemon juice
10 ounces frozen
    raspberries (or 1 pint
    fresh raspberries)
    Sugar to sprinkle over
    raspberries as needed

1/2 cup sugar
1/2 cup flour
1/4 teaspoon nutmeg
1/2 cup (1 stick) unsalted
    butter
    Whipping cream,
    lightly whipped, or
    milk for topping

PROCEDURE:

Preheat oven to 375°. Peel, core and slice apples. Place in a buttered 9" glass pie pan. Sprinkle lemon juice over apples. Drain raspberries and sprinkle over the apples. (If raspberries seem especially tart, sprinkle a little sugar over fruit before adding topping.) Mix the 1/2 cup sugar, the flour and nutmeg in a bowl. Cut the butter into small pieces and add to flour mixture. Using your finger tips, work the butter in until mixture is crumbly. Cover fruit with this mixture. Bake for 25 minutes or until fruit is bubbly and top is golden brown. Serve warm with lightly whipped cream or milk, if desired.

This is a basic fruit "crumble" recipe which can be varied endlessly by using other fruits or combinations thereof. You may also vary amount of sugar and flour topping to taste.

Betty Vale
Parent, Elizabeth Vale '92 and Susannah Vale '95

"Too Easy" Food Processor Pie Crust

Yields 1 pie crust

INGREDIENTS:

1 1/2 cups white flour
1/2 teaspoon salt
1/2 cup (1 stick) butter
cut in small pieces

1 egg yolk
3 tablespoons cold water

PROCEDURE:

Put flour, salt and butter in bowl of food processor fitted with metal blade. Pulse On/Off button so butter and flour mix and become "granular". Keeping the food processor going, add egg yolk and cold water. Dough will form a ball. Remove and wrap in wax paper. Refrigerate for 30 minutes before rolling out into pie shape.

Do not substitute margarine for butter. Treat yourself and use the real thing!

Susanna Smith
Parent, Troy Smith '97 and Adam Smith '98

Flaky Pie Crust

Yields 4 9" pie crusts

INGREDIENTS:

- 1 egg
- 1 tablespoon white vinegar
- Water
- 4 heaping cups white flour

- 1 1/2 cups lard (or 1/2 cup solid vegetable shortening and 2 sticks margarine)
- 1 teaspoon salt (1/2 teaspoon if using margarine)
- 1 teaspoon baking powder

PROCEDURE:

Put egg and vinegar into a 1-cup measuring cup. Then add water to the level of 3/4 cup. Mix with a fork until well-blended. Mix remaining ingredients together with pastry blender (or process with On/Off button in food processor) until lumps are the size of peas. Add the wet ingredients to the dry mixture and mix just until blended. (Do not over-mix). Form dough into 4 balls, wrap in wax paper and chill in refrigerator for approximately 2 hours before using. (Seal tightly in plastic wrap to freeze).

Freezes well up to 6 weeks. This recipe will be flakier if lard is used but obviously healthier if margarine is used. Adapted from an old family recipe.

Carole Mills
Parent, Sara Mills '97

Basic (Always Flaky) Pie Crust

Yields 1 double crust for 9" pie

INGREDIENTS:

2 cups all-purpose flour
1/2 teaspoon salt
3/4 cups (1 1/2 sticks)
  very cold or frozen
  unsalted butter

3 tablespoons margarine
  or chilled vegetable
  shortening
1/4 cup ice water

PROCEDURE:

Put flour and salt in bowl of food processor fitted with steel blade. With a knife on a cutting board, quickly slice the butter and margarine into tablespoon size pieces. (Do not handle too much or butter will soften.) Add butter and margarine pieces to flour. Process with On/Off mode a few seconds until mixture resembles course meal. With the machine On, add the ice water drop by drop, mixing briefly, until dough begins to stick together. (Overworking the flour releases the gluten and causes the dough to be sticky and tough.) Remove dough and divide in half. Press each half into a ball and flatten slightly with the heel of your hand. Wrap and chill if not using immediately. (To use dough after chilling, let warm at room temperature for at least 15 minutes.)

Roll out 1 of the dough "balls" on a lightly floured pastry board or marble. Sprinkle top of dough with flour. Roll to 1/8" thick and slightly larger than pie plate. Line pie plate and crimp or flute edges as desired. Chill if not filling immediately. Roll out second half of dough for top (or wrap tightly and freeze for later use).

Work quickly! Cold butter/margarine and very brief handling and processing of flour are the key ingredients of flaky pastry. Worth the effort because so much better than store bought!

Betty Vale
Parent, Elizabeth Vale '92 and Susannah Vale '95

Strawberry Pie

Serves 6 to 8

INGREDIENTS:

3 to 4 cups fresh strawberries
1 9" baked pie shell
1 1/2 cups water

1 1/2 cups sugar
1/4 cup corn starch
1 3-ounce package strawberry jello

PROCEDURE:

Wash and stem strawberries. Fill pie shell with strawberries. In a small saucepan, combine the water, sugar and cornstarch and bring to a boil, stirring, until clear. Remove from heat and add the jello. Mix until well-blended. Cool slightly and pour over berries. Refrigerate and eat when set.

This recipe can be used with any fresh berries. One of our favorites is blueberry with berry jello. Quick and easy. Serve with whipped cream if desired.

Marilyn Ott
Parent, Carter Ott '94

Mother's Fresh Peach or Strawberry Pie

Serves 6

INGREDIENTS:

1 baked 9" pie shell

Glaze:
2 peaches, peeled and
   finely sliced
1/2 cup sugar
2 tablespoons
   cornstarch
2/3 cup water
Pinch salt
1 tablespoon lemon juice

1/4 teaspoon almond
   extract
1 tablespoon butter or
   margarine

3 to 4 cups sliced, ripe, fresh
   peaches (uncooked)
2 cups (1 pint) whipped
   cream
Nutmeg to taste

PROCEDURE:

Bake pie shell. (Poke bottom and sides with fork so it won't puff up.)

Glaze: Combine the 2 sliced peaches, sugar, cornstarch, water, salt and lemon juice in a saucepan. Stir frequently over medium heat, until thickened and clear. Remove from heat and add the almond extract and butter (or margarine). Stir.

Slice fresh fruit into pie shell. Dribble warm glaze over fruit and refrigerate for 1 to 1 1/2 hours before serving. Whip cream and pile around edge of pie before serving. Sprinkle nutmeg lightly on whipped cream.

This pie, which also can be made with strawberries, raspberries, blackberries or ollalieberries (or a mixture of any of these), is always a huge hit from May through September. It is tart and cold, quick to make and very refreshing on a summer evening. It has been a favorite of mine since I can remember and now is loved by my own family. Do not make too far ahead or crust gets soft.

Martha Bybee Vlahos '55

Apple Pie

Yields 8" pie

INGREDIENTS:

Pie Pastry: (Makes 2 8" double crust pies)
1/2 cup lard
1/2 cup Crisco
3 cups flour
1 egg
5 tablespoons milk
1 teaspoon cider vinegar
1/2 teaspoon salt

Filling: (For 1 8" pie)
2 tablespoons flour
6 cups peeled and sliced green apples
1 1/2 cups sugar
3/4 teaspoon cinnamon
1/2 teaspoon nutmeg
Dash salt
2 tablespoons butter

1 tablespoon milk, for brushing on top pastry

PROCEDURE:

Pie Pastry: Cut the lard and shortening into the flour with a pastry cutter or forks. Mix the egg, milk, vinegar and salt together, then add to the flour and mix briefly until dough is formed. Divide the dough into 4 pieces, flattening each into a thick disk. Refrigerate 30 minutes before rolling out, or wrap in plastic and freeze.

Preheat oven to 425°.
Filling and assembling pie: Roll the bottom crust of the pie and place in an 8" pie plate. Combine the flour and apples. Combine the sugar and spices and mix thoroughly into the apples. Place apples in the pie crust and dot with the butter. Roll out the top crust, make several slashes in the crust and top the apples with it, crimping the edges. Brush the top of the pie with milk. Bake for 45 minutes.

Line the bottom of the oven with foil to catch the drips.

Molly Hannan
Parent, Mimi Hannan '92

Fresh Blueberry Pie

Yields 9" pie

INGREDIENTS:

Pastry for double crust
pie:
2/3 cup solid vegetable
shortening (Crisco)
2 cups sifted all-purpose
flour
1 teaspoon salt
5 to 7 tablespoons cold water
Filling:

2 boxes fresh blueberries
(4 to 6 cups)
3/4 cup sugar
3 tablespoons flour
Dash ground nutmeg
1 teaspoon lemon juice
1 tablespoon butter

Sugar for sprinkling
crust (optional)

PROCEDURE:

Preheat oven to 400°. Cut shortening into flour and salt with pastry blade in food processor until mixture is like small peas. Pour cold water in a stream into mixture while processor is running. Mixture will form a ball. Divide in half. Flatten on lightly floured surface and roll from center to edge. Line 9" pie plate with rolled out pastry round.

Combine blueberries, sugar, flour and nutmeg. Fill pastry-lined pie plate. Sprinkle with lemon juice and dot with butter. Roll out other half of pastry. Adjust top crust and seal. Cut slits to allow steam to escape. Sprinkle sugar on crust (optional). Place on cookie sheet (to catch fruit juice) and bake for 15 minutes. Turn temperature down to 350° and bake for 45 minutes or until top is slightly browned.

Wonderful with vanilla ice cream on the side. You may add 3 tablespoons of tapioca in place of the flour as thickening for the fruit. Other fruit pies may be made with this recipe (e.g., raspberry, peach, apricot, or apple; be sure to add 1 teaspoon cinnamon for an apple pie).

Patricia Clark
Parent, Ryan Clark '92 and Ashley Clark '95

Slice of Lemon Pie

Serves 8

INGREDIENTS:

1 9" pie crust, unbaked
1 1/2 cups granulated sugar
3 tablespoons flour
1/4 teaspoon salt
1/3 cup soft butter (or margarine)
3 eggs, well-beaten
2 tablespoons grated lemon peel
1/2 cup cold water

3 lemons peeled and sliced <u>very</u> thinly (I use food processor fitted with slicing blade), seeds removed
2 tablespoons medium crystal sugar*

* **These are the large sugar sprinkles you can find in cookie decoration section of the store. I use white or yellow.**

PROCEDURE:

Preheat oven to 375°. Use your favorite pastry for pie crust, roll out and line 9" pie plate. In a large bowl stir granulated sugar with flour, salt, butter (or margarine), eggs, grated peel and cold water until thoroughly blended. Stir in sliced lemons last. Carefully pour in pie crust. Arrange lemon slices so they are at the top and evenly spaced so they look pretty when baked. Bake for 25 minutes. Then sprinkle crystal sugar on top and bake for 10 minutes more. Cool.

If I have extra crust, I make short strips, cut into 1" to 2" lengths and twist to place on top of pie before baking. I also have made lattice, or cut out little shapes or letters for fun. I really hate to make pie crust, so I usually just buy the pre-made ones in the deli section and put in my own pie plate and serve with just the sugar sprinkles on top.

Chris Young
Parent, Dana Young '87 and David Young '96

Pear Tart

Serves 10

INGREDIENTS:

Crust:
1 3/4 cups all-purpose flour
   1/2 cup (1 stick) unsalted
       butter, ice cold, cut
       into pieces
   1/4 cup sugar
     1 egg
   1/2 teaspoon ice water
   1/2 teaspoon vanilla

Filling:
   1 cup sugar
   6 tablespoons all-purpose
     flour
   3 eggs
   1/2 cup (1 stick) butter
   4 Bartlett pears, peeled,
     cored and sliced 1/4"
     thick
     Powdered sugar to
     sprinkle on top

PROCEDURE:

Preheat oven to 375°.
Crust: Combine flour, butter and sugar in a food processor and mix using On/Off turns for a few seconds until mixture resembles coarse meal. In a small bowl, mix together the egg, water and vanilla until well-blended. Add the egg mixture to the flour mixture and continue mixing until dough is crumbly. (Can also be mixed by hand.) Turn dough into an 11" tart pan. Carefully press dough into pan covering bottom and up sides. Refrigerate while preparing filling.

Filling: Combine sugar, flour and eggs in large bowl and whisk until smooth. Melt butter in medium skillet over high heat until foamy and golden brown. Slowly whisk melted butter into sugar mixture. Set aside.

Arrange pear slices side by side in circle in crust. (Make 1 circle around outside edge and another circle inside. Place pears very close together.) Pour melted butter mixture over pears. Bake until crust and filling are brown, 30 to 40 minutes. Serve warm or at room temperature. Before serving, sprinkle with powdered sugar.

Mrs. Jack Lucas
Grandparent, John Spanos '98

Blackberry Tart

Serves 8

INGREDIENTS:

Crust:
5 ounces finely minced nuts
1/2 cup (1 stick) butter
1/4 cup sugar
1 1/2 cup flour
1 egg
1 teaspoon vanilla

Filling:
1 tablespoon unflavored gelatine
1/4 cup water
1/2 cup sugar
1/2 cup red raspberry or blackberry jelly
3 cups fresh or frozen blackberries

PROCEDURE:

Crust: In a food processor, chop nuts with steel blade until finely minced. Add other ingredients and mix until well-blended. Press into a 10" tart pan which has a removable bottom. Chill 30 minutes. Preheat oven to 350°. Bake for 15 to 20 minutes.

Filling: Soften gelatine in the water. In a saucepan, combine sugar and jelly and cook over very low heat until sugar and jelly are melted and thoroughly mixed, about 7 minutes. Add berries and simmer until berries lose their crunch but not their shape and get coated with the sugar/jelly mixture (1 to 2 minutes for fresh berries; 3 to 5 minutes for frozen). Remove from heat and add gelatine, stirring gently (being careful not to crush berries) until gelatine is dissolved and thoroughly blended. Cool. Pour into crust and chill.

Prepare ahead so the tart has time to set. Delicious with whipped cream. My favorite breakfast!

Sandra Bogart '70

Sweet Potato Pie

Yields 10" pie

INGREDIENTS:

1 10" unbaked pie crust
1 3/4 cup mashed cooked
    sweet potatoes
1 teaspoon salt
1 cup white granulated
    sugar
1 teaspoon ground
    cinnamon
1/2 teaspoon ground
    nutmeg

1/2 teaspoon ground
    ginger
1 1/2 cups evaporated milk
3 eggs, slightly beaten
1 tablespoon butter,
    melted
1 teaspoon vanilla

PROCEDURE:

Preheat oven to 400°. Fit pie crust into 10" pie pan. Make decorative edges using tines of a fork or by pinching edges to form scallop design. Set aside. Spoon the mashed sweet potatoes into a large mixing bowl. In a small bowl, combine salt, sugar, cinnamon, nutmeg and ginger. Stir these dry ingredients into mashed potatoes until dry ingredients are completely dissolved. In the small bowl, stir together the milk and the slightly beaten eggs, then add to mashed potatoes. Stir gently with wire whisk until mixture is smooth. Stir in the melted butter and vanilla extract. Slowly pour the pie filling into prepared crust, being careful not to slop the filling onto the edges of the crust. Carefully place the filled pie dish into the oven on a center shelf.

Bake for about 15 minutes until crust is very lightly brown. Then lower the heat to 325° and cook for 30 to 40 minutes until pie filling is set. Check pie after 25 minutes. If edges are browning too quickly, cover edges with strips of aluminum foil. You can test pie filling by inserting the tip of a stainless steel knife halfway between the edge and center of the pie. If the knife comes out clean, the pie is ready to remove from the oven. The center will continue to cook as pie cools.

Let stand for 2 hours, then serve with dollops of whipped cream sprinkled with chopped pecans. Delicious alone or with a hardy cup of coffee.

Anna Roseboro
Faculty, English Department

Swiss Walnut Pie

INGREDIENTS:

Crust:
2 cups flour
3/4 cup butter
1/3 cup sugar
1/4 teaspoon salt
1 egg
1 teaspoon water

Filling:
1 1/2 cups white sugar
2 tablespoons honey
1/2 cup half and half
2 cups walnuts

PROCEDURE:

Crust: With pastry blender (or 2 knives) cut butter into dry ingredients. Beat egg and water and add all but 1 tablespoonful to pastry. (Reserve the 1 tablespoon for brushing the pastry before baking.) Mix well. If too soft to roll, chill for 10 to 15 minutes. Roll dough to fit 8" round cake pan. (I use disposable ones.) Line the pan with the dough. Save some dough for cut out shapes to decorate top of pie. (I usually use Christmas tree cookie cutter.)

Filling: Preheat oven to 350°. Caramelize sugar (melt over medium heat and continue to cook until light brown). (I use an electric fry pan.) Stir frequently as it burns easily. Turn off heat. In a small saucepan slightly warm the honey and half and half. Add slowly to caramelized sugar which will froth a bit and get hard. Turn heat on low to remelt sugar mixture. Add broken nuts. Stir until sugar mixture is all melted again. Remove from heat and pour onto crust. Put cut-outs on top (it is not necessary to completely cover top). Brush edges and cut-outs with remaining egg and water mixture. Bake at 350° for 20 minutes. Turn heat up to 375° and cook for 20 more minutes until crust is golden. Remove from oven and cool.

Serve with whipped cream, ice cream or plain (the way I like it best). Keeps well on shelf. Can be mailed. I often double the crust recipe and roll out for 3 pies and triple the filling recipe and make 3 at a time. Caramelizing the sugar is the time consuming part. If you have extra crust, roll out and make cut-out cookies. Sprinkle them with cinnamon and sugar and bake about 10 minutes in 300° oven. Children like making these cookies and the dough doesn't get tough with rerolling.

Jeanie Fawcett Merrill '42

Buttermilk Pie

Yields 9" pie

INGREDIENTS:

Uncooked 9" pie shell
1/2 cup (1 stick) butter
2 cups sugar
3 tablespoons flour

3 large eggs
1 1/2 cups buttermilk
1 teaspoon vanilla
Dash of nutmeg

PROCEDURE:

Preheat oven to 350°. Prepare pie shell using your favorite recipe or one of the pastry crust recipes at the beginning of the pie section of this cookbook (pages 474-476). Cream butter; add sugar and flour and mix well. Add eggs, buttermilk, vanilla and nutmeg and mix well. Pour filling into pie shell. Bake pie for 50 minutes or until pie sets.

This is a very old family recipe.

Mrs. Shelman Porter
Grandparent, Lauren Porter '96

California Mud

Serves 15

INGREDIENTS:

Crust:
1 cup flour
1/2 cup (1 stick)
    margarine, softened
1/4 cup ground nuts

Filling:
8 ounces cream cheese,
    softened

1 cup powdered sugar
1 teaspoon vanilla
1 12-ounce container
    Cool Whip
2 3-ounce packages
    instant lemon
    pudding
3 cups milk
1/4 cup chopped nuts

PROCEDURE:

Preheat oven to 375°.
Crust: Mix together the flour, margarine and nuts. Pat into a 9" x 13" pan and bake 15 minutes. Cool.

Filling: Cream the cream cheese, powdered sugar and vanilla together. Fold in 1 cup of the Cool Whip and spread over cooled crust. Beat the 2 packages of instant lemon pudding with milk until thick. Spread over cream cheese mixture and add remaining Cool Whip over pudding. Sprinkle with nuts. Chill.

This is a take-off on "Mississippi Mud" but after our California granddaughter visited and made the pie we renamed it "California Mud". You could use a vanilla wafer or graham cracker crust. If you are in a hurry to serve, cut the milk to 2 1/2 cups.

Ruth Wood
Grandparent, Erin Wood '98

Sour Cream Pie

Serves 6 to 8

INGREDIENTS:

1 **cup raisins**	**Pinch salt**
1 **cup (1/2 pint) sour cream**	1 **9" baked pie shell**
3/4 **cup brown sugar, packed**	**Meringue:**
3 **egg yolks**	3 **egg whites**
1/2 **teaspoon cinnamon**	1/4 **teaspoon baking powder**
1/2 **teaspoon cloves**	6 **tablespoons sugar**
1/8 **teaspoon nutmeg**	

PROCEDURE:

Preheat oven to 325°. Mix together raisins, sour cream, brown sugar, egg yolks, cinnamon, cloves, nutmeg and salt in a heavy pan and cook over medium heat, stirring frequently until thick, about 8 minutes. Pour into 9" baked pie shell.

Meringue: Beat egg whites with baking powder until partially stiff. Beat in sugar 1 tablespoon at a time. Continue beating until whites are stiff and form a sharp peak. Spoon onto pie. Be sure to cover top completely, up to all edges. Bake in oven until meringue is golden. Be sure to cool away from a draft, for it will weep.

Anne C. Oliver
Grandparent, Josh Oliver '96 and Hunter Oliver '98

Pecan Oatmeal Pie

Serves 8

INGREDIENTS:

2 eggs, beaten
1/4 cup (1/2 stick) butter
    or margarine, melted
1/2 cup granulated sugar
1/2 cup white Karo syrup
1/2 cup pecans

2/3 cup uncooked oatmeal
    (quick or regular)
1/8 teaspoon salt
1 teaspoon vanilla

1 unbaked 9" pie shell

PROCEDURE:

Preheat oven to 350°. Mix all ingredients together and pour into an unbaked 9" pie shell and bake until firm, 45 to 50 minutes.

Very rich and delicious.

Rachel Gorski
Grandparent, Tyler Cooper '96X and Megan Cooper '98

Pecan Cups

Yields 24 to 30

INGREDIENTS:

Shells:
3 ounces cream cheese
1/2 cup (1 stick) butter
1 cup flour

Filling:
3/4 cup packed brown
    sugar
1 egg
1/8 teaspoon vanilla
1 tablespoon butter
1 cup pecans

PROCEDURE:

Preheat oven to 375°. Mix first 3 ingredients together until well-blended and mold into "cups" in a mini muffin tin. Combine next 5 ingredients and put a small amount of filling in each "cup" (fill about 1/2 full). Bake for 25 minutes.

Galen Cooper
Parent, Tyler Cooper '96X and Megan Cooper '98

Heavenly Pecan Pie

Serves 6 to 8

INGREDIENTS:

Crust (for 2 pies):
2 cups flour
1/4 teaspoon salt
Just less than 3/4 cup
   Crisco
4 tablespoons ice water

Filling:
3 eggs
2/3 cup sugar
1/3 teaspoon salt
1/3 cup butter, softened
1/2 teaspoon vanilla
1 cup dark corn syrup
1 cup pecans

PROCEDURE:

Crust: Put flour, salt and Crisco in mixing bowl. Cut Crisco into flour with 2 knives until pea size balls form. Add the water; mix into dough with fingers. Form dough into a large ball, divide and roll out on floured surface. Line 9" pie plate with 1/2 of the dough.

Preheat oven to 350°.
Filling: Mix all ingredients (except pecans) in food processor or by hand if desired. Stir in the pecans and pour into unbaked pie crust. Bake for 45 minutes.

This pie is delicious and very easy to prepare. Serve warm with vanilla ice cream or frozen yogurt

Nancy Gordon
Parent, Lindsay Gordon '95 and Allison Gordon '98

Chocolate Pecan Tart

Serves 16 to 20

INGREDIENTS:

Crust:
1 cup (2 sticks) unsalted butter
2 cups flour
1/2 cup sugar
1/8 teaspoon salt

Filling:
1/2 cup (1 stick) unsalted butter
1/2 cup granulated sugar
2 tablespoons whipping cream
4 tablespoons flour
2 1/2 cups pecan halves

Chocolate Glaze:
6 ounces semisweet chocolate
3 ounces unsweetened chocolate
1 1/2 cups whipping cream
1 tablespoon unsalted butter

Garnish:
1 cup (1/2 pint) whipping cream, whipped

PROCEDURE:

Preheat oven to 375°.
Crust: Put crust ingredients in food processor and blend. Pat into bottom and sides of 12" metal tart or quiche pan (with removable bottom). (You will not use all of mixture for a 12" pan.) Bake in preheated oven until barely brown (12 to 15 minutes). Set aside.

Filling: In a saucepan melt the butter, sugar, whipping cream and flour and stir over low heat until blended. Add the pecans and stir to coat. Pour into cooled tart shell and spread carefully with a fork to distribute pecans evenly over bottom of shell. Straighten pecans that are on their ends; try to have most lie flat or sideways, not on end. Bake 20 to 25 minutes until caramelized. Remove from oven and cool completely.

Chocolate Glaze: Melt chocolates, cream and butter over low heat stirring frequently. Cool to room temperature and with a large spoon, distribute chocolate over the pecan tart. Chocolate will settle down and around the pecans. You may poke the nuts and lift them slightly to let the chocolate flow around. Cool and pre-cut before decorating with whipped cream or decorate and cut afterwards.

Garnish: Pipe (with a piping bag) the firmly whipped cream on top in any design you like. I use rosettes around edge and in center.

When I take this to a buffet or party, I pre-cut tart into very small slices (16 to 20) before I garnish each portion with whipped cream. The slices are so thin they can be picked up like a bar or cookie. This tart may be frozen.

Linda Strauss
Parent, Barbie Strauss '89

French Silk Chocolate Pie

Serves 12

INGREDIENTS:

1 baked 9" pie shell
1/2 cup (1 stick) butter
1/2 cup sugar
1 ounce unsweetened chocolate (or more)
1 teaspoon vanilla
2 eggs

Topping:
1 cup (1/2 pint) whipping cream
Powdered sugar (to taste)
2 teaspoons instant coffee powder (or to taste)

PROCEDURE:

Prepare pie shell using your favorite recipe or one at the beginning of the pie section of this cookbook (pages 474-476). After baking, set aside to cool. Cream butter. Gradually add sugar. Cream thoroughly. Melt chocolate in top of a double boiler. Remove from heat and cool slightly. Add melted chocolate and vanilla to butter mixture and blend well. Add eggs, 1 at a time, beating 5 minutes after each addition. Pour into cooled pie shell. Chill.

Topping: Whip the cream. Stir in powdered sugar and instant coffee powder to flavor. Top pie with this mixture.

Refrigerate pie until serving time. It will become soft if left out of refrigerator too long.

Jennifer Swanson '90

Cool Chocolate Mint "Angel" Pie

Serves 8

INGREDIENTS:

1/2 cup granulated sugar
1/8 teaspoon cream of
 tartar
2 egg whites
1/2 cup chopped nuts
 (pecans best)

3/4 cup semisweet mint-
 flavored chocolate
 chips
3 tablespoons hot water
1 teaspoon vanilla
2 cups (1 pint) heavy
 cream, whipped

PROCEDURE:

Preheat oven to 275°. Sift sugar and cream of tartar. Beat egg whites until stiff but not dry! Add sifted ingredients very slowly, beating constantly, until smooth and glossy. Use this to line the bottom and sides of a well-greased 9" pie plate (keeping center hollowed out to a 1/4" thickness. Do not cover rim of pie plate). Sprinkle chopped nuts onto the meringue. Bake 1 hour or until light brown. Cool.

Melt chocolate in double boiler. Stir in water. Cook until thickened. Cool slightly, then add vanilla. Whip 1 cup of the cream and fold into chocolate. Carefully turn this mixture into the meringue shell and chill 2 to 3 hours. Before serving, whip remaining 1 cup of cream and spread on top. Chill before serving.

A delicious dessert which can be made well ahead of a time-consuming meal.

Jacqueline Bethune '83

Chocolate Pie

Serves 8

INGREDIENTS:

Graham Cracker Crust:
1 1/4 cups graham cracker crumbs
2 tablespoons sugar
1/4 cup (1/2 stick) butter, melted

Filling:
7 ounces chocolate chips
1/2 cup milk
1 teaspoon vanilla
32 marshmallows
Pinch salt
1 cup (1/2 pint) whipping cream
Additional whipping cream for topping

PROCEDURE:

Preheat oven to 350°.
Crust: Mix crumbs, sugar and butter. Press mixture firmly and evenly against bottom and sides of an 8" pie pan. Bake for 10 minutes. Cool.

Filling: Heat first 5 ingredients in a double boiler until melted. Set aside and let mixture cool. Whip the cream and add to the mixture. Pour into cool crust. Keep in refrigerator <u>overnight</u>. Add additional whipped cream to top of pie when serving.

Very rich and delicious.

June A. Yarborough
Grandparent, Taylor Price '99

Toffee Chocolate Pumpkin Pie

Yields 10" pie

INGREDIENTS:

1 unbaked 10" pie crust
5 ounces unsweetened
  chocolate
1 tablespoon dark rum
3/4 cup water
1/2 cup sugar
2 eggs plus 1 egg yolk,
  slightly beaten
1 cup (packed) dark
  brown sugar

1 1/2 cups cooked pumpkin,
  fresh or canned
1 cup (1/2 pint)
  whipping cream
1/4 teaspoon cinnamon
1/4 teaspoon cloves
1 1/2 teaspoons flour
1/2 cup pecans

PROCEDURE:

Prepare pie crust using your favorite recipe or one at the beginning of the pie section of this cookbook (pages 474-476). Line 10" pie pan and place in refrigerator until filling is prepared.

Preheat oven to 350°. Over low heat in a heavy saucepan or in a double boiler, melt the chocolate with the rum and water. Stir with a whisk to blend thoroughly. Remove from heat, add the sugar and whisk until the mixture is smooth. Set aside to cool slightly. In a large mixing bowl, place the eggs, brown sugar, pumpkin, whipping cream, spices, flour and the cooled chocolate mixture. Stir with a wooden spoon until all the ingredients are incorporated. Spread the pecans over the bottom of the unbaked pie crust. Pour the chocolate pumpkin mixture over. Bake the pie for 55 minutes. A knife inserted into the middle of the pie will come almost but not quite clean. Cool on a rack.

This pie is much like a dense dark chocolate mousse deepened with richness and moistness of pumpkin. Cinnamon and cloves combined with brown sugar and rum give the pie an expected subtlety. Serve at room temperature with a good vanilla ice cream or rum-flavored whipped cream.

Marianne Engle
Parent, Lindsey Engle '94 and Jordan Engle '98

Peanut Chocolate Dessert

Serves 15

INGREDIENTS:

1/2 cup (1 stick) butter or
    margarine, softened
1 cup all-purpose flour
1 cup finely chopped dry
    roasted peanuts
8 ounces cream cheese,
    softened
1/3 cup peanut butter
1 cup powdered sugar
1 12-ounce carton
    frozen whipped
    topping, thawed

1 3-ounce package
    vanilla instant
    pudding mix
1 3-ounce package
    chocolate instant
    pudding mix
2 3/4 cups milk
1 1.2-ounce milk
    chocolate candy bar,
    shaved

PROCEDURE:

Preheat oven to 350°. Cut butter into flour until mixture resembles coarse meal. Stir 2/3 cup of the chopped peanuts into flour mixture. Press peanut mixture into a 9" x 13" x 2" baking pan. Bake for 20 minutes. Cool crust completely. In a medium bowl combine cream cheese, peanut butter and powdered sugar. Beat until fluffy. Stir 1 cup of the whipped topping into cream cheese mixture. Spread over crust. Chill.

In a medium bowl combine pudding mixes and milk. Beat 2 minutes at medium speed of electric mixer. Spread pudding over cream cheese layer. Spread remaining whipped topping over pudding layer. Sprinkle the top with shaved chocolate and the remaining 1/3 cup chopped peanuts. Store in refrigerator.

Refrigerate until ready to serve.

Barbara Riggs
Aunt, Chris Donaldson '93 and Leslie Donaldson '95

Death by Chocolate I

INGREDIENTS:

- 1 recipe chocolate brownies baked in a 9" x 13" pan
- 1/4 cup Kahlúa (optional)
- 2 3-ounce packages chocolate mousse, prepared

- 1 8-ounce container whipped topping
- 8 Heath bars, crushed
- 1 cup chopped pecans

PROCEDURE:

Prepare brownies. Cool in pan and poke holes. Pour Kahlúa over brownies. Remove brownies from pan, crumble and place half of the pieces in large serving bowl. Prepare mousse and divide into 2 portions. Spread half of the mousse over the crumbled brownies. Spread half the container of whipped topping over the mousse. Sprinkle half the crushed Heath bars and pecans over the topping. Repeat layers. Refrigerate and allow to set for several hours or overnight for flavors to mingle.

Better if made a day ahead to allow flavors to mingle. A trifle bowl makes a beautiful presentation.

Linda Shick Juwvipart '72

Death by Chocolate II

Serves 6 to 8

INGREDIENTS:

24 ounces finest
    semisweet chocolate
1 cup (2 sticks) unsalted
    butter
8 tablespoons sugar
8 egg yolks
5 ounces chopped
    hazelnuts
10 egg whites

Custard Sauce
    (1 1/2 cups):
1/2 cup milk
1/2 cup cream
1 vanilla bean
3 egg yolks
1/4 cup sugar

PROCEDURE:

Break up chocolate into small pieces and melt in double boiler with butter, stirring until smooth and completely melted. Remove from heat, let cool, but do not allow to harden. Add sugar and mix well. Add egg yolks one by one, mixing well after each addition. Add 1/2 of the hazelnuts and mix thoroughly. In a large bowl beat egg whites until very stiff. Fold egg whites into the chocolate mixture, delicately keeping the maximum amount of volume in the egg whites. Butter a 2-quart loaf pan and pour the mixture into the pan. Sprinkle the remaining hazelnuts over the top of the mixture. Cover with plastic wrap and refrigerate for at least 1 day. Unmold by dipping pan into warm water for a few seconds. Slice about 1/2" thick and serve on top of custard sauce.

Custard Sauce: In a saucepan scald the milk and cream with a vanilla bean over medium heat without stirring. (It will scald when tiny bubbles form around the edges of the pan. DO NOT BOIL.) For more vanilla flavor, cut the vanilla bean lengthwise. Beat the egg yolks and sugar together until thick and pale in color; stir gradually and constantly into the hot liquid. Blend well. Cook in double boiler, stirring constantly until sauce thickens enough to coat a spoon. DO NOT BOIL. If desired you can strain the sauce through cheese cloth to remove the dark flecks from the vanilla bean. Cool to room temperature to serve with the chocolate loaf.

To serve, put enough custard sauce on the dessert plate to cover, then place a slice of the chocolate loaf in the center of the sauce.

This chocolate loaf must be made at least 1 day ahead. The custard sauce is best if made same day it is being eaten. Very rich! Fairly easy but very impressive.

S. Ronai White
Parent, Nicholas White '97

Heavenly Hash Dessert

Serves 12

INGREDIENTS:

  1 large angel food cake
  12 ounces chocolate
     chips
  4 eggs, separated

  2 cups (1 pint) whipping
     cream (or prepared
     whipped topping)

PROCEDURE:

Break angel food cake into pieces (a little larger than bite size) and place in a serving bowl. Melt chocolate chips in double boiler or microwave oven. When cooled, pour melted chocolate into a medium size mixing bowl. Add the egg yolks, slightly beaten and mix well. In another bowl, beat egg whites until stiff. Fold into chocolate mixture. Whip cream and fold into chocolate mixture. Pour over cake, tossing until coated. Refrigerate until ready to serve (preferably overnight).

This recipe has been in the family for 50 years and has been a great favorite of all the kids. I have eliminated the extra 2 tablespoons of sugar originally called for. I use prepared whipped topping instead of whipped cream for lower fat content.

Sharon Arbelaez
Parent, Erica Arbelaez '99

Ice Box Pudding

Serves 8 to 10

INGREDIENTS:

  3 ounces German
     chocolate
  6 tablespoons sugar

  4 1/2 tablespoons cream
  6 eggs
  24 lady fingers, halved

PROCEDURE:

In a double boiler, melt chocolate, sugar and cream over boiling water. Separate egg yolks and whites. Beat egg yolks well. Add about 1/4 cup of hot chocolate mixture to eggs, stirring constantly. Add egg mixture to chocolate mixture in double boiler, stirring constantly. Cook until custard is thick enough to coat a spoon. Remove pan from heat and stir until cool. Beat egg whites until stiff and fold into chocolate mixture. In a 2-quart rectangular loaf pan with straight sides, make alternate layers of chocolate and lady fingers, starting and ending with chocolate. Refrigerate <u>overnight</u>.

Very rich. Serve small portions. You'll think you'll want more, but don't do it. This is an old family favorite. Just the name "ice box" tells you it's old.

Jill Lecoq
Staff, Business Office

Steamed Pumpkin Pudding

Serves 8

INGREDIENTS:

1/2 cup vegetable oil	1/4 teaspoon baking
1 1/2 cups sugar	powder
2 eggs	3/4 teaspoon salt
1 cup canned pumpkin	1/2 teaspoon each:
1 2/3 cups flour, sifted	Cloves, cinnamon,
1 teaspoon baking soda	nutmeg, allspice

PROCEDURE:

Beat oil and sugar in mixer until combined. Add eggs 1 at a time while beating. Add pumpkin and mix well. At low speed beat in flour, baking soda, baking powder, salt and spices until just moistened. Pour into greased 1 1/2-quart steamer mold. Cover with foil (or lid). Place mold on rack in Dutch oven or steamer. Pour 1" boiling water into Dutch oven and cover. Steam over low heat for 2 hours or until toothpick inserted in center of pudding comes out clean. Remove mold from Dutch oven and remove foil (or lid). Let stand 5 minutes. Unmold.

Great with dollops of whipped cream dusted with cinnamon. A tasty Christmas season dessert. I use a crock pot with rack for steamer.

Sarah Henriksen
Parent, Nicholas Henriksen '98

Baked Lemon Pudding

Serves 4 to 6

INGREDIENTS:

1 cup sugar
1/2 cup flour
1/2 teaspoon baking
   powder
1/4 teaspoon salt
3 eggs, separated

1/2 cup lemon juice
2 teaspoons grated
   lemon peel
2 tablespoons butter,
   melted
1 1/2 cups milk

PROCEDURE:

Preheat oven to 375°. Sift dry ingredients (saving 1/2 cup sugar). Beat egg yolks until light yellow. Add lemon juice, peel, melted butter and milk. Beat well. Stir in dry ingredients and beat until smooth. Beat egg whites and remaining 1/2 cup sugar until stiff. Fold gently into lemon mixture. Pour into greased 2-quart casserole. Place in pan of warm water in oven. Bake for 45 minutes to 1 hour. (Middle should be somewhat soft or runny.) Serve at once while still warm.

Also good cold.

Anne Gilchrist
Parent, Jennifer Gilchrist '94

Hills' Cornstarch Pudding

Serves 6

INGREDIENTS:

2 cups milk
2 tablespoons
   cornstarch

1/2 cup sugar
2 eggs, separated
1 teaspoon vanilla

PROCEDURE:

Warm milk in medium saucepan. In the bowl of an electric mixer combine cornstarch and sugar with egg yolks and beat until light yellow in color. Continue beating while slowly adding 1/2 cup of the warm milk. Pour egg mixture into hot milk and stir to blend. Continue stirring and cooking over medium-low heat until pudding thickens. (Be careful not to burn.) Remove from heat. Stir in vanilla. Beat egg whites until stiff. Fold egg whites into pudding. Cool for 5 minutes and serve.

This was my dear father's favorite dessert. It's quick and easy and all ages love it. It was my great-grandmother's recipe.

Kimberly Miller
Parent, Camden Miller '94X, Trent Miller '96, Derek Miller '98

Southern Boiled Custard

Yields 4 to 5 cups

INGREDIENTS:

4 eggs yolks
2 tablespoons
cornstarch

3/4 cup sugar
2 teaspoons vanilla
4 cups whole or 2% milk

PROCEDURE:

Separate egg yolks and whites. Whisk egg yolks until blended. Add cornstarch, sugar and vanilla to 1 cup milk and mix well. Pour this mixture into egg yolks. Add remaining milk. Cook over medium heat, stirring, until liquid comes to a boil. Custard will be thick enough to cover a spoon. Pour into serving bowl. Allow to cool to luke warm and serve or refrigerate.

This is good served over fresh fruit, or sprinkled with coconut. It can also be poured over big chunks of angel food cake in a flat container and put in refrigerator to cool. Cake soaks up custard and is "to die for".

Susanna Smith
Parent, Troy Smith '97 and Adam Smith '98

Coffee Bavarian Cream

Serves 6 to 8

INGREDIENTS:

1 envelope (1 tablespoon)
   gelatine
3/4 cup cold water
1 cup strong, hot coffee
3/4 cup sugar

1 teaspoon vanilla
   extract
2 cups (1 pint) whipping
   cream, whipped

PROCEDURE:

Soak the gelatine in cold water. Add hot coffee, then add sugar and vanilla. Stir to blend well. Cool in refrigerator. When beginning to thicken, remove from refrigerator, beat until smooth and add to whipped cream, folding in completely. Put in large serving bowl, or in 6 to 8 small dishes. Refrigerate until set (several hours).

This is a very easy, but very elegant dessert. Can be decorated with whipped cream, chocolate curls, or grated chocolate.

Jennifer Pearson McGough '62

Burnt Cream

Serves 6

INGREDIENTS:

2 cups (1 pint) whipping
   cream
4 egg yolks
1/2 cup sugar

1 tablespoon vanilla
3 teaspoons sugar for
   topping

PROCEDURE:

Preheat oven to 350°. In a saucepan, heat cream over low heat just until it bubbles at edge of pan. With an electric mixer, beat egg yolks and sugar until thick, about 3 minutes. With mixer on medium speed gradually beat cream into egg yolks. Stir in vanilla and pour into custard cups. Place cups in baking pan that has 1/2" water in it. Bake until knife inserted in center comes out clean, about 45 minutes. Remove cups and refrigerate until chilled. Sprinkle each cup with 1/2 teaspoon sugar. Place on top rack under broiler and melt sugar. Chill.

Can be made a day ahead

Ann Payne
Parent, Ashley Hobbs '92 and Tyler Hobbs '95

Crème Brulée

Serves 6

INGREDIENTS:

6 egg yolks	**2 teaspoons vanilla**
1/2 cup sugar	**extract**
2 cups (1 pint) heavy	**1/2 cup light brown sugar**
cream	
1 cup (1/2 pint) half and	
half	

PROCEDURE:

Preheat oven to 350°. Beat egg yolks and sugar together thoroughly. Scald cream and half and half by placing in heavy saucepan over medium-low heat. Remove pan from heat just before bubbles form on the surface and the mixture comes to a boil. Slowly beat egg yolks and sugar into cream mixture. Add vanilla extract. Pour into individual soufflé dishes. Place dishes in shallow pan of hot water in oven. Bake for 30 minutes or until a silver knife inserted in center comes out clean. Cool thoroughly to room temperature. Sprinkle surface with very thin layer of light brown sugar. Put under broiler. Watch carefully! Sugar will melt to a thin crust in a minute or two and will burn in another few seconds. Serve at room temperature.

Always impressive. Great for New Year's Eve dinner.

Martha Dennis
Trustee and
Parent, Jendy Dennis '94, Andrew Dennis '97, Evan Dennis '97

Caramel Flan

Serves 8

INGREDIENTS:

1 cup sugar
8 large eggs
2/3 cup sugar
1/2 teaspoons salt

2 12-ounce cans
   evaporated milk
2 teaspoons vanilla
1 tablespoon brandy

PROCEDURE:

Preheat oven to 350°. Begin boiling water to use for pouring around flan. Carefully caramelize the 1 cup sugar in a heavy skillet. Cook over medium heat until a syrup forms and turns golden brown. Pour the hot caramelized liquid into a 9" x 5" x 3" loaf pan. Turn and tip the pan to coat sides and bottom. In a large bowl beat the eggs until well-blended and light yellow. Add sugar gradually, beating well after each addition. Add remaining ingredients and mix well. Pour this mixture into the caramel coated pan and set into a larger pan. Pour boiling water into larger pan until it comes about 2" up on flan. Bake for 1 hour or until a silver knife inserted in center comes out clean. When done, leave in pan to cool to room temperature.

When cool, cover with plastic and refrigerate <u>overnight</u>. When ready to serve, run a knife around edges and invert onto a serving plate.

This recipe must always be made a day ahead and allowed to set in refrigerator <u>overnight</u>. Delicious!

Kristen Druker
Faculty, History Department and
Parent, Mara Druker '99

Rizogalo
(Greek Rice Pudding)

Serves 6

INGREDIENTS:

3/4 cup rice
3 cups water
Pinch of salt
4 cups (1 quart) milk
5 egg yolks
3/4 cup sugar
Grated peel of 1
orange (or lemon)

Raisins (optional) to
taste
1 teaspoon vanilla
Cinnamon
Whipped cream or
milk, to accompany
(optional)

PROCEDURE:

Parboil rice uncovered in 3 cups of water with a pinch of salt for 10 minutes; drain. Scald the milk (heat over low heat to just below a simmer), add drained rice and cook covered over low heat, stirring occasionally for 35 minutes. Beat egg yolks with the sugar. Remove the rice mixture from the fire and slowly stir in the egg yolks, mixing well. Add orange or lemon rind (or a combination of both); return to low fire and stir constantly until creamy and thick (3 to 5 minutes; be careful not to burn). (Raisins may be added if desired.) Add vanilla, mix well and pour into dessert glasses or dessert bowls. Sprinkle generously with cinnamon and allow to cool to room temperature.

After pudding has reached room temperature, cover with plastic wrap and refrigerate for 2 to 3 hours before serving. Serve with whipped cream or milk if desired.

Delicious hot or cold; most seen to prefer it cold. Great with a cup of coffee or tea.

Themis Chryssostomides '97

Chocolate Soufflé

Serves 4 to 6

INGREDIENTS:

2 1/4 cups milk
3/4 cup sugar
6 tablespoons flour
6 eggs, separated
3 additional egg whites

6 ounces unsweetened chocolate, melted and cooled
1 1/2 tablespoons sugar
Confectioners' sugar to sprinkle on top

PROCEDURE:

Preheat oven to 350°. Scald milk in a heavy saucepan. In a mixing bowl, blend the 3/4 cup sugar, flour and egg yolks until smooth. Stir in a few tablespoons of the hot milk, then stir egg yolk mixture into hot milk. Bring the mixture to a boil over low heat, stirring constantly or beating with a wire whisk. Beat in the chocolate. Set aside.

Beat the 9 egg whites until stiff but not dry. Then beat in the 1 1/2 tablespoons sugar. Fold half the egg whites lightly but thoroughly into chocolate mixture. Add remaining egg whites and fold in lightly but leave some streaks of white still visible. Turn into an ungreased 1 1/2-quart soufflé dish. Bake 30 to 35 minutes or until well-puffed and dry on top. Sprinkle with confectioners' sugar and serve immediately.

Chocolate heaven! Serve with ice cream, if desired.

Martha Dennis
Trustee and
Parent, Jendy Dennis '94, Andrew Dennis '97, Evan Dennis '97

Chocolate Fondue

Yields 1 1/3 cups

INGREDIENTS:

8 ounces semisweet or
   milk chocolate (or
   chips)
1/2 cup light cream
2 tablespoons coffee
   liqueur
1/2 teaspoon instant
   coffee crystals
1 to 2 tablespoons peanut
   butter (optional)

For dipping:
1 pint strawberries
1 banana, cut into bite
   size pieces
1 apple, cut into bite
   size pieces
1 loaf angel food cake,
   cut into bite size
   pieces
Marshmallows

PROCEDURE:

Cut chocolate into small pieces (or use chips). In saucepan over low heat melt chocolate with cream, stirring constantly. Remove from heat. Stir in remaining ingredients. Make sure instant coffee is completely dissolved. Pour mixture into fondue pot or chafing dish. Place over low heat. Serve with assorted fruit, angel food cake and/or marshmallows.

Our family loves the addition of peanut butter for a different taste. We sometimes omit the coffee flavors (liqueur and instant) all together. A real treat.

Alison Dahlbo '97

Amaretto Mousse

Serves 8 to 10

INGREDIENTS:

5 eggs, whites and yolks
  separated
1/2 cup sugar
  Pinch salt
1 teaspoon vanilla
1 cup milk

1 envelope gelatine
2 tablespoons cold water
2 cups (1 pint) heavy
  cream, whipped
  Amaretto liqueur

PROCEDURE:

In a bowl beat the egg yolks with the sugar until the mixture is light yellow. Add a pinch of salt. In a saucepan, combine the vanilla and milk and bring to a boil. Gradually add the milk mixture to the beaten yolks, mixing thoroughly. Return the mixture to the pan and heat over a slow fire, stirring constantly. Heat thoroughly but DO NOT BOIL. Remove from heat. In a separate bowl, soften gelatine in the cold water. Add to the milk and strain mixture through a fine sieve. Cool in a bowl of ice (but do not allow mixture to congeal and become lumpy). Fold in the whipped cream. Beat the egg whites until stiff and fold into mixture. Add 2 to 3 ounces of Amaretto. Pour into a serving bowl or individual glasses. Chill in refrigerator. Before serving, float 1 to 2 tablespoons of Amaretto on each portion.

A rich "special" dessert that is worth the effort!

Joni Ann Ganley
Parent, Brendan Ganley '99

Pumpkin Mousse

Serves 6 to 8

INGREDIENTS:

1 cup sugar
1 envelope unflavored
    gelatine
3/4 teaspoon cinnamon
1/4 teaspoon freshly
    grated ginger
1 1/2 cups milk
1 3/4 cups sour cream

14 ounces canned
    pumpkin
1/3 cup orange liqueur or
    orange juice
3/4 cup whipping cream
6 to 8 candied or chocolate
    covered orange peels
    (optional)

PROCEDURE:

Reserve 2 teaspoons of sugar. In a 2 to 3-quart pan, mix remaining sugar, gelatine, cinnamon and ginger. Add 1/2 cup milk and stir often over medium-high heat, until milk is steaming. Add remaining milk, the sour cream, pumpkin and liqueur. Set pan in ice water and stir often until mixture just begins to set, approximately 20 minutes. (If mixture gets too stiff, stir over heat to soften.)

Whip cream with reserved 2 tablespoons of sugar until soft peaks form. Cover and chill 1/3 cup of the whipped cream until ready to serve. Fold remaining whipped cream into the pumpkin mixture. Divide the mousse evenly among 6 to 8 wine or martini glasses. Lightly cover and chill in the refrigerator until set, at least 4 hours, but not more than a day. When ready to serve, garnish each glass with a dollop of reserved whipped cream and a candied or chocolate covered orange peel.

Barbara Angelucci Giammona '77

Strawberry Sorbet

Serves 4

INGREDIENTS:

    4 cups strawberries
1/4 cup water
    Sugar to taste

PROCEDURE:

Purée strawberries in a blender or food processor. Strain to eliminate most of the seeds and add water and sugar. Pour into a shallow metal pan or bowl, cover and freeze until solid. Remove from freezer when solid, let stand at room temperature for a few minutes. Spoon into bowl of food processor or electric mixer. Purée or beat until smooth and slushy. Place in individual serving bowls, stemmed glasses or a suitable covered storage container and return to freezer until serving time.

There is no trick to sorbet. Its simplicity is its elegance. The recipe remains the same for almost any fruit, with sugar (or fruit syrup) added to taste for tart fruits, such as lemons and limes. Certain canned fruits also make very good sorbets: Try (drained) canned pears with a dash of "Poire" liqueur or (drained) canned peaches with a dash of Armagnac and black pepper.

Neely Swanson
Parent, Reid Swanson '94X

Pineapple Sherbet

Serves 6

INGREDIENTS:

4 cups (1 quart) low fat
    buttermilk (strained)
3/4 cup sugar
  1 20-ounce can crushed
    pineapple with
    natural juice

2 egg whites (or 1 to
  1 1/2 cups lite
    whipped topping)
2 teaspoons vanilla

PROCEDURE:

Combine buttermilk, sugar and pineapple and mix until well-blended and sugar is melted. Pour into a 2-quart dish. Freeze until mushy but not solid. Whip egg whites (or use whipped topping) and stir gently into pineapple mixture with vanilla until blended. Cover and freeze. To serve, let defrost slightly for several minutes.

Very easy to make and absolutely delicious!

Peggy Diehl Candler
Aunt, Jeff Deems '91 and Jeremy Deems '94

Summer Lemon Sherbet

Serves 6 to 8

INGREDIENTS:

1 1/4 cups sugar
  1/3 cup freshly squeezed
      lemon juice
    2 eggs
    2 cups (1 pint) milk
      (whole or low fat, <u>not</u>
      nonfat)

Grated peel of 2
  lemons
2 to 3 drops yellow food
  coloring (optional)

PROCEDURE:

Combine sugar and lemon juice. Stir or beat well. Add the 2 eggs, continuing to beat. Add the milk, grated lemon peel and 2 drops of yellow food coloring (optional) and beat a little more. If not yellow enough, add 1 more drop food coloring. (Should be pale lemon yellow, not bright yellow.) Pour into freezer tray and freeze until mushy (2 to 4 hours). Return to mixer and beat well until lumps are gone. Refreeze until hard.

Serve as dessert course on a perfect La Jolla summer evening, preferably on the patio! With or without a cookie! To remove from tray it is easiest to use knife and small spatula. I serve in sherbets or even on flat dessert plates.

Melesse W. Traylor
Parent, Kerry Traylor '80, Robin Traylor '85, John Traylor '88

511

Pumpkin Bombe

Serves 12

INGREDIENTS:

1 1-pound can pumpkin
1 cup brown sugar
2 teaspoons cinnamon
1/2 teaspoon nutmeg
1/4 teaspoon ground
   cloves
1/4 teaspoon salt

2 quarts vanilla ice
   cream
Pecans to garnish
Warm mincemeat
   sauce to accompany,
   if desired

PROCEDURE:

In a large mixing bowl, blend pumpkin, brown sugar, spices and salt. Cut ice cream into chunks. With mixer on low speed, beat ice cream into pumpkin mixture until smooth and well-blended. Pour ice cream mixture into a 10 or 12-cup mold. Plunge spatula down through ice cream several times to release air bubbles. Freeze at least 24 hours. Unmold onto chilled plate. Return to freezer long enough to firm up edges. (May be stored in freezer for up to 1 week.) Garnish with pecans, cut in wedges and serve with warm mincemeat sauce if desired.

This has been our Thanksgiving dinner dessert for the last 20 years. Everybody loves it!

Anne-Marie Lloyd Caple '57

Marshmallow Cream Dip

Yields 1 1/2 cups

INGREDIENTS:

8 ounces cream cheese
1 7-ounce jar
    marshmallow cream
6 Maraschino cherries,
    chopped

Small amount cherry
    juice to get color you
    want

PROCEDURE:

Beat all ingredients in mixer until well-blended.

Serve with strawberries or spread on date nut bread. Recipe from my friend Lisa Krueger.

Jeanette Ruchlewicz
Parent, Brian Ruchlewicz '97

La Jolla Fudge Foggies

Yields 16 2" x 3" rectangles

INGREDIENTS:

- 1 **pound bittersweet (or semisweet) chocolate, finely chopped**
- 1 **cup (2 sticks) unsalted butter, cut into tablespoons**
- 1/3 **cup strong brewed coffee**

- 4 **large eggs**
- 1 1/2 **cups granulated sugar**
- 1/2 **cup all-purpose flour**
- 8 **ounces (about 2 cups) walnuts, coarsely chopped**

PROCEDURE:

Position rack in the center of the oven and preheat to 350°. Line a 9" x 13" pan with double thickness of aluminum foil so that the foil extends 2" beyond the sides of the pan. Butter the bottom and sides of the foil-lined pan. In the top of double boiler set over hot (not simmering) water, melt chocolate, butter and coffee, stirring frequently, until smooth. Remove the pan from the heat. Cool the mixture, stirring it occasionally, for 10 minutes.

In a large bowl, using a hand-held electric mixer set at high speed, beat the eggs for 30 seconds, or until foamy. Gradually add the sugar and continue to beat for 2 minutes, or until the mixture is very light and fluffy. Reduce the speed to low and gradually beat in the chocolate mixture until blended. Using a wooden spoon, stir in the flour. Stir in the walnuts. Do not overbeat the mixture. Scrape the batter into the prepared pan and spread evenly. Bake for 25 to 30 minutes, or until the foggies are just set around the edges. They will be moist in the center. Cool the foggies in the pan on a wire rack for 30 minutes. Cover the pan tightly with aluminum foil and refrigerate <u>overnight</u> or for at least 6 hours.

Remove the top foil and run a sharp knife around the edge of the foggies. Using two ends of the foil as handles, lift the foggies out of the pan. Invert the foggies onto a large plate and peel off the foil. Invert them again onto a smooth surface and cut into 16 rectangles.

Great when individually wrapped in colored cellophane and tied with a bright ribbon. They are an unforgettable rich delight.

Kristen and Malcolm (Lon) Mitchell '76

Peanut Butter Balls

Yields approximately 100

INGREDIENTS:

3 cups Rice Krispies
1 pound powdered sugar
2 cups creamy peanut
  butter
1/4 pound (1 stick) butter
  or margarine, melted
  (or half of each)

Chocolate Coating:
1/2 bar (2 ounces) paraffin
1 8-ounce bar Hershey's
  sweet chocolate
1 6-ounce package
  chocolate chips

PROCEDURE:

Place Rice Krispies in a large bowl and crush slightly. Mix in powdered sugar.
Add peanut butter and blend well with hands. Add melted butter/margarine and
again blend well with hands until dough sticks together. With a well-rounded
teaspoon of dough in the palm of your hand, roll dough into smooth balls. If the
dough becomes too dry and crumbly, add a little more melted butter/margarine
and blend. Store in metal containers with tight lids and refrigerate for several
hours or overnight before beginning the next step.

Chocolate Coating: Melt paraffin in top of double boiler. Add Hershey bar and
chocolate chips. Stir occasionally until all ingredients are completely melted.
With cover on, heat sauce for 2 to 3 minutes more. Stir until very smooth. With
toothpick, dip 1 ball at a time in chocolate sauce. Hold the ball over the sauce
until it stops dripping, also giving the chocolate time to set a little. Invert ball on
waxed paper. Twist the toothpick to remove it. Let cool for at least 1 hour before
handling.

*Store in refrigerator in metal container. Can be made at least a month in advance --
they keep excellently. Leslie and Inis first experienced these delectable
confectioneries at the school in 1974 when a student brought them in for a bake sale.
The student kindly shared the recipe with them and Leslie began the tradition of
making several recipes at Christmas-time and bringing them to school for the faculty
and staff. When Leslie left the school in 1984, Inis carried on the tradition which she
still does to this day (even though she has been retired from her position at the school
for several years). Inis says that the faculty and staff begin reminding her in
October each year that they are looking forward to the legendary Peanut Butter Balls
and hope they will appear come Christmas. Inis also reports that these balls are
very time consuming to make (4 hours) but well worth the effort.*

Leslie Sissman Evans, Former Head of Lower School
and
Inis Clark, Former Secretary to Head of School

English Toffee I

Yields 1 pound

INGREDIENTS:

1 cup sugar
1 cup (2 sticks) butter
2 tablespoons water
1 teaspoon vanilla

2 4-ounce bars Hershey
   chocolate
1/4 cup chopped almonds

PROCEDURE:

Combine and cook sugar, butter and water in a heavy pan to 300°. (Use candy thermometer to measure temperature.) Remove from heat and add 1 teaspoon vanilla. Stir to blend. Spread mixture on a cookie sheet. Break Hershey bars into pieces and place evenly on top. After chocolate melts, spread it to a thin coating. Sprinkle with chopped nuts. Cool <u>overnight</u>. Break into pieces.

Ellin Todd '68

English Toffee II

Yields 4 pounds of candy

INGREDIENTS:

2 cups sugar
1 1/2 cups (3 sticks) butter
4 tablespoons water
2 tablespoons light corn
   syrup

3 cups slivered almonds,
   toasted
12 ounces milk chocolate
   (or semisweet) chips

PROCEDURE:

Combine sugar, butter, water, corn syrup and 1 cup of the toasted slivered almonds in heavy saucepan. Heat over medium-high to high heat, stirring constantly until candy thermometer reaches 300° (hard crack stage). Pour onto 11" x 17" teflon cookie sheet. Spread to edges. Let cool. Melt 1 bag of chocolate chips and spread over cooled candy. Grind remaining toasted almonds and sprinkle half of them over chocolate. Refrigerate until chocolate hardens (1 to 2 hours).

Remove from refrigerator. Lift sheet of toffee carefully and turn over in pan and return to room temperature. Melt remaining chocolate chips and spread over candy. Sprinkle remaining ground almonds over top. Refrigerate approximately 2 hours to let chocolate harden. Remove and break into bite size pieces.

Best kept refrigerated. Also freezes very well and keeps indefinitely!

Pam Frazer Kelly '61

English Toffee Candy

Yields 100+ pieces

INGREDIENTS:

2 cups (4 sticks) butter	12 ounces Nestle's chocolate morsels
2 cups sugar	
1/2 teaspoon salt	2 1/2 ounces sliced almonds, chopped

PROCEDURE:

In a heavy saucepan place butter, sugar and salt on high heat. When butter is melted, turn heat to medium. Attach candy thermometer. Make sure it does not touch the bottom of the pan. Heat sugar mixture to 310° (HARD CRACK). Stir constantly while heating. Pour candy mixture onto cookie sheet and cool (may be placed in refrigerator to speed up the process). In a medium saucepan melt chocolate morsels and spread half of melted chocolate on hardened candy on one side. Sprinkle half of chopped nuts over the chocolate layer. Cool. Turn over candy and repeat chocolate and chopped nuts procedure. Cool. Break candy into bite size pieces to serve.

This has been a Christmas tradition in our household for almost 20 years. This candy will stay edible for weeks. Enjoy.

Kimberly Miller
Parent, Camden Miller '94X, Trent Miller '96, Derek Miller '98

Divinity Candy

Yields 64 1" squares

INGREDIENTS:

2 1/2 cups sugar
   1/2 cup hot water
   1/2 cup corn syrup

2 egg whites, beaten
   until stiff
1 1/2 cups chopped pecans
   Oil for greasing pan

PROCEDURE:

Mix sugar, water and corn syrup together in a saucepan and cook until the liquid forms soft ball in cold water. (Test by dropping a small bit of liquid into cold water.) Beat the egg whites until very stiff. Pour 1 cup of the sugar mixture over egg whites, beating all the while. Cook the remainder of sugar mixture until it forms a hard ball in cold water. Pour this over the egg whites, beating until thick. Add nuts and mix well. Pour into an 8" x 8" greased pan. Then cool and cut into squares.

Freezes well.

Bodie Schmidt
Grandparent, Brenna Fleener '98

Grandmother's Divinity

Yields 30 to 35 pieces of candy

INGREDIENTS:

2 1/2 cups sugar
1/2 cup water
1/2 cup light Karo syrup
2 egg whites
1 teaspoon vanilla

1/2 teaspoon almond or
black walnut extract
Almond or black
walnut halves to
correspond with
extract flavoring

PROCEDURE:

Bring sugar, water and syrup to hard ball or 260° on candy thermometer. As syrup mixture is cooking, beat egg whites with electric mixer to soft peak. Pour half of the syrup mixture slowly into the egg whites while beating with the mixer. When thoroughly blended, add flavorings. Return second half of syrup to burner and heat to soft crack or 280°. Pour syrup slowly into the egg white mixture while beating and continue to beat until mixture reaches semi-hard peak and begins to lose its gloss. Can fold nuts in at this time or reserve and place 1 nut half on top of each individual drop. Working quickly, use a tablespoon to drop candy in individual pieces onto wax paper.

May also decorate with candied cherries or other fruits as well as candy toppings. Store in airtight container.

Joanne Callan
Trustee and
Parent, Megan Callan '91

Bishop's Family Recipe

Serves whole family

INGREDIENTS:

Friendship	**Hope**
Thoughtfulness	**Charity**
Kindness	**Gaiety**
Loyalty	**Laughter**
Faith	

PROCEDURE:

Preheat oven to Warm.

Take 1/2 cup of Friendship, add 1 cup of Thoughtfulness and cream together with a pinch of powdered Kindness. Mix in gently a large dash of Loyalty (very important).

Add the vital ingredient of Faith. Sprinkle generously with Hope and Charity. (Some days, double the Hope and Charity...a Mother and Father's secret for a well-raised, finished product.)

Be sure to add a spoonful of Gaiety that sings, with the ability to Laugh at little things and overlook the non-essential items. Bake in a good-natured pan and serve repeatedly.

If prepared properly, will last for a lifetime.

Edith Thompson
Parent, Anthony Thompson '95

Index

Happy cooking!

We hope that our school family's favorite recipes
will soon become your favorites too!

You may obtain additional copies of this cookbook
for your family and friends
by filling out the attached order forms
or by stopping by
The Bishop's School Alumni Office
at the address below.

The cookbook is a joint project of
The Bishop's School
Parents' Association and Alumni Association.

All proceeds from the sale of the cookbook are contributed to
The Bishop's School Faculty Endowment Fund.

The Bishop's School family thanks you for your support.

The Bishop's School Cookbook
7607 La Jolla Boulevard
La Jolla, CA 92037
(619) 459-4021

The Bishop's School Cookbook
7607 La Jolla Boulevard
La Jolla, CA 92037

Additional copies of this cookbook may be purchased at
The Bishop's School Alumni Office at the address above.
If you wish to have copies mailed to you, please use the form below.

MAIL ORDER FORM

Name_____

Address_____

City_____**State**_____**Zip**_____

I would like to order_____**cookbooks at $15.00 each**   _____

Postage and Handling
To California addresses, $4.00 per book (includes CA sales tax)   _____
To other U.S. addresses, $3.00 per book   _____
To Canada or Mexico addresses, $4.00 per book   _____
To all other countries,
    Surface: $4.00 per book   Air: $12.00 per book   _____

                                                                       TOTAL   _____

ALL ORDERS MUST BE PREPAID.
Please make check or money order payable to
The Bishop's School Cookbook
and send with completed form to the address above.

This cookbook is a joint project of
The Bishop's School Parents' Association and Alumni Association.
All proceeds from the sale of the cookbook are contributed to
The Bishop's School Faculty Endowment Fund.

The Bishop's School Cookbook
7607 La Jolla Boulevard
La Jolla, CA 92037

**Additional copies of this cookbook may be purchased at
The Bishop's School Alumni Office at the address above.
If you wish to have copies mailed to you, please use the form below.**

MAIL ORDER FORM

Name_____

Address_____

City_____**State**_____**Zip**_____

I would like to order_____**cookbooks at $15.00 each**   _____

Postage and Handling
To California addresses, $4.00 per book (includes CA sales tax)   _____
To other U.S. addresses, $3.00 per book   _____
To Canada or Mexico addresses, $4.00 per book   _____
To all other countries,
    Surface: $4.00 per book   Air: $12.00 per book   _____

                                       TOTAL   _____

**ALL ORDERS MUST BE PREPAID.
Please make check or money order payable to
The Bishop's School Cookbook
and send with completed form to the address above.**

This cookbook is a joint project of
The Bishop's School Parents' Association and Alumni Association.
All proceeds from the sale of the cookbook are contributed to
The Bishop's School Faculty Endowment Fund.

The Bishop's School Cookbook
7607 La Jolla Boulevard
La Jolla, CA 92037

**Additional copies of this cookbook may be purchased at
The Bishop's School Alumni Office at the address above.
If you wish to have copies mailed to you, please use the form below.**

MAIL ORDER FORM

Name_____

Address_____

City_____State_____Zip_____

I would like to order_____cookbooks at $15.00 each   _____

Postage and Handling
To California addresses, $4.00 per book (includes CA sales tax)   _____
To other U.S. addresses, $3.00 per book   _____
To Canada or Mexico addresses, $4.00 per book   _____
To all other countries,
    Surface: $4.00 per book   Air: $12.00 per book   _____

                         TOTAL   _____

**ALL ORDERS MUST BE PREPAID.
Please make check or money order payable to
The Bishop's School Cookbook
and send with completed form to the address above.**

This cookbook is a joint project of
The Bishop's School Parents' Association and Alumni Association.
All proceeds from the sale of the cookbook are contributed to
The Bishop's School Faculty Endowment Fund.

The Bishop's School Cookbook

7607 La Jolla Boulevard
La Jolla, CA 92037

**Additional copies of this cookbook may be purchased at
The Bishop's School Alumni Office at the address above.
If you wish to have copies mailed to you, please use the form below.**

MAIL ORDER FORM

Name_____

Address_____

City_____**State**_____**Zip**_____

I would like to order_____**cookbooks at $15.00 each**   _____

Postage and Handling
To California addresses, $4.00 per book (includes CA sales tax)   _____
To other U.S. addresses, $3.00 per book   _____
To Canada or Mexico addresses, $4.00 per book   _____
To all other countries,
     Surface: $4.00 per book   Air: $12.00 per book   _____

                                        TOTAL   _____

**ALL ORDERS MUST BE PREPAID.
Please make check or money order payable to
The Bishop's School Cookbook
and send with completed form to the address above.**

This cookbook is a joint project of
The Bishop's School Parents' Association and Alumni Association.
All proceeds from the sale of the cookbook are contributed to
The Bishop's School Faculty Endowment Fund.

The Bishop's School Cookbook
7607 La Jolla Boulevard
La Jolla, CA 92037

**Additional copies of this cookbook may be purchased at
The Bishop's School Alumni Office at the address above.
If you wish to have copies mailed to you, please use the form below.**

MAIL ORDER FORM

Name_____

Address_____

City_____State_____Zip_____

I would like to order_____cookbooks at $15.00 each   _____

Postage and Handling
To California addresses, $4.00 per book (includes CA sales tax)   _____
To other U.S. addresses, $3.00 per book   _____
To Canada or Mexico addresses, $4.00 per book   _____
To all other countries,
    Surface: $4.00 per book   Air: $12.00 per book   _____

                                      TOTAL   _____

**ALL ORDERS MUST BE PREPAID.
Please make check or money order payable to
The Bishop's School Cookbook
and send with completed form to the address above.**

This cookbook is a joint project of
The Bishop's School Parents' Association and Alumni Association.
All proceeds from the sale of the cookbook are contributed to
The Bishop's School Faculty Endowment Fund.

Notes

Notes

Notes

Notes

Notes

Notes

Notes

Notes

Notes

Notes

Notes

Notes